TURN THE
BEAT AROUND

TURN THE
BEAT AROUND

The Secret History of Disco

PETER SHAPIRO

Faber and Faber, Inc.

An affiliate of Farrar, Straus and Giroux

New York

Faber and Faber, Inc.
An affiliate of Farrar, Straus and Giroux
19 Union Square West, New York 10003

Owing to limitations of space, all acknowledgments for permission to reprint previously published material can be found on page 367.

Library of Congress Cataloging-in-Publication Data
Shapiro, Peter, 1969–
    Turn the beat around : the secret history of disco / Peter Shapiro.— 1st ed.
        p.   cm.
    Includes discography (p.   ), bibliographical references (p.   ), and index.
    ISBN-13: 978-0-571-21194-4
    ISBN-10: 0-571-21194-1 (hardcover : alk. paper)
    1. Disco music—History and criticism.   2. Popular culture—History—20th
    century.   I. Title.

ML3526.S5 2005
306.4'8424'0973—dc22   2004024211

Designed by Jonathan D. Lippincott

www.fsgbooks.com

1   3   5   7   9   10   8   6   4   2

To Rachael

CONTENTS

ACKNOWLEDGMENTS

Thanks to everyone involved in this project, whether by providing inspiration, granting interviews, helping me chase down leads, or feeding my vinyl jones: Nile Rodgers, Sooze Plunkett-Green, Bob George, Danny Wang, Danny Krivit, Michael "Lucky Strike" Corral, Tom Moulton, Ian Levine, Daniele Baldelli, Cherry Vanilla, Vicki Wickham, Barry Lederer, Bob Blank, Quinton Scott, Toni Rosano, Drew Daniels, Martin Schmidt, Dan Selzer, Chris at Dfiledamerica, Jeff Chang, David Toop, Sasha Frere-Jones, Mike Rubin, Dave Tompkins, Philip Sherburne, Rob Michaels, $mall ¢hange, Jonathan Buckley, and Mark Ellingham. Sections of this book have appeared in different form in *The Wire*, and I'd like to thank my editors there (Tony Herrington, Rob Young, and Chris Bohn) for allowing my theoretical ramblings on disco to appear in such an august journal.

Thanks to my agent, David Smith, and my editors, Denise Oswald and Lee Brackstone. Extra special thanks to my wife, Rachael, for putting up with my ridiculously late nights and the creeping monster that is my record collection; for cracking the whip; and for giving me never-ending amounts of support.

TURN THE
BEAT AROUND

THE ROTTEN APPLE

A dance is the devil's procession, and he that entereth into a dance,
entereth into his possession.   —St. Francis de Sales

Hello from the gutters of N.Y.C. which are filled with dog manure, vomit,
stale wine, urine and blood.   —David Berkowitz

Fee fie fo fum
We're looking down the barrel of the devil's gun
Nowhere to run
We've got to make a stand against the devil's gun.   —CJ & Co.

To many, disco is all about those three little words: "Halston,
Gucci, Fiorucci." Others undoubtedly have images of long-
legged Scandinavian ice queens in metallic makeup and dresses
"cut down to there" dancing in their heads. Or maybe it's the tête-
à-tête between Andy Warhol and Bianca Jagger in the VIP room of
Studio 54, each trying to outdo the other with their looks of super-
cilious boredom. Disco is all shiny, glittery surfaces; high heels and
luscious lipstick; jam-packed jeans and cut pecs; lush, soaring, swooping strings and Latin razzmatazz; cocaine rush and quaalude wobble.
It was the humble peon suddenly beamed up to the cosmic firmament
by virtue of his threads and dance moves. Disco was the height of
glamour and decadence and indulgence. But while disco may have

sparkled with diamond brilliance, it stank of something far worse. Despite its veneer of elegance and sophistication, disco was born, maggot-like, from the rotten remains of the Big Apple.

In the early 1970s, the words "New York City" became a shorthand code for everything that was wrong with America. Movies like *Midnight Cowboy*, *The French Connection*, *Taxi Driver*, *The Panic in Needle Park*, *The Prisoner of Second Avenue*, *The Out-of-Towners*, *Dog Day Afternoon*, *Shaft*, *Across 110th Street*, and *Death Wish* depicted a city on the brink: a cesspool of moral and spiritual degradation; a playground for drug dealers, pimps, and corrupt cops; the government an ineffectual, effete elite running its fiefdom from cocktail parties in high-rise apartments seemingly miles above the sullied streets; the only recourse for the ordinary citizen to grab a gun and start shooting back. As *New York Times* film critic Vincent Canby wrote, "New York City has become a metaphor for what looks like the last days of American civilization. It's run by fools. Its citizens are at the mercy of its criminals who, often as not, are protected by an unholy alliance of civil libertarians and crooked cops. The air is foul. The traffic is impossible. Services are diminishing and the morale is such that ordering a cup of coffee in a diner can turn into a request for a fat lip."[1]

Only a few years earlier, in 1967's *Barefoot in the Park*, the city was the setting for young love and newlywed highjinks. Sure, the Bratters' Greenwich Village apartment was small and cramped, but the conspicuously beautiful and well-scrubbed Robert Redford and Jane Fonda could scamper about Washington Square Park without shoes and have picnics if they needed to escape. By 1971, the newlyweds would've been played by Ernest Borgnine and Karen Black, and walking barefoot in any of the city's parks would have got them one-way tickets to Mount Sinai for a tetanus shot. How did things change so quickly?

To fully comprehend New York in the seventies, it's necessary to look at where the previous decade and its progressive agenda fell off course. The liberal experiment of the 1960s was fueled by the youthful enthusiasm and swaggering confidence of a generation that had never known anything but the greatest prosperity the world had ever seen. But as soon as the economic conditions that had made the Great Society possible started to falter, the dreams turned into disillusionment, the promises became retractions, and the sweeping

4

vision became blinkered and myopic. The civil rights marches devolved into "race riots," "flower power" wilted and turned into "the year of the barricades,"[2] and "groovy," "peace," and "love" were traded for "Up against the wall, motherfucker."[3] Two of the figureheads of the Old Left, Martin Luther King and Robert F. Kennedy, were assassinated in the spring of 1968, and a few weeks later the full force of the Chicago Police Department was unleashed on protesters outside of the Democratic National Convention. Vietnam, numerous ecological disasters, and oppressive mores turned young people against the scoundrels running the government and big business, and against the Establishment in general; meanwhile, the previous generation was bemoaning the lack of respect for authority and the loss of "values." In response, both the Left and Right became increasingly militant and increasingly intractable in their positions. Gone were the beloved communities of the civil rights marchers, protest singers, antiwar activists, and Woodstock nation, and their spirit of inclusion, participation, and democracy in action. Instead, the onset of the 1970s brought identity politics, special-interest groups, EST retreats, armed street gangs, "corporate rock," tax revolts, and a politics of resentment, and attendant with all of this feelings of alienation, resignation, defensiveness, frustration, and betrayal. A kind of siege mentality replaced the "great consensus" that had previously characterized American life.

Although Harlem and the Brooklyn neighborhood of Bedford-Stuyvesant erupted into riot on July 18, 1964, when a police officer who had shot and killed a black teenage boy two days earlier was exonerated, New York's 1960s "race riot" was relatively small (one dead and one hundred injured) compared to the riots that ravaged other American cities like Detroit, Los Angeles, and Newark. Nevertheless, the scars were just as deep. As with these other cities, New York had experienced enormous demographic changes since the 1930s. Northern cities like New York, Chicago, and Philadelphia were the goal for millions of poor rural African Americans who migrated northward during the 1930s and '40s.[4] In 1965, the immigration quota laws that effectively prevented anyone who wasn't from Western Europe from entering the country were relaxed, allowing huge numbers of Asians, Latin Americans, and Afro-Caribbeans to enter the United States—so much so, that by the mid-1980s, there were more first-generation blacks from the West Indies in New York City than African Americans who were born in the United States.[5] Unfortunately for New York, the vast majority of these newcomers were unskilled workers, and they arrived at exactly the time the manufacturing industries that had formerly provided them with jobs started to decline—a downturn that was exacerbated by a recession that began in the late 1960s and would hit New York harder than any other metropolitan area.[6] To further compound the problem, this influx of immigrants was concurrent with a massive exodus of the city's white population to the suburbs.[7] White flight coupled with the recession meant that the city's tax revenues shrunk drastically—at exactly the same time that the municipal government was forced to dramatically increase its budget.[8]

While the ranks of the city's bureaucracy necessarily swelled, services were cut proportionally in order to pay for the expansion of the municipal government. The city stopped investing in infrastructure and could barely pay its most important employees. Sanitation workers staged strikes during summer heat waves, turning the Big Apple into a festering trash heap tended by the city's twenty-five million rats. To save on overtime payments, firefighters "were dispatched to blazes in dial-a-cabs to relieve those ending their shifts."[9] Cynical, underpaid policemen fought a losing battle with crime: Between 1966 and 1973, New York's murder rate jumped a staggering 173 percent and rapes 112 percent.[10] The Knapp Commission Report, issued in December 1972, said that police corruption "was an extensive, department-wide phenomenon that included cops selling heroin, ratting on informants to the mob, and riding shotgun on drug deals."[11] A new priority for police officers was the result: "Stay out of trouble and avoid the appearance of corruption."[12] "[A] proactive police department that kept order on the streets by showing a strong street presence" suddenly became "a reactive department that patrolled neighborhoods by car instead of foot."[13] The subways were ceded to the muggers and thugs; and if you weren't physically assaulted, you were visually besieged by the graffiti writers' brutal and aggressive tags and burners. The one area where police resources were significantly expanded was in the battle against the drug epidemic: Drug offenses that had been previously punishable by probation and a stay at a residential drug treatment program now carried with them mandatory minimum prison terms.[14]

The result was a creeping blue funk that swept over the city, instilling everything with a sense of dread and foreboding. As *The New York Times*'s David Burnham wrote, "The fear is visible: It can be seen in clusters of stores that close early because the streets are sinister and customers no longer stroll after supper for newspapers and pints of ice cream. It can be seen in the faces of women opening elevator doors, in the hurried step of the man walking home late at night from the subway. The fear manifests itself in elaborate gates and locks, in the growing number of keyrings, in the formation of tenants' squads to patrol corridors, in shop buzzers pressed to admit only recognizable customers. And finally it becomes habit."[15]

Meanwhile, landlords began a concerted, if largely unorganized, campaign of disinvestment in an effort to overturn the city's rent control regulations and to squeeze every inch of profit they could out of their properties. As "desirable" tenants fled to the suburbs, rather than accept controlled rents from the city for low-income tenants, landlords neglected their maintenance responsibilities, stopped providing utilities, refused to pay taxes, and eventually indulged in arson on their own properties, leaving vast areas pockmarked with burned-out buildings, destroying communities and neighborhoods in the process.[16] The worst ravaged area was the South Bronx (the communities of Mott Haven, Morrisania, and Hunts Point), a few square miles just over the Willis Avenue Bridge from Manhattan that had been abandoned to the drug abusers, street gangs, and roving packs of wild dogs, and largely left for dead. Dr. Harold Wise of the neighborhood's Martin Luther King Jr. Health Center called the place "a necropolis."[17]

In the late '60s, organizations like the Black Panther Party and Nation of Islam attempted to act as the sheriffs in these urban ghost towns, but their influence was waning in the face of the FBI's COINTELPRO (a massive covert action program that sought to "neutralize" what FBI director J. Edgar Hoover called "Black Nationalist hate groups" and "the greatest threat to the internal security of the country").[18] The void left in their wake was filled by street gangs like the Black Spades, Savage Skulls, Roman Kings, Javelins, and

Seven Crowns to which disenfranchised young African-American and Hispanic men turned in droves.[19] By 1973, there were 315 gangs with more than 19,000 members in New York City.[20] Even though many of these gangs evolved into politicized empowerment groups like the Young Lords Party and the Real Great Society (which grew out of the Lower East Side Dragons and the Assassins) and started to attack the drug dealers who ravaged their neighborhoods with heroin, the gangs' association with violence and their intimidating presence colored the city with a steely brutality. As Nelson George noted, "Civil rights, self-sufficiency, protest, politics . . . all of it faded for those trapped in the shooting galleries of the body and the mind."[21]

New York's members of the Silent Majority who had swept Richard Nixon into power in 1968 felt like they were being outnumbered and ignored, and reacted with fear and resentment. Their response to growing black militancy, the antiwar movement, bra burning, major demographic change, and hedonistic hippies "tuning in, turning on, and dropping out" was America's thermidorean reaction and prompted *Time* magazine to name the Middle American as its Man and Woman of the Year in 1969.[22] The Middle American was the square heartlander who rallied around Old Glory and still believed in Mom, baseball, and apple pie; he was the anti-intellectual narrator of Merle Haggard's "Okie From Muskogee" who doesn't "smoke marijuana . . . take trips on LSD [or] burn [his] draft card down on Main Street [because he likes] livin' right and being free"; she was the mother concerned about kin and decency who put an "Honor America" bumper sticker on the family car. These Middle Americans were the ones responsible for a law in West Virginia that absolved the guilt of any policeman involved in future deaths of antiwar protesters or race rioters, the ones who defied almost two hundred years of separation between church and state to encourage their kids to pray in a public school in Netcong, New Jersey.

Despite being that den of iniquity and vice so close to decadent Europe and the seat of the Northeastern liberal elite, New York City had its own Middle Americans—the working-class white ethnics who lived in the outer boroughs. They were, as described by New York City mayor John Lindsay's biographer Vincent J. Cannato, "men and women descended from German, Irish, Italian, Polish, Greek and Jewish immigrants who were either civil servants (teachers, firemen, policemen), union members (welders, electricians, carpenters), or members of the petite bourgeoisie (clerks, accountants, small businessmen). Their culture was middlebrow, traditional and patriotic."[23] They were enshrined in popular culture by *All in the Family*'s Archie Bunker, who became the country's favorite TV character as soon as he appeared in 1970. His vision of America was "the land of the free where Lady Liberty holds her torch sayin' send me your poor, your deadbeats, your filthy . . . so they come from all over the world pourin' in like ants . . . all of them free to live together in peace and harmony in their separate little sections where they feel safe, and break your head if you go in there. That there is what makes America great!"[24]

The Bunkers were traditional Democratic voters who had grown disenchanted with the liberal experiment of the 1960s and blamed it for tearing apart the fabric of American society. One particular target of their ire was the welfare program, which in the popular imagination had become permanently associated with African Americans and had exploded out of control.[25] But since welfare did nothing to address the real problems of ghetto life, racism, and endemic poverty, urban African Americans continued to protest vociferously their social and economic conditions. "But," as writer Peter Carroll noted, "these complaints seemed particularly outrageous to working-class whites, who themselves teetered on the brink of economic disaster."[26] In a chilling article in *New York* magazine, veteran New York newspaperman Pete Hamill wrote that the white working and lower middle classes "see a terrible unfairness in their lives and an increasing lack of personal control over what happens to them." Instead of turning to the government or the unions or community groups for help, they were increasingly arming themselves, forming vigilante groups, and talking of a race war. Hamill ominously warned that "All over New York City tonight, in places like Inwood, South Brooklyn, Corona, East Flatbush and Bay Ridge, men are standing around saloons talking darkly about possible remedies. Their grievances are real and deep, their remedies could blow this city apart."[27]

Even though the prophesied race war never happened, on May 8, 1970, their grievances bubbled over into physical violence. A group of about two hundred construction workers carrying crowbars and hammers descended on a gathering near City Hall of one thousand students who were protesting the deaths four days earlier of four students who were killed by members of the National Guard at an anti-war protest at Kent State University in Ohio. Chanting "All the way, USA," they beat the protesters with their helmets, tools, and steel-toed work boots to the accompaniment of applause from the suited and tied executives at the brokerage houses overlooking the square. "Bloody Friday" was only the beginning of two weeks of virulent flag-waving, pro-Nixon demonstrations that were known as the "Hard Hat Riots" and culminated on May 20, when between 60,000 and 150,000 construction workers and their allies marched down the Canyon of Heroes in lower Manhattan in a tickertape parade.[28]

The "Hard Hat Riots," however, weren't so much prowar rallies as they were potent symbols of class resentment. The working class felt the effects of the military action in Vietnam much more strongly than the middle-class families whose children were safely ensconced in college, where they were protected from the draft. Peter Carroll recalled "one worker whose son was serving in Vietnam lament[ing] the inability of poorer boys to 'get the same breaks as the college kids. We can't understand,' he added, 'how all those rich kids—the kids with beards from the fancy suburbs—how they get off when my

---

THE OCEAN HILL TEACHERS' STRIKE

If one event epitomized the stress and strife of New York in the late '60s and early '70s, it was the series of strikes called by the United Federation of Teachers in 1968. In May, thirteen teachers, five assistant principals, and one principal were dismissed from their positions at Junior High School 271 in the Ocean Hill–Brownsville school district in Brooklyn. The recently elected district school board was the result of an experiment in community control over schooling in an effort to help improve the quality of education in an area that had shifted rapidly from a predominantly Jewish neighborhood to a predominantly African-American and Puerto Rican one. Almost all of the educators who were fired were Jewish, while the school board was almost entirely black. In perhaps the only sector of the employment market where Jews and African Americans competed for the same jobs, tensions were high, and accusations of racism and anti-Semitism flew from

son has to go over there and maybe get his head shot off.' "[29] While their sons were dying on the killing fields of Southeast Asia, members of the working class were dying at similar rates back home. In 1970, there were 14,200 deaths in the workplace, while thousands more suffered chronic illnesses resulting from workplace exposure to dangerous substances like asbestos. In construction work (one of the country's most dangerous occupations), this misery was compounded by the fact that in 1970, 30 percent of the construction workers in the United States were unemployed at one time or another, largely due to reductions in public works programs caused by inflation and budget cuts.[30]

And nowhere were these cutbacks more severe than in New York. As stagflation—the economic condition of rising inflation, intractable unemployment, and near-zero economic growth that defies almost every theory of classical economics—reared its ugly head, due to a swelling bureaucracy, increasing municipal operating expenses, and escalating debt-service costs (principally paying interest on city-issued bonds), the city had accumulated a $3 billion budget deficit by 1975. In May of that year, Gotham reached financial meltdown when the institutions that had been underwriting the municipal bonds used to pay the city's costs decided to stop lending money to such a high-risk enterprise as the city of New York.[31] Facing default, the government of New York State created the Municipal Assistance Corporation (MAC), which was chaired by banker Felix Rohatyn.

---

all corners in the dispute. A little over a decade after Arkansas governor Orval Faubus had called in the National Guard to prevent black students from entering a school in Little Rock, black parents were now blockading the school to prevent the dismissed teachers from entering. In protest, the city's teachers' union called a series of strikes that severely disrupted the school calendar and bitterly divided the city. Its most profound effect was the severing of the bond that had existed between blacks and Jews, who had played a huge role in the civil rights movement. Previously, Jews had thought of themselves, and perhaps more crucially were thought of, in a racially nebulous way. But during this dispute, their racial identification became definitely "white," and they even formed previously unthinkable alliances with New York's Catholic communities. The result was that for the next three-plus decades, New York's Jewish community became much more conservative, and the city's traditional liberal alliance was broken.[32]

MAC would issue long-term, high-interest bonds backed by municipal revenues in order to pay off the city's creditors. But this help came with a condition—sacrifice. The city slashed services, fired sixty-three thousand municipal employees (including fifteen thousand teachers and four thousand hospital workers)—"the first municipal layoffs since the Depression";[33] closed firehouses; increased transit fares from 35 to 50 cents a trip; and ended the free tuition offered at the City University of New York to all graduates of New York City high schools. On October 30, 1975, after the city had failed to persuade the federal government to help bail it out of its fiscal crisis, the *Daily News* ran a headline that effectively summed up the rest of America's feeling toward Gotham: "Ford to City: Drop Dead."

But while the remains of New York's infrastructure were withering away, its artists and musicians produced a groundswell of creative activity that aimed to reclaim the city. In the spaces left by deindustrialization and disinvestment, they forged their own communities outside of the traditional industry-backed and commercially oriented channels. Just as avant-garde artists like Nam June Paik, Joan Jonas, and Gordon Matta-Clark were making works in tune to the new topography of New York and were busy turning the abandoned warehouses of SoHo (at the time it was still called "Hell's Hundred Acres") into the world's most vibrant artistic community, musicians were seeking their own form of rapture from within the city's crumbling cast-iron skeleton. The "loft jazz scene" saw free jazz musicians gather in disused loft spaces like Studio We, Studio Rivbea, and Ali's Alley that were owned by the musicians themselves[34] in order to hone a seemingly structureless, searching sound that was dubbed "ecstatic." Young rock musicians, especially those from the outer boroughs, who congregated at old theaters like the Mercer Street Arts Center and sleazy dives like Max's Kansas City reacted against the increasingly bloated, corporate nature of rock by stripping down the music to its barest essence of attitude and noise and by finding enlightenment in the discarded ephemera of trash culture. Young kids at outdoor parties in the parks in the Bronx would find their own nirvana by isolating the two or three bars of utter musical perfection on obscure albums and extend the pleasure indefinitely by manipulating two copies of the same record on a pair of turntables that were usually powered by illegally tapping into the city's power grid. And, in fading hotels and former churches, gays, blacks, and Latinos were feeling the exaltation of the damned as they danced to a new style of syncretic music that was being pieced together by the clubs' DJs. This glittering beast that eventually rose on sateen wings from the burrows of the Big Apple's worm-eaten core was disco.

"GO WHERE THE ACTION IS, THAT'S WHERE THE IN-CROWD LIVES"
A Prehistory of Disco[35]

The disco may very well be "where the happy people go," as the Trammps insisted in 1976, but in reality the discotheque and discontent go together like glitterballs and rhinestones. Not just in the sense of dancing one's blues away (which, of course, is part of it), but also in the fact that disco—that music now most redolent of cheery knees-ups and good-time girls dancing around their handbags— could have emerged only from the dark underground of a society teetering on the brink of collapse. Indeed, the disco scene of the 1970s—with its wanton cocaine and casual sex gluttony, its devotion to baroque indulgence in the face of staggering inflation, its aging celebrity has-beens desperately trying not to waste away (or at least do so elegantly), its sense of partying hell for leather tonight because you're not going to know where you stand tomorrow—often conjured nothing so much as the degeneration of Weimar Germany. It's ironic, then, that the ancestral roots of disco culture and the very notion of the discotheque (the combination of two French words, *disque*, meaning "record," and *bibliothèque*, meaning "library") can be traced back to Nazi Germany and Nazi-occupied Paris during World War II.[36]

On March 25, 1939, Adolf Hitler signed a law that made it compulsory for all boys between the ages of fourteen and eighteen to join the Hitlerjugend, or Hitler Youth, and all girls of the same age to join the Bund Deutscher Mädel (German Girls' Federation). Around the same time, an alternative youth movement started in Hamburg and quickly spread across Germany. The Swing Jugend (Swing Kids) were one of a number of loosely organized youth groups or movements that, in their own small ways, opposed the relentless and draconian homogenization that Hitler enforced in order to foster youth that would serve Germany forever. The Swing Kids were mostly middle- and upper-class (and, it must be stressed, largely apolitical) youths who wore long whips of hair (in direct contravention of the order that men must wear military-length hair) and "long, often checked English sports jackets, shoes with thick light crepe soles, showy scarves, homburg hats";[37] some even carried umbrellas in imitation of the British foreign secretary at the time, Anthony Eden. The female Swing Kids, meanwhile, wore long, flowing hair and penciled eyebrows, lipstick and nail polish. Naturally, the Nazis were scandalized by such wanton displays of Hollywood-influenced degeneracy, as true German women had a "pure" beauty and kept their hair in Heidi braids.

Even more of an affront to Nazi sensibilities, though, was the Swing Kids' taste in music: degenerate "Americano nigger kike jungle music"[38] created by African Americans and disseminated by the Jewish-dominated media industries. The Swing Kids would dance in an outrageous fashion (linking arms, jumping up and down, jitterbugging to the point of physical exhaustion, one woman often dancing with two men at the same time) to the "hot" sounds of Louis Armstrong and Nat Gonella. However, it wasn't easy for the Swing Kids to dance: Not only did the organization of professional musicians under the Nazis, the Reichs Music Chamber, travel around the bars in search of swing music and then alert the Gestapo, but the leader of the SS and the chief of police, Heinrich Himmler, issued a police order preventing adolescents from loitering after dark or attending dances after 9 p.m. Gatherings of Swing Kids were therefore largely clandestine affairs hastily organized around a vacant spot and the availability of a portable gramophone and a connoisseur's collection of swing records.

These swing parties may not have had any ultrasuede jackets, dry-ice-covered dance floors or party whistles, but they are the source point of the disco aesthetic. While people had been dancing to recorded music for years at American bars and roadhouses that had jukeboxes or, even earlier, piano rolls, both jukeboxes and piano rolls were serviced by distribution companies that chose the music themselves. The gatherings of the Swing Kids mark the first instance that a disc jockey played music of his own choosing and not necessarily what was in the hit parade, tailored to a specific crowd of dancers in a nondomestic setting.[39] Add to this the frightening cultural climate, the almost-outlawed subculture, vivid dress sense, a politics of pleasure, uninhibited sexuality, and complex relations to class, and if they only had a primitive mixer and a drum machine, the Swing Kids might have invented disco thirty years early.

There were also pockets of Swing Kids in Vienna and, especially, in Paris, with its long connection to American jazz musicians and "le jazz hot," where they were known as Les Zazous. Taking their name from nonsense syllables scatted by Cab Calloway, the Zazous, like their German counterparts, often came from the upper middle class, smoked Lucky Strikes, and greeted each other with the phrase, "Ça swing!" According to jazz historian Mike Zwerin, "Zazou boys wore pegged pants with baggy knees, high rolled English collars covered by their hair, which was carefully combed into a two-wave pompadour over their foreheads, long checked jackets several sizes too large, dangling key chains, gloves, stick-pins in wide neckties with tiny knots; dark glasses and Django Reinhardt moustaches were the rage. The girls wore short skirts, baggy sweaters, pointed painted fingernails, hair curled to their shoulders, necklaces around their waists, bright red lipstick."[40] On Sundays, even during the Nazi occupation, they took portable record players to small restaurants and cafés in outlying areas of Paris, played their favorite swing records, and danced.

With their loud music and refusal to take anything seriously, the Zazous had become such a headache to the authorities that on June 14, 1942, the head of the collaborationist Jeunesses Populaires Françaises sent squads of thugs on "search-and-destroy" missions in the Quartier Latin, the Champs-Élysées, and the suburb of Neuilly-sur-Seine. Their objective was to cut the hair of any Zazous they could lay their hands on.[41] Later that year, when the Nazis started to force Jews to wear the yellow Star of David, some of the Zazous wore yellow stars with "Zazou" or "Swing" scrawled across them as a rather unfortunate celebration of what they interpreted as Nazi kitsch.[42] This gesture certainly didn't help matters any when, in late 1942 and 1943, the Nazis arrested several hundred Swing Kids and Zazous in both Germany and Paris and sent them to work camps.

While such cherished Parisian institutions as the Moulin Rouge, One Two Two, and Maxim's continued to operate during the Occupation largely to serve Nazi officers, and Hitler encouraged Paris's famous nightlife to remain vital because he thought such wanton decadence would hasten French defeat, the Zazous, members of the Resistance, and intellectuals had to dodge the gestapo, informants, and road blocks to assemble and discuss strategy at more (often literally) underground spots. One such meeting place was La Discothèque, a tiny basement club on rue de la Huchette, one block south of the Seine in the Fifth Arrondissement (the Quartier Latin), which, according to Albert Goldman, opened during the Occupation.[43] While the soldiers of the Wehrmacht got their jollies at the nightclubs of the Pigalle, and the Nazi propaganda machine targeted "educated" Parisians by bringing the very best of Berlin's renowned classical music community to Paris, here, on a street where the revolutionary tyrants Robespierre, Saint-Just, and Marat had met to discuss the founding of the Committee of Public Safety that intimidated the country during the French Revolution with its campaigns of surveillance and violence, patrons would exorcise the demons of another reign of terror through the sacrament of alcohol and the testifying spirit of American jazz records. According to Goldman, patrons could order a record at the same time as they ordered a drink.

As the war raged on, however, with resources diverted elsewhere, the bans on dancing and public assembly were gradually enforced less and less and *"les bals clandestins"* flourished in private homes and in bars in the Quartier Latin and in the shadow of the Arc de Triomphe near the place d'Étoile.[44] Many of these bars copied La Discothèque's format: Some brave soul would get his hands on a primitive PA system and a gramophone, lay some cables in a vacant basement, and set up a makeshift club. Entry to these clubs was often speakeasy style: A hatch in the door allowed the proprietor to check out the prospective client and ask him for the day's password or membership credentials. Once inside, the patron could listen or dance to jazz records until the early hours of the morning.

Even after the Occupation ended, though, the basement hovel remained so popular that it became the template for a uniquely

European form of nightlife. Given the rationing of the postwar years and the fact that the public service model of broadcasting became firmly entrenched in Europe (as opposed to the capitalist free-for-all it was in the United States), the discotheque became the only venue in which adventurous listeners could hear music that was outside a prescribed "national culture." Furthermore, where their American comrades could simply take the A train over to Fifty-second Street and on any given night hear Erroll Garner or Charlie Parker at the Three Deuces, Art Tatum at Club Downbeat, and Count Basie at Club Troubadour, European jazz fans' distance from their heroes led them to sanctifying the record as an almost holy artifact, as opposed to the live performance itself.

Perhaps the most important of the postwar nightclubs was Paul Pacine's Whisky à Go-Go. He opened the club sometime around 1947–48 on the site of the old Plancher des Vaches, where, according to future club impresario Regine Zylberberg, the nightclub custom of marking a bottle of whiskey with the customer's name was started.[45] The club on the rue de Beaujolais, right behind the Palais Royale in the First Arrondissement, was set in a tiny cellar that had three levels, and when there were thirty or forty people inside it felt like the black hole of Calcutta. The club was decked out in Scottish kitsch—all tartan and whiskey cases, inspired by the Ealing comedy *Whisky Galore*, called *Whisky à Go Go* in French—but, interestingly, what truly set the club apart was that it was the first place in France to have a jukebox. Even in the land that invented the discotheque, this was a major draw and the club was soon the most celebrated in Paris.

In 1953, Pacine moved the club to a new location on rue Robert Estienne, near the Champs-Élysées. Regine Zylberberg, a Belgian Jew who had escaped the Nazis by hiding in a convent for two years and who then worked as a coat-check girl at the club, convinced Pacine to let her take over the old location, which was lying dormant. According to her autobiography, she was a one-woman show there: "I could lay my hands on a barmaid, disc jockey, cloak room attendant and bouncer straight away, no problem; I did it all myself . . . I had a dozen hands, six legs and four eyes. I was a Jack-of-all-trades; I welcomed people in, gave them a drink, put the records on, and chucked out undesirables. My domain? A cellar on three levels.

As you came in there was the bar, where ten people could get a drink, provided they stepped on each other's toes. Down five steps to the second level where there were four tables and a banquette. Five steps further down was the dance-floor, which also served as the bottle-store. With more than 40 people in the place you got asphyxiated . . . By the end of the first month, I had 30 or so regulars, and by the end of the second the place was busting at the seams . . . After three months, we extended into the cellar next door . . . We had a contrasting mixture at the club, but it was effective. We danced the cha-cha, the meringue [sic] and of course rock 'n' roll. I'd bought some rock records before it became fashionable, and when people started talking about it I got them out and everyone went wild."[46]

No longer the haunt of Resistance fighters and fugitive intellectuals, the discotheque was now a celebrity hangout. Among the flashy guests that Zylberberg boasts of were Zsa-Zsa Gabor, Sacha Distel, Darryl Zanuck, Louis Malle, Françoise Sagan, and Claude Terrail, the proprietor of the legendary Parisian restaurant Le Tour d'Argent. Yes, this was the birth of the new socially promiscuous Eurotrash. But with the first nonstop, transatlantic flights beginning in the late 1950s, they had a kinder term back then for Europe's roaming elite, the jet set (or, in French, *les locomotifs*). The jet set also had dozens of clubs that followed in the Whisky's wake, tailored especially for them: Chez Castel, New Jimmy's, Le Privé. These were the kind of places where the host would cheerfully natter away in English with Omar Sharif but pretend he didn't speak a word of English as soon as an uncouth American businessman arrived at the door trying to get in.[47]

The most important of these clubs was Regine Zylberberg's Chez Regine, which opened in 1958 and was a far more fabulous affair than the Whisky. The club was funded by the Rothschilds and counted Brigitte Bardot, Salvador Dalí, Rudolf Nureyev, and Georges Pompidou among its regular visitors. It was here that Zylberberg introduced the theme party to nightlife with the Jean Harlow night, which required women to wear white satin dresses to gain entry—some even had their Rolls-Royces painted white for the occasion. The discotheque had indeed come a very long way from its origins. During the 1968 student uprisings, the students pushed through barricades to confront the police just outside of Chez Regine on the boulevard du Montparnasse in the Sixth Arrondissement. Zylberberg led frightened guests like Dior designer Marc Bohan, shipping heir and future virulent right-wing commentator Taki Theodoracopoulos, and Françoise Sagan through the clouds of tear gas and up the back stairs to her apartment above the club. As Zylberberg recollected to *New York* magazine, "Taki complained, 'I want to go outside! I want to see the war in France!' Two minutes later, he was back, and banging down the door—'Let me in, Regine!' Idiot! While the sirens blared outside, the whole group whiled away the night, dancing and drinking champagne."[48]

While offering minor royalty and pampered society types refuge from the marauding hoi polloi, Chez Regine also introduced the world outside of North America to the twist, and in so doing became the first true discotheque to be associated with a dance craze. According to legend, on an autumn night in 1961, the cast of the traveling production of *West Side Story* visited Chez Regine. Apparently one cast member had with him a few twist records, including Chubby Checker's version of Hank Ballard's "The Twist" and Joey Dee and the Starliters' "Peppermint Twist," and played them that night at the club. Soon all of fashionable Europe was swiveling its hips.

The twist is important not only because of its relationship to the discotheques, but also because it fomented a revolution in the style of dancing, one that would be crucial to the culture of disco. Even half a decade after Elvis first thrust his pelvis and Chuck Berry did his first duck walk on American television, much of the world was still fox-trotting around ballrooms and cocktail lounges. As Albert Goldman says, "The Twist smashed forever the old dance molds and established an entirely new style for social dancing; a solo rather than a partner dance; a stationary rather than a traveling step; a simple motion, like toweling yourself, that anyone from a three-year-old to your grandmother could learn to do."[49] Goldman, though, overstates the case. Ever since the plantation dance known as the cakewalk—which originated with slaves in Florida and featured couples parodying the pompous manner of white society with exaggerated high steps and arched backs—became popular among whites, American social dancing has been markedly different from its European counterpart, which retained its connections with courtly dancing for much longer. By the time ragtime, and accompanying dance steps like the turkey trot, the grizzly bear, and the bunny hug, burst out of Chicago's saloons and bordellos at the turn of the century, white Americans had long been used to adopting the more exuberant dance styles of African Americans. The big apple, a group participation dance that originated in South Carolina in the 1930s, featured solo dancers surrounded by a circle of eight to ten people. Teenage rock-and-roll fans had been performing semipartner line dances like the stroll, the walk, and the madison, and largely solo steps like the shake, the shimmy, and the shag at "record hops" for a few years before the twist took off.[50] However, unlike most of these short-lived dance crazes, the twist really was a cultural moment rather than a fleeting fad, so much so that even President John F. Kennedy was hosting twist parties at the White House.

While for most American teenagers the twist began with Chubby Checker's first appearance on *American Bandstand*, for mainstream Americans of an older generation, the twist started at a Times Square dive owned by Shirley Cohen called the Peppermint Lounge at 128 West 45th Street. In 1961, the New York press started to report that celebrities like Judy Garland, Tallulah Bankhead, Noël Coward, and Marilyn Monroe had been spotted doing the twist at this seedy sailor bar and gay pickup joint attached to the Knickerbocker Hotel. The music was provided by the house band, Joey Dee & the Starliters, and the media frenzy was such that by December, the group's "Peppermint Twist" was #1 in the *Billboard* chart.

Inevitably, the stars and the in crowd got bored of slumming it, and several more upscale discotheques were soon set up to cater to their every whim. There was Olivier Coquelin's swishy Le Club on Fifty-fifth Street and Sutton Place, which was designed to look like the alpine ski lodges he used to run in Europe; Bradley Pierce's Ondine at 308 East 59th Street; Shepheard's in the Drake Hotel at Park Avenue and Fifth-sixth Street; L'Interdit and Le Directoire in the Gotham Hotel at Fifty-fifth Street and Fifth Avenue; and on Fifty-fourth Street and Second Avenue was the famous El Morocco, which had transformed itself from a nightclub featuring live entertainment into a discotheque and was so fabulous that it was chosen as the site to hold perhaps the most bizarre fund-raiser in the history of American politics, the Discotheque for LBJ in 1964, in which the terminally old-school Texan President Lyndon Johnson attempted to acquire some of the hip cachet of his former boss, JFK.

But even with the most powerful man in the world among your clientele, nothing is guaranteed in clubland, and El Morocco's decline forced it to move to a different location. After Richard Burton ditched her in favor of Elizabeth Taylor, Sybil Burton opened Arthur in May 1965 on the site of the old El Morocco with an investment of $88,000 provided by eighty-eight backers (including Rex Harrison, Julie Andrews, Leonard Bernstein, Mike Nichols, and Lee Remick) who each contributed $1,000.[51] Named after George Harrison's quip to a reporter who asked him, "What do you call your hairstyle?" in A Hard Day's Night, Arthur brought to New York a taste of swinging London and, more important, it foreshadowed the caste-destroying social aesthetic that could have become one of disco's biggest gifts to world culture. Although the prospective clubgoer still needed something that could only be inherited (i.e., beauty) in order to catch the eye of doorman Mickey Deans and gain access to the world beyond the club's fabled velvet ropes, Arthur was the first step in the undoing of the jet set—it was no longer good enough just to have a name or money. However, in a glaring example of the truism that subcultures always end up reproducing the culture they try to escape, by granting admission based on the sexual proclivites of the doorman, Arthur set the precedent for the disco culture born from the resistance to the Nazis to enshrine its own peculiar form of body fascism. Sybil Burton and Deans also dabbled in a bit of social genetic engineering; they were after the right mix: a handful of celebrities like Judy Garland, Leonard Bernstein, Liza Minnelli, and Diana Vreeland; a pinch of pretty young things in miniskirts, bell-bottoms, and Nehru jackets; a soupçon of outrageous night people; and the merest hint of prostitutes and hustlers. This was the beginning of that all-important night world concept that would be elevated to an art form a decade later by Studio 54's Steve Rubell.

The concept of the mix was taken one step further by Arthur's disc jockey, Terry Noel. Noel had been one of the house dancers at the Peppermint Lounge during its heyday, and he understood both the highs and lows of the three-minute pop single. While the immediacy of the traditional single got people onto the dance floor in a hurry, its abrupt ending got them off just as quickly. With Arthur's fairly sophisticated sound system and two turntables at his disposal, Noel became the first DJ to mix records, to blend, say, Smokey Robinson & the Miracles, the Mamas and the Papas, Otis Redding, and the Rolling Stones as part of one continuous flow. Now there was no abrupt ending, no jarring halt to your favorite song, no excuse, other than physical exhaustion, to stop dancing. This may have been the dawn of the psychedelic era and the beginning of "head music," but no musical innovation had so catered to the body since the advent of the drum.

Arthur struck a singular pose in New York nighlife. Unlike the Olde Worlde vibe of most of New York's nightspots, Arthur was a brash Pop Art laboratory filled with bold blocks of primary colors, Plexiglas, and smoked mirrors; the drinks were served in goblets. This was not your granddad's wood-paneled gentlemen's club, a lavish dance palace of the 1920s and '30s, or the exotic fantasia where you took the missus or the mistress to get a bit of the other. It was something thoroughly modern and totally new, and New York's nightspots quickly followed suit. In response, Coquelin and Borden Stevenson (the son of onetime Democratic presidential candidate Adlai Stevenson) opened the Cheetah at Broadway and Fifty-third Street. It didn't get more over the top than the Cheetah: an eight-thousand-square-foot dance floor surrounded by garish lighting, a movie theater, a TV room (with one color television), a reading room (complete with library) for any bookworms who had somehow stumbled in, a clothes shop, and vendors making their way through the crowd hawking Nathan's hot dogs at 50 cents a pop.

Offering a slightly more sophisticated menu (although the onion soup and Sole Kathleen were cooked at home by owner Nilo DePaul and brought in frozen to be reheated on the premises), Aux Puces was a French restaurant on Fifty-fifth Street between Park and Madison avenues that provided a bridge between Old World elegance and the brash new Pop Art decor. From the outside, it looked like your run-of-the-mill faux Parisian bistro. "You had to *know* there was more behind it," says Kathy Dorritie, one of the club's DJs who would later gain fame under the name Cherry Vanilla as a member of the cast of Andy Warhol's shocking stage show *Pork*, as David Bowie's publicist, and as a punk icon in her own right. "Many people had no idea. You knocked on a big wooden door and David

Smith either let you in or told you there was a private party going on back there and turned you away. Getting in depended on your being known, beautiful, sexy, famous, a drug dealer, a madam, whatever David decided was going to make the night divine."[52] Once inside, Aux Puces was a reflection of the anointed ones' glitter and dazzle: It was filled with mirrored coffee tables painted with astrological signs surrounded by velvet banquettes and a mirrored fireplace. There were a few chandeliers and birdcages dangling from the already low ceiling and fake palm trees dotted around the floor to add a hint of natural color. "The dance floor was quite small," says Dorritie, "but that was the fun of it. Everyone was jammed in together, bodies touching bodies, padding joints, snorts of coke, poppers. That's what everyone liked about it." The music played by Dorritie and fellow DJ Jay Martin was a hipper, less uptight selection than that spun by Terry Noel at Arthur: a mix of soul (Motown, Aretha Franklin, Lee Dorsey, Lorraine Ellison), rock (Jimi Hendrix, Janis Joplin, and Iron Butterfly's "In-A-Gadda-Da-Vida"), and oddities like "word-jazz" maestro Ken Nordine and French yé-yé girls like Françoise Hardy and Sylvie Vartan.

Although the distaff discaire would soon become a rarity in New York nightlife, Dorritie had an almost equally hip counterpart in British expatriate Ann Henry, who spun at downtown's only society discotheque, Salvation! on Sheridan Square. Like Arthur and Aux Puces, the scene inside Salvation! was largely the creation of doorman Mike Quashie, a limbo instructor from Trinidad, who let in plenty of Greenwich Village freaks to provide entertainment for the magnates, fashion designers, and their admirers who frequented the place. As the crowd of suits and women sporting Native American chic (headbands and deerskin miniskirts) attempted to do the booglaoo to the Doors on the tiny dance floor, Henry would also control the lights, projecting parameciumlike fractals onto the club's white walls.

The wild fantasyscapes of Arthur, Cheetah, Salvation!, and Aux Puces paralleled the development of the multimedia aesthetic that began during the early to mid-1960s. With technology encroaching on art, and vice versa, the old divide between high and low culture started to crumble. Art movements like Fluxus (neo-Dadaists attempting to challenge the notion that works of art are fixed objects through mixed-media works like found poems, mail art, "aktions," performance art, etc.), Jonas Mekas's Expanded Cinema (in which film's relationship with the screen and the theater was called into question with the use of slideshows, music, and lights), and Allan Kaprow's "happenings" (improvised theatrical events that emphasized the experiences and sensations of the audience) not only questioned the nature of "art" but also the role of the spectator. The previously passive audience of art and cinema was now being asked to become part of the process, part of the work of art. This, in turn, paralleled the rise of the hippie counterculture and its championing of "mind-expanding" drugs that allegedly heightened sensitivity and fostered feelings of connectedness. Andy Warhol's jarring discotheque environment Exploding Plastic Inevitable (with music provided by the Velvet Underground and film projections, strobe light show, and patterned slides designed by Warhol and assistant Dan Williams) and the hippie "be-ins" ("gatherings of the tribes" featuring poetry, lectures, rock bands, impromptu bongo jam sessions, child care provided by the Hell's Angels, Timothy Leary playing patty-cake with little girls, and so on) combined the multimedia aesthetic with the sensory overload of psychedelic indulgence.

Of course, in the sphere of dance music the dancers had always been part of the spectacle. Predominantly black clubs like the Territorial Club on 125th Street in Harlem, the COCP social club on Fulton Street in Brooklyn, the Dom (below the Electric Circus on St. Mark's Place), Nell Gwynn's Taverne across the street from Grand Central Station, and Gary Catus's Third World Gallery at 144 Fifth Avenue combined aspects of the house/rent parties of the 1920s and '30s with the African-American tradition of the "jook" (a kind of communitarian party that emerged in the postemancipation South where new dance steps were taught and exchanged between people from different regions) to create atmospheres that were halfway between a bar and someone's house. The focus at the gatherings was firmly on the dance floor, with the dancers essentially the star performers. As Sly Stone sang in 1970, "Everybody is a star," and as Sybil Burton's notion of the "mix" indicates, this idea of the audience being the true star of the show would become one of the most subversive aspects of disco culture.

The notions of the "happening" and the "be-in" were quickly

assimilated into the club culture of the time and embodied most outrageously at the opening gala for the Electric Circus, housed in the old Polish National Hall at 23 St. Mark's Place, on June 27, 1967 (as well as trapeze performers and performance artists, the club featured a blinding light show and a sound system so powerful that New York City's electric supplier Con Edison had to lay a special cable underneath the street just to power it).[53] But these ideas were expressed perhaps most perfectly, most bizarrely at a club at 429 Broome Street in SoHo, which at the time was still largely a no-go area full of abandoned warehouses and bad street lighting. Opened in 1968, Cerebrum was effectively the world's first chill-out club. John Gruen in *Vogue* described an evening there: "At the door, a young man dressed in outer-space silver greets you with enormous gentleness and asks you to remove all your clothes . . . Now, as you and your date stand in pristine nakedness, a lovely young girl helps you into a voluminous, shimmery garment—a kind of silken flowing toga with hood that is cool and delectable to the touch—and leads you through a dark, carpeted corridor into a large softly lit room. Continuous music varies from Indian contemplative to hard-rock soul; on the walls, multicolored projections.

"It is a white room," he goes on. "There are no tables and chairs. You sit communally on heavily carpeted 'islands,' each designed to accommodate up to six persons . . . No one talks. The idea is to 'experience.' In a short time your guide returns with a goblet filled with *water*. This is your drink and it must be shared with your date—only one glass a couple. With it comes a large plate of marshmallows . . . Later still, the guide comes and sits with you. She has with her a tube of heavily scented hand lotion, and begins to anoint your hands with it."[54]

Of course, not every club was as sedate as Cerebrum. The club housed at 407 West 43rd Street between Ninth and Tenth avenues in the Hell's Kitchen section of Manhattan would eventually become one of the most celebrated and outrageous clubs in the long and colorful history of New York nightlife. Arnie Lord opened the Church, which was indeed housed in a former German Baptist church, at the tail end of the 1960s as perhaps the most over-the-top of all of the hippie sensoriums. Lord "had the diabolical idea of decorating it for a Witches' Sabbath. Opposite the altar was a huge mural projecting a terrifying image of the devil, his eyes drawn so that wherever you stood, his baleful orbs were glaring down upon you. Around the Evil One was a flight of angels with exposed genitalia engaging in every known form of sexual intercourse. Before the altar with its broad marble communion table and imposing range of organ pipes stood the long-haired DJ preparing the disco sacrament. With the throw of a switch he could black out the hall and illuminate it eerily with lights shining through the stained-glass windows. His communicants firked around or laid back on the pews, which had been arranged around the walls as banquettes."[55] As a sop to the building's former occupants, the DJ would often play the theme song from *Jesus Christ Superstar*—lighting up each of the stained glass windows as he did.[56]

Even though the place was an old Baptist church, Lord's choice of decor attracted the ire of the New York archdiocese of the Roman Catholic church, which temporarily suspended their centuries-long feud with the spiritual descendants of Martin Luther and branded the Church a blasphemy. The Catholic church managed to persuade a judge to grant an injunction against the club, forcing it to close down, but not for long.

The pressure exerted on the Church's gates by the sybaritic hordes was so great that it quickly reopened under the name the Sanctuary, with plastic grapes covering the cherubs' unmentionables, but it was now the clientele rather than the decor that was desecrating this former house of God. The club's ownership, having fallen into financial straits, was taken over by a flamboyant gay couple called only by their first names, Seymour and Shelley, and the crowd changed accordingly. While the gay rights movement was ignited a couple of miles away at a bar called the Stonewall Inn in Greenwich Village,[57] the Sanctuary, whose crowd was also peppered with Broadway actors (due to the club's location near the theater district) and hip straights, would prove to be one of the sites of gay liberation's first full flowering. No longer the victims of unchecked police harassment, with the birth control pill slowly changing people's minds about the function of sex and a climate of "I'm OK, You're OK" liberal tolerance, the Sanctuary's gay crowd turned the former house of worship into a bacchanalian pleasure palace. "It was here that the Bump got its start,"

Goldman wrote, "only it wasn't the cute little hip-hugger, tushie-touching step that it became in the straight world. It was a frank pantomime of buggery. Two boys could get into it together or twenty could make up a daisy chain."[58] The sex wasn't confined to the dance floor, nor was it confined to simulation. There were constant orgies in the toilets, and the club would be eventually closed down in 1972 because its patrons regularly used the hallways of neighboring buildings for impromptu "bump" sessions.[59]

The orgiastic spirit of the Sanctuary was intensified by the music, a triumphal march of syncopated drums and keyboard fanfares—the ceremonial accompaniment to a tribal rite of intiation for people who were just beginning to conceive of themselves as a group, as a unified whole. There was Motown (particularly the Four Tops' "Don't Bring Back Memories," a 1969 track that presaged the direction soul would take in the '70s in its dynamics, percussion, and instrumentation if not its maximialism, and the slower "Still Water [Peace and Love]") and James Brown and Aretha Franklin and Sly & the Family Stone and Booker T. & the MG's, to be sure (after all, what was a dance party without the black voices and rhythms that made it all possible?), but the most striking aspect of the Sanctuary sound was the predominance of a heavily percussive psychedelia: Babatunde Olatunji's pan-African drumming and chanting on "Jin-Go-Lo-Ba (Drums of Passion)"; the conga-heavy Latin- and Afro-rock of Santana and Osibisa; the jazz-rock of Brian Auger; Cat Mother and the All Night News Boys' "Track in 'A' (Nebraska Nights)" (a fairly directionless, sullen hippie jam coproduced by Jimi Hendrix that becomes a wild, almost gamelanlike[60] fire dance with the Phantom of the Opera on keyboards at the seven-minute mark); the Marketts' surfbeat takeoff of the evergreen "Apache" called "Out of Limits"; British freakbeat band Timebox's amphetamines-'n'-strings rave-up of the 4 Seasons' "Beggin'"; high-energy Detroit rock meeting the Stax rhythm section on Mitch Ryder's *The Detroit/Memphis Experiment*; and the horny, musky, cowbell-heavy "Mongoose" by Elephant's Memory. An evening at the Sanctuary would always finish with the Doors' epic of oedipal rage and pharmacological lunacy, "The End."

The DJ's name was Francis Grasso and he almost single-handedly created what would become disco's sonic hallmarks. DJs before Grasso played whatever was popular at the time. Grasso, on the other hand, was playing African music that was recorded in 1959 in the early '70s and playing obscure British imports that he had to bug record shops to order specially for him. Grasso's taste in percussive rock especially created the nexus that would eventually establish disco as its own musical genre, as something distinct from either soul or funk. Many of the records he championed were funky but definitely not funk: They weren't as aggressive in either attitude or rhythm, and they often sounded as if they were wrapped in a patina of alienation. One of his favorite records was Little Sister's "You're the One," a record produced by Sly Stone and featuring his sister Vanetta Stewart, Elva Melton, and Mary Rand. With an almost demonic voice repeating the title phrase over and over again, a deracinated James Brown horn chart, and a heavy, plodding bass line–driven groove that quickly reasserts groove's literal meaning as a rut over its metaphorical, rhythmic meaning, the track would presage Stone's move from token poster child for the hippie movement to dark chronicler of the African-American condition at the turn of the 1970s.

But it wasn't just the playlist that was revolutionary, it was what Grasso did with his records that helped define disco as a style and not just a place you went to hear records. Although Terry Noel was the first DJ actually to mix records, it was Grasso who would make the DJ set a unified whole rather than a collection of individual records. Fittingly, Grasso had replaced Noel as the DJ at a club on Central Park South called Salvation II one night in 1968 (when Noel showed up late), and it was here that he hit upon the idea of the DJ mix as "a journey," as one continuous piece of music that the DJ himself created out of ready-made parts. Grasso's signature mix of the percussion breakdown of Chicago Transit Authority's "I'm a Man" with Robert Plant's orgasmic moans and Jimmy Page's eerie guitar effects from the middle section of Led Zeppelin's "Whole Lotta Love" compounded the ultramasculine atmosphere of the Sanctuary and set in motion the notion that a good DJ was a gifted musician in his or her own right and that a turntable and a mixer were his or her instruments. Grasso is generally credited as being the first DJ to beat mix (to sonically overlap two records so that their drumbeats are synchronized), and he introduced the technique of slip-cueing (holding the record about to be cued in place while the turntable underneath spins, so that the record can be started exactly where you want at the exact millisecond you want it started).[61] He used this technique to extend the dancers' pleasure potentially indefinitely by playing two copies of the same record on two turntables,[62] lengthening the grooves of such crowd favorites as James Brown's "Hot Pants" or Abaco Dream's "Life and Death in G & A" (another Sly Stone record).

It was a thrilling, intensely physical sound, particularly when blasted through the mammoth stacks that the Sanctuary had acquired from the rock band Mountain. The physical experience of the music was heightened by the pharmacopoeia provided by the dealers who mobbed the club and provided patrons with poppers, quaaludes, and Seconal.[63] As journalist Peter Braunstein writes, "The drugs of the psychedelic 60s, particularly LSD, were now supplanted by the 'body high' drugs of the 1970s. Predominant in the gay disco scene were poppers, amyl nitrate vials, used originally by angina sufferers, which when broken open and inhaled caused a precipitous drop in blood pressure and near-loss of consciousness [amyl nitrate was originally used in the gay community as a means to enhance orgasm]. Poppers coexisted with that other quintessential 1970s club drug Quaalude, which suspended motor coordination and turned one's arms and legs to Jell-O."[64] Borrowing the concept from the "events" of the psychedelic underground where groups like the Grateful Dead would craft their sets to coincide with the peaks and valleys of the acid trip, Grasso would program his "journeys" in such a way that they would maximize the effect of the narcotics of choice.

With Grasso playing a kind of music that tempered the "head music" of the psychedelic era with "tribal" percussion that connected more with the feet and groin, and with the accompanying drugs moving away from mind-expanding psychedelics toward those that delivered a body high, the Sanctuary marked the transition between the expanded consciousness espoused by travelers going "further" in the 1960s and the near loss of consciousness that many commentators said characterized the solipsistic 1970s. Disco was a retreat back into the body—both the newly liberated body of its prime constituents and the body politic. As Peter Carroll wrote, "Rhetoric ran freely in 1970—rhetoric about the war and about peace, rhetoric about social injustice and possibility. There was also considerable rhetoric about rhetoric."[65] After wars and traumatic events, American popular music has always returned to the body as a locus of meaning and turned its back on language: After the Civil War, barn dances and square dances were all the rage, and this was also when burlesque dancing began in the United States with the vaudevillean skirt dance; the end of World War I saw the dawning of the Jazz Age; World War II heralded rock and roll.

But disco wasn't simply an escape from the language that had divided America, it was at the same time an embodiment of the very tensions and schisms that the rhetoric sought to express and resolve. Disco was at once about community and individual pleasure, sensation and alienation, orgy and sacrifice; it promised both liberation and constraint, release and restraint, frivolity and doom. Disco was both utopia and hell.

"COME ON OVER TO MY HOUSE
AND LET'S HAVE SOME FUN"
The Loft

Throughout its history, disco was trapped between worlds. It wasn't just caught in the tug-of-war between the opposite poles of gay and straight, black and white—though that, of course, was part of it. Disco's very birth was the result of the big bang between contradictory impulses: exclusion and inclusion, glamour and dilapidation, buying in and dropping out, engagement and withdrawal, earnestness and frippery. Born just as the great liberal experiment of the post-Depression years started to be dismantled and as the '60s hangover of disillusionment began, disco was seen by many commentators as the death knell for community and the harbinger of narcissism. There was at least one disco pioneer, however, who still believed in the '60s dream, that the Summer of Love wasn't over, that love could still save the day.

David Mancuso was born in 1944 and grew up in a Catholic orphanage in the upstate town of Utica, New York. The orphanage was run by a Sister Alicia, who would often hold parties for the children where she would play records in a room decorated with balloons and crepe paper.[66] When Mancuso wasn't in a celebratory mood he would spend time in the surrounding countryside "listening to birds, lying next to a spring and listening to water go across the rocks. And suddenly one day, I realized: What perfect music. Like with the sunrise and sunset, how things would build up into midday. There were times when it would be intense and times it would be soft and at sunset, it would get quiet and then the crickets would come in. I took this sense of rhythm, this sense of feeling."[67]

Mancuso brought this sense of the ebb and flow of the country idyll with him to the concrete jungle of New York City in 1965. While spending time in the antiwar, civil rights, and gay rights movements, Mancuso started to further explore his love of sound at his illegal loft space amid the abandoned warehouses at 647 Broadway, just north of SoHo. "I was always into sound, and I was more into the psychedelic sound in jazz, R&B, and all that stuff," Mancuso told London's XFM radio station. "I started making tapes where what I would do was take a song, and as soon as the song ended I would put some kind of sound effect and then the next record would come. I would do it like that, so it was always a continuous flow of some kind of sound information. And I would invite my friends over and we would have only big parties this time because I had this big space, and it'd be 100 people. And it started to happen more and more frequently."[68]

On Valentine's Day 1970, Mancuso decided to make his parties a bit more formal. The Love Saves the Day party was heralded by an invitation decorated with a reproduction of Salvador Dalí's *The Persistence of Memory*. While there was undeniably a hint of Timothy Leary about the proceedings (Mancuso uses Leary terms like "Bardo" and "set and setting" to describe his party philosophy, and there are stories aplenty about the punch and the fruit being spiked with LSD), Mancuso was also aiming at something more innocent, more childlike. As his invitation-only parties (which soon became members-only parties, with free membership) began to take off, the symbol of what would soon become known as the Loft shifted from Dalí to *Our Gang* (Spanky, Alfalfa, Buckwheat, Darla, et al.). Mancuso didn't serve alcohol, only juice and food, which were included in the $3 admission fee (Mancuso's motto was "life is a banquet"[69]). "The ceiling was hung with colored streamers and balloons," wrote Vince Aletti, describing the interior of Mancuso's home-cum-club. "Other balloons bobbed around on the floor and in the next room there were tables covered with bowls of fruit punch, nuts and raisins, bananas, small candies, and gum . . . it was like being at someone's—everyone's—birthday party."[70] In the corner of the main room there was a Christmas tree with its fairy lights on year-round. Mancuso controlled the party from a booth above the dance floor that was designed like an old Wurlitzer jukebox.

It may have begun on Valentine's Day during the tail end of the "free love" era, but that kind of love was never the focus of the Loft. After all, the back room hadn't been invented yet. While the party was predominantly gay and far from sexless, it was not particularly cruisy and was far more racially integrated than most of the gay parties at the time. Unusually, there was also a significant female presence at the Loft. Even destitute members weren't turned away—they were simply asked to write an IOU. "I remember going when it was $3.99 and they'd actually give you the penny back," recalls frequent visitor Danny Krivit.[71] Part Saturday night/Sunday morning hippie commune, part surrogate family, part Southern jook, the Loft represented the beloved community of the 1960s protest movements but had pleasure, beauty, and connectedness as its goals rather than social justice. Its success at achieving these goals can be measured by the fact that by 1975 Mancuso could remember only three small items being stolen from his house since he started running the weekly parties.[72] Of course, this was also the beginning of the eternal, unresolvable contradiction of the dance music scene. On one hand, Mancuso was preaching inclusivity and innocent positivity; on the other, his party was members-only and defiantly underground—you had to be in the know even to be aware of its existence. It may not have been elitist like the jet-set discotheques, but in its own way it was just as exclusive.

Where Francis Grasso was dazzling dancers at the Sanctuary and the Haven with his skill and working them to surging peaks of musk and sweat, Mancuso was using similar techniques to almost the opposite effect. According to Aletti, "Dancing at the Loft was like riding waves of music, being carried along as one song after another built relentlessly to a brilliant crest and broke, bringing almost involuntary shouts of approval from the crowd, then smoothed out, softened, and slowly began welling up to another peak."[73] If Grasso defined disco as a certain kind of rhythmic drive, Mancuso created its lushness, its elegance. But Mancuso was no baroque sybarite; he wasn't after symphonic grandeur but rather warm textures that caressed the dancers, grooves that swelled and broke like tides lapping the shore. "He played records at a volume that was just below loud, so you had to train your ears to listen harder," Krivit says.[74] Mancuso was an audiophile, and with Alex Rosner, an electronics engineer who escaped Nazi Germany through Schindler's list, he created the Loft's legendary sound system. With highs that shimmered (thanks to Rosner's array of tweeters that faced north, south, east, and west) and lows that cocooned the dancers, Mancuso was tuning into what he called "that natural rhythm, that three-billion-year-old dance— I just applied it through these artificial means which were amplifiers and records."[75] This almost Buddhist approach to sound was rounded off by Mancuso's legendary Koetsu record cartridges, which were designed by a Japanese painter who also made samurai swords.

While Mancuso and Grasso shared many songs on their playlists— James Brown's "(Get Up I Feel Like Being a) Sex Machine," Olatunji's "Jin-Go-Lo-Ba (Drums of Passion)," Little Sister's "You're the One"—Mancuso would play them in a different way: He would let them build and crash, rather than focusing on, and extending, the groove. These more percussive records would also be tempered by odder, often more ethereal selections. "The Loft had a real vibe, and they were playing records that I had bought and was really into, but I used to get a lot of trouble for playing," Krivit says. "People would come up to me like, 'What are you doing? This is stuff you play at your house.' I almost started to believe that and lose faith in my own taste and had to second-guess myself and play a little safer. Once I went to the Loft, I thought, 'Wait a minute, these exact records that I love are the peak records there. I gotta stop catering to these other people and concentrate on what I'm into' . . . A perfect example is War's 'City Country City.' Mandre's 'Solar Flight' was a good example of a record that people used to look at me like I'm playing drum 'n' bass in the '60s or something.

'You can't dance to this. There's no way you can dance to this, it's just impossible.' And yet I go to the Loft and people just go nuts to it."[76]

As DJ Larry Levan reminisced to Steven Harvey in 1983, "I used to watch people cry in The Loft for a slow song because it was so pretty."[77] An early Loft standby that had the dance floor in tears was a recording of the *Missa Luba* by Les Troubadours du Roi Baudoin, a group of forty-five young Congolese boys singing a Christian mass in a distinctly African style under the direction of Belgian Father Guido Haazen. No less spiritual, though rather less celestial, was Exuma's "Exuma, the Obeah Man," a funked-up junkanoo tune that offered an almost postmodern slant on the Caribbean religion of Obeah in a manner not dissimilar to Dr. John's take on New Orleans voodoo. Perhaps the strangest Loft record of all, though, was Diga Rhythm Band's "Sweet Sixteen." While the record featured only an array of percussion instruments, "Sweet Sixteen" was no rousing stomper or infinite trance circle. Rather, it was dominated by marimbas and vibes and could almost have been an extended Martin Denny or Les Baxter jam session; even when the group got down and dirty, it sounded more like the music to a free-movement class for expectant mothers at some New Age spa than a fierce rhythmic throwdown for urban sophisticates. Its tie-dyed vibes could be explained by the fact that the Diga Rhythm Band was the project of Grateful Dead drummer Mickey Hart.[78]

Of course, Mancuso wasn't one of the architects of the disco aesthetic because he managed to play slow songs without clearing the dance floor. He is credited with introducing what may very well be the foundation of the disco sound to New York's DJ community. Unlike either James Brown funk or the emerging sound of the Philadelphia International label that dominated the black music scene in 1972, Eddie Kendricks's "Girl You Need a Change of Mind" was an expansive track that slowly surged and then broke down (twice) and then built itself back up instrument by instrument throughout its eight-minute duration. There was no concentrated burst of percussive blare or gloopy sweetening to undercut the slow-burning groove, just the organic ebb and flow that Mancuso first heard sitting by a stream in upstate New York.

A further crucial disco component and Mancuso discovery was another hypnotic yet utterly celebratory record, "Soul Makossa" by Cameroonian jazzman Manu Dibango. Mancuso found the obscure imported forty-five in a West Indian record shop in Brooklyn in 1972 and played it frequently at the Loft.[79] With Mancuso attempting to replicate the gentle flux of nature with his DJ sets, the swirling, mesmerizing rhythms of "Soul Makossa" fit in perfectly. While the track was only four and a half minutes long, it made clear the link between the African trance ritual of "Jin-Go-Lo-Ba (Drums of Passion)" and the James Brown groove. This elongation and elastication of the funk was the disco aesthetic in a nutshell, and other African variants on this theme (Fela Kuti's "Shakara" and "Expensive Shit," Osibisa's "Music for Gong Gong," Black Blood's "AIE (A'Mwana)," and Buari's "Advice From Father") would become minor disco classics. The response to the first few airings of "Soul Makossa" was such that the few copies of the record in New York quickly sold out. One copy found its way to Frankie Crocker, a DJ at WBLS, the biggest black radio station in New York at the time, who played it on heavy rotation, creating such a buzz that at least twenty-three cover versions of "Soul Makossa" (including versions by Afrique, All Directions, Simon Kenyatta, Babatunde Olatunji, Nairobi Afro Band, the Ventures, the Gaytones, and the Mighty Tomcats—not to mention Armando Trovajoli's reversioning of the song as "Sessomatto" for an Italian sex farce of the same name; the song became a cult disco hit when it was reissued in the States by West End) were rushed out to feed demand for this now impossible-to-find record. Eventually, Atlantic licensed the record from French label Fiesta and it reached the bottom of the American Top 40 the following year.

Mancuso's crusades didn't stop there, though. In 1973, while in Amsterdam, he stumbled across a record that appealed to him because it had a track called "Wild Safari" that sounded like it might feature tribal percussion. The album was the delirious and rather silly funk-rock debut by a group of Spaniards, led by drummer Fernando Arbex and percussionist Tito Duarte, called Barrabas. Tracks like "Wild Safari" and "Woman" were heavily percussive cod-Latin rock with loony vocals in a style very similar to that of another European funk-rock group that was popular among New York DJs, Norway's

Titanic. The sound was redolent of the first cheap European package holidays and of traveling the hippie trail to Ibiza. More important, the English-as-a-second-language lyrics made the songs unintentionally camp, and the slightly stilted but strangely funky grooves were a refreshing change from the straight and narrow of most Anglo-American rock. Once again, the Barrabas record was wildly popular with the Loft's dancers, so Mancuso phoned the Spanish record company and arranged to sell the records at cost at the Loft because he simply wanted to spread the joy he found in their music.

Mancuso had proved that discotheques could sell records. The problem was that most of the record industry hadn't caught on yet. Back in the days when *Rolling Stone* was still a novelty, when MTV was inconceivable, the promotional machine of the record biz concentrated almost exclusively on radio. The club DJ was an afterthought. While Mancuso was credited with starting the ball rolling on "Soul Makossa" and Le Jardin spinner Bobby "Bobby DJ" Guttadaro was given gold records for his contribution to making Love Unlimited Orchestra's "Love's Theme," Carl Douglas's "Kung Fu Fighting," and Disco Tex & His Sex-O-Lettes' "Get Dancin'" hits, disco DJs were generally given short shrift by the record labels. With its ties to consumerism and quantifiable audience figures, radio DJing was an honest, respectable business; the club DJ was an underworld pariah who only brought unwanted focus on the seamier side of the music business and was dealt with accordingly. With his communitarian ideals, Mancuso wanted to change this and set about organizing New York's DJs in 1975. With fellow DJs Steve D'Aquisto (Tamburlaine, Broadway) and Paul Casella (Hollywood), and journalist Vince Aletti, Mancuso chartered the Record Pool in June at his new Loft at 99 Prince Street.[80] The idea was that the record companies could save money by sending promotional material to one centralized office and wouldn't have to deal with the DJ rabble coming to their offices in search of free records; the DJs would get all the new records without having to trek around the city and without being rejected because their club wasn't important enough.

Many of the DJs who were part of the Record Pool were inspired to spin because of Mancuso and the Loft. Nicky Siano, Larry Levan, Frankie Knuckles, David Rodriguez, and Tee Scott were all "Loft babies" who became the second generation of disco DJs, the ones who built on the foundations of Mancuso and Grasso and codified the sound and attitude of disco. David Rodriguez (along with Michael Cappello) was the DJ at the original Limelight (on Seventh Avenue between Christopher and Bleecker streets) in 1972. Making records like Betty Wright's "If You Love Me Like You Say You Love Me" and the Pointer Sisters' "Yes We Can Can" literally talk to each other by making them answer or complete each other's phrases, Rodriguez was perhaps the first of the storyteller DJs, linking his records thematically rather than by beat or groove. Rodriguez was also one of the DJs to introduce the cod-Latin style of Titanic's "Rain 2000." Cappello, on the other hand, was perhaps more technically gifted and more rhythmically intuitive. Paul Casella spun alongside Richie Kaczor at Hollywood at 128 West 45th Street (on the site of the old Peppermint Lounge). Both gained reputations for their prowess at mixing (or, more precisely, slip-cueing) with primitive equipment, and picking up a trick from Grasso, one of Casella's most popular transitions was mixing the short conga break of the Doobie Brothers' "Long Train Runnin'" into the J. Geils Band's reggae-ish "Give It to Me." Levan, Knuckles, and Scott, all of whom played the Continental Baths (the most opulent pleasure palace of gay New York at the time) at one time or another during the early '70s, would really make their mark on the scene from the mid-1970s onward.

The most important of these "Loft babies" was Nicky Siano. Siano was a young kid from Coney Island in love with music who first went to the Loft at age fifteen. The following year he landed a DJ gig at a club called the Round Table but was so unimpressed with the setup that he decided to open his own club in the Loft's image, but with a commercial imperative. Securing financing with the help of his brother, Siano opened the Gallery (also called the This & That Gallery) on Twenty-second Street between Sixth and Seventh avenues in 1973 (the club later moved to 172 Mercer Street). If Francis Grasso was the Chuck Berry of the turntables, Siano was the Jimi Hendrix. Siano built on Grasso's innovations and took them to new realms of expressivity and intensity. Playing on three turntables (while controlling the club's lights with foot pedals), he would take records like Gloria Spencer's gospel stormer "I Got It" and stretch it completely out of shape. Siano would work the crowd up to fever pitch by playing two copies of "I Got It," extending until breaking point the beginning where Spencer screams over the piston-pumping cymbals that would become familiar a few years later from both the Isley Brothers' "Fight the Power" and, more bizarrely, Black Sabbath's "Supernaut." He achieved a similar crowd response when he mixed MFSB's "Love Is the Message" (which he turned into "the national anthem of New York"[81]) with a sound-effect record featuring a jet plane taking off.[82] Siano was also credited with pioneering the use of varispeed turntables in club DJing. Previously the preserve of the avant-garde (John Cage's *Imaginary Landscape No. 1* uses a varispeed turntable to create an eerie tone poem portraying an Yves Tanguy–style topography), the vari-speed turntable enabled Siano to create a world that was just as far-fetched as that of the avant-gardists, but he used it to create order and neatness rather than wild, other-worldly sounds. Taking advantage of the turntable's ability to vary its speed, and thus the pitch and tempo of the record it's playing, Siano was able to craft mixes and blends that were almost letter-perfect. In Siano's hands, the transitions between songs were no longer the awkward herky-jerky, sputtering dance floor moments (like trying to change gears without using the clutch) they used to be; they were now taut, well-defined, and smooth—kind of like the ideal male body on the dance floor. It would be hard to overstate the impact of this on the DJing scene. A whole new world was created; reputations were destroyed and made in the flash of a cross-fade.

Siano also shaped the direction of what would soon be called disco music. He loved deep, deep bass and had Alex Rosner design him a sound system with forbiddingly dark, bowel-quaking bass re-production and crossover points on his mixing board so he could isolate the treble, midrange, and bass of a record. Siano's sound was reflected in the spartan decor of his club. Although it was decorated with streamers and balloons à la the Loft, the Gallery had minimal lighting that would be used only during key moments of certain songs. The occasional rhythmic flashes of light would punctuate the festivities, paralleling the surging energy of the records, and carry the dancers out of the penumbra up to heights of dizzying incan-descence. More than any DJ before him, Siano homed in on the break. While the percussive breakdowns of records were focal points in the sets of Grasso and Mancuso, Siano pushed this aesthetic over the top. Grasso and Mancuso both built up to the breaks, but Siano attacked them right from the get-go and played his favorite parts of a record over and over and over and over again by using two copies at once. Like the free jazz cats who congregated in similar loft spaces to explore parallel limits of physical and spiritual release, punk rockers accelerating three chords into immolating infinity, and Bronx hip-hoppers contorting themselves into new shapes by dancing to their own, more explosive break beats, Siano created a dark whorl of sound, a vortex of tribal drums and propulsive bass murmurs that was at once exhilarating and menacing.

But he also loved over-the-top female vocals, and if anyone can be credited with bringing the diva to the dance it is Siano. Records featuring either rousing, "gonna wash that man right out of my hair," don't-do-me-wrong vocals, or breathy, soft-focus coos of postcoital bliss by Gloria Spencer, Genie Brown, Faith, Hope & Charity singer Zulema, Ecstasy, Passion & Pain, Thelma Houston, Minnie Riperton, Diana Ross, and LaBelle all got extensive airings at the Gallery. In essence, Siano was the bridge between the intense, rather serious music of the earliest days of disco and the cheery music of airheaded levity that it became in the popular imagination. The characteristic interplay between the sheer ecstasy or thrilling exorcism of the vocalist and a creeping, dark undertow that marked out the very best disco music was first pinpointed by Siano.

"YOU'RE JUST THE RIGHT SIZE"
The Art of the Mix and the Development
of the Twelve-inch Single

While DJs always wanted longer records with longer percussive passages (one of the many reasons why album tracks, rather than singles, were so important in the earliest days of disco), Nicky Siano's mixing advances at the Gallery made this even more imperative. The traditional seven-inch forty-five is difficult to handle when in the middle of the fray of a DJ set. On top of that, its tight, compressed grooves wear out faster than those on albums and they just don't sound as good in a big room with lots of space to fill. The whirling dervish trance ritual that was developing in these New York clubs also demanded extended tracks of a more diffuse, prolonged intensity than the standard three-minute wham-bam-thank-you-ma'am pop single—dancing from midnight until six in the morning at the Loft or the Gallery was a very different proposition from the midday blood-sugar rush of the sock hops or the drunken, stumbling toga parties of old.

One of the first people to recognize this new paradigm was, ironically, an old music biz hand who had left the industry in disgust at its duplicitousness and was pursuing a career in modeling instead. Yet however much he was identified as Camel's answer to the Marlboro Man or the face of classic tailors Hart, Schaffner & Marx, Tom Moulton always identified himself through music. "Without music I'm dead," he says. "That's my whole life. That's who my lover is, that's who my mistress is, that's everything."[83]

Moulton grew up in Schenectady, New York, about thirty-five miles down the road from David Mancuso in Utica, and was a music buff from a very young age. "I was always used to hearing the white versions of the black songs, but when 'Earth Angel' by the Penguins came out, oh, my God," he reminisces. "I thought, 'Oh, Lord, that's really something.' The next record I really went nuts over was 'Slippin' and Slidin'' by Little Richard, and I thought, 'Uh-oh, something's happening here because white people sure don't play like that.'"[84] His love of black music eventually led to a job in sales and promotion for King Records from 1959 to 1961, where he worked with James Brown, Freddie King, and Hank Ballard.

But after similar jobs with RCA and United Artists, Moulton got fed up with "the bullshit, the ass-kissing, the insincerity" and started working for the Bookings and, later, the Ford modeling agencies. "There was this guy John Whyte who was at the same agency I was and owned the Botel on Fire Island [a predominantly gay summer community about fifty miles from New York City]," Moulton remembers of the fateful event in 1972 that would change not only his life but eventually the entire course of music history. "A friend told me I should go out there and check out the music that people were dancing to [at the Sunday Tea Party]. So I went out there and I thought, 'Okay, this is very Villagey, bohemian.' And they're listening to *soul* music. I'm watching these white people really getting off on this music. And I'm really observing them, and, of course, all the songs are like two and a half, three minutes long, and I notice how everything is like 'one-two-three-four,' and they'd always leave the floor on 'one.' They'd always walk off [because the clumsy mixing interrupted the momentum and flow]. I'm thinking, it's a shame, 'cause you could almost sense an emotional reaction there, but it wasn't long enough to get it out. So I thought, 'I'm going to try something.' And I went to John and said, 'You got a tape machine, right? I'm going to try something and see if it works.'"[85]

The result of his experimentation was a forty-five-minute tape of perfectly mixed music with no skips, no awkward transitions, nothing played at the wrong speed, no DJ saying, 'Whoops!' It took him eighty hours to make. "But it was flawless," Moulton beams. He spent his two working weeks painstakingly reediting, recrafting, and blending with a razor blade, Scotch tape, and varispeed turntable records by Ann Peebles, Syl Johnson, the Detroit Emeralds, and obscure records on tiny labels that he found in Oakland, California. "He would do it on an old Wollensak recorder," recalls Barry Lederer, a DJ and soundman who sometimes watched Moulton at work. "Since he couldn't blend [i.e., he didn't have a mixer], he would actually count out the beats of a song with his feet, and as it came to the end he would make the next song come in on the right one, two, three, four, beat . . . and this worked."[86] He doubled the length of the records and stretched out the grooves so that the dancers just couldn't hide (or walk off the floor). "It was mostly new stuff," Moulton remembers, "stuff that I liked, but I knew there were certain songs that had that 'I've gotta get up and move to this no matter what.' I'd always start with that kind of a song where people would want to dance to that, and then you could start taking them on this trip. What I would use was this varispeed and start speeding up slowly so you'd never know. And then I go into the next song, so that by the end of the forty-five minutes you could peel them off the walls, they were screaming and yelling."

Well, that didn't exactly happen when Moulton gave the tape to Whyte. As Moulton recalls: "He wouldn't play it. John hands the tape back to me and says, 'Don't give up your day job.' So I had the tape in hand and I was sitting waiting for the boat to take me back to the mainland. This guy came over to me and said, 'Did somebody just die?' I said, 'Why?' 'I've never seen anyone look so down in my entire life. What's the matter?' I kind of explained the story to him. He says, 'Listen, I don't do the music here [at the Sandpiper restaurant and bar], but my partner does. If you want, I'll give him the tape and see what happens. Give me your phone number and address and we'll send it to you.' I said, 'Okay.' I forgot about it. A couple of weeks later, I get this call at quarter to one in the morning. 'Hello.' 'They hate the tape.' And I said, 'Oh, okay.' I guess I was on the wrong track here. The next night—I should say the next morning—I get a call at two in the morning. It sounds like someone in a stadium. 'They love the tape.' I hung up, thinking these people are sick. They call back like five or six times, and I keep hanging up. The next day, I get a call: 'Hi, my name is Ron Malcolm and I love your tape.' 'But someone called me on Friday.' 'That was me.' 'I thought you said they hated the tape.' 'They did . . . You know when people come out here on a Friday night, they gotta fight the city traffic, then the Long Island Expressway, then they gotta take a boat. They just want to come down. They don't want to come down to things they don't know. They want things to be familiar. The next day, they're ready to party, and they want some new stuff. That's why yours worked so well because you got them with the one song and then you took them somewhere they'd never been before. What I'd like you to do is do a tape a week.' And I was like, 'Forget it. I don't work eighty hours a week for anybody. That's very difficult to do.' He said, 'We'll give you five hundred dollars a tape.' I said, 'You can give me ten thousand a tape, that's not the problem. It's time.' He said, 'Can we work out an arrangement where you give us an hour-and-a-half tape just for Memorial Day, the Fourth of July, and Labor Day?' 'Oh, okay. I think I can do that.' I didn't realize how fast those holidays come. I just got one done and then it's the Fourth of July. I had to make a living too. I said, 'This is crazy. How did I agree to do this?' That's basically how it got started, but I had no idea what I was doing. I just had this idea to do something a certain way, and it worked. When I think about it now, I really had a lot of balls to do something like that."[87]

At around the same time as Moulton started making his tapes for the Sandpiper, the sale of reel-to-reel tapes of DJ sets started in New York City. These tapes, which the DJs often made as backups in case something went wrong with their turntables, sold for between $30 and $75 apiece. Claiming that Manhattan's trendy beauty parlors and cafés that wanted an alternative to Muzak for background music were the main customers of the tapes, *Billboard* magazine, the voice of the American record industry, decried the copyright violation inherent in the practice and the illegality of the trade.[88]

Soon enough, though, the record companies wanted in on the action. The first "legitimate" mixed compilation was Spring's *Disco Par-r-r-ty*, which was released in 1974. "There's a new spirit at work here," the liner notes trumpeted. "Something more in tune with the spirit of the times . . . and the tastes of the *now* audience . . . A spirit which has pulled out all the stops . . . We're having a party and everybody's invited."[89] While the selection of tracks was a pretty accurate reflection of what was being played in discotheques at the time—Barry White, James Brown, Joe Simon, the Chakachas, and the Peppers—the "mixing" was pretty appalling (the songs just scrunched together as if they were on a crowded bus and there was no DJ credited on the album, not that any self-respecting discaire would have wanted to be associated with it) despite the claim that the album was "tight and distinctive . . . professional and polished . . . never contrived or stylized."[90] Needless to say, it couldn't hold a cross-fader to one of Moulton's meticulously crafted tapes.

Perhaps because of such atrocities, Moulton's tapes were garnering him attention from some of the record companies attuned to New York's club life. "Because I used to be in the record business, I would go to different companies and ask them for instrumentals of certain records to see if I could do a little stretcharoo here and there because I've got to make these tapes longer," Moulton says. "So I did it to a song called 'Dream World' [by journeyman Oklahoma soul singer Don Downing]. And the label [Scepter] said, 'Do you think you could do that in the studio?' I went, 'I really don't know. I've only been in a studio a couple of times and that was back in the sixties at RCA.' So I did it, and I noticed that the song is so short. I said, 'How am I going to make it longer? Oh, I'll just do this and blah blah blah. But I can't do that because it modulates. How am I going to get around that?' . . . I'm listening and listening and listening. I said, 'What if I take out the strings, take out this, take out this. God, I gotta take out everything.' Finally, I said, 'Wait a minute, all that's left is the percussion. Maybe I can raise the congas a little bit, then just kind of groove, and then all of a sudden come in with the bass line.' I wanted to build it back up so that it sounded like it modulated again. Of course, it didn't. Everyone to this day says it modulates twice. Oh, no, it don't, only once." The label liked what Moulton did and asked him to perform a similar trick with B. T. Express's "Do It ('Til You're Satisfied)." "The group hated what I did to that record, they absolutely hated it," he declares. "I saw them on *Soul Train* when it was the number one song. [Imitates Don Cornelius] 'We're talking to B. T. Express. Their record is 5:35 and the radio stations are playing it.' 'Yeah, that's the way we recorded it.' Oh, I wanted to kill them. They kept saying, 'Oh, you put the organ in the middle.' Man, I wanted to kill them I was so mad."[91]

Moulton wasn't just elongating records to meet the demands of the dance floor. Holing himself up in his living room, Moulton was toying and playing with these records, using his equalizer to boost the bottom end and adding breaks to create disco extravaganzas out of three-minute pop songs. The first side of Gloria Gaynor's 1975 album, *Never Can Say Goodbye*, was an eighteen-minute mix of her first hit, "Honey Bee," the Clifton Davis–penned title track, and a cover of the Four Tops' "Reach Out, I'll Be There." "I speeded ['Honey Bee'] up a bit, but what that does is it puts things up in a higher range and makes the drums a little brighter," Moulton told *Black Music* magazine. "It makes the voice a little higher, and if you roll off the bottom and put more highs on the voice, you can almost make like she's really screaming, like she's really into the record. I've done that with a lot of records, where it sounds like they're singing their ass off, but they're not 'cause it's done technically."[92]

Whatever studio alchemy Moulton was up to, the industry wasn't interested. Instead, it was obsessed with the effect the longer records might have on radio play and its well-established promotional machines. The success of records like "Do It ('Til You're Satisfied)" led the December 14, 1974, edition of *Billboard* to trumpet, "Discos Demand Five-Minute Singles" on its front page. A survey found DJs and club owners bemoaning the industry's slow response time to the increasing importance of the discotheque as a medium for breaking records and its seeming lack of interest in satisfying the clubs' needs for longer records with breaks and builds. While independent labels like Scepter and Roulette believed they garnered extra sales by releasing versions of Don Downing's "Dream World" and Moment of Truth's "Your Love" (also a Moulton "stretcharoo") with a "radio mix" on one side and a longer, club-friendly mix on the flip, the majority of the industry was happy with the status quo. As is always the case in the music biz, though, an accident would force the record companies' hand.

Sometime in early 1975, after doing an edit of Al Downing's "I'll Be Holding On," Moulton took the mix to New York's Media Sound to be mastered onto a seven-inch metal blank as a reference disc. However, they were out of them and had only twelve-inch blanks left, so Moulton and engineer José Rodriguez used one of those instead. "Oh, my God, boy was that so hot," Moulton enthuses, remembering the sound when they first played the twelve-inch. "It just made the regular forty-fives sound like such shit. The levels were so much . . . the dynamics, the bass, the everything, the volume was like . . . playing something that was fifth generation and all of a sudden you're playing the master tape." For Moulton's next edit, "So Much for Love" by Moment of Truth for the Roulette label, he went one step further and gave some test pressings to DJs like Richie Kaczor and David Rodriguez. Although not released commercially until 1976 (by Salsoul), this was the very first twelve-inch single. Several promotional twelve-inches followed in quick succession: Scepter released Bobby Moore's "(Call Me Your) Anything Man" in June 1975; Warners issued a special promotional one-sided twelve-inch version of Calhoon's "(Do You Wanna) Dance Dance Dance" in July; Atlantic countered with Barrabas's "Mellow Blow" and Ace Spectrum's "Keep Holding On" in August; also in August was Moulton's mix of Good Times star Ralph Carter's "When You're Young and in Love" on Mercury.

Of course, the twelve-inch single not only allowed for a more defined bass sound and greater volume, but the format's much less constraining temporal restrictions allowed for seemingly infinite possibilities of restructuring songs. However, none of the mixers of the original twelve-inches seemed to grasp this—most were pretty formulaic, prefab extensions. It wasn't until one of disco's maverick geniuses got his first remix commission that this would change, and that the new format would get a work worthy of releasing to the general public. Released a week before Salsoul's pressing of "So Much for Love" in May 1976, Walter Gibbons's radical restructuring of the veteran Philadelphia vocal group Double Exposure's "Ten Percent" was the first commercially available twelve-inch. While primeness has been thrust upon it simply for being first, "Ten Percent" would deserve accolades even if it were the 137th twelve-inch single. Gibbons, the resident DJ at Galaxy 21 at 256 West 23rd Street, was almost universally revered on the disco scene for his heavily percussive DJing style that was nearly as reliant on sliced-and-diced breaks as the hip-hop DJs in the Bronx. People called Gibbons's style "jungle music." The consumately professional (and commercial) Moulton's reedits were often merely reconstructive plastic surgery, a simple matter of extension and reduction. Gibbons's mixes, on the other hand, were as much about deconstruction as reconstruction. The first minute and forty seconds of "Ten Percent" is as intoxicating an experience as recorded music has to offer: all champagne bubbles and gooey chocolate cake. Beginning with the ur-disco beat (a few seconds of hissing hi-hats and galloping kicks enveloped by serpentine congas) punctuated by the sharpest string edit you will ever hear, the track is then transmuted into ambrosia when Gibbons isolates TG Conway's unctuous keyboard. Gibbons not only extends the track from three minutes to more than nine, but turns it into a Philly fantasia (the record was produced by the mainstays of the Philadelphia International house band MFSB, Earl Young, Ron Baker, and Norman Harris) of orchestral swoops, pinpoint details and intense but almost soothing breaks.

His 1977 remix of Loleatta Holloway's "Hit and Run" was equally remarkable. This wasn't a cut-and-paste job like "Ten Percent," though. Here, he had access to the multitrack tapes, enabling him to rebuild the song from scratch, which he did. Excising large portions of the record, including several minutes of Holloway's vocals, Gibbons shifted the focus of the track from hokey love song to burning stormer with Holloway, one of disco's most charismatic and individual vocalists, reduced to nothing but vamps and exhortations. Other early Gibbons landmark mixes include the percussion frenzy of Anthony White's "Block Party" and the Salsoul Orchestra's "Nice 'n' Naasty."

Gibbons was very different from the other drama queen DJs. A shy, introverted guy from Queens, he came alive on the turntables and was perhaps the most technically gifted of all the disco spinners. Picking up from where Siano left off, Gibbons looped his favorite percussion breaks (Freddie Perren's "Two Pigs and a Hog" from the *Cooley High* soundtrack, Jermaine Jackson's "Erucu" from the *Mahogany* soundtrack, Rare Earth's "Happy Song") seemingly endlessly and cut back and forth between records like a hip-hop DJ. He was also perhaps the first to make his own reel-to-reel edits of his favorite records.[93] But even as he sliced and diced records on the turntables, Gibbons never lost sight of the message. "Walter was completely message oriented," remembers Danny Krivit. "You didn't hear mixed messages, you didn't hear a record say one thing and then another say something completely different and chop the message off. He went with the flow with that . . . He also had a sound system that he was really working and at that time not a lot of people were proficient at that. He kind of customized the songs as he went on, like he was writing tracks."[94]

But Gibbons was also a deeply troubled soul, and the same demons that drove him to become a born-again Christian in 1979 probably led him to explore the darkest recesses of inner space in the studio via the shape of dub effects and techniques. Like dub's high priest, Lee "Scratch" Perry, Gibbons seemed to believe that the mixing board was imbued with mystical properties and was a pathway to some cosmic netherworld. Gibbons's astonishing 1978 remix of Bettye LaVette's "Doin' the Best That I Can" is the pinnacle of his (and probably all of disco's) dub experimentation. Slowing the track to an absolute crawl and stripping it like an abandoned car with the remains scattered across eleven minutes, Gibbons somehow made the record funkier and more danceable. Sort of like the most cloying Motown B side in dub, "Doin' the Best That I Can" is almost antidisco in the way that Gibbons palpably heaps scorn on producer Eric Matthews's worst instincts by constantly undercutting the saccharine strings, judiciously using dropout and echo, importing his own rhythms, and essentially reversing the entire arrangement. This isn't to say that Gibbons isn't capable of going over the top, though. In disco's long and glorious history of excess only the completely irrelevant use of slap bass about two-thirds of the way through A

Taste of Honey's "Boogie Oogie Oogie" can top the totally gratuitous half-second proto-House percussion fill Gibbons throws in at around the two-minute mark.

"Doin' the Best That I Can," however, would be one of Gibbons's last contributions to disco for some time. His spiritual rebirth in Seattle in 1979 led him to stop playing records that were not uplifting. While disco contained many trace elements of gospel and, thanks largely to David Mancuso, preached positivity and loving your brother, during its heyday in 1978–79 it was focused almost exclusively on sex, and Gibbons wanted nothing to do with that. As a result, Gibbons disappeared from the scene for several years, playing gospel records and mixes of Philadelphia instrumentals with his own Christian-message vocals over the top at his own house parties. But when he did reappear in the mid-1980s, it would be with records whose effects are still reverberating today.

"COME AND GET THESE MEMORIES"
The Parallel Universe of Northern Soul

It's well past midnight on a Saturday night/Sunday morning in a relatively unkempt, unlicensed venue in a ghostly part of town. In a tiny, claustrophobic, dimly lit room, a sweaty, heavily drugged, overwhelmingly male crowd is executing athletic spins and leaps in time to Brenda Holloway's Motown stomper, "Just Look What You've Done." The crowd seems hell-bent on partying, trying to escape their skin with a fanatical fervor. They're equally devoted to the records the DJ is playing, a series of Motown-style soul songs with a pounding 4/4 beat and a surging heartbreak melody, but with brittle instrumentation that often sounds like someone stifling tears.

It's a scene straight out of any number of New York's underground discotheques of the early 1970s. Yet this dance floor exorcism was taking place thousands of miles away and several years earlier. The site was the Twisted Wheel club at 6 Whitfield Street in central Manchester, England, on any weekend in the mid- to late 1960s. This was the birth of a strange phenomenon that would come to be called "Northern Soul," in which young men from the industrial wastelands of the north of England worshipped American soul records—the rarer and more obscure the better—with a zeal and piety that would shame anyone but the most devout religious followers. Over the next several years, the culture of Northern Soul would not only parallel the nascent disco scene in New York but profoundly influence it as well.

Even more than being a nation of shopkeepers, Britain has always been a nation of collectors. Ever since New Orleans and Dixieland jazz were superseded by swing in the early 1930s, the United Kingdom has seen numerous small collector cultures dedicated to preserving and obsessively documenting African-American musical styles that have fallen out of favor with black Americans. The original "keepers of yesterday's blues" (as Amiri Baraka/LeRoi Jones called them in *Blues People*) were dubbed the "moldy figs," but successive cultural guardians got progressively less stuffy and hipper. The coolest of them all were the Northern Soul devotees.

The United Kingdom's soul scene was an outgrowth of London's jazz scene and started developing in the very early '60s at clubs like the Flamingo (a former Jewish social club beneath the Whisky à Go-Go on Wardour Street that held all-nighters on weekends that were popular with recently arrived West Indian immigrants and American GIs stationed in Britain) and the Scene in Ham Yard in Soho where DJ Guy Stevens would play a combination of urban blues like B. B. King, the lounge blues of Mose Allison, and the Hammond organ jazz of Jimmy Smith. It was this strange and explosive combination of fanatic DJs/collectors/curators, immigrants from the African diaspora, and American armed forces personnel that would define not only Northern Soul but also the next forty years or so of European popular music.

At around the same time as the soul clubs were taking off, the very posh Ad-Lib opened in Soho in February 1964. Unlike its continental cousins, however, the Ad-Lib wasn't just the domain of Hooray Henrys and glittery contessas. Journalist Anthony Haden-Guest described the Ad-Lib as "'the chosen haven for the gilded mafia of the pop scene, with its nightly Beatle or Stone, and the supporting fashion-photographers, satyrs in this urban Arcady.' It was in the discos of mid-sixties London that you could actually see society morphing into new shapes. They were the arenas where artists and photographers from the middle or working class, like David

Hockney, David Bailey, and Terry Donovan, designers like Mary Quant and Ossie Clark, and a hairdresser like Vidal Sassoon met with the young of the smart set on equal terms."[95] While this was the first step in the undermining of the British class structure, the liberation from a predetermined life path led to an extreme self-regard in the first generation of British young people that weren't effectively morphed into their parents by the time they finished school. "[Manager John] Kennedy hung large mirrors everywhere," wrote journalist George Melly of the club's interior. " 'A club needs movement,' is how he puts it, but I feel he realised, whether consciously or not, that the whole hippy movement is obsessively narcissistic. They don't dance for each other's benefit but for their own. Kennedy told me he never got over his amazement at the indifference of the men. 'The girls at the Ad-Lib,' he said, 'they're such little dollies, but where do they come from? You don't see them anywhere else. And they dance so sexily, but for all the reaction they get they might as well not be there."[96]

This narcissism achieved its peak with the Mods. The Mods wanted to turn their backs on traditional gray old England and its bleak Victorian factories belching out acrid smoke on its cloth-capped workers and their shabby council houses. The Mods did this by wearing made-to-measure suits with continental cuts and bright Fred Perry shirts, riding Italian Vespa scooters and cutting their hair à la Jean-Paul Belmondo. If it meant spending two weeks' worth of wages to get the right shirt in order to achieve the right look, then so be it. Of course, such extreme aestheticization found its way to music, and the ultimate Mod, antitraditionalist music at the time was black American music like James Brown's "Night Train" or Martha & the Vandellas' "Come and Get These Memories."

As soul music became a more mainstream proposition thanks to the hit-making prowess of Motown, though, the Mods began to search for more obscure records that would set them apart from the pop flock. The most influential DJ in this regard was Roger Eagle of the Twisted Wheel. As early as 1965, Eagle was searching out soul records that were rare even in America: Chubby Checker's "(At the) Discotheque," the Sapphires' "Gotta Have Your Love," Darrell Banks's "Open the Door to Your Heart," the Flamingos' "The

Boogaloo Party," Earl Van Dyke's "Six by Six." With the exception of "Open the Door to Your Heart," these records—and most of the records that really moved the dance floor at the Twisted Wheel—all had that monolithic, stomping, four-square Holland-Dozier-Holland Motown backbeat and uplifting tempo and chords (usually masking the pain of the lyrics) in common. They were high-energy rave-ups that fit the amphetamine atmosphere of the Twisted Wheel perfectly. This unique subculture now had its signature sound that would remain unchanged for years, and in 1970 it would finally get a name when in an article for *Blues & Soul* magazine journalist and leading light of the British soul scene Dave Godin coined the term "Northern Soul" to distinguish it from the funkier, more contemporary soul music that was being played at clubs in London.

Many of the ultrarare records that would fuel the Northern Soul scene were "discovered" by Ian Levine, the son of two well-off Blackpool club owners. His parents' comfortable financial position enabled him to travel to the United States at a time when foreign holidays were still a rarity for the vast majority of the British population, and it was on these trips, usually to Miami, that Levine found the records that gave birth to a subculture. "When my parents were sunning themselves on the beach, I was getting on a bus going round these ridiculous areas, going through various warehouses looking for records, going through hundreds of thousands of old forty-fives," he says. "There was a . . . Miami Goodwill where the radio stations would donate all their old records. There were a quarter of a million records there with no jackets, all loose, and that's where I found all the stuff, on Flagler Street in Miami."[97]

Levine was at first supplying his records to DJs at both the Twisted Wheel and then the Blackpool Mecca, watching with delight as the countless hours he spent scouring junk shops uncovering records like J. J. Barnes's "Our Love Is in the Pocket," Rose Batiste's "Hit and Run," and Pat Lewis's "No One to Love" resulted in dance floor gold. In 1971, he finally became a DJ in his own right at the Mecca and one of the biggest names on the scene. But Northern Soul was an aesthetic dead end, an ultraconservative, anachronistic sound that was doomed to cause its own demise. Levine was determined to keep the spirit alive, however. "By '73, '74, we'd exhausted the supply of these unknown sixties records," he says. "We'd

found most of the good ones at that time, and what we were finding were substandard. We weren't playing any records that were
new; all the records we were playing were from the sixties or three
or four years earlier. What changed it all was a record I heard on the
radio in Miami by the Carstairs called 'It Really Hurts Me Girl' on
Gene Redd's label, Red Coach, which was all set to come out distributed by Chess Records, but Chess folded and went into liquida-
tion. Because they went under, the record never came out. It took
me six months to find a copy. It had a very primitive, early disco
beat, but it had a very throaty, intense Northern Soul vocal, really
seriously powerful vocal. The record became a kind of anthem and
it changed the Northern Soul scene around. So suddenly, people
were craving these kinds of records."[98]

Levine was satisfying this hunger for newness with records like
Patti Jo's "Make Me Believe in You" and First Choice's "The House
Where Love Died"—records that were equally important in New
York—as well as pure Northern obscurities like the Montclairs'
"Hung Up on Your Love," Marvin Holmes's "You Better Keep Her,"
James Fountain's "Seven Day Lover," the Anderson Brothers' "I Can
See Him Loving You," and Kenny Smith's "Look What's Happening
to Your People." "This is all around '74, and these were all obscure
early disco records on little, tiny labels that no one could get hold
of," Levine continues. "Suddenly, the Northern scene split into two
factions: the purists who went to a club called the Wigan Casino
who wanted to hear the sixties stuff and didn't want to hear this
new disco stuff, and what we were doing at Blackpool Mecca, which
was playing these kind of disco records. It was swerving more to-
wards disco but not out-and-out trashy disco like Silver Convention, but proper soul records with a disco flavor. I became fascinated
by this, and this is when I went over to America and met Tom
Moulton. After 1975, Blackpool Mecca was pretty much all New
York disco."[99]

In 1975, Levine started to record his own tracks, first with the
veteran New York soul group the Exciters, then with four young
singers he discovered in Chicago: L. J. Johnson, James Wells, Evelyn
Thomas, and Barbara Pennington. He tailored these records specifically for the Northern Soul scene, but their contemporary sound

TURN THE BEAT AROUND

turned off many dancers. In a weird foreshadowing of the disco sucks "movement," a faction of clubgoers started the "Levine Must Go" campaign, which culminated in Levine's car being attacked by a mob that attempted to smash the windows. The ugliness he encountered led him to turn his back on the Northern scene and concentrate on disco, a move that would eventually have a huge impact on the shape of dance music in the aftermath of disco.

While the Northern Soul scene was fetishizing obscure objects of desire, in London a homegrown of sorts soul scene was very slowly starting to emerge. The first black soul artist to perform regularly in the United Kingdom was probably Mel Turner, an American who had sung with one of the various Five Crowns lineups that eventually became the Drifters before he moved to Britain in 1960, where he performed in a style similar to Clyde McPhatter. A few years later, African-American GIs stationed in Britain started to form bands—Geno Washington & the Ram Jam Band, Herbie Goins (and later Ronnie Jones) & the Nightimers—as did Caribbean immigrants (Jimmy James & the Vagabonds, Mac and Katie Kissoon).

These singers' deracination collided head-on with musicians who played Motown and Stax like they were reading from a fake book and pop hacks from Denmark Street (London's Tin Pan Alley) who insisted on putting moon-June-spoon and showbiz glitz into soul's gospel-derived vernacular. It was a strange, uncomfortable combination, perhaps best exemplified by the Foundations and their transatlantic hits "Baby, Now That I've Found You" and "Build Me Up Buttercup." Even though lead singer Clem Curtis was from Trinidad, he sounded like he was singing phonetic English. The music was similarly awkward, with Allan Warner's reggae-derived guitar chank sitting uneasily with Tom Jones horn charts and cod-Motown rhythms. Unwittingly, the group had stumbled on the formula that, with minor alterations, would define a peculiar strain of popular music that would become known as Europop.

With its streamlining of black music's funkier excesses in order to make it palatable for people raised on schlager and Vera Lynn, Europop's convergence of African-American rhythms and blue notes with European melodic sensibilities would have enormous implications for disco. The combination of driving rhythm and indulgent artifice was, of course, a perfect expression of the emerging gay aesthetic, but it was also a hallmark of the thermidorean reaction to the '60s—the retreat from "consciousness" into the blank innocence that characterized much of the first half of the '70s. The apotheosis of the early Europop style was Johnny Johnson & the Bandwagon's "Blame It on the Pony Express": all tortuous metaphors, singsong strings, and a Motown beat that was more of a dull thud than strutting stomp. The irony was that the group was entirely American and had only just relocated to the United Kingdom after the British success of "Breaking Down the Walls of Heartache" in 1968. "Blame It on the Pony Express" was played at some New York clubs when it was released in 1970 and, aside from bringing Euro to the New World, it introduced what would become another disco convention: the contrast between a husky male baritone and self-consciously pretty music.

Of all the early British Europop groups, none was more important than the Equals. A multiracial band from Hornsey, north London, the Equals were led by Eddy Grant, who had moved to London from British Guyana at the age of twelve. Their first single, "Hold Me Closer," was released in 1966, but no one would notice until the following year when the flip side, "Baby, Come Back," became a number one hit in both the Netherlands and Germany. "Baby, Come Back" was the perfect Europop record: a singer with a seemingly tentative grasp of English, a bubblegum (before the fact) melody, a metronomic beat, a trebly guitar that predates Elvis Costello and the Go-Go's by more than a decade, and even a bit of ska thrown in at the end. As their 1976 single put it, they were "Funky Like a Train." In 1970, though, they would achieve disco locomotion with "Black Skin Blue-Eyed Boys." With its relentless energy (you lose your breath just listening to it, let alone dancing to it), driving, ultrafast bass line, rock-solid drums, woodblock percussion, and punchy, Santana-ish guitar style (creating the early Europop style that would be copied by Titanic and Barrabas), "Black Skin Blue-Eyed Boys" was one of disco's earliest floor fillers and one of its first anthems.

The Equals may have been sui generis, but Europop inevitably fell totally into the hands of the hacks. As arranger/producer Gerry Shury told *Black Music* magazine, "cutting black artists in England was a whole different concept, and you had to make them sound pop to make them acceptable."[100] Shury had arranged and produced British hits in this mock soul style for the Fantastics (formerly an American doo-wop group called the Velours), the Pearls, and Sweet Dreams. Sweet Dreams was a duo of reggae singer Tony Jackson and Polly Brown, a white singer who occasionally performed in blackface. Shury would produce "Up in a Puff of Smoke" for Brown in 1974, and the record got significant play in New York discos thanks to Brown's Diana Ross impersonation and a crunching kick drum/bass/synth bottom end that would point the way to Amii Stewart's Eurodisco classic "Knock on Wood."

In 1974, Shury hooked up with a producer known as Biddu. Biddu was born in Bangalore, India, in 1944 and moved to England in the late '60s after a stint with the Indian version of the Rolling Stones. While struggling to make it as a singer-songwriter, Biddu worked as a chef, making doughnuts at the American embassy. In 1971, he started working at Nova Studios in Marble Arch with unknown British-based soul artists like the Lollipops, the Jesters, Tyrone & Carr, and Lon Satton. All of the records he made there imitated the Motown beat and became big on the Northern Soul scene. In 1974, Biddu was working with journeyman Jamaican soul singer Carl Douglas on a song called "I Want to Give You My Everything," and they needed a flip side for the single. Douglas suggested one of his own self-penned numbers, and in the remaining ten minutes of studio time, the song was arranged by Shury, sung by Douglas, and recorded by Biddu. The song, of course, was "Kung Fu Fighting," the record that kicked the door in for Eurodisco in the United States.

In 1975, Biddu would create the prototype for the deluge of Eurodisco epics with his disco version of Michel Legrand's theme song to the movie *Summer of '42*. Complete with wah-wah guitars, hyper skipping hi-hats, and sweeping strings, it was little more than a brazen rip-off of Philadelphia International's MFSB (see Chapter 4), but the discos ate it up. More ham-fisted quasi-orchestral schlock followed in the form of "Rain Forest," "Jump for Joy," and "Blue-Eyed Soul," but their strange combination of deluded grandeur and wink-wink-nudge-nudge suggestiveness made them the ideal background music for clumsy singles bars pickups. Having soundtracked so much bad sex during his career, it was perhaps inevitable that Biddu was chosen to compose the theme for the Joan Collins flick *The Stud*. Biddu's other claim to fame was that he foisted Tina Charles upon the world (Biddu called her a "white ball of fire").[101] Charles had already annoyed hundreds of thousands of Britons with her overenunciated faux blues vocals on the *Top of the Pops* cover albums and her vocals on 5000 Volts' "I'm on Fire" (which was somehow reminiscent of Cossacks dancing at a provincial disco in Staffordshire), but when Biddu crafted "I Love to Love (But My Baby Just Loves to Dance)" for her (with a band that included the men who would terrorize the world as the Buggles, Trevor Horn and Geoff Downes), she became inescapable.

While the British soul scene helped create the blueprint and the foundation for the disco craze of 1977–79 with its lost-in-translation version of African-American music, this was only the beginning of its influence. From the birth of Europop and the culture of the collector through the specter of the cult of Mod hanging over *Saturday Night Fever* to the birth of Hi-NRG, Northern Soul, with its throbbing beat and stilted take on Motown, would cast a long shadow over disco.

"I'M JUST AN OUTLAW, MY NAME IS DESIRE"

Disco and Sexuality

Do you think homosexuals are revolting? You bet your sweet ass we are.
                                        —Gay Liberation Front

If you've got them by the balls, their hearts and minds will follow.
                                        —John Wayne

Music is the connective tissue between protest, rebellion, violence, sexual awareness and community.   —Lydia Lunch

It's 11:30 p.m. on a weekend night in 1970, and in the basement of the old Ansonia Hotel on Seventy-fourth Street and Broadway an unknown singer named Bette Midler takes the makeshift stage by the swimming pool and performs a camped-up version of the scandalous Duke Ellington number "Sweet Marijuana." Not only is Midler the only woman in the enormous room, but all the men, including her pianist, Barry Manilow, are wearing nothing but towels slung low on their hips. Of course, the men frolicking in the pool aren't even wearing towels. While most of the crowd is either rapt by Midler's vampy rendition of Bessie Smith's "Empty Bed Blues" or hoping to cure their own by cruising the packed dance floor, others are ignoring the show and working out on the exercise equipment in this health-club-cum-nightspot. All of this activity, however, is merely a sideshow to the club's main purpose—sex. Sex of the most vehement, uninhibited kind. While most of the rampant fornication was hidden from view in the Finnish and Russian saunas, steam rooms, massage parlors, private cubicles, and showers, one visit to the candy machine cured any misapprehension that this was anything but a coitus cloister. Alongside the expected Snickers and Three Musketeers bars, the vending machine dispensed sachets of K-Y jelly. The in-house VD clinic was also a pretty good indicator of where the club's priorities lay.

This fleshpot was the legendary Continental Baths, which was opened by former cantor and Fuller Brush salesman turned entrepreneur Steve Ostrow in September 1968. Gay-oriented bathhouses had existed in New York since at least the turn of the twentieth century, when gay men started to frequent the Everard Baths (inevitably nicknamed the "Ever Hard" Baths) on West Twenty-eighth Street, but the Continental Baths marked the beginning of a new era. Instead of the secretiveness and seediness usually associated with the bathhouses, Ostrow was relatively open about his baths and aimed them at an upmarket crowd, advertising them as recapturing "the glory of Ancient Rome." Ostrow's all-male health club was festooned with that ultimate symbol of early '70s luxury—the rattan wing chair—while the glass pillars lent his pleasure palace a classical grace. It was a rather different form of "classicism," though, that made the Continental Baths truly important. While the first shots in the battle for gay civil rights were fired in 1966 by the Mattachine Society, a group of gay Communists that split from the main party because of their unwillingness to recognize homosexuality as part of the struggle,[1] the Caligula-like scenes at the Continental Baths marked the first defiant steps of an out and proud gay *sexuality*. This was not a claim on citizenship or belonging, but a confrontational demand by a group of pariahs[2] to be accepted on their own terms and a ritualistic celebration of those terms. Disco was born in the rubble of New York, but it was in this pungent hothouse atmosphere that disco really started to take shape.

The multigenre musical cluster fuck constructed by the wandering ears and fingers of the early DJs mirrored the delicious promiscuity of the bathhouses. Their smooth blends and segues were emblematic not only of a newfound group identity but also of a newly liberated pleasure principle that exploded out of its shackles with such intensity that it wanted to keep going full-bore all night long without stopping. It was a music and a scene of prodigious physicality, an embrace of a previously forbidden body and pushing that body to the absolute limits. Disco was all about breaking the bonds of shame that had imprisoned gay men for centuries. It was a declaration that pleasure didn't have to be inextricably meshed with guilt and self-loathing. *The Kinsey Report* and Masters and Johnson may have showed people that there was more to sex than the missionary position, there may have been communes and ashrams promoting "free love," John Sinclair's White Panther Party may have advocated "dope, guns and fucking in the streets," but never before had a popular culture moment so wantonly wallowed in the pit of carnal depravity as disco.

Despite all of the marches on the Capitol, all the flag burnings and bra burnings, all the sit-ins and the be-ins, the most radical social change that occurred in the 1960s was wrought not by hippies, yippies, or civil rights marchers, but by chemists. With the possible exception of the airplane and the personal computer, no twentieth-century invention had such a profound impact on American life as the birth control pill. Hitting the market in 1960, the Enovid-10 pill swept through a nation of bluestockings and Puritans with the force of a category-five hurricane. "The widespread use of the Pill at the beginning of the sixties made sex simpler, more accessible and seemingly less consequential," wrote gay historian Charles Kaiser. "It also encouraged public acceptance of a truly radical notion for a prudish nation: the idea that sex might actually be valuable for its own sake. The idea represented a sea change in the way millions of Americans of all orientations thought about copulation."[3]

The full ramifications of this revolutionary new attitude were felt in the early '70s. The first few years of the decade saw an explosion of sex in mainstream heterosexual popular culture: It was the era of the suburban swinger and wife-swapping parties; Dr. Alex Comfort's best-selling erotic manual, *The Joy of Sex*, was first published in 1972; Erica Jong's roman à clef, *Fear of Flying*, was published in 1973, and its shockingly frank depictions of female sexuality and casual sex incited huge debate; the first "big-budget" porn flick, *Deep Throat*, caused a sensation in January 1972 when it was released and has allegedly grossed hundreds of millions of dollars since; the slightly more respectable *Last Tango in Paris* (1972) and the Warren Beatty bedroom farce *Shampoo* (1975) both brought controversial sexual practices to mainstream cinema. But it wasn't just hetero heart-throbs like Beatty who were enjoying all the benefits of looser sexual mores. As Kaiser wrote, the birth control pill and the attitude it fostered "was *the* fundamental philosophical leap, *the* indispensable step before homosexual sex could gain any legitimacy within the larger society."[4]

While the Continental Baths was a debauchee's paradise, legitimacy was the operative word there. Perhaps because Ostrow was a bisexual with a wife and a daughter (who both helped out at the club), the Continental Baths never quite became as truly wild as later bathhouses like Man's Country, St. Mark's Baths, or First Avenue Baths did. Ostrow's entertainment program ensured that sex was never the only focus of either the club or its patrons, much to the chagrin of clubgoers like writer Edmund White, who complained that when Midler performed "everybody stop[ped] their sexual activities to listen to her."[5] With the success of the shows (aside from Midler and Manilow, performers like LaBelle, Peter Allen and, umm, Wayne Flowers and Madame attracted notoriety from their appearances there), Ostrow decided in 1971 to turn the dance floor into a discotheque when there was no one on stage. The first DJ was Don Finlay, who was soon replaced by Bobby DJ Guttadaro, whose mixes

---

With the aroma of musk and spunk perfuming the air so strongly in the '70s, it was perhaps inevitable that the Continental Baths was eventually resurrected as a swingers' club. Plato's Retreat opened on September 23, 1977, in the same basement location and re-created the Baths' notorious hedonism for straight people. While the swimming pool remained—Plato's Retreat even followed New York City regulations and had a lifeguard on duty—the glory holes in the showers were filled in, the saunas and steam rooms were replaced with a Jacuzzi big enough for sixty people, and the exercise room was transformed into the "Orgy Room," whose floor was covered from wall to wall in mattresses. While numerous celebrities—Sammy Davis Jr., Richard Dreyfuss, Rodney Dangerfield, Wolfman Jack, ex-Yankee Joe Pepitone, the who's who of the '70s porn industry—dropped by to check out the scene and usually remained clothed and chaste (aside from the porn stars, of course), most of the clubgoers followed the old Baths tradition and walked around in nothing but a towel.

of uptempo but highly polished soul helped make the club into the hottest nightspot in New York. When Guttadaro left the Baths for the super-hip Le Jardin, the Baths became something of a DJ academy with Joey Bonfiglio and future dance music legends Larry Levan and Frankie Knuckles manning the wheels of steel.

The charged atmosphere on the dance floor and the growing fame of the performances[6] meant that heterosexuals wanted to join in the fun. Of course, that meant the intrusion of women into this beefcake Eden. In late 1972, women were allowed into the club on Saturday nights, but they had to remain fully clothed—there was no women's locker room. While "slumming it" had existed since at least the 1920s, when the Cotton Club became all the rage, the Continental Baths was perhaps the first gay venue to be ferociously cruised by the cultural tourists. The craze reached its peak in 1973, when the Metropolitan Opera's Eleanor Steber gave a "black towel" concert at the Baths and the souvenir towels were available for purchase at Bloomingdale's. By the following year, much of the hard-core gay crowd that the Continental Baths originally attracted had fled to bathhouses that didn't feel the need to put on shows to attract a more upscale clientele, and Ostrow was forced to close his club.

With its rapid rise among the sexually voracious club cognoscenti, explosion into mainstream prominence, and subsequent detumescent fizzle into commercial blandness, the Continental Baths

---

The club was presided over by portly, middle-aged divorcé Larry Levenson, who could often be found mud wrestling with some of the waitresses. He usually sported a jacket emblazoned with "King of Swing" on the back and he boasted that he bedded some twenty thousand women during his reign. While most of the action was happening in the side rooms and the Orgy Room, there was a dance floor— presided over by former Le Jardin DJ Bacho Mangual—and one of the city's best sound systems. However, dancing wasn't really the order of the day, and certainly no opera singers ever performed at Plato's Retreat. In 1980, when the owners of the Ansonia Hotel wanted to turn the building into luxury condos, the club was forced to relocate to an old warehouse at 509 West 34th Street. Then, in 1981, Levenson was found guilty of skimming the receipts and evading income tax and was sentenced to prison, where he was visited by porn star Ron Jeremy, who showed up with a bevy of starlets. The writing was on the wall for the club, however, and with the emergence of the AIDS crisis it was finally shut down in November 1984.

encapsulates in a way the history of disco in miniature. The wild, unbridled carnal energy that characterized the Baths buzzed throughout New York nightlife and lit up the discos that followed in the Baths' wake. Disco's surging bass lines and pulsating rhythms carried this sexual dynamism out of the back room, onto the dance floor, and into the streets, where it filtered into style, community action, and protest.

The Stonewall Inn wasn't the likeliest of places to host a revolution. The dingy Mob-run firetrap at 53 Christopher Street in the West Village didn't even have running water. It was the kind of place where instead of repairing the disconcertingly regular fire damage, the owners of the bar would just put up a new coat of black paint to hide the smoke burns. The establishment, which was frequented by drag queens and students, was so dirty and dingy that it was the suspected source of a hepatitis epidemic in the winter of 1969.[7] Nevertheless, this unlicensed "bottle club" seemed to be a bit of a celebrity hot spot. The bar's log, which, according to the law, everyone had to sign, showed that Elizabeth Taylor and Judy Garland visited several times each night.

"Judy Garland" even visited on Friday, June 27, 1969—the night of her funeral. So too did half a dozen policemen under the command of Deputy Inspector Seymour Pine. Although the Stonewall had been raided by the cops on numerous previous occasions, this night was different. The standard practice was that the owners would be notified in advance of any raid (the Stonewall forked over two thousand dollars a week in payoff money to the local precinct[8]), but no one was warned that night that the NYPD would be enforcing the state's archaic laws regarding the fraternizing of homosexuals. Even though the raid was a surprise, they still managed to flash the warning lights in time for people to stop dancing, and the cops arrested only a few drag queens (out of the two hundred or so patrons) for violating the statute that bar-goers' attire had to be gender-appropriate.

The scene outside the bar was initially festive, with a crowd "composed mostly of Stonewall boys who were waiting around for friends still inside or to see what was going to happen. Cheers would go up as favorites would emerge from the door, strike a pose, and swish by the detective with a 'Hello there, fella.'"⁹ Soon enough, though, the mood turned darker when the police got rough with some of their prisoners. Instead of the docility that usually accompanied such incidents, the crowd started throwing both pennies and insults at the cops. "Limp wrists were forgotten," Lucian Truscott IV wrote in *The Village Voice*. "Beer cans and bottles were heaved at the windows, and a rain of coins descended on the cops."¹⁰ Or, as the New York *Daily News* reported it, "Queen power exploded with all the fury of a gay atomic bomb. Queens, princesses and ladies-in-waiting began hurling anything they could lay their polished, manicured fingernails on . . . The lilies of the valley had become carnivorous jungle plants."¹¹

The riot lasted until about four in the morning, with four policemen getting injured and thirteen protesters arrested. The numbers might not have been any worse than a typical Friday night punch-up at a rowdy bar in Brooklyn, but Stonewall served as a catalyst for political awakening as surely as Rosa Parks sitting in the front of the bus in Alabama. Just as soul music came to voice the pride and assertiveness that accompanied the civil rights struggle, disco quickly became the sound of this new movement. As the cultural adjunct of the gay pride movement, disco was the embodiment of the pleasure-is-politics ethos of a new generation of gay culture, a generation fed up with police raids, Victorian laws, and the darkness of the closet. That this new movement was born on the night of Judy Garland's funeral couldn't have been more appropriate.

Of the numerous political groups that formed in the immediate wake of the Stonewall uprising, perhaps none was as important to the history of disco as the Gay Activists Alliance. Founded on December 21, 1969, by Arthur Bell, Arthur Evans, Kay Tobin Lahusen, Marty Robinson, and Jim Owles, the GAA operated under the slogan "Out of the closet and into the streets." In accordance with their slogan, the GAA pioneered direct action techniques (called "zapping") in the quest for gay rights: members shouted "Gay Power" during a speech by Mayor Lindsay on April 13, 1970, they staged sit-ins at *Harper's Magazine* after it ran an article by Joseph Epstein that declared, "If I had the power to do so, I would wish homosexuality off the face of the earth," they hosted one of the first shows on public access cable television, and they blockaded the George Washington Bridge. After a prolonged campaign launched by the GAA, in December 1971 the superannuated laws that regulated homosexual admissions and ratios at New York nightspots and restaurants were changed.

However, almost as soon as the GAA won its campaign to allow gay men to dance together as couples, couple dancing became as old-fashioned as the Judy Garland camp of the preliberation era. Mirroring the backroom and bathhouse bacchanals that accompanied liberation, the ability to dance with a single partner was immediately skipped over in favor of an orgy of multiple partners. Ironically, one of the first places this dance floor debauch occurred was at the GAA's Firehouse. Opened on May 6, 1971, in an old fire station at 99 Wooster Street in SoHo, the Firehouse was Manhattan's first gay and lesbian community center. Painted bright red, the Firehouse was famous for its intense and frighteningly earnest political meetings, but a hint of frivolity entered into the premises when it hosted dances from 9 p.m. to 3 a.m. on Saturdays. Typically, the politicos didn't really get music, and the first few parties were fairly stolid affairs despite the $2 admission price, which got you free drinks for the evening. When Barry Lederer (who was not affiliated with the group or particularly involved in gay activism) was hired as the DJ, however, the parties took off, and even though the Firehouse had four floors, it got so crowded that there were safety fears. Lederer was playing what he calls "heady, drug-oriented music"[12]— slightly dark funk records like the Equals' "Black Skinned Blue-Eyed Boys," Bill Withers's "Harlem," and Billy Sha-Rae's "Do It." The new gay dance floor wasn't just interested in mirroring bathhouse promiscuity, it also wanted a longer, more intense, more trancelike experience, something different from the old three-minute jukebox chop-and-change routine. "I was mixing records," Lederer remembers. "However, since I was new, I was not the greatest. Luckily, the music transcended my mistakes."[13]

In 1972, Lederer left and was replaced by Richie Rivera, who played until the dances began to fizzle out in 1973 when the GAA came under heavy criticism for being overwhelmingly white, for marginalizing its lesbian contingent, and for targeting too heavily Mayor Lindsay, who was generally liked in the gay community. On

October 8, 1974, the Firehouse was destroyed in an arson attack that still hasn't been solved.

In part, the GAA lost momentum because, in a sense, the rise of the discotheque made activism largely irrelevant. It was never going to change discrimination enshrined in law, but disco culture was the most effective tool in the struggle for gay liberation. Disco didn't have to hit anyone over the head with slogans or bore you into submission with earnest missives; its "message" was its pleasure principle. Disco was born of a desire that was outlawed and branded an affront to God and humanity, so its evocation of pleasure was by necessity its politics, and by extension its politics was pleasure. The percolating sexual energy and communitarian spirit of the early discos were the perfect antidote to the lingering '60s hangover—the gay-derived sense of theatricality and refusal to peer beneath the surface were instantly understandable to anyone tired of the denim solemnity of the Woodstock Nation.

Even more than winning friends and influencing people, though, disco was emblematic of a new kind of political resistance, of what French theorists and psychoanalysts Felix Guattari, Gilles Deleuze, and Guy Hocquenghem call a "revolution machine." As opposed to the individual expressions of desire in capitalist societies that necessarily force one to view the world in either/or structures, Guattari and Deleuze proposed a collective linking of libidos and desires that would open up innumerable possibilities for sexuality other than the oedipal death drive of capitalism.[14] Liberated from social, economic, and political forces, desire is set free and humans become pure "desiring machines" that interface with any and every other "machine" with no hang-ups, no repression, no constraints. The group grope of the disco dance floor, the anonymous antics of the back room, and the heedless hedonism of the bathhouses were probably as close to such a polymorphously perverse paradise as humans will ever get.

We are all pied pipers, tempted to gather here by irresistible things.

—Tarjei Vesaas

When you conjure the image of a disco fleshpot in your mind's eye, a rural, coastal, carless idyll of rolling sand dunes, big surf, and sassafras trees teeming with sapsuckers probably aren't the first things that come to mind. Add to that the fact that this fairy-tale locale is reachable only by ferry and didn't even have electricity until the early '60s and it would seemingly rank right up there with Nouakchott, the capital of Mauritania, as a hotbed of dance music. Nevertheless, if disco had a second home outside of New York City, it was here in Fire Island, a tiny strip of land off the coast of Long Island about fifty miles from the Big Apple.

For centuries, Fire Island was little more than a lighthouse and a refuge for smugglers, but in the 1920s it became a bohemian enclave when writers, musicians, and showbiz types started to congregate on this relatively isolated barrier island to escape the clutches of Prohibition. Most of their activity centered around the tiny community of Cherry Grove, which quickly became a popular resort for gays and lesbians thanks to the bohemian atmosphere and lax policing. In the 1940s, Cherry Grove was populated in the summer by such prominent figures as Christopher Isherwood, Tennessee Williams, W. H. Auden, Carson McCullers, and Patricia Highsmith, and the Grove's outrageous theme parties, drag theatrics, and camp aesthetic made it the most famous gay and lesbian resort in the world. By the 1960s, much of the community's social life revolved around the Sea Shack hotel and restaurant. Owner Jimmy Merry added a dance hall to the hotel when his establishment finally got electricity, and people would dance the lindy to old rock-and-roll records.

After the 1969 summer season, the Sea Shack was sold to Ted Drach and Tiger Curtis, who enlisted the help of former Broadway dancer Michael Fesco in transforming the old dance hall, which was nicknamed "the Boom Boom Room." Fesco stripped out the Boom Boom Room's old stereo system, lightbulbs, and Christmas lights in favor of mirror-paneled walls (perhaps the first nightspot to use them), a DJ booth, and a lighting system that was synchronized with the music. Named after Tarjei Vesaas's novel of the same name, the Ice Palace opened on Memorial Day weekend in May 1970 and was an instant success.

Word spread fast about the Ice Palace, and its format was copied two weeks later by Ron Malcolm and Gene Smith, the owners of the Sandpiper restaurant in the Pines, another predominantly gay community located across the sand dune from Cherry Grove.[15] The

Pines was a newer community and attracted a much more affluent, less bohemian crowd than Cherry Grove. And true to the Pines' upward mobility, the Sandpiper, a restaurant that would turn into a disco at 11 p.m., soon trumped the Ice Palace thanks to DJ Don Finlay, who started playing records like Marvin Gaye's "What's Going On" there in 1971. "It was pure magic," Barry Lederer says about that summer. "It was just the height of dancing, especially knowing the condition we were in [i.e., drugged up to the gills] . . . Don was absolutely incredible. Everyone could not wait to go out on Friday and Saturday to dance. It was one of those magic summers, and I consider it a highlight of music in my life."[16]

The following summer Lederer started to spin at the early evening tea dances at John Whyte's Botel in the Pines, and Tom Moulton started making tapes for the Sandpiper (see Chapter 1). Moulton's tapes would eventually be replaced by DJs Roy Thode and Tom Savarese. Meanwhile, in the Grove, Bobby DJ Guttadaro was reasserting the Ice Palace as Fire Island's preeminent disco with his infectious, high-energy party mixes. Both Lederer and Guttadaro played acetates of "Love's Theme" by Love Unlimited Orchestra months before it was played on the radio, and their championing of the record—and, of course, the reaction of their audiences—made it the first "disco" record to become a #1 hit. In many ways, "Love's Theme" was the perfect disco record: its unabashed celebration of "beauty" and lushness and its complete willingness to go over the top in the pursuit of that goal; its swooning strings; its groove, which is somehow at once the least funky thing this side of Phil Collins and as redolent of sex and spunk as Ron Jeremy's basement; and, ultimately, its utter lasciviousness. More than that, though, it was the perfect Fire Island record. Its string zephyrs and almost singsong lilt hit you like a sea breeze, while its slow-grind rhythm and wah-wah riff gave it a tribal quality perfect for shirtless boys enjoying their first carefree summers of freedom.

In many ways the Fire Island clubs were even more of a fairyland than the original New York discos. The Ice Palace, Botel, and the Sandpiper weren't escapism so much as pure, unadulterated fantasy. Here, on this island of astounding natural beauty seemingly light-years away from the real world of discrimination and homophobia, hundreds of tanned, toned men gathered together to dance and have sex in the Meat Rack[17] without the watchful eyes of the state or the church gazing down on them. Fire Island was a place where the wildest fantasy—from the extravagant theme parties of the old Cherry Grove to the wanton abandon of the new Rack—could be acted out without fear that anyone from the straight world would find out about it. This idea of cloaked permissiveness would soon pervade not only the gay discos of New York City but also the celebrity palaces like Studio 54, where anything could happen under the dim lights of the VIP areas and no one would ever be the wiser.

While Francis Grasso and David Mancuso laid down the basic framework of the disco sound in the city, the Fire Island crowd's reaction to the music spun by Guttadaro, Moulton, and Lederer helped create disco's intensity. By 1972, the dancers at Fire Island had become particularly discerning—whistling and stomping if they enjoyed a record and abandoning the floor or even booing if they didn't—and this almost symbiotic relationship between crowd and DJ became one of the hallmarks of gay disco. The bodies, the drugs, the heat, the sweat, the sunrises, and the throb of the music all conspired to create a heated sense of nowness, a sense that nothing existed outside of that room. No past, no future, no promises, no regrets, just right now and those strings from "Love's Theme" cascading all over you and prickling your skin.

The real fantasy that Fire Island peddled, though, was that of class, particularly in the Pines. Not only was the Pines crowd a more affluent group of people than those that congregated in Cherry Grove, they were better connected, they were prettier, they spent more time in the gym. It was a very incestuous scene, and it was in this tiny enclave that the "clone" look was born. In its original incarnation, the clone was invariably butch, well toned, ruggedly handsome, with short hair and a well-trimmed mustache, and he usually wore a flannel shirt and Levi's. The uniform was accompanied by a shared attitude about sex and sexual partners. To the clone, sex was a sport—with definite winners and losers—and partners were viewed as mere conveniences or vehicles, if not outright opponents. The hypermasculine, hypersuccessful clone was the reaction to decades of popular culture characterizing gay men as effeminite or as somehow failed men. While the multiple bedroom conquests, macho exterior, strange tribal individualism, and flaunting of achievement sought to prove that the gay man was a "real" man, the clone was also the ultimate expression of Deleuze and Guattari's desiring machine, only with the capitalist death drive very much intact. Spreading quickly from its Fire Island base, the clone stereotype was exalted—in the form of gay porn star Al Parker and the stable of Colt models—as the ultimate in manhood.

The clone quickly replicated itself in New York City. In December 1972, Pines habitués David Sokoloff, Jim Jessup, and David Bruie opened a small club on the tenth floor of 151 West 25th Street. The three were designers who had made names for themselves throwing lavish theme parties on Fire Island, the most famous of which featured an erupting volcano constructed on a barge that floated just off the coast of where their house was situated. Their Manhattan club was more restrained—gray industrial carpeting, white walls, and big flower arrangements, nothing else—but no less memorable. This minimalist setting where the people functioned as the decor became the template for nearly all underground discos, gay or straight, that followed.

Most of the "decor," however, matched the walls. Very few people of color and fewer women attended the Tenth Floor. "It was definitely a Pines crowd and a drug crowd," recalls Barry Lederer. "The Tenth Floor, and soon other subsequent gay clubs followed, started the attitude you had to be hot, muscular, etc."[18] And with this crowd came the attendant look. As novelist Andrew Holleran wrote in his fictionalized account of the early days of disco and of the people who frequented the Tenth Floor, "We had our web belts and painter's jeans, our dyed tank tops and haircuts, the plaid shirts, bomber jackets, jungle fatigues, the all-important shoes."[19]

The clone aesthetic wasn't just maintained by the tribal decorations, however. Sokoloff, Jessup, and Bruie imitated not only David Mancuso's loft location but his members-only creed as well. Where Mancuso's membership policy was largely pragmatic (a way of managing the crowd that came into his own home and as a way of circumventing the city's building and licensing codes), the Tenth Floor's membership policy was more reminiscent of old grande dame discotheques like Le Club—its purpose was to keep the hoi polloi out. The Tenth Floor effectively functioned as the gentlemen's club of the gay elite. As Tenth Floor regular Bill Ash said, "It reminded me of the 400, New York society in the 19th century."[20] In other words, the Tenth Floor represented the four hundred people who "mattered" in gay society in the early 1970s.

Ironically, the DJ at this lily-white scene was black. Although he made his name by programming the music for Halston's catwalk shows, Ray Yeates was one of the most experimental and uncompromising of the early DJs. His most famous record was Area Code 615's "Stone Fox Chase," an utterly bizarre record made by Nashville's most famous session musicians that sounded like the backwoods family in *Deliverance* jamming with the percussionists from the Last Poets records (it was also the theme song of the BBC's very old-guard rock show *Old Grey Whistle Test*—context was everything in disco). Yeates's outrageousness, however, didn't always go down well, particularly when it was the result of prodigious drug intake. "It was like he thought that the drugs would carry over his mistakes," Lederer says, "but they didn't . . . The crowd was very picky and really wanted it their way, and could be bitter if they didn't get it."[21]

Yeates's erratic performances and eccentric taste in music notwithstanding, experimentation wasn't really the order of the day at the Tenth Floor. While the sex and pharmacological ingestion were anything but, the conservatism that detractors would later claim characterized disco probably started here. Every attempt to move outside of an established culture succeeds only in reconfirming it, and with its embrace of masculine norms (albeit magnified to the nth degree), social hierarchy, and segregation, this was certainly true of the Tenth Floor. Two different strains of music would eventually emerge from this disco discrimination. One strand would retain a connection to the musical miscegenation started at the Loft and carried on by clubs like the Gallery, Better Days, and Paradise Garage. The other would blanch disco, not so much by bleaching its black roots but by striving for superhuman perfection, by pushing the clone aesthetic to its furthest possible limits in an attempt to attain a machinic state of grace. This search for physical transcendence would entail two things: an ever-escalating tempo (eventually mutating into a separate genre called Hi-NRG) and the exclusion of the imperfect. This attitude started at the Pines and the Tenth Floor, but it really took flight at the Flamingo.

TURN THE BEAT AROUND

The Flamingo was opened in December 1974 by the Ice Palace's Michael Fesco. Fondly remembered by most regulars as a gay utopia, the Flamingo, although situated on the second story of the Ayer Building at 599 Broadway (next door to the Gallery), was one step above the Tenth Floor. From the day it opened to its final party on February 15, 1981, the Flamingo was the premier gay club in New York, if not the entire world. It was the A-list to end all A-lists (according to legend even Calvin Klein had to call in favors to get a membership, which was priced at $600 a year[22]). Before weight lifting had become commonplace in gay culture, the profusion of chiseled, sculpted bodies at the Flamingo was like a Tom of Finland fantasy come to life. The intense, incredibly sexually charged atmosphere was described by journalist Andrew Kopkind as "extraordinarily assaultive; I have felt trapped forever in a theater of sound, of flesh, like a character in Buñuel's *The Exterminating Angel*, unable to leave a party even after its positive appeal has fled."[23]

Like the Tenth Floor's, the decor was extremely minimal—with a pantheon of gods to rival Olympus, who needed it?—but it was constantly changing. The banquettes were rearranged every week, the artwork on constant rotation, the lighting always reconfigured. The loft space in which the Flamingo was situated was half a block long, fifty feet wide, with very high ceilings (and huge windows that were always kept open) and no supporting beams to clog up the dance floor or make redecoration a hassle. Fesco also brought with him the Fire Island tradition of theme parties, and once a season the Flamingo would host its famous Black, White, and Cowboy Parties. Writer Edmund White described one of the club's Black Parties: "We went dressed in the requisite color, which turned out to mean leather to most celebrants. As we entered the club at one in the morning (the doors had opened at midnight) I saw a roomful of husky men, many of them shirtless, sipping beer or Coke and casually watching the entertainment: on raised trestles along one wall, hired musclemen garbed as centurions or deep sea divers or motorcyclists. They struck conventional body-building poses . . . 'This place is all about touching,' someone told me. 'They kept fiddling with the design till they got it right, till everyone had to slip and slide against everyone else.' . . . The blending of the records, the estimation of the crowd's mood, the choice of music were superb—the most discerning I'd come across anywhere . . . The mirrored panels were frosted over with condensed sweat."[24]

Whatever color costumes the crowd wore, it was always a white party at the Flamingo. And like the Tenth Floor, the DJs were often the only people of color in the place. The first season (the Flamingo shut down every summer, when the majority of its regulars went to Fire Island) the DJs were Armando Galvez, Luis Romero, Vincent Carleo, Ray Yeates, Frank Monteagudo, Bobby DJ, and Frank Hudon. While Galvez was a permanent fixture at the Flamingo, it would really become associated with two DJs: Howard Merritt (who started in 1976) and Richie Rivera (who started in 1977). The two essentially functioned as a musical good-cop/bad-cop routine, with Merritt playing the good-times, bubbleheaded high-energy music (Odyssey, Barry White) and Rivera playing slightly darker, more electronic and tribal music like Le Pamplemousse's "Le Spank," "Kings of Clubs" by Chocolat's, and Roy Ayers's "Running Away." The two DJs catered to both of the main pharmacopoeias prevalent at the Flamingo: cocaine/speed (Merritt) and, surprisingly, angel dust (Rivera).

Before moving to the glamorous surroundings of the Flamingo, Rivera DJed at one of New York's least salubrious discos. After leaving the slightly uptight Firehouse in 1973, Rivera moved about as far as he possibly could in the opposite direction. The Anvil, at 500 West 14th Street in the heart of Manhattan's meatpacking district, was originally a go-go bar that had female dancers during the day to cater to the meat packers and male dancers at night. The Anvil soon turned

Despite the notoriety of the Tenth Floor and the Flamingo, New York's gay discos weren't all temples of elitism. Even though it was a members-only club as well, 12 West had a far more diverse clientele—it even let in women. 12 West was opened in 1975 in a former plant nursery at 491 West Street (right across the street from the notorious Pier 48) by Cary Finkelstein and Alan Harris. The three-story space featured an arcing roof with wooden beams that made it a far superior acoustic environment than most New York discotheques. Sound system designers Barry Lederer and Peter Spar (Graebar) took advantage of this and created one of the most celebrated systems in New York. Unlike the equally famous systems at the Loft and Paradise Garage, which focused on the bass, 12 West's

TURN THE BEAT AROUND

completely male when it realized how many gay men came in during the day and left as soon as they saw the women. The premises upstairs from the Anvil was a fleapit hotel where many drag queens lived.

The Anvil occupied two floors. Downstairs, there was a small theater where it screened porno flicks and the notorious unlit back room. "There was sawdust all over the floor and it smelled like an old barn down there," remembers frequent visitor Ian Levine. "Everything that could have gone on in the world went on downstairs at the Anvil."[25] Upstairs was the bar area and small dance floor that was presided over by Rivera. Although the Anvil had an excellent sound system—the first to be designed by Graebar—it probably didn't matter what Rivera played because, aside from the go-go dancers, the place was usually so packed with people that you could barely move, let alone dance. Unlike the Tenth Floor or the Flamingo, the Anvil, particularly the back room, was democracy—in its crudest, most basic form—in action. It was a plebiscite of the flesh: In the dark there were no class signifiers and the participants operated on a level playing field with the only law being "any hole will do."

The Crisco Disco, at 510 West 15th Street, followed the Anvil's egalitarian lead, although you had to pass a speakeasy-style entrance in order to be allowed in. It was pretty sleazy, with wanton open sex and drug use. The DJ booth, usually helmed by Michael Haynes or Frank Corr, was a mock-up of a giant can of Crisco, but with all the leather boys prowling the club it was pretty clear that Crisco was no longer about Mom and apple pie. "Of course, the Crisco was used for all sorts of nefarious purposes," says Levine. "At Crisco's, more probably than the Anvil, they were drugged out of their mind, com-

---

Graebar system had a "sweeter" sound—thanks to the twenty high-frequency tweeters suspended in a grid above the dance floor and the woofers that cleverly used the room's curves to disperse the bass tones throughout the space—that was more in line with the high-energy music favored by 12 West's crowd and DJs. The original DJ at the club was the consummately professional Tom Savarese, who blended the high camp of the Ritchie Family with more straightforward commercial tracks like Tavares's "Heaven Must Be Missing an Angel" and Candi Staton's "Young Hearts Run Free." Savarese was replaced by Jimmy Stuard, who died in the Everard Baths fire in 1977, Alan Dodd, and Robbie Leslie.

pletely drug fucked. No one ever got to go home with anyone because they were just out of it."[26]

However, both the Anvil and the Crisco Disco paled in comparison to what was probably the Mount Rushmore of filth, the Mineshaft. Situated at 835 Washington Street, again in the aptly named meatpacking district, the Mineshaft was where the Al Pacino movie *Cruising* was set. Instead of a DJ, the club used tapes and the music was darkly erotic and rather unsettling in the cold light of day. Dancing was definitely not a major concern. A room off to the side of the main area was filled with glory holes cut into the wall, a row of shoeshine chairs and benches, with cans of Crisco beside them. A downstairs room was equipped with all manner of S&M paraphernalia and a big tub for watersports. "The Anvil looked like a vicarage compared to the Mineshaft," remembers Levine. "It was a real Dante's *Inferno*."[27]

"YOU MAKE ME FEEL MIGHTY REAL"
Sylvester and the San Francisco Sound

Disco wasn't about the stylized romantic love of classic pop or even soul, but overwhelming ecstasy, the complete and utter joy of being able to take pleasure from something that only a few years ago was forbidden. Of course, disco loved showbiz and was as stylized in its own way as any other genre of music, but the intensity of the (particularly gay) discotheque experience—the relentless rhythm, the poppers, the tight jeans, the mood manipulation of the DJs, the strobe lights—punctured the veneer of pop conventions. This carried over into the disco records themselves. Records like Donna Summer's "Love to Love You Baby" and "I Feel Love" (see Chapter 3) or Loose Joints' "Is It All Over My Face?" (see Chapter 6) reduced pop's Tin

---

The premier black gay club of disco's early days was Better Days in the Times Square area at 316 West 49th Street. The club opened in 1972, with Bert Lockett as the DJ. When she refused to play a request for the boss's wife one night, she was fired. Lockett was replaced by Tee Scott, who began his DJing career at the Candy Store on Fifty-sixth Street. Better Days was in a rough part of town and the clientele was almost exclusively black. The owner was cheap—but with admission prices as low as they were (as late as 1980, the $3 fee on Wednesday nights got you three drinks

TURN THE BEAT AROUND

Pan Alley conventions to a series of orgasmic moans and coos and translated decades of coquettish, flirty, ambiguous lyrics into a single mantra. If there was one artist, though, who truly exemplified disco's new language of ecstasy it was Sylvester, whose use of his gospel-trained falsetto in the service of gay desire and pleasure is surely the most radical rewrite of pop's lingua franca ever attempted.

This isn't to say that the out-and-proud Sylvester didn't have antecedents or contemporaries in the R&B world, however. While many of the female classic blues singers of the 1920s were well-known bisexuals (Bessie Smith, Ma Rainey, Alberta Hunter), the most outrageous performer of the era was Frankie "Half-Pint" Jaxon, a vocalist who performed with such jazz/hokum artists as the Harlem Hamfats, Tampa Red, Thomas Dorsey, Punches Delegates of Pleasure, and his own Hot Shots. Jaxon, who was barely five feet tall (thus his nickname), wore a skullcap, twirled a baton, was alleged to have been gay and performed very risqué material in a high falsetto dressed as a woman. Before Little Richard took the rock-and-roll world by storm with his shriek and makeup (and long before he came out), R&B duo Charlie & Ray performed their minor hit "I Love You Madly" (1954) to each other unabashedly on stage—they won the amateur night at the Apollo for five straight weeks thanks to their performances. Tony Washington of the mid-1970s Washington, D.C.–based vocal group Dynamic Superiors was gay and would sing "Me and Mr. Jones" in concert. In 1975, on the Motown subsidiary Gaiee, Charles "Valentino" Harris released "I Was Born This Way," "a half-baked plea for tolerance dressed in mid-'70s disco bounce"[28] (it was rerecorded in 1977 by future preacher Carl Bean).

While he certainly wasn't the first musician to openly address his homosexuality, Sylvester wasn't just a sideshow act tolerated because he was amusing, nor did he sing facile, feel-good anthems.

---

as well) it was hard not to be—and Scott had to bring in his own equipment. But because of this, Scott was forced to experiment, which would pay handsome dividends. Scott claims to be the first DJ to use three turntables,[29] and his facility on a relatively primitive setup enabled him to become one of disco's greatest mixers. The crowd at Better Days was fiercely loyal to Scott and would blow whistles as a sign of appreciation at high points during his mix. In 1973, Scott gave future DJ legend Frankie Knuckles his first gig on Monday and Tuesday nights at the club.

Merging the mechanical, piston-pumping beats that started in clubs like the Flamingo with the gospel/R&B tradition that gay white disco often seemed to try to break free from, Sylvester united the two main strains of disco. But in doing so, he went way beyond either. Sylvester propelled his falsetto far above his natural range into the ether and rode machine rhythms that raced toward escape velocity, creating a new sonic lexicon powerful, camp, and otherworldly enough to articulate the exquisite bliss of disco's dance floor utopia, but also sensitive enough to recognize that the dance floor could just as often be hell.

Sylvester James was born in Los Angeles in 1947 to a middle-class family. Like most singers of his generation, he learned his craft in church, and at age eight he toured the South, performing on the gospel circuit. His grandmother was Julia Morgan, a blues singer in the '30s, and by his teens, the music of her contemporaries Bessie Smith and Billie Holiday had supplanted gospel as his first love. Morgan also instilled a love of the theater in her grandson. In his late teens, Sylvester left home, changed his name to Ruby Blue, and lived as a woman for a few years on the Sunset Strip.

He moved to San Francisco in 1969 and joined the cross-dressing hippie revue troupe the Cockettes, which debuted on December 31, 1969, at the Palace Theater in North Beach. While many of the members (who were neither all gay nor all male) of the Cockettes had beards and dressed like women—but with motorcycle jackets and boots—or like bizarre combinations of Carmen Miranda and Robinson Crusoe, Sylvester's performances were more carefully observed impersonations of people like Josephine Baker than the acid-fueled, *épater le bourgeois* shenanigans of the rest of the troupe. Thanks to the group's notoriety, Sylvester quickly became an underground star. When the Cockettes split up in the summer of 1972, Sylvester starred in a cabaret show called "Women of the Blues" at the Rickshaw Lounge in San Francisco's Chinatown, where he performed piano blues and jazz standards from Bessie Smith, Billie Holiday, Lena Horne, Josephine Baker, and Ethel Waters.

At the Rickshaw Lounge he was discovered by *Rolling Stone* publisher Jann Wenner, singer Boz Scaggs, and jazz musician Ben Sidran, which led to a recording deal with Blue Thumb records. His two records for Blue Thumb—*Sylvester and the Hot Band* (with the Pointer

Sisters singing backup), aka *Scratch My Flower* because it had a scratch-and-sniff sticker on the cover that smelled of gardenias, and *Bazaar*—featured fairly typical rock instrumentation with Sylvester doing his helium gospel bit on top while he covered Neil Young, James Taylor, and Gram Parsons. Sylvester's cottony falsetto was an uncomfortable match with guitars, however, and both albums had an unpleasantly astringent quality and, unsurprisingly, bombed. More interestingly, at around the same time, Sylvester sang backup for the extraordinarily feisty Betty Davis (Miles Davis's ex-wife) on two tracks from her self-titled debut album.

Even though he idolized singers like Cissy and Thelma Houston, Sylvester hated disco music until a trip to Europe in 1975 changed his mind. Sylvester stopped performing in a cabaret or rock style and, with singer Martha Wash, he began to sing straightforward gospel-soul. While performing at a nightclub called Palms on Polk Street, Sylvester was "rediscovered" by Harvey Fuqua (a former member of the vocal group the Moonglows and a producer for Marvin Gaye), who had come to see backup singer Wash. Fuqua signed Sylvester to his Honey label, which was distributed by Fantasy, and produced *Sylvester* in 1977. "Down, Down, Down" was pretty formulaic first-wave disco—surging strings, galloping bass line, awkward horns—and the workmanlike arrangement made Sylvester's voice sound weak, but it did have energy and pace, and the song became a modest club hit in New York. It was a version of Nickolas Ashford and Valerie Simpson's "Over and Over," though, and it propelled Sylvester toward disco superstardom. Rather than the dance floor heat with which he would become associated, "Over and Over" was a guitar-and-bass slow burn whose intensity came from impassioned vocals by Sylvester and his great backup singers, Wash and Izora Rhodes. The track's warmth and its gospel-styled peaks and message ("You can't be somebody's lover until you're somebody's friend") made it a staple at the Loft.

1978's *Step II* brought Sylvester temporarily into the mainstream. The album's first single, "Dance (Disco Heat)," was a fairly mindless but irresistible disco bounce-along that featured Rhodes and Wash (now known as Two Tons o' Fun) and reached the American Top 20 at the peak of disco fever. Although the follow-up, "You Make Me Feel (Mighty Real)," barely creeped into the Top 40, it is

Sylvester's greatest record. "You Make Me Feel (Mighty Real)" was originally recorded as a midtempo, piano-driven gospel tune. According to legend, Sylvester was scheduled to do a performance at San Francisco's celebrated City disco (on the corner of Montgomery and Broadway in North Beach) and was rehearsing "You Make Me Feel (Mighty Real)" in the club's basement when lighting engineer Patrick Cowley, who was getting a little bit of fame on the city's disco scene for his astonishing sixteen-minute bootleg remix of Donna Summer's "I Feel Love," asked if he could do a similar treatment to Sylvester's song. Sylvester agreed, and the result was an epochal record in disco history. With its synth licks, mechanized, galloping bass line, computerized hand claps, and uptempo drumbeats, "You Make Me Feel (Mighty Real)" is the genesis of the disco subgenre known as Hi-NRG and the cornerstone of gay disco.

Where much gay disco, though, had the insistent perkiness of a high school pep rally and often conjured nothing so much as the image of two particularly buff bobble-head dolls doing the bump with one another, "You Make Me Feel (Mighty Real)" interrogated the African-American musical tradition and asked what "realness" is supposed to mean to gay black men who, alienated from almost all of society, were forced to hide their true identities for most of their lives. The chicken shack of R&B and gospel's storefront church got renovated by Cowley's synthesizers, while at the same time Sylvester ruffled the detached exterior of synth-pop with an intense expression of rapture. The way Sylvester sang "I know you love me like you should," moving up to a register so high that it can be completed only by a synth whoosh, might be disco's ultimate diva moment.

After "You Make Me Feel (Mighty Real)," Cowley began to play a bigger role in Sylvester's music. Cowley was the driving force behind the disco concept album *Stars*. Unlike the sprawling double and triple albums of the progressive rock era, *Stars* had only four tracks—"Stars (Everybody Is One)," "Body Strong," "I (Who Have Nothing)," and "I Need Somebody to Love Tonight"—but they pretty much summed up the entire disco experience. While Cowley is associated with a relentlessly uptempo sound, he proved his genius on "I Need Somebody to Love Tonight," a slow and moody sci-fi–reggae track that, along with the Peech Boys's "Don't Make Me Wait," is one of disco's greatest expressions of longing.

"I Need Somebody to Love Tonight" was an aberration for Cowley, however. As San Francisco mixer/producer Casey Jones told producer/singer David Diebold, "Patrick Cowley came along and basically created a sound in music that became known around the world as a San Francisco identity sound. It was a druggy sound. It was an 'up' sound. The whole scene in San Francisco at the time pretty much revolved around 'up' drugs. The entire gay disco scene has in fact, since the mid- to late '70s, been influenced by music which would complement their drug highs. The drug of choice in high energy markets has always been speed of one sort or another. Patrick created a synthesized sound that would enhance a drug induced high and the song which really launched that sound was 'Menergy.'"[30]

"Menergy" was originally released in 1981, and although it was an aural fantasy of a futuristic club populated entirely by cybernetic Tom of Finland studs, the record was remarkable not for its passion or stink, but for its hygiene. The song talked about the "boys in the back room lovin' it up, shooting off energy," but the production—synth vapor trails, hand claps like a cracking bullwhip, melodies that recall "They don't wear pants on the other side of France," mechanically processed vocals, background clave rhythms sped up so fast that any sense of swing or Latin flair was banished—was so clinical that a back room was the last thing it conjured. While it flew along at 120-something bpm, you couldn't imagine breaking a sweat to it, it was so clean. It was camper than Jeanette MacDonald and Nelson Eddy singing the "Indian Love Call" to each other, but it was also somehow incredibly composed, unwitty, and nonswishy. This bordering-on-sterile style continued on other Cowley productions for his Megatone label: Sylvester's "Do Ya Wanna Funk," Paul Parker's "Right on Target" (with a cover of the Seeds' "Pushin' Too Hard" on the B side!), and his own "Megatron Man" and "Sea Hunt."

That Cowley's production style was so antiseptic is not surprising given that he moved to San Francisco from Rochester, New York, in 1971 in order to study electronic music at the City College of San Francisco. The lab-coated atmosphere of the academic music world rubbed off on him, and Cowley would continue to treat synthesizer music as a scientific experiment until his career was cut short when he died of AIDS in November 1982. Diebold, however, suggests another reason for the dirtless and often bloodless vibe of

Cowley's recordings. In San Francisco "there has always been the distinction between the dance club and a public sex utility," he writes. "There are no correlations between The Sanctuary in New York with its black mass murals and orgiastic congregation and the pristine, clean (and even conservative) Dreamland. The balconies at The Saint in New York (which entertain every sort of sexual union) are nothing at all like the balconies at Trocadero [Transfer] (which are generally used for sitting and viewing the dance floor)."[31] The San Francisco disco scene was very button-down even if nearly everyone on the dance floor had his shirt off. And although the city's biggest star was African American, San Francisco's discotheques were overwhelmingly white.

The Bay Area's ultimate disco was the Trocadero Transfer at 520 Fourth Street. The club was huge—like Studio 54 it was housed in an old television studio—with a four-thousand-square-foot dance floor, above which dangled a cluster of a dozen or so mirror balls. The club's original DJ was Gary Tighe, but the DJ who took it to prominence was Long Island native Bobby Viteritti, who spun there from 1977 to 1981. Like fellow Long Island DJs Wayne Scott, Howard Merritt, and Roy Thode, Viteritti played in the high-energy, thoroughly professional style developed at the Flamingo. Like many of the great New York DJs, Viteritti made his own reel-to-reel edits of popular tracks, but he emphasized the midrange rather than the bass, making for a cleaner, more consistently upful sound. This was enhanced at the Trocadero by another Graebar sound system whose four coffin speakers, despite their name, propelled the music away from the dark depths. Viteritti was also famous for playing an hour or so of downtempo records—torch songs, jazzy R&B ballads like Marlena Shaw's cover of Diana Ross's "Touch Me in the Morning," and almost always Cerrone's "Call Me Tonight"—to bring the crowd down after several hours of dancing at a cardiac-inducing pace. During this part of the set, the lights were turned down, submerging the club in blackness, creating a seamy, sexually charged atmosphere. The "sleaze music" set would soon become a hallmark of many gay after-hours clubs.

Despite the early morning popularity of sleaze music, high-energy dance music was the bread and butter of Frisco disco. Aside from Megatone, which was run by Patrick Cowley and Marty Blecman, San Francisco's main gay disco label was Moby Dick. Founded by DJ

Bill Motley and Victor Swedosh, the owner of the Moby Dick bar in the Castro, Moby Dick records were in a more "classic" disco style—horn charts, swelling strings, surging (real, not synthesized) bass lines—only with the jackhammer tempo de rigueur at the city's clubs. The label is best known for Motley's Boys Town Gang records, perhaps the campest (or kitschest, depending on your worldview) records ever perpetrated on humanity. The group's first release, "Cruisin' the Streets," was one of the first records not by Rudy Ray Moore to feature a warning label ("May contain material not suitable for children or the prudish"). It was easy to see why: "You can find anything you're looking for / You might find a big ol' boy, nine inches or more / It's all true I promise you, it might make you sore." The music and the vocal performance by local cabaret singer Cynthia Manley were as cartoonish and ridiculous as the Village People, but the heavy-breathing interlude and the lyrics meant that it would never cross over to middle America.

The flip side of "Cruisin' the Streets" was a medley of "Remember Me" and "Ain't No Mountain High Enough," two Motown standards written by Ashford and Simpson. Previously, Motley, along with DJ Trip Ringwald, had included Martha & the Vandellas' "Come and Get These Memories" as part of their vapid sing-along "Bitchin' 50s Medley" on Disconet, even though the track was recorded in 1963. On the surface, there doesn't seem to be much connection between the glories of Motown and Boys Town Gang's trashy disco potboilers. But Motown not only provided the archetype for gay disco's teenage-crush heartbeat momentum, it also laid the foundation for its hot flashes and heroic heartbreak. The connection was made explicit when Hi-NRG came to be defined as its own genre.

"PRIMITIVE DESIRE"
Hi-NRG

Conjuring both the racing heart and the swelling rush of blood, the rhythm of the gallop had been used to connote sexuality since at least 1866, when Jacques Offenbach used the beat to connote gay Paris in his operetta *Gaîté Parisienne* (aka the can-can).[32] However, when jazz and blues started to reshape popular music, the gallop was largely replaced by the concept of swing. It wasn't until Motown merged R&B arrangements with gospel's Holy Roller stomp on records like the Supremes' "Love Is Like an Itching in My Heart" that the giddyap came back to pop music.

As we have already seen, it was Europeans, particularly men from the north of England, who really latched onto the cantering drumbeat pioneered by Motown session men like Benny Benjamin, Richard "Pistol" Allen, Uriel Jones, and Jack Ashford. When Giorgio Moroder and his Munich Machine synthesized the gallop (see Chapter 3) and took it to new levels of robotic precision, the cybernetic sound quickly became the soundtrack of the gay underground. Fittingly, it took a Northern Soul luminary to figure out how to bring back some soul into gay disco's marauding man-machine.

After Ian Levine was hounded out of the Northern Soul scene because of his embrace of disco, he eventually moved to London and became the DJ at the legendary Heaven club in the arches underneath Charing Cross Station. "We opened the club [on December 6, 1979] with the two Dr. Buzzard's Original Savannah Band albums at a very low level, very quiet and everyone didn't know what the hell this was all about, quiet, music and no dancing," Levine remembers. "Suddenly, we plunged the place into darkness at exactly twelve o'clock. An actor called Doug Lambert came on the microphone and said [takes on a deep husky voice], 'In the beginning there was darkness, and God said, "Let there be light," and there was light.' And there was a little twinkle of light. 'God created man and man created Heaven.' Then we put on the 'Vertigo' part [of Dan Hartman's 'Relight My Fire'], the discordant bit at the beginning, and as it rose up and got to the 'bow-bow' part, all these lasers and neon lights came on, and the place went wild."[33]

With Levine being one of the few DJs in the country who could mix, Heaven quickly became the biggest gay club in Britain, if not in Europe. The problem was that, like the Northern Soul scene, the Heaven sound just as quickly got stuck in a rut. "The big record at Heaven was Dan Hartman's 'Relight My Fire'—that's when we brought the big fans out and two thousand people had their hands in the air screaming," Levine says. "It was electrifying. But there weren't enough records coming out that could capture that magic, so we started making our own."[34]

The first record Levine tailor-made for Heaven was Miquel Brown's "So Many Men, So Little Time," released in 1983 on a tiny label operated out of the Record Shack record shop in Soho. "I had been at the Circus Maximus in L.A. and I saw a guy wearing a T-shirt that said, 'So many men, so little time,' and I was like, 'One day I want to make a record with that title,'" Levine recalls. "The concept was I sat down with my cowriter and arranger, an Irish guy called Fiachra Trench, and I played him 'Relight My Fire' and I said, 'I want this kind of choppy piano, big powerful chords, and the idea is a woman is going to sing, instead of "I love you, I want you, you're the man of my dreams," I want the opposite. I want "I wake up next to this man and say, 'Who are you?'" It's so naughty but nice and everyone'll love it.'"[35]

Everyone did love it—to the tune of two million copies, according to Levine. While it had the aerobic rhythm that had come to define the body-beautiful gay culture and, as Levine puts it, the "naughty but nice" sexuality, "So Many Men, So Little Time" also added a hint of grit to the sanitary quality that Cowley had brought to the discotheque. It was a synth-dominated track, but "So Many Men, So Little Time" was more "musical" than the San Francisco sound—it was more melodic and you could actually hear another instrument besides the kick drum. "By the late seventies, there was an obsession with the separation of sound," Levine says of the prevailing disco sound he was reacting against. "They would take the bass drum and key out all the other sounds, the snare, the hi-hat. They'd use very primitive sound techniques to isolate one sound (now you can do it much more effectively on a computer). Basically the bass drum would just go *boom-boom-boom*, and they'd take out all the ambient sound and just wallop that up. You had the early makings of electronic music by treating the live sounds. What it started to do was demusicalize it."[36]

In addition to the melody and dramatic chords, Levine decided to use a singer who had some grain to her voice as opposed to the plasticity of singers like Cynthia Manley and Paul Parker. While Brown didn't have much range, the strain in her vocals at the high notes was reminiscent of honest-to-goodness soul pleading. And although the arrangement was indeed a Dan Hartman rip-off, particularly with the countdown (reminiscent of his "Instant Replay") and the nearly identical piano chords to "Relight My Fire," "So Many Men, So Little Time" resembled Northern Soul classics like Sandi Sheldon's "You're Gonna Make Me Love You" or Sister Sledge's "Love, Don't You Go Through No Changes on Me" or the Sapphires' "Gotta Have Your Love." "The concept was, go back and do things that you love, but always find a slightly new angle on them, but keep that beat there," Levine says. "Forever keep that beat."[37]

After "So Many Men," Levine produced records like Earlene Bentley's "The Boys Come to Town" and "I'm Living My Own Life," Eastbound Expressway's "Primitive Desire," and Laura Pallas's "Emergency" all in a similar style. In 1984, Levine gave the new subgenre a name with a record by one of his old Chicago discoveries, Evelyn Thomas. "After having such a big hit with 'So Many Men,' I wanted to make an anthem to the music," he says. "I fused the rhythm of the Village People, 'In the Navy,' *chun-chun-chun-n ch-chun-chun-chun-n* with the hand claps, cowbells, and chords that Frankie Goes to Hollywood had just developed with 'Relax,' but theirs was much rockier, and metronomic fours bass going *doong-doong-doong-doong* right on the beat. It really is a fusion of sixties Northern Soul, seventies disco, and eighties electronics rolled into one."[38] The record was "High Energy," and it became Levine's biggest hit, reaching #5 on the British charts.

Soon abbreviated as Hi-NRG to make it more in keeping with its mechanical beat, the sound would come to dominate not only gay dance floors but the British pop charts as well. Given the genre's

---

At the same time as Hi-NRG was being developed in San Francisco and England, a New York producer was coming up with his own version of the sound. Where the San Francisco sound took shape from Patrick Cowley's roots in academic electronic music and Hi-NRG was an electronic update of Northern Soul, Bobby Orlando's brand of Hi-NRG was greatly influenced by a youth spent idolizing glam punkers the New York Dolls. Listen to Orlando-produced records like the Flirts' "Jukebox," Roni Griffith's "Mondo Man," or her cover of Roxy Music's "Love Is the Drug," and the bubblegum moon boot stomp of glitter rock is inescapable.

Unlike Cowley or Levine, though, Bobby O (as he was generally known) wasn't part of the gay disco scene. According to *The Face*, in fact he was a rampant homophobe who once pulled out of buying a house when he found out that the

TURN THE BEAT AROUND

Northern Soul roots, it's unsurprising that most of its main auteurs were former soul boys. Wigan Casino DJ Kev Roberts would produce Velvette's "Nothing Worse Than Being Alone," Linda Lewis's "You Turned My Bitter Into Sweet," and Yvonne Gidden's "In Orbit"—all Hi-NRG remakes of Northern Soul classics; Ian Stevens had a hit with Hazell Dean's "Searching"; and then Pete Waterman, as part of the Stock-Aitken-Waterman production team, would become one of the biggest forces in the British music industry with a style based entirely on Hi-NRG.

While Hi-NRG took over the European pop charts in the late '80s, it was virtually ignored in the United States except on the gay dance floors of San Francisco and New York. Even though Levine would mix most of the records put out by Frisco's Megatone label, if Hi-NRG had a home at all in America, it was at what may be the most famous gay discotheque ever: the Saint. The club was opened by Bruce Mailman on September 20, 1980, in the old Fillmore East at 105 Second Avenue. The dance floor was an enormous 4,800 square feet, and thirty-eight feet above it was an aluminum dome seventy-six feet in diameter. The place was so spectacular that people gasped the first time they set their eyes on it. "In the opaque surface of the dome they had like a diver," remembers Levine, who was a frequent visitor. "It was like a three-D hologram and I don't know how they did it. It looked like he was going up and then he'd go *shoom* down to the ground, and then all the lights would just go *voom* from every direction."[39]

In the center of the dance floor was a tower affixed with around

previous owner was gay.[40] Bobby O, a rich kid from suburban Westchester County, was an unrepentant capitalist, a guy who would get into bed with anyone as long as it would make him a buck. Loving Alice Cooper, ABBA, and Giorgio Moroder equally, Bobby O saw a hole in the market when disco died in America in 1979, and he exploited it mercilessly with a steady stream of crass records—sometimes dozens a month—with the same synthesized clave and dramatic keyboard stabs from Griffith, the Flirts, Hotline, Claudja Barry, Oh Romeo, Hippies With Haircuts, the He-Man Band, etc., etc. Bobby O records were huge in the Benelux countries, particularly his records with Divine: "Shoot Your Shot," "Native Love," and "Jungle Jezebel." Orlando is most famous, though, for helping to launch the Pet Shop Boys by producing "West End Girls" and "One More Chance" for them in 1984.

fifteen hundred lighting fixtures, including a planetarium projector responsible for the image of the diver. The Saint, designed by Charles Terrel, was the most technologically sophisticated club of its time—not just in the lighting but in its sound system (yet another Graebar) as well. The 26,000-watt sound system, which had nearly five hundred speakers, was driven by an unheard-of thirty-two amplifiers. The club was incredibly expensive to run (it cost $4.2 million just to renovate the space) and had to be packed every Saturday just to break even. Luckily for Mailman, the Saint attracted something like five thousand visitors every weekend, and it became such a phenomenon that both 12 West and the Flamingo had to shut down because it was so popular, and so popular with the "right" people—the largely white gay middle class.

The Saint was legendary for the live performances held there—Bonnie Tyler played decked out in black leather, Sarah Dash sang "Sinner Man" dressed in a wedding gown—but it was the DJs who drew the A-list gay crowd there with such fervor. Alan Dodd was the DJ on opening night, and the club had a huge roster of DJs—Terry Sherman, Sharon White, Jim Burgess, Roy Thode, Michael Fierman, Chuck Parsons, Tony Devizia, Wayne Scott—but the Saint was really associated with Robbie Leslie and Shaun Buchanan. Leslie had learned DJing at the Sandpiper on Fire Island (under the watchful eyes of Wayne Scott and Howard Merritt) and at clubs in Florida where Bobby Viteritti played before moving to San Francisco. With this training, Leslie was an excellent mixer who, like his mentors, emphasized the midrange over the low end. Leslie played records like Carol Jiani's "Hit and Run Lover," Passenger's "Hot Leather," Kelly Marie's "Feels Like I'm in Love," and Brainstorm's "Lovin' Is Really My Game," but his biggest records were the Saint's unofficial theme songs: "Souvenirs" by Voyage and "Hold on to My Love" by Jimmy Ruffin.

Buchanan also learned from Viteritti. Buchanan, a British DJ, was famous for his "sleaze" sets, which were pioneered by Viteritti at the Trocadero Transfer in San Francisco. As well as Hi-NRG, Buchanan played New Wave records like China Crisis's "Working With Fire and Steel" and Sleeping Lions' "Sound of My Heart" before his "sleaze" records like Johnny Bristol's "Do It to My Mind," Talk Talk's "It's My Life," and Miquel Brown's "Close to Perfection." "Shaun

Buchanan was the best," Levine claims. "He was absolutely fantastic, the best taste in music you've ever heard . . . He played with the crowd; he pulled the strings. He used them as puppets to lift them up and . . . he was an absolute craftsman."[41]

True to its name, the Saint rapidly attracted a truly devoted following. "By the time the Saint was at its peak, it was a religion to people," says Levine. "It was fuck yourself up senseless with drugs because you'd go at midnight and you'd still be dancing at noon the next day. Then they would go completely out of their minds to the St. Mark's Baths [which were also owned by Mailman]. St. Mark's Baths had like seven floors, and there was always about two thousand people in there at any one time. It was like something out of a Roman painting—all these chiseled bodies, like Michelangelo's *David*, all of them. They'd walk around with just a towel hanging around their shoulder, not around them. If you didn't have a body like that it was embarrassing, because so many of them did. The religion part of it, starting Monday, was recovery time. Monday to Saturday in the gym, every day, eating healthy, zero body fat. They completely worked on their bodies like a temple just to fuck it up on the weekend . . .

"It was amazing," Levine continues. "You'd go to Vinyl Mania [a record shop] on a Monday, and all these queens would be like, 'Did you hear what Shaun Buchanan did' or 'what Robbie Leslie did with that record?' And they'd be analyzing and criticizing. They'd remember every mix, they were so in tune with what was going on. They'd criticize someone, 'Oh, he should have never mixed this into that. He lost it, he lost the atmosphere.' It was obsessive. The problem with the Saint was that it stagnated. There were certain records that were part of the religion—like both sides of the Cut Glass record 'Without Your Love' and 'Alive With Love,' Theo Vaness's 'Sentimentally It's You,' Voyage's 'Souvenirs.' If a DJ dared not play them, they were castigated for it. So what you got were these religious followers of a mentality that couldn't break away from it, and the same moldy old records got played year in, year out. But there was a magic about the Saint; it was very special. I went to the closing party in 1988. It was a three-day event [it ran from April 30 to May 2]. Marlena Shaw was on and Thelma Houston and Candi Staton. It was packed for three whole days. We would go back to the hotel, sleep, go back, still packed, still dancing. Amazing. It was so packed at the closing party, I don't understand why they had to close."[42]

Part of the reason the club had to close was what was originally called "Saint's disease," named "in honor of the downtown discotheque favored by the most beautiful and sought-after men of all—because so many of the best-looking were among the first to die."[43] Despite the ritual of going to the Baths afterward on Sunday morning/afternoon and the notorious balcony that brought the Anvil's basement up to the penthouse, the Saint was more than just an enclosed Central Park Ramble with music. "We didn't know we were dancing to the edge of our graves," Rodger McFarlane, the executive director of the Gay Men's Health Crisis, told *The New York Times* about his days as a Saint devotee. "It was the headiest experience I've ever had in my entire life. And it is unrivaled still. It was liberating, spiritually uplifting."[44]

3

"LIKE CLONES AND ROBOTS THAT WE ARE"

Automating the Beat

The adaptation to machine music necessarily implies a renunciation of one's own human feelings.   —Theodor Adorno, 1941

We have grown used to connecting machines and funkiness.
      —Andrew Goodwin, 1988

O n their 1979 album *Uncle Jam Wants You,* George Clinton's groove collective Funkadelic conceived of themselves as a funk militia, a phalanx protecting Afro-America from an outside invasion. This invading force was disco, and Uncle Jam and company were "the army with the mission to rescue dance music from the blahs." Disco, they argued, was boring, it didn't go anywhere, it just stayed on the same 4/4 beat forever. A funk fan, however, was "a dancing interpretation of the meaning of syncopation / She's a big freak, got to be freak of the week / Don't give her that one move groovalistic / That disco sadistic / That one beat up and down it just won't do / Don't give her that forever and ever foreplay / She's not looking for the short way / She's got to reach the point where she gets off." Disco, in other words, was a cocktease that offered no climax. For Clinton, disco was the "Placebo Syndrome," a pale imitation of funk whose machine rhythms were a fake substitute for the pleasure principle. Its sexless grooves were denuding black music of its funk and, by extension, black people of their humanity. As we have seen, though, disco's endless throb turned plenty of people on and got most of them off. Disco may have been attempting to artic- ulate a new kind of sexuality, but its insistence on machinic rhythms was hardly unprecedented. In fact, the standardized meter and me- chanical beats of disco can be traced back to the very birth of African- American popular music, and even the growth of Clinton's beloved funk music can't escape this history.

The rhythms of modern popular music were born in the late nine- teenth century in New Orleans's Congo Square, where brass bands composed of freed slaves and immigrants from Haiti and Cuba would congregate on Sundays. Not as well trained as the mixed-race Creole bands that enjoyed white patronage, the black bands developed a style of playing that was hotter (more rhythmically charged) than the European brass-band style played by the Creoles. These gather- ings were the first battles of the bands, and the group that played the hottest would take the second line with it as it marched in vic- tory. The second line were the people who marched behind the band and clapped, stomped, and shouted along with the music. The second line soon became an established rhythmic pattern. A combi- nation of John Philip Sousa with Latin American clave patterns, this syncopation became one of the primary sources not only of jazz, but just about every form of African-American music.

With its emphasis on regimentation and rigidity in order to foster the discipline necessary to create the perfect killing machine, march- ing band music is at the root of dance music's proximity to mecha- nization. Even in the hands of the funkiest cats the Big Easy had to offer, the second line pattern couldn't escape its roots in regimen- tation. With his conversion of the marching band style to the drum kit, New Orleans beatsmith Earl Palmer is the father of funk, yet rigidity and bounce were never very far away from one another when he played. Although it wasn't issued until 1991, his drumming on Dave Bartholomew's "Messy Bessy," which was recorded in 1949, sounds like the font of modern rhythm. Palmer's controlled torrent of triplets and snare rolls anticipated not only rock and roll and the funk of James Brown and the Meters, but surf music and the Burundi beat fad as well—and all this from a sound that probably wasn't all that different from a fife and drum band leading the Minutemen against the Redcoats at the Battle of Concord in 1775.

Even more martial was Palmer's angular version of the Mardi Gras beat on Eddy Lang's 1956 single "I'm Begging With Tears," but the ground zero of the militarism metaphor was Jesse Jaymes's "Red Hot Rockin' Blues" from 1958. Palmer's percussive volleys were so punishing on this and Eddie Cochran's "Somethin' Else" from the following year that Palmer was recruited by Phil Spector to join his wrecking crew and help create the wall of sound. The drill-sergeant precision of Palmer's drumming was primarily responsible for the creation of rock and roll's monolithic backbeat—check his jackhammer pounding behind Fats Domino and Little Richard.

Palmer's backbeat may be the archetype of rock and roll, but the ultimate rock rhythm wore a tartan tux and was played on a homemade square guitar and maracas. A mathematical formula for the Bo Diddley beat might read something like: (John Lee Hooker + 1/2 Gene Krupa) × (hambone + clave). Within this equation is basically the entirety of American popular music, and the Bo Diddley beat has been at the heart of everything from the British Invasion to disco (check Shirley and Company's "Shame, Shame, Shame" or Kiss guitarist Ace Frehley's dance floor crossover "New York Groove"). While Louisiana has its own version of this souped-up "shave and a haircut, two bits" rhythm, the Slim Harpo beat, the roots of the Bo Diddley beat proper are also in New Orleans. Long before Miami and New York had Hispanic populations to speak of, Latin rhythms took hold in New Orleans's cosmopolitan melting pot. With the city's significant numbers of Caribbean immigrants, the practices of voodoo and Santeria were widespread throughout New Orleans and so were the cross rhythms that were used to summon the loas and orishas. Eventually, the clave, the basic 3/2 pattern that was the backbone of this music, spread outside the shrines and was integrated into the brass bands.

Part of the reason the marching band sound was so popular in New Orleans was that a large number of decommissioned soldiers ended up there after the Civil and Spanish-American wars, making brass instruments readily available. Elsewhere, though, people couldn't afford tubas or drums, so they created bass lines by blowing into empty moonshine jugs and made beats by thrashing cheap guitars. The rhythm of life in most of America was created by the railroad, and prewar blues and country records were often little more than imitations of the locomotive using jugs and guitars: the Memphis Jug Band's "K.C. Moan" from 1929, Lead Belly's "Rock Island Line" and "Midnight Special" from 1940, Darby & Tarlton's "Freight Train Ramble" from 1929, and Bill Monroe's "Orange Blossom Special" from 1941. As the funkafied marching-band sound advanced up the Mississippi from New Orleans, it was smelted with these piston-pumping train rhythms, and the Bo Diddley beat was born. With its chugging momentum, Diddley's first single, "Bo Diddley" in 1955, established his trademark rhythm. Everything, including the guitar that imitated both wheels on a track and a steam engine going through a tunnel, was at the service of the beat. "Bo Diddley" may have sounded a bit like *The Little Engine That Could*, but by 1956's "Who Do You Love?" and 1957's "Hey Bo Diddley," the Bo Diddley beat had all the forward motion of a newfangled diesel locomotive.

Like Bo Diddley, the German group Kraftwerk created the end of the century's most enduring rhythms by mimicking a train. Where Diddley's guitar was a steam engine moving off in the distance, the synth lick on Kraftwerk's 1977 "Trans-Europe Express" was the Doppler effect trail left by a Japanese bullet train. Strangely, though, the beat huffed and puffed just like the maracas of Diddley's sidekick, Jerome Green. The reasons for this were twofold. First, by boarding the "Trans-Europe Express," Kraftwerk wasn't trying to escape this mortal coil like the prisoner in Lead Belly's "Midnight Special"; it was celebrating industry's ability to bring people together, its power to efface boundaries. Second, it was a demonstration of just how much the German power plant intuited the very essence of the machine. As Kraftwerk's Ralf Hutter told journalist David Toop, "Sit on the rails and ch-ch-ch-ch-ch. Just keep going. Fade in and fade out rather than trying to be dramatic or trying to implant into the music a logical order which I think is ridiculous. In our society everything is in motion. Music is a flowing artform."[1]

Kraftwerk wasn't approximating only the machine pulse, but its very logic (if such a thing is possible)—the ultimate trance of perfect repetition. This is perhaps most apparent in the full twenty-plus-minute version of 1975's "Autobahn." That characteristic swingless rhythm of much Krautrock, especially the drumming of Neu!'s Klaus Dinger (a former member of Kraftwerk), was called "motorik," and this was writ large on "Autobahn," where the pulse just flowed and surged constantly on cruise control. Both "Autobahn" and "Trans-Europe Express" were underground disco hits and were, perhaps more surprisingly, very popular in the black ghettos of New York, Detroit, and Miami. Detroit Techno artist Carl Craig said that Kraftwerk "were so stiff, they were funky,"[2] while the Great Peso from early hip-hop crew the Fearless Four called Kraftwerk "our soul group."[3] That Kraftwerk was so important to many African-American musicians speaks not only of the profound dislocation that postindustrialization and the fetishization of communication technologies wrought on the black community but also of the fact that, despite all appearances to the contrary, Kraftwerk touched on something deep in the roots of all music. The trance ritual is as ancient as humans themselves, and the eternal rhythm loop that could transport you across its waves of sound was the goal of the very first person to beat two rocks together. For Kraftwerk, these rocks were now machines. As Hutter told Toop, "We came from little train sets and *Elektrobaukasten*—the post-war generation with these little electric toy boxes. You immediately become child-like in your approach."[4] As with most of disco's practitioners and celebrants, Kraftwerk was discovering the wonder, the elemental in the all-night flow motion of the machine. The ultimate aim of disco's own trance ritual wasn't the zombielike catalepsy that the naysayers claimed, but the most exquisite ecstasy. Despite its own machine roots, rock was man's attempt to master his sonic surroundings—"to implant into music a logical order"—disco was a ravishing surrender to the clockwork throb.

Another reason disco attracted so much scorn was that it was the combination of the seemingly utterly inhuman sound of Kraftwerk and the genre that is alleged to be the most organic—funk. According to its definition, funk is supposed to be greasy, dirty, stinky, redolent of sex—the epitome of earthiness. However, although funk is perceived of as being loose and free-flowing, the truth is that it's as rigid as any time-regulated servomotor. Yet again, with his metronomic precision, Earl Palmer laid down the ground rules for funk. The finest exponent of the New Orleans swing that would eventually mutate into funk, though, was Charles "Hungry" Williams. As the drummer behind Huey "Piano" Smith and the Clowns on records like "High Blood Pressure," "Little Liza Jane," "Everybody's Whalin,'" and "Rocking Pneumonia and the Boogie Woogie Flu," Hungry took the marching-band gumbo flavor into more polyrhythmic directions. Hungry swung like crazy, but however far out he went, he never forgot "the one." "Everything on the one" is funk's only commandment, and people who break it have their own circle in hell—a dentist's waiting room where they'll sit for all eternity listening to Perry Como.

Hungry taught Clayton Fillyau, drummer on James Brown's *Live at the Apollo*, the New Orleans mandate, and in his hands the James Brown beat was born. On Brown's 1962 single "I've Got Money"—perhaps the most intense and electric record of his entire career—Fillyau's lightning-speed syncopated chatter notes behind the main beat are the foundation of funk drumming. Fillyau, and every drummer who followed him, hit "the one" with digital accuracy—if he didn't, he'd get fined. From the impeccably shined shoes to the precision-tooled beats, every one of Brown's bands was a well-oiled machine. With Brown policing funk's cardinal rule like Draco and the hard-and-fast strictures governing the rhythm, you didn't really need postpunk groups like Gang of Four to make obvious the connection between funk and control.

Funk really started to take shape on 1964's "Out of Sight" with drummer Melvin Parker's rim clicks and the rest of the band basically sitting on the vamp. However, it was Brown's next single, "Papa's Got a Brand New Bag," that truly changed the face of music. For all of the naturalism that racists and Cartesians like to ascribe to Brown, the bone-rattling effect of "Papa" was largely due to the fact that the master tape was sped up, thus giving the record a claustrophobic feel that made the blaring horns, piercing guitar, and ricocheting rhythm section that much more intense. At the same time as "Papa" is all about glare and flamboyance (the horns, Brown reducing the gospel vocal tradition to nothing but the falsetto shrieks and guttural roars, the "chank" of the guitar, which is probably the genesis of reggae), it also posits the once anonymous bottom end (the bass and drums) as the be-all and end-all of music. The first rule of this new Brownian motion was that nothing—not even melody, harmony, structure, or texture—can usurp the primacy of the pulse. Brown's new music was, in effect, Kraftwerk before the fact, just without the conceptual baggage. Disco's never-ending beat would be unthinkable without "Papa's Got a Brand New Bag."

Probably the funkiest drummer to ever zing a Zildjian, the Meters' Joseph "Zigaboo" Modeliste brought both the New Orleans tradition and the JB beat to hitherto unimagined levels of dexterity. He may sound like an octopus behind the kit, but the reason he's such a bad-ass is that he keeps time like a Swiss quartz—it's not for nothing the band's called the Meters. Ziggy played on LaBelle's *Nightbirds* album, the record that truly subsumed funk into disco. On the album's two best tracks, "What Can I Do For You?" and "Lady Marmalade," Ziggy's drums are distinctly flat and angular, the N'orlins swing is only implied. Given funk and soul's marching-band roots, this kind of severe regimentation was inevitable.

The hit factory at Motown got close to assembly-line interchangeability, particularly in its rhythm sections, and this was brought to the fore with what are often considered the first disco records. Eddie Kendricks's 1972 single "Girl You Need a Change of Mind" was disco's prototype even though its main beat, which was a snare rather than a kick, was a bit too human (the drummer is noticeably late a couple of times during the track). The following year, with the Temptations' "Law of the Land," producer Norman Whitfield made his apocalyptic funk even more dystopic with a strict 4/4 drumbeat that embodied the inevitability of human nature described in the song. The skipping hi-hats, the subtle but crucial conga fills, the hand claps, the dubby effects Whitfield puts on the horns, the hooky string lines, the deracinated gospel keyboards—this was almost the entirety of disco in five-minute microcosm. It was the rigid main beat, however, that really marked "Law of the Land" as a break from the soul continuum. Picking up on cues from Sly Stone and James Brown, Whitfield had broken from the Motown mold in the '60s by inserting spaces in between the beats; the relentless, clockwork beat of "Law of the Land," however, was perhaps his most Motown-like beat, albeit updated for a world quickly getting used to the certainties of the machine.

Motown's greatest rhythm mechanic, however, never even recorded for them. Hamilton Bohannon used to drum in the Motown touring band, and when the label left Detroit for Los Angeles in 1971, Bohannon stayed behind in the Midwest. No one has taken "groove" as literally as Bohannon—there are no peaks, no builds, no intensity anywhere in the records he made for Brunswick from 1974 to 1976. Perhaps because of his time at Motown, Bohannon made dance music like an assembly-line worker—his hypnotrance rhythms were so monotonous you could get repetitive strain injury listening to them. Willie Henderson was a producer and arranger at the Chicago offices of Brunswick from 1968 to 1974 before he decided to start his own Now Sound label. There must have been something in the water in the Windy City during that time, because Henderson's "Dance Master"—a favorite at the Loft—had the same machinic inevitablity as Bohannon, the same drone of the downtrodden funk worker. Rahiem LeBlanc, the guitarist of New York's Rhythm Makers (note the workmanlike name), had the same sound as Bohannon and Henderson—what Bo Diddley would sound like given a wah-wah pedal and a flanger—but Herb Lane's keyboards were far too engaging to make their disco classic, "Zone," quite as hypnotic. What "Zone" did have, though, was the most metronomic cowbell ever—you can almost hear drummer Kenny Banks counting off to himself every quarter-note hit. Without the Eno-esque ignorability factor, this numbing regularity was taken up by "the human metronome," Chic's Tony Thompson.

Ironically, though, for all the talk of the disco robots removing humanity from black music, *the* disco beat is probably the least mechanistic of any of the rhythms mentioned so far. The battery for almost all of the classic Philadelphia International records, drummer Earl Young and bassist Ronnie Baker, were two of the most influential rhythm players of the '70s. With the help of engineer Joe Tarsia, they experimented with all sorts of techniques in order to achieve the marvelously rich and full sound that characterized Philly soul. Baker would wrap a rubber band around his bass strings at the bridge in order to get a thumpy sound that not only anchored but propelled the music forward. Young, meanwhile, placed a wallet on his snare drum to give it a certain dynamic. Tarsia was obsessive about microphone placement, drum tuning, and which bass drum beater was the right one for a particular sound. All of these peculiar elements came together on Harold Melvin and the Blue Notes' "The Love I Lost." The song originally began life as a ballad, but the session wasn't working until producer Kenny Gamble told the musicians to let rip and crank up the tempo. Young unleashed a war dance on the kick drum with a shuffle on the snare, but instead of echoing this pattern on the cymbals, Young used a trick he had first used a few months earlier on an obscure record by the Fantastic Johnny C, "Waitin' for the Rain." Picking up a thing or two from jazz drummer Max Roach, Young accented the off-beats using an open hi-hat. The result was the hissing hi-hat sound that has dominated dance music ever since this record was first released in September 1973. The first drummer to pick up on this hi-hat pattern was New York session drummer Allan Schwartzberg. His beat on Gloria Gaynor's version of "Never Can Say Goodbye" (and his later work on records like the Joneses' "Sugar Pie Guy," Disco Tex & His Sex-O-Lettes' "Get Dancin'," and the Wing and a Prayer Fife and Drum Corps's "Baby Face") ensured that the sibilant cymbal would become one of the hallmarks of disco.

"LES FRONTIÈRES SONT OUVERTES"
Eurodisco

With such a strong presence of automated beats and mechanical rhythms throughout the history of African-American music, the disco naysayers were on unsteady ideological turf when they criticized its repetitiveness and machinelike qualities. After all, they couldn't very well denigrate their own beloved funk. So they found a scapegoat. It came from Europe like a marauding Ostrogoth in clodhoppers and a three-piece polyester leisure suit, and its name was Eurodisco. Journalist Nelson George described Eurodisco as "music with a metronomelike beat—perfect for folks with no sense of rhythm—almost inflectionless vocals, and metallic sexuality that matched the high-tech, high-sex, and low-passion atmosphere of the glamorous discos that appeared in every major American city."[5] Funk historian Rickey Vincent further characterized the dreaded Eurodisco parasites as "producer-made tunes [that] generally lacked any sense of sequence—beginning, buildup, catharsis, release—yet they were simple and catchy enough to bring rhythmless suburbanites and other neophytes flocking to plush dance clubs at strip malls from coast to coast."[6] Just as Native Americans thought that if you photographed them, they would lose part of their soul, the defenders of funk thought that if you made drumbeats with machines, music would lose its soul. Eurodisco was tainting the pure gene pool of black music with its goose-stepping stomp beats and beer-hall sing-alongs, and taming James Brown the way Pat Boone had wrapped Little Richard in a woolly grandpa cardigan. While there was no doubting that Eurodisco was seemingly made for the Stepford Wives and air-headed California girls aspiring to be Farrah Fawcett, it was equally true that many Eurodisco hits were practically note-for-note remakes of earlier records by Barry White, MFSB, and the Temptations.

The history of Eurodisco is inseparable from the history of the drum machine and the click track (the metronome beat that now plays in the headphones of all studio musicians while they're laying down a track). The first electronic drum machine, the Wurlitzer Side Man, was released in 1959. The Side Man was designed as an ac-companiment for solo organ players, and even significant advances like the Kent K-100 and the Keio Donca-Matic remained the pre-serve of albums like *Ken Demko Live at the Lamplighter Inn* until the early '70s, when Sly Stone made the drum machine as expressive as a guitar or piano. Stone was an organist, and when he locked him-self in the studio to record that masterpiece of pessimism and defeat, *There's a Riot Goin' On*, he took one of these primitive rhythm boxes to keep him company. But it wasn't just for practical reasons: The machine's stammering, staggered, punch-drunk quality was the perfect foil for lyrics like "Feels so good inside myself, don't want to move."

The most famous early drum machine hit, though, was born of purely pragmatic concerns. Timmy Thomas was a lounge musician who played at the club he owned in Miami, where he used a Lowrey organ and one of these beat boxes. His 1972 "Why Can't We Live Together?" was essentially the same version that you would have heard any night at his club—just Thomas sobbing about racial in-justice, almost funky organ playing not dissimilar from a jaunty cin-ema keyboard player, and a spooky bossa nova–ish preset beat. The instrumental flip side, "Funky Me," tackled the rhythm box on its own terms and featured a beat eerily reminiscent of Suicide's earliest records. Incidentally, a carbon copy of the rhythm box beat from

"Why Can't We Live Together?" would reappear, chained to a slowed-down Bo Diddley rhythm, on one of disco's founding moments, George McCrae's 1974 smash hit, "Rock Your Baby," which was produced by Thomas's former booking agent, Harry Wayne Casey (aka KC from KC and the Sunshine Band). Sylvia and the Moments ("Sho Nuff Boogie") and Shuggie Otis ("Island Letter") soon followed with their own "sophisticated" and trippy-tropical takes on the primitive drum machine groove. Strangely, though, the drum machine was used on these records precisely because it didn't reproduce the uniform sound of a conveyor belt (heck, you could get Ringo Starr to do that). Instead, it sounded exotic, otherworldly, inebriated.

It wouldn't be until the dawn of Eurodisco in the mid-1970s that the drum machine would live up to its name. Thanks to the Common Market, broadly similar social democratic governments, and the onslaught of the American pop culture machine, the distinct national identities of Europe began to dissolve after World War II. The lingua franca of this new pan-European identity became a combination of the deracinated Motown stomp beat first developed in the north of England, the sunny cod-Latino holiday music first developed by Titanic and Barrabas, and the bubblegum music started in the United States by Jerry Kasenetz and Jeff Katz as an antidote to the "serious" rock music of hippiedom. Europop was relentlessly chipper, hyperstylized music that reflected the boundless optimism of a European union that would end all continental wars, the homogenized blandness of a culture run by bureaucrats, and the retreat into safety of a continent that was reeling from terrorist organizations like the Baader-Meinhof gang and the Red Brigade. It was lowest-common-denominator music, and its message could be understood by anyone, even if you had to wade through swamps of bad diction and even worse syntax to get there. It was a kind of musical Esperanto—designed for everyone yet seemingly loved by no one (at least in public). Europoppers hardly needed the drum machine to make their rhythms more metronomic (check the Equals' early Europop classics "Baby, Come Back" and "Viva Bobby Joe" for proof), but when Eurodisco producers discovered the drum machine, the nightmare vision of a unified Europe was realized: The Germans were the drummers, the Belgians were the bassists, the Swedes were the singers, the French and the Italians were the producers, and everyone but the British wrote the English-language lyrics.

When the rhythm box fell into the hands of producers in Munich and Düsseldorf, it became the stern taskmaster it was always designed to be—"a regulator to tighten the pulse,"[7] as journalist David Toop called it, and any derivation from a strictly regimented 4/4 was absolutely forbidden. Academic Walter Hughes has called disco "a form of discipline" in which, along with body building and safe sex, gay men turned the practices of regulation into acts imbued with eroticism. Hughes writes that disco "takes the regular tattoo of the military march and puts it to the sensual purposes of dance music."[8] Of course, as we have seen, this had happened in popular music all along, but with its own self-awareness, insistence on the 4/4 beat, and the development of the synthesizer and the drum machine, disco explicitly played on this aspect, perhaps never more obviously than on Donna Summer's "Love to Love You Baby."

Little more than Donna Summer simulating an orgasm or twenty over a background of blaxploitation cymbals, wah-wah guitars, a funky-butt clavinet riff, some synth chimes, and what could be the most lifeless drums ever recorded (courtesy of a Wurlitzer Side Man), "Love to Love You Baby" was the aural parallel of the newly respectable porn industry. Even without Summer's moans and heavy breathing, this would have been the case. Thanks to a thousand terrible love scenes in blaxploitation flicks, that wink-wink-nudge-nudge guitar riff had become permanently associated with a couple getting down in a wood-paneled room with leopard-skin throws and astrological bric-a-brac, while the piercing synth fills represented the more "spiritual" side of fornication. But it was that bloodless jackhammer beat that really screamed *Debbie Does Dallas*. Rock critic Dave Marsh once compared rock and roll's backbeat with the rhythm of onanism, but this was the sound of a professional grimly, resolutely performing his task until it was time for relief, particularly in the song's seventeen-minute marathon version.

The original three-and-a-half-minute version of "Love to Love You Baby" was extended into a minisymphony at the behest of Casablanca Records chief Neil Bogart. "He liked the song so much he wanted to have a long version of it," producer Giorgio Moroder told David Toop with some amusement in 1992. "And that's when I did the 17-minute one. The official story is that he was playing it at a party and people wanted to hear it over and over. I think the real one was more like the bad story. He was doing something other than dancing."[9] Instead of just padding out the track, Moroder elongated it by using a new bass line as a tidal bridge between segments, creating waves that surged, climaxed, and crashed every four minutes or so. Moroder had applied the motorik autobahn aesthetic to the human body, and the resulting cyborg permanently changed the character of music.

While "Love to Love You Baby" was Eurodisco's most perfect expression, the calling card of this new subgenre was released several months earlier, in January 1975. Like so many Europop records, Silver Convention's "Save Me" used the archetypal Motown pounding rhythm and tensile bass line as a starting point but erased any hint of gospel fury and righteousness or chicken shack sweat and sex from its structure, leaving only an anodyne bouncy castle for the air-headed vocalists to bop around in. What marked this out as something slightly different, however, was the prominence granted to the bass line and the way the string section was used. As Silver Convention producer Michael Kunze told *Billboard*'s Adam White and Fred Bronson, "At that time, a lot of disco music featured brass. We knew we had a problem there because there were no suitable brass players in Munich, but we had a very strong string section."[10] Where records from Philadelphia International and Barry White had used strings to connote luxury and upward mobility, Kunze and coconspirator Silvester Levay had flipped that notion on its head by using the most "European" instrumentation (courtesy of some slumming players from the Munich Philharmonic) as a replacement for disco's "bluesiest" element.

This became more pronounced on Silver Convention's next two singles, "Fly, Robin, Fly" and "Get Up and Boogie," where the strings became more scything, more punchy, blaring almost (although the ones on "Get Up and Boogie" were a bit like hoedown fiddles). Gone were the Motown bass line and the percussion fills; they were replaced by a robot's version of the walking bass line (like following a square pattern on the floor) and rigid, four-square drums courtesy of Keith Forsey (and a Side Man). Despite the echo effects, vocalists

Penny McLean, Ramona Wolf, and Linda Thompson were so flat they sounded like heads without torsos, like there was no resonating chamber for their voices. While the chorus of "Fly Robin Fly" had Silver Convention's characteristic string stabs, the bridge used disco's more standard lush sweeps and swoops (which borrowed extensively from Love Unlimited Orchestra's "Love's Theme")—but on top of cymbal hits that sounded a lot like Kraftwerk's ch-ch-ch-ch.

Despite the assertion of Rolling Stone's Abe Peck that "the musicians [on Silver Convention's Save Me album] are so low profile that their record company could not identify them when asked for a photo caption,"[11] with his motorik cymbals and almost oompah drums, Forsey became the Earl Young of Eurodisco. While his beats were relentless, more often than not his drum sound resembled someone playing two rolls of paper towels. Perhaps because of this rather weak sound, Forsey was a master of negative space: Listen carefully to his rhythms—the funk and swing reside in the area between the drum hit and the bass line. Forsey's "I shall not be moved" style was probably developed as a reaction to his first notable gig—percussionist for commune Krautrock noodling freaks Amon Düül II. With less regard for structure than a toddler banging a piano, Amon Düül II jammed for hours on end, changing styles and time signatures at the drop of a hat and with no regard for logic or flow. It was enough to make anyone a stickler for order, and Forsey quickly became a 4/4 obsessive-compulsive. Giorgio Moroder, Michael Kunze, and Silvester Levay may have been Eurodisco's architects, but Forsey was its foundation. Aside from Silver Convention, Forsey anchored records by almost everyone in the Euro pantheon: Donna Summer, Boney M, Giorgio Moroder, Munich Machine, Roberta Kelly, Trax, Suzi Lane, Sparks, Claudja Barry, Dee D Jackson, Madleen Kane, Patrick Juvet, and Gaz.

While the British-born Forsey was the piston for the Munich Machine, the other major Eurodisco center, London's Trident Studios, was dependent on a combustion engine from France. Parisians Jean-Marc Cerrone and Alec R. Costandinos first attracted attention when three hundred copies of Cerrone's "Love in 'C' Minor" (which they cowrote), a brazen, sixteen-minute rip-off of "Love to Love You Baby," were mistakenly sent to New York as record store returns and found their way into the hands of local DJs. While it featured some very familiar saccharine strings, cheesy synth motifs, wah-wah riffs, and choruses of G-spot vocals, "Love in 'C' Minor" did make some important adjustments to the "Love to Love You Baby" template. Where "Love to Love You Baby" was about Donna Summer's pleasure, "Love in 'C' Minor" was Cerrone's own adolescent fantasy in which some guy called "Cerrone" with the world's largest trouser bulge ("I tell you money ain't all he's got a lot of. He just turned around, look at the front of him . . . That ain't no banana") picks up three women at a singles bar and proceeds to satisfy them all . . . at once. And, as if to drive the point home, Cerrone reinforced that pounding kick drum sound pioneered by Forsey, moved it way up in the mix, and sped it up about 30 bpm. Aside from being faster, Cerrone and Costandinos's productions (with help from arranger Don Ray) were richer in texture than the Munich sound, heaping on the strings and FX with abandon.

Cerrone and Costandinos first worked together in 1972 as part of a band called Kongas, which supplied party music for the jet set in St. Tropez. Working on the template first developed by Barrabas and Titanic, on records like "Anikana-O" and "Africanism/Gimme Some Lovin'," Kongas fused pan-Latin percussion, Santana-style screaming keyboards, chunky bass lines, and frankly ridiculous he-man vocals in a language faintly resembling English. This faux Latin/Afro-rock sound was the more percussive but no less sterile flip side of the more charcteristic Eurodisco sound. Largely thanks to producers Ralph Benatar and Jean Kruger (who later went to Paris to work with the Gibson Brothers, Ottawan, and Italian-Egyptian diva Dalida), Belgium was the true home of this style, with records by the Chakachas ("Stories" and "Jungle Fever"), Black Blood ("AIE [A'Mwana]," "Chicano [When Philly Goes to Barcelona]," and "Wela Wela"), Nico Gomez ("Baila Chibiquiban"), Chocolat's ("King of Clubs," "El Caravanero"), and Two Man Sound ("Qué Tal America").

Despite this flirtation with syncopation, Cerrone, a former musician with Club Med (probably where he got his taste for concupiscence), spent most of his career exploring the relationship between technology and lust and trying to convince himself that he could answer yes to Philip K. Dick's eternal sci-fi question, "Have you ever made love to an android?" He tightened his grip on the-king-of-disco-porn crown with records like the follow-up to "Love in 'C' Minor," the not quite as lewd but equally orchestral "Cerrone's Paradise," the quiet storm "Time for Love," and "Rocket in the Pocket," which undercut its tale of masterful cocksmanship with half-man/half-machine vocals that would make Gary Numan proud. Cerrone's flirtation with electronics was perhaps inspired by the French love for cheesy robot music: Jean-Jacques Perrey and Gershon Kingsley, the Peppers' "Pepper Box," Hot Butter's "Popcorn," Space's "Magic Fly," Jean-Michel Jarre's "Oxygène," Lilo's "The Banana Split," and Jacno's "Rectangle" have all been hits in France. Maybe with this in mind, Cerrone's best record saw him briefly change from directing aural skin flicks to becoming a sonic John Carpenter. "Supernature" turned the old "the freaks come out at night" tale into a bizarre sci-fi parable where laboratory mutants destroy the humans that created them. In other words, through the transformative power of disco (and especially that oscillating synth line that was largely ripped off from Donna Summer's "I Feel Love"), the freaks shall inherit the Earth.

Cerrone 3: Supernature was not the only disco concept album to emerge from Trident Studios. When a spoiler cover of "Love in 'C' Minor" (by the Heart and Soul Orchestra) came out in the United States before Cerrone's version could get decent distribution, Costandinos (who was also being pushed into the background by a limelight-hogging Cerrone) complained to Casablanca and was promptly offered a production deal to keep him sweet. Costandinos (who had previously produced records for Andy Williams, Paul Anka, and Demis Roussos) responded by following the blueprint of "Love in 'C' Minor" and creating disco's most opulent fantasies for the groups Love and Kisses, Sphinx, and the Syncophonic Orchestra (essentially aggregations of London session musicians including Alan Hawkshaw, Don Ray, Katie Kissoon, Madeline Bell, and Sue Glover). Costandinos's most opulent production was undoubtedly Love and Kisses' staging of *Romeo & Juliet*, which was one of the first albums to be recorded using forty-eight-track technology.

Costandinos was born Alexandre Kouyoumdjiam in Cairo, Egypt, in 1944 to a Greek mother and Armenian father, spent his adolescence in Australia, and moved to Paris when he was twenty-two. Like Cerrone (whose father was an Italian who fled to France to escape

Mussolini) and the biggest Eurodisco group of them all (at least on their home continent), Boney M, which was made up of four West Indian session singers under the direction of über-producer Frank Farian, Costandinos had a hybrid heritage that was the perfect background for Eurodisco success. His schlocky epics where the singers were more wooden than the inflexible rhythms, where the string section never stopped zinging, where the melodies bored into your skull with more determination than an Andrew Lloyd Webber tune epitomized the feeling of enforced joy that Eurodisco promoted. Of the seemingly hundreds of producers who followed Costandinos's blueprint, the most original was probably Russian-born Boris Midney. Instead of Shakespeare, Midney plundered Carlo Collodi's *Pinocchio* (complete with song titles like "Don't Leave Me Hanging" and "I Am Attached to You") and instead of trying to out-irritate Lloyd Webber, he remade his *Evita* as the dance floor schmaltz it begged to be. Midney's one moment of utter transcendence was Beautiful Bend's "Boogie Motion," perhaps the only time Eurodisco managed to incorporate a bit of sass into the vacant vocalists who were the subgenre's raison d'être (plus perhaps the goofiest bass line ever).

If there was a pied piper of Eurodisco leading the blankly grinning masses over the cliffs, though, it was probably Simon Soussan. Ironically, most of his records were recorded in America. Soussan, a French American of Middle Eastern heritage, was a legendary record collector and a notorious presence on Britain's Northern Soul scene, accused of taking advantage of fellow collectors and bringing the scene into disrepute with his dodgy covers of soul favorites. When he entered the discotheque, the results were predictably disastrous. Soussan hooked up with Dick Griffey, the booking agent for *Soul Train*, and under the name Shalamar recorded "Uptown Festival," a fairly horrific medley of Motown hits ("Going to a Go-Go," "It's the Same Old Song," "I Can't Help Myself," "Stop! In the Name of Love," etc.) over a pile-driver kick drum that would have given even Keith Forsey a migraine. Another Soussan-produced medley was recorded by Kansan singer Pattie Brooks. "Pop Collage Medley" was a diabolical fusion of Hot Butter's "Popcorn," Steam's "Na Na Hey Hey Kiss Him Goodbye," and Los Bravos' "Black Is Black." Brooks's biggest hit was "Girl Don't Make Me Wait," a sort of *Fiddler on the Roof* version of a song written by Philly International's Gamble and Huff. Toward the end of the '70s, though, Soussan's penchant for overripe strings and shudderingly loud bass drum was tamed by the synthesizer, and records like Arpeggio's 1979 "Love and Desire" and French Kiss's 1979 "Panic" became important hallmarks for the Hi-NRG sound of the 1980s.

The keyboardist and drummer on many of the early Soussan sessions were Laurin Rinder and Michael Lewis, two longtime session men and fugitives from the hard rock band Joshua. With their own production deal for AVI (American Variety International), Rinder and Lewis jazzed up the Eurodisco sound for an American audience with records by El Coco, Le Pamplemousse, Saint Tropez, and Sweet Potato Pie. However, as Rinder told Bernard Lopez, "We were scared to death that someone would find out about us . . . We were very legitimate guys. We were rock and rollers and when someone said 'You wanna do Disco?' we thought it was the biggest cop-out that you could possibly ever do."[12] Perhaps another reason they were embarrassed was that many of their records borrowed liberally from other records: Le Pamplemousse's "Le Spank," which attempted to cash in on the Chicago dance craze the spank, swiped its intro and bass line from Barry White's "It's Ecstasy When You Lay Down Next to Me," while their Tuxedo Junction project (discofied versions of big band classics like "Chattanooga Choo Choo," "Take the A Train," "Begin the Beguine," and "Tuxedo Junction") owed more than a little to the glitterball nostalgia of Charlie Calello and Dr. Buzzard's Original Savannah Band. The duo's finest moment was El Coco's "Cocomotion," a pastiche of every disco style you could care to name with hi-hats that made explicit the connection between Earl Young and Kraftwerk and, on the twelve-inch version, the hand claps of the gods.

The ultimate rapprochement of Eurodisco and the American original, though, came from a group from Australia and their Turkish producer. Arif Mardin had resuscitated the Bee Gees' sagging career in 1975 with the album *Main Course*, which found Barry, Maurice, and Robin Gibb trying their hand at Philly soul–inspired songs rather than the dated Beatles and folk harmonies of their previous records. The following year they recorded the similarly styled "You Should Be Dancing" at Criteria Studios in Miami. While Dennis Byron's kick drum sound was watertight and the cowbells were suitably metronomic, the track's Euro feel was tempered by the conga-heavy break. There were also horns and chicken-scratch guitar riffs galore—you would have never heard that in Munich. What made the track so European in feel, though, was the bass line, which was clearly developed after listening to one polka record too many. The superball bass line poings and bounces so much it could have been lifted straight off of a happy hardcore track recorded in Rotterdam in the early '90s.

As redolent as this bass line was of lederhosen and Maypole dancing, it was actually originally developed by one of the goddamn funkiest players ever to pluck the round wounds, Sly & the Family Stone's Larry Graham. While Graham is credited with inventing the technique of slap bass, and his abuse of the strings with a thumb that must have been made of steel provided new ways for bravura players to show off, his principal innovation had the exact opposite effect. With its deceptively simple, singsong vision of racial harmony, "Everyday People" topped the American R&B charts in February 1969. While Sly was begging for tolerance because we're all "Everyday People," Graham grounded his equality plea with a bass line that anyone with two hands and opposable thumbs could play. Graham certainly didn't invent the one-note bass line on "Everyday People," but he made it perfectly acceptable in the framework of funk by doubling every eighth-note he played, giving it a lurching but incredibly propulsive quality—sort of like popping the clutch on a car.

On the Jackson 5's 1975 remake of the Supremes' "Forever Came Today," Motown stalwart Brian Holland took this technique one step further. Instead of the note merely repeating, the slurred note was now doubled in a different octave.[13] While relentlessly robotic, the bass line on "Forever Came Today" also has a galloping quality—the Four Horsemen of the Apocalypse riding grimly forward toward Doom. This bass line is the backbone of nearly everything we now think of as disco: Diana Ross's "Love Hangover," Thelma Houston's "Don't Leave Me This Way," Village People's "San Francisco (You've Got Me)," Donna Summer's "Try Me, I Know We Can Make It" and, of course, the Bee Gees' "You Should Be Dancing." While some 60 to 70 percent of all disco records used some variation of this bass line, T-Connection's 1977 hit, "Do What You Wanna Do," is maybe its ultimate expression. During the main part of the song, bassist Kirkwood Coakley fleshes the riff out a bit with some slap runs, but during the breakdown the bass becomes dizzyingly hypnotic and incredibly precise. It's then doubled by a keyboard riff that follows the blueprint to the letter. While the Bahamian T-Connection thought of itself as a funk band and not a disco band, this was effectively the first step in the Frankenstein creation of Hi-NRG, the ultimate automaton boogie that would attempt to sever disco's connection with funk.

UTOPIA—ME GIORGIO

The more we study Art, the less we care for Nature.   —Oscar Wilde

And these ideas the writers are having about us using machines and becoming like machines—they must be making a joke. I know for sure that we are and maybe, as I think you say in English, we are having the last, longest laugh.   —Giorgio Moroder

About five months after T-Connection's "Do What You Wanna Do" provided the basis for Hi-NRG's shell, this barely nascent genre would receive its brains, bolts, and electric charge. With its dentist drill synths, perforator tom-toms, scalpel edits, and oscillator bass line (created with a digital delay), Donna Summer's "I Feel Love" seemingly had more to do with a hospital operating room than one of disco's pleasure palaces. Nevertheless, it topped *Billboard*'s disco chart for three weeks and reached #6 and #9 on the the pop and R&B charts respectively in the summer of 1977. Synthesizer-based records were hardly shocking by 1977, but where records by Kraftwerk, Tangerine Dream, Emerson, Lake & Palmer, and Tonto's Expanding Head Band had used Moogs and Arps to imagine the whooshing speed and gurgling weirdness of a possible future, and kitschy novelty records by Jean-Jacques Perrey and Hot Butter had poked fun at this brave new world, "I Feel Love" was probably the first record to consider what implications the machine would have on the human body.

Motion, escape, and fantasy had all been ascribed to the synthesizer before "I Feel Love," but never corporeal pleasure or sexual
gratification. With Summer's mock-operatic fake-orgasm vocals
set against an entirely synthesized background of syn-drums, stereo-
panned percussion effects, and a Moog playing that galloping bass
line from "Do What You Wanna Do," "I Feel Love" was a masterpiece of mechanoeroticism. Set loose in this baco-foil hall of mirrors, Summer sings about the pleasures of the flesh as if she were
disembodied, or at least lying back and thinking of Munich. The
epitome of the cocaine chill and metal gloss (your teeth hurt after
listening to it) of the '70s, "I Feel Love" could have better encapsulated the decade's obsession with the detachment of anonymous sex
only if the record was sheathed in latex. On the other hand, though,
never before had a record throbbed so tremulously, so basely, yet at
the same time been so rapturous that there was almost a holy purity
about it. Producers Giorgio Moroder and Pete Bellotte surrounded
Summer in a crystal and steel synth cathedral, and she responded
by sounding far more like Aled Jones than any sexy soul vixen.
Summer is frosty and distant, but she also has a beatific serenity that
approaches the angelic.

"I Feel Love" was in many ways a perfect soul record. Its confla-
tion of God and sex is surely as powerful and complex as anything
by Ray Charles, Marvin Gaye, or Al Green; it's just that it's not informed by the Baptist church but by something more akin to the
Carmelite order. However, it was also the record that effectively set
disco adrift from the soul continuum. The gospel tradition is almost
a "faith to power," if you will—do right by God and He will take you
over—and this transferred over to soul. Summer's was an ecstasy
of surrender. While the Holy Rollers and Pentecostals often found
themselves possessed by the spirit, it was only temporary. Summer,
on the other hand, sounded like an Eastern mystic completely sub-
mitting her will to the glories she had just experienced.

Compare this to the third great electronic record of 1977 (after
"I Feel Love" and Kraftwerk's "Trans-Europe Express"), Parliament's
Funkentelechy vs. the Placebo Syndrome, a comic book funk fantasy
that pits Star Child ("the protector of the pleasure principle") in
a battle to the death with Sir Nose D'Voidoffunk. The album is

densely populated with all manner of synth squiggles and, on "Flash Light," a preposterously funky Moog bass line that was made by stacking notes on top of each other, creating a springy sound of profound depth. Star Child's principal weapon in this battle in the "zone of zero funkativity" is the "Bop Gun," which features the lyric, "Turn me loose, we shall overcome." The reference to the civil rights struggle was unmissable: The "Bop Gun" was Parliament mastermind George Clinton's metaphor for the life-affirming power of dancing in the face of the pleasure-denying, sexless Puritans and the charlatan "urge overkill" peddlers who ran America. In Clinton's hands, the machine and gospel tradition not only marched hand in hand, but the two fused to become a weapon—anything but Summer's submission. The album's textures and scenario screamed "science fiction," but the album was all about "realness"—dig that title!—where true black music struggled against joyless funk poseurs.

"I Feel Love," conversely, relished its "unreality"; its denial of the human element meant that it was that much closer to the surrender, oblivion, nirvana that the song is about. Inevitably, the keepers of black music deemed it too robotic, too sterile, too unnatural; James Brown might have sung about being a sex machine, but actually embodying one was a step too far. Whether it was intentional or not, here was a record that challenged (if not directly confronted) almost every stereotype of blackness there was. Yes, Summer sounded thoroughly oversexed, but she was not the dirty blues mama or sensuous soul sista of old. Nor was she after Miles Davis's "cool" or the poise of Jerry "The Iceman" Butler—this wasn't detachment as mastery but something far more ethereal. The music may have throbbed and had a pulse like a racing heartbeat, but "I Feel Love" was almost devoid of the physicality so often attributed to black people. There was no athleticism, no bump and grind, no sweat, no blood.

Of course, as both a mongrel genre that was pieced together from disparate styles and impulses and the expression of an outlaw minority throwing off the shackles of repression that were forged in the immutable steel of Nature, disco was skeptical of the "certainties" of the material world. "I Feel Love" once and for all banished the naturalism ascribed to dance music. Pissing on the concept of biology from a great height, Moroder and Bellotte had the African-

American Summer playing a Teutonic ice queen with a machine heart singing about biology's most fundamental act while surrounded by the most synthetic textures ever heard on a record. With songs like this and those of Sylvester (and the entire Hi-NRG genre), disco fostered an identification with the machine that can be read as an attempt to free gay men from the tyranny that dismisses homosexuality as an aberration, as a freak of nature.

From the *Imaginary Landscapes* of John Cage through Walter/Wendy Carlos, Throbbing Gristle, Sylvester, and Patrick Cowley to the contemporary transgendered interventions of Terre Thaemlitz and Matmos's digital reshaping of the world, electronic music has been used as a vehicle to express sexual transgression, as a way of transforming society. As the most visible aspect of this largely invisible history, disco used the fantastic sounds of the new machinery to imagine a brave new world of sexuality. The hypnotic, otherworldly quality of the timbres and the rigidly insistent mechanistic throbs of the Moog and Arp synthesizers used by disco producers like Moroder, Cowley, and Bobby O summed up an aesthetic that sought to upset the "natural" order of things. As the outgrowth of both electronic experimentation and James Brown's rhythmic dictum, disco was also very much a search for perfection. The metronomes, synths, sequencers, and drum machines created a music of delicious absolutism—the aural parallel to gay culture's eroticization of discipline and its sole focus on process rather than result (procreation). Disco is the ultimate cyborg music, the ultimate coupling of organism and machine. In this way disco is a parallel to academic Donna Haraway's championing of the cyborg as a way to undermine the "biological-determinist ideology" that stands in violent opposition to both the women's and gay rights movements. "The cyborg is a creature in a post-gender world," Haraway writes. "It has no truck with bisexuality, pre-oedipal symbiosis, unalienated labour, or other seductions to organic wholeness through a final appropriation of all the powers of the parts into a higher unity. In a sense, the cyborg has no origin story in the Western sense . . . The cyborg is resolutely committed to partiality, irony, intimacy, and peversity. It is oppositional, utopian, and completely without innocence . . . Nature and culture are reworked; the one can no longer be the resource for appropriation or incorporation by the other. The relationships for forming wholes from parts, including those of polarity and hierarchical domination, are at issue in the cyborg world. Unlike the hopes of Frankenstein's monster, the cyborg does not expect its father to save it through a restoration of the garden; that is, through the fabrication of a heterosexual mate, through its completion in a finished whole, a city and cosmos. The cyborg does not dream of community on the model of the organic family, this time without the oedipal project. The cyborg would not recognise the Garden of Eden."

There is a ghost in disco's cyborg machine, though: camp. "I Feel Love" was as camp as a pink poodle wandering onto the set of a Busby Berkeley musical. Never before, with the possible exception of Eartha Kitt, some of the French yé-yé girls, or the most over-the-top Dionne Warwick production, had a record so reveled in its own artifice. Summer swoons like the woman in Rossetti's *Beata Beatrix* or Millais's *The Crown of Love*, utterly rapt by some power greater than herself. Summer is hardly the epicene figure so venerated in the camp aesthetic, but her femininity is so exaggerated (as it was on the back cover of the *Love to Love You Baby* album, where she's decked out in white Victorian/Southern belle finery, on a swing covered with pink flowers in a pastiche of Rococo painter Jean-Honoré Fragonard's *The Swing* or Jeanette MacDonald sitting on the same swing being wooed by Nelson Eddy in *Naughty Marietta*) that her gender is dissolved into the sexless synths.

Although she supposedly learned to sing in church, Summer's extreme stylization owes more to the Great White Way than to gospel's "Milky White Way"—there's a reason that she had to travel to Europe to make it on the *schlager* circuit. Disco's naysayers criticize disco singers for having more in common with Broadway vocalists than with soul's more "authentic" expressionists. With Summer they've got a point—her phrasing wasn't all that different from Ethel Merman's or Barbra Streisand's—but this is the very reason she was crowned "the queen of disco." The fact is, with one or two exceptions (1982's "State of Independence," where Quincy Jones's *West Side Story*–style production suited her to a T, and 1983's "She Works Hard for the Money," in which the brittle synth stabs and guitar runs paralleled Summer's eggshell vocals), Summer ain't a good singer—listen to her version of "Could It Be Magic," where she gets cut by both Barry Manilow and, umm, Take That. What kept

Summer out of both the canon of camp and the soul pantheon was that none of her records (particularly "I Feel Love") had the anguish, the torture, the wrestling match between guilt and desire that mark out the greatest divas.

However, with apologies to Loleatta Holloway and Grace Jones, disco wasn't about divas; disco was producer's music par excellence, and with Donna Summer disco found its ultimate blank canvas. As Summer told Anthony Haden-Guest, "That was Marilyn Monroe singing ['Love to Love You Baby'], not me. I'm an actress. That's why my songs are diverse."[14] Summer was an unknown singer from Boston, Massachusetts, who was in the Munich production of *Godspell* in 1973 when she met Giorgio Moroder. Their first record together, 1974's "The Hostage," was a big hit in both France and the Netherlands, but it had nothing to do with disco and sounded like something you might find on the *Kids from Fame* soundtrack. Moroder's first attempt at disco was on his kung fu craze cash-in effort, Roberta Kelly's "Kung Fu's Back Again" in late 1974, but it was when he decided to imitate the Philly soul sound with that German backbeat you just can't lose on, an answer record to Serge Gainsbourg and Jane Birkin's "Je T'Aime . . . Moi Non Plus," that this pop hack was transformed into the prophet of dance floor automation.

In its own way, Summer's "Love to Love You Baby" is just as robotic as "I Feel Love." Quite aside from the relentless dull thud of its machine-assisted drumbeat, there's a distinctly pushbutton (pun not entirely intended) quality to Summer's vocals. Meanwhile, those icy keyboard fills in the background are strangely reminiscent of the ghostly antisepticity of the Jupiter probe sequence of *2001: A Space Odyssey*. Moroder claims that Philly soul was his inspiration for the arrangement, but it sounds like a dead ringer for the Temptations' "Masterpiece," which is from the same album as (and features similar production to) "Law of the Land."

Summer quickly grew tired of playing the sex machine, however, as her born-again Christian values increasingly conflicted with her status as disco's queen. She retreated into standard pop fare like "Love's Unkind," "I Love You" (though both of these had a certain German overlord quality about their rhythms), "Last Dance," and, gasp, "MacArthur Park." As Moroder told journalist Vince Aletti, "She wouldn't sing about this, she wouldn't sing about that. Having her biggest hit with a sexy song, she was suddenly saying that she wouldn't sing that type of song any more, and then she insisted on having a song about Jesus on her album."[15] As an Italian from Val Gardena in the Dolomites, whose culture has more in common with Germany than the red-sauce-and-pasta stereotype of Italy, and as a musician whose first big hit was a German-language bubblegum-style cover of Sir Douglas Quintet's roots-rock standard "Mendocino," Giorgio Moroder had his own history of ambivalence and culture clash. Being stranded between cultures meant that Moroder was not only an excellent mimic, but that electronic music's quality of erasing "roots" and classification held a particular allure for him, and when Summer decided to play it safe, Moroder kept the electronics for himself.

Of course, Moroder had a history with the synthesizer well before he met Summer. His 1972 album, *Giorgio*, featured a song called "Son of My Father" that would be covered a few months later by slumming English glam rockers Chicory Tip and become the first pop #1 to feature a Moog. Intriguingly, the album also had a song called "Automation," but he reserved the true robot schtick for his 1975 album, *Einzelganger*, which was composed almost entirely of hopelessly corny vocodered vocals. During this time he also worked with Agnetha Fältskog and Bonnie Tyler, and musing on what might have happened had he not met Donna Summer is just too awful to bear. You might get an idea from his extraordinary 1976 solo album, *Knights in White Satin*. His version of the Moody Blues song (part of a fourteen-minute suite that takes up side one) does feature some of the most preposterous, unbearably kitschy, just god-awful vocals this side of Richard Harris, but the music was definitive Munich sound—clockwork cowbell kick drum from Keith Forsey, bouncy bass doubled by the Moog, blocky piano chords, and utterly transporting strings—and became a hit on the campest dance floors. The album also included the single entendre of "I Wanna Funk With You Tonite"—easy listening as Hi-NRG, and possibly the most Motown of all of his bass lines.

More letter-perfect Munich sound came in the form of two albums released, with tongue firmly in cheek, under the name Munich Machine. The real machine music, though, came with his 1977 album, *From Here to Eternity*, whose back cover boasted, "Only electronic keyboards were used on this recording." On the title track he combined the bass pulse of "I Feel Love" with Kraftwerk's synth vapor trails, while on the suite of "Faster Than the Speed of Love" / "Lost Angeles" / "Utopia—Me Giorgio" he again reinvented synthesized rhythm by volleying the solid drum machine pattern with what sounded like pins and needles ricocheting around a cake tin, presaging both the android descarga (a salsa jam session) called Latin freestyle and techno's drum machine calculus. Unlike "I Feel Love," though, there was no tension at all, not even a hint of ambivalence. *From Here to Eternity* was a headlong rush into computer hyperspace, *Tron* without the dystopian urge, shiny, happy music for the shiny, happy people of the health-and-efficiency-crazed 1980s. Of course, there was something a bit *Stepford Wives* about it all, but like a cat or a baby you couldn't help but be transfixed by the sheer radiance of the synth effects.

As journalist Angus MacKinnon ponted out in a 1978 profile, "This affable and amiable man is not, I surmise, a conceptual metaphysician. He is a producer and, above all, a businessman."[16] Perhaps this is why he was so eminently qualified to define the sound and gloss of '80s pop with *From Here to Eternity* and 1979's $E=MC^2$. Moroder's last great record was "Chase" from his soundtrack to Alan Parker's film *Midnight Express*. "Chase" used the same materials and virtually the same sounds as "I Feel Love" to conjure the adrenaline rush of terror and loss of control as the film's protagonist was arrested by Turkish police for drug smuggling. Strangely, it was a big disco hit, and Moroder created the template for that peculiar strain of dance music based on the dark side of nightlife, on fear, on bad drugs, on worse sex. Away from the dance floor, Moroder's music becomes like Tangerine Dream's score for *Risky Business*— there's a hint of alienation, but it's the alienation of privilege and not giving a fuck. It's the alienation of the salesman. Of course, there's something vital about electrobubblegum music giving the finger to the pretense and portent of rock, something liberating about its utter detachment from meaning and the discrimination of "value." But without the community of the dance floor, it all rings rather hollow. The machine needs social interaction just as much as humans do.

"ZIPPIN' UP MY BOOTS, GOING BACK TO MY ROOTS"

Disco and the Soul Continuum

If history tells us anything about the black experience it is that the different
expressions of black protest tend often to be a by-product of economic
class position.   —William Julius Wilson

One night in mid-1974 at the Gallery, Nicky Siano mixed
LaBelle's feverish, desperate, ultrapercussive, shockingly direct plea for justice and unity, "What Can I Do for You?,"
into MFSB's lush, but no less rousing or straight-ahead, jazzy flower-
child mantra, "Love Is the Message," and the crowd went berserk.
Perhaps no other single moment in the history of disco sums up the
tumultuous changes that the new aesthetics of the dance floor and
the post–civil rights generation would have on the soul continuum.
Here was a gay Italian man mixing together two African-American
records that each in its own way severed black music's historical
connection to the gospel tradition for a crowd that couldn't have
had less use for the church's message of doin' right by Jesus if they
were there to hear one of the satanic black masses of DJ Anton
LaVey.

"The triumphs of the black civil rights movement in the first
half of the decade—especially the March on Washington in 1963 and
the passage of the Civil Rights Act in 1964—provided the blue-
prints for a much broader national liberation, first for women, then
for gays and eventually for practically every other oppressed group

in America," Charles Kaiser wrote.[1] With the civil rights and Black Power movements providing not only the inspiration and impetus for the gay liberation movement but also its basic structure, sloganeering,[2] and models for collective struggle, it should come as no surprise that the black music of the period would become the soundtrack to gay liberation. And, with the often less than savory views on homosexuality in the Black Power movement in particular, there should be no further surprise that subtle changes would be made to the formula.

Although it didn't feature either a shudderingly deep bass sound or diva vocals, "Love Is the Message" was in many ways the perfect Siano record thanks to its play of light and dark, the constant shift between groove and goofiness, and the tension between fluidity and unrepentant cheesiness. MFSB was the house band of Philadelphia International Records, the single most important influence on the sound of disco, and "Love Is the Message" first appeared on their 1974 album, *TSOP*. The track is almost completely devoid of blue notes—the slurry sax is so schlocky that it's somewhere between a Vegas lounge act and the yuppie cabaret of Sade, Spandau Ballet, and George Michael's "Careless Whisper"; the vocalists are so anodyne they could be from Munich; the churchy organ (which sounds awfully close to the roller-rink eighty-eights of Dave "Baby" Cortez) gets only a couple of look-ins and is completely swamped by the sweetening—and so syrupy that if you discovered that Lawrence Welk orchestrated it you wouldn't be all that surprised. Yet it's a record that is as epochal as "Mystery Train" or "Johnny B. Goode" or *Sgt. Pepper's Lonely Hearts Club Band*, a record that delineates a cultural and musical shift as surely as any acknowledged rock masterpiece. Almost the entirety of the next thirty years of dance music comes from this single record: the cheery bonhomie, the cloying fantasy of the good life, the doe-eyed spirituality, the cushiony, enveloping bass sound, the string stabs, the adoration of jazzy chords and jazz as a sound rather than process, the keyboards like pools of liquid mercury, the mantra as lyric. While the musicians were aiming for St. Peter's harps, for music that soared like angels, it was certainly an earthly paradise that they were envisioning. This was no primeval Garden of Eden or the pristine "milky white way" of heaven; it was more like a luxury high-rise penthouse—a rather different kind of triumphant march to the skies, a different kind of crossing over.

LaBelle's "What Can I Do for You?," meanwhile, is gospel as theater—the production values and brassy, over-the-top singing scream supper-club revue. While gospel has always had its fair share of showmanship, LaBelle's campy, overwrought virtuosity (particularly when combined with the Starchild outfits) is far closer to Vegas than it is to vespers. While the song retained traditional soul's view of love as salvation, "What Can I Do for You?" seemed primarily concerned not with dignity and basic humanity but with quality of life. Gospel's ideal of noble struggle was replaced by an assertiveness, a stridency, a squawky friction (by the end all you hear is "What can you do for me?") that was alien to the solemnity and the turning of the other cheek of the gospel-inspired civil rights movement. Patti LaBelle, Nona Hendryx, and Sarah Dash sang "What Can I Do for You?" far more like Mick Jagger demanding satisfaction than Mahalia Jackson stoically moving on up a little higher.

"What Can I Do for You?" was on the album *Nightbirds*, which also featured their breakthrough record, "Lady Marmalade." The forcefulness and sexual forthrightness of the album stood in sharp relief to the prissiness and cuteness of so many girl groups. Of course, LaBelle started life as the Blue-Belles, one of those typical girl groups wearing ludicrously frilly dresses and singing songs like "Down the Aisle (Wedding Song)" and, um, "Danny Boy," but when they came under the stewardship of Vicki Wickham, a British woman who had previously produced the classic television show *Ready Steady Go* and managed Dusty Springfield, they metamorphosed into a feminist rewrite of the girl group blueprint. "It was my concept," Wickham says. "I did know that the sixties girl groups were over—this was 69 going into 70—and they were having a hard time. The Ronettes, the Supremes, the Shirelles, and on and on, nobody was really doing anything—it was a whole new day. I also, though I absolutely loved that type of music, didn't know that world particularly well. What I did know was a rock world, and so to combine the two seemed very natural to me. They had the greatest voices, they could perform on stage. If we took some of the more familiar rock type of attitudes, that would be a good combination."[3]

Instead of the usual girl group fodder like "Down the Aisle (Wedding Song)," Wickham had the group singing rock songs like the Rolling Stones' "Wild Horses," the Who's "Won't Get Fooled Again," and Cat Stevens's "Moonshadow." And with this rock approach came the rock uniform. "The thing that I really did wrong was at the beginning to put them into jeans and T-shirts because I thought we can't do the same old dresses and wigs and all of this," Wickham admits. "It really was dismal. I mean they looked pretty bad and it was horrible of me. Thank god for someone called Larry LeGaspi, who came to a show and said, 'You are doing it all wrong. I make costumes.' I said, 'We've got no money.' He said, 'Don't worry. I'd be delighted. I have friends, I can do it. If you let me dress them, you don't have to pay at the beginning.' And he came up with this whole concept—the silver, the feathers, everything—and it was wonderful. And that was what was missing . . . He was right, that these three women were larger than life. When you put the three of them together, the moment they opened their mouths everyone would just go, 'Oh, my God.' It was just enormous, their presence on stage . . . He saw this much more than I did: If we put them in wonderful clothes, they can carry it and that's what's needed. And indeed it was. I was trying to attract attention to them with the lyrics and the concept. Of course, what I was missing was the visuals."[4]

With the visuals in place, LaBelle started to attract a following among New York's disco denizens. "Even when they were playing the Village Gate or the Bitter End, folky sort of places, the gay audience started to come," Wickham remembers. "And, of course, with the costumes, that endorsed them as a potentially interesting diva group." LaBelle's gay following eventually led them to play regularly at the Continental Baths. "The Baths came about because there was a woman who used to come around to the recording sessions who was dating the drummer and she would sit in the corner," Wickham explains. "One day she said, 'I'm going out to L.A. to do the Johnny Carson show.' We really didn't know who she was and we said, 'Oh, my God, why are you on the Johnny Carson show?' 'Well, I perform and I sing.' And it was Bette Midler. Bette went into the Baths before us, and one day she said to me, 'The girls really should play the Baths, they'd love it.'"[5]

While the space age glitz of LaBelle's image went down a storm with the gay community, it didn't always jibe with the sentiment of their lyrics. "People want truth or nothing at all," they sang on "What Can I Do for You?" "People want sincerity and nothing more." Here in a nutshell was the conflict of African-American popular music in the 1970s: selling out versus tuning out, fantasy versus "reality," movin' on up versus movin' on out. With the basic battle for civil rights and integration seemingly won, African-American music moved away from the influence of the church to an emphasis on the here and now. It was time for America to deliver on its promises; it was time for something solid and tangible and real. However, when the assurances came due, they were revealed as nothing more than lip service. With this shift from hope to disillusionment, black music began to eschew the integrationist aesthetic and practice of Southern soul and started to question the illusions of American society, to search beneath the veneer of the American dream and its myths and promises, to catalog the betrayals. Representing both the last gasp of the integrationist drive and the first breath of cultural nationalism, postsoul disco favorites like LaBelle were caught in this crossfire.

"YOU CAUGHT ME SMILIN'"
The Smiling Faces Trope of Seventies Soul

In December 1963, at the beginning of a long New England winter, graphic artist Harvey Ball was commissioned by the State Mutual Insurance Company of Worcester, Massachusetts, to design a feel-good campaign to boost morale among the workers. What Ball came up with was two dots above an inverted arc on a vivid yellow, beaming sun background. The company initially printed up one hundred badges, but they proved so popular that Worcester was soon overrun with these caricatures of vacant cheerfulness. Ball's fee for designing what is probably, aside from the cross and the swastika, the world's most iconic symbol: $45 (even adjusted for inflation, that ain't much more than a couple hundred bucks).

However, despite the local success of Ball's figure and its subsequent use in numerous advertising campaigns across the United

States, smiley was truly born seven years later, a few hundred miles away in Philadelphia. In September 1970, two brothers, Bernard and Murray Spain, were looking for a way to make a quick buck. With America entrenched in the Vietnam War and riven by protests, generational conflict, and racial unrest, Bernard stumbled upon the image that summed up America's Nixonite reaction to the '60s in some old ad campaign. Bernard put the smiley on a badge and Murray came up with the slogan "Have a Happy Day," which soon mutated into "Have a Nice Day." Echoing such mantras of bland optimism as "Turn that frown upside down" and "A day without a smile is like a day without sunshine," the "Have a Nice Day" campaign swept a country that was desperately trying to put the '60s behind it and was looking more and more like *The Stepford Wives*, *Logan's Run*, and *Dawn of the Dead* every day. The Spain brothers hooked up with New York button manufacturer N. G. Slater and the smiley face became the fad to end all fads, replicating the Worcester craze but on a national level. By 1972, some fifty million smiley badges had been produced, not to mention all the other paraphernalia the image appeared on.[6]

But as smiley was zombifying the country, narcotizing it with an empty, blissful grin, a group of musicians recognized the symbol as the pernicious little yellow devil that it was. After centuries of betrayals and lies, the smile, handshake, and pat on the back are no longer ways of sealing a social contract. Instead, they become things to fear, temporary placations mollifying rage and resentment, until the inevitable U-turn, retraction, and cutback come. For African Americans in the early '70s, the Cheshire Cat grin was all that was left of the promises of the '60s—the substance of which had long since vanished into thin air, gone up in smoke like the ghettos of Watts, Detroit, and Pittsburgh. Instead of turning their frowns upside down and grinning and bearing it, soul artists of the early '70s engaged in a remarkable conversation centered on the "smiling faces" trope, an imagistic minefield that played confidence games with centuries of caricatures, the beaming faces of the white liberal establishment promising civil rights and integration, Nixon's dirty tricks gang and, yes, smiley himself. Invariably, these smiling faces told lies, but rather than being simple protest shorthand for the duplicitousness of the ofay oppressor that worked in a similar way to other pop music tropes—like, say, stoner/doom rock's "Witchfinder General" trope (derived from the great Vincent Price flick of the same name, also called *The Conqueror Worm*), which attacks the hypocrisy of squares and Moral Majority types—it is infinitely more complex and confusing, filled with self-loathing, and hectors any number of targets. Whether the central theme of the song or merely a seemingly thrown-away line, the image of "smiling faces" was universally wrapped up in some of the tensest music ever made in the stunning succession of soul records that used it, creating the ultimate expression of paranoia and elevating the answer song tradition above the level of kitsch.

Motown producer extraordinaire Norman Whitfield was perhaps the first to see smiley as the lobotomized, jaundiced, signifyin' so-and-so that he really was. But before he did this, he laid the groundwork for soul's interrogation of America's "Have a Nice Day" positivity. Soul may have blasphemed the church by using the language of salvation in the service of worshipping the flesh, but it never really strayed that far from the flock. Motown's relentless optimism, the NAACP platitudes of the Impressions, the "dignity" of the Southern soul singers, the theatrical arrangements and singing of New York soul: Change a word here and there, and there's nothing to mark this "devil's music" from the gospel-based tradition of positivity and noble struggle. In 1968, though, Whitfield broke this bond by creating a sound that had more to do with the starkness of ancient spirituals like "Motherless Children" and pretty much defining the strain of paranoid soul that dominated black radio in the late '60s and early '70s with Marvin Gaye's version of "I Heard It Through The Grapevine." Whitfield had written the song with Barrett Strong in the summer of 1966, and Smokey Robinson & the Miracles, the Isley Brothers, and Gladys Knight & the Pips all recorded or released versions before Gaye. Even though Knight's gospelly, Aretha Franklin–influenced version reached #2 on the American charts, it was Gaye's version that would eventually become the classic. Gaye's "Grapevine" was recorded in February 1967, six months after the versions Whitfield had cut with the Miracles and the Isleys. With Gaye, however, Whitfield slowed the tempo down, way down. In fact, he cut it in half. The new tempo created a coiled tension that perfectly suited the stinging string arrangement of Paul Riser, Earl Van Dyke's somber Wurlitzer organ lines, and Richard "Pistol" Allen's drums-along-the-Mohawk tom-toms. Gaye's performance is every bit the equal of the arrangement. In order to get Gaye to sound truly intense, Whitfield used a trick that would come to characterize his productions: He set the song in a key that was beyond the singer's natural range, so that he had to strain to reach the notes. The result was the greatest performance of Gaye's career, unifying all of his gospel training and earthly sensuality in one sustained cry of desperate passion.[7]

Inevitably, the Motown brass hated it. At the label's legendary Quality Control sessions they would play the current pop Top 5, and in order to be released as a single a new song had to be able to segue neatly into one of them. Needless to say, "Grapevine" sounded like nothing else at the time and even went so far as to abandon nearly all the conventions of the Motown sound. (Holland-Dozier-Holland's towering triptych of paranoia with the Four Tops— "Reach Out I'll Be There," "Standing in the Shadows of Love," and "Bernadette"—while working in slightly similar terrain, still kept the driving beat that was Motown's signature and thus escaped censure.) Motown boss Berry Gordy refused to release the song until they relented to Whitfield's pleading and used it as filler on Gaye's August 1968 album, In the Groove. The song would have died a quiet death were it not for Chicago's legendary disc jockey E. Rodney Jones. The WVON spinner abandoned his usual singles format and played the album track on his show and the phones wouldn't stop ringing. Gordy finally agreed to release "Grapevine" as a single on November 30, 1968.

It quickly became Motown's biggest-selling single up to that point, and was #1 for seven weeks. Nineteen-sixty-eight was the year that both Martin Luther King and Bobby Kennedy were assassinated, the year that the Vietnam War became the longest military conflict in American history, the year that Chicago policemen savagely beat hundreds of protesters at the Democratic National Convention. It was also the year when the National Advisory Commission on Civil Disorders, appointed by President Lyndon Baines Johnson and under the leadership of Illinois governor Otto

Kerner, delivered its report on the causes of the race riots that had swept major American cities during the mid-1960s. The commission found that the United States was "moving toward two societies, one black, one white—separate and unequal." The report recommended initiatives aimed at improving education, employment opportunities, housing, and public services in black urban communities. Most radically, it recommended a system of "income supplementation." This was perhaps the strongest acknowledgment by the federal government that America was, indeed, a racist society and that the grievances and anger of urban African Americans were justified. However, by the time "I Heard It Through the Grapevine" was released, Nixon was in power and the backlash had begun. The Kerner report became yet another promise that had gone up in smoke. "I Heard It Through the Grapevine" captured the mood of the country as a whole, and most especially the African-American community. Originally based on a motif inspired by Ray Charles, the new simmering, moody, scary, paranoid "Grapevine" now seemed to connect the slang expression back to its roots as a term for the means of communication that blacks used during the Civil War. The rumors, the whispers, the uncertainty, the fear— they were all summed up by "I Heard It Through The Grapevine."

"Grapevine" was far from Whitfield's only run-in with Motown's rather conservative Quality Control. When he first heard Sly & the Family Stone's amalgam of soul and rock, Whitfield immediately knew that was the sound of the future. Unfortunately, no one else at Motown did. Nevertheless, Whitfield got his chance to experiment when the Temptations' lead vocalist, David Ruffin, left the group in 1968. Whitfield drafted in white session guitarist Dennis Coffey to add wah-wah guitar to his increasingly dense and tense productions. Along with Sly Stone, Whitfield's "psychedelic soul" records with the Temps would change the course of black music for the next several years: "Cloud Nine," "Runaway Child, Running Wild," "Don't Let the Joneses Get You Down," "I Can't Get Next to You," "Message From a Black Man," and "Ball of Confusion."

Whitfield continued along the same path with Edwin Starr's stentorian 1970 #1, "War"—surely the most assertive pacifist statement ever. By this time, Whitfield's vision had been vindicated, and black radio was awash with darker and more political songs: Jerry

Butler's "Only the Strong Survive," the Chi-Lites' "(For God's Sake) Give More Power to the People," Stevie Wonder's "Superstition," Bill Withers's "Who Is He (And What Is He to You?)" (particularly in its ten-minute-plus wah-wah epic incarnation by Creative Source).

Among the most potent of this new wave of radical soul was Paul Kelly's "Stealin' in the Name of the Lord." While many of the other tracks relied upon moody production for their vibe, Kelly's track was remarkable for the directness of his attack and even more so for its target. "Stealing in the Name of the Lord" featured a straightforward gospel arrangement, with a Sister Rosetta Tharpe–influenced guitar figure front and center, a Holy Roller piano line, and a rousing choir. It could've easily been the Edwin Hawkins Singers' follow-up to "Oh Happy Day," except Kelly wasn't singing about a happy day and the song wouldn't have been played in any church in the world. Kelly was sermonizing against manipulative religious charlatans like Father Divine who preyed upon the desperation and willingness to believe of the poorest part of the population: "This man'll walk up to you / And look you in the eye / Put his hand on your shoulder / And tell you a big fat lie / He'll tell ya, 'God's gonna bless you children if you put your faith in me' / Then he'll pass the tray while the choir's singing 'Nearer My God To Thee' / Step in the line / Can ya spare a dime? / I heard him say, 'Step right on up good people / Can you drop a buck?' / That man is stealin' in the name of the lord." The secular and sacred strains of African-American music have never seen eye to eye, especially since soul singers appropriated gospel's language of religious ecstasy to articulate the pleasures of the flesh, but the antagonism of "Stealin' in the Name of the Lord" was unique.

Perhaps even more remarkable was another Whitfield masterpiece, the Temptations' "Papa Was a Rollin' Stone." Unlike "Stealin' in the Name of the Lord," whose attack was specific, "Papa Was a Rollin' Stone" seemed to criticize everyone, at least everyone male. With a bass line that was more of a black hole than a groove, a frenetic wah-wah guitar part, and just about the most dramatic arrangement imaginable, "Papa Was a Rollin' Stone" was a searing interrogation of black male stereotypes. The song was actually recorded first by the coed vocal trio the Undisputed Truth, but, as with many of the records of this period, the message was that much stronger coming from voices that seemed to represent the people being critiqued. The Temps' lead singer at this point was Dennis Edwards, a powerful tenor almost as forceful as Edwin Starr, and the lyrics undercutting his machismo made for a startling contrast, a technique that would also be used on many of the records on the Philadelphia International label (see below).

The limits and constraints placed on male behavior are constantly variable, always contested, and forever in flux in any community. But ever since the publication of what has become known as the Moynihan report in March 1965, masculinity had been a hot-button issue for African Americans. In his controversial report, "The Negro Family: The Case for National Action," future Democratic senator Daniel Patrick Moynihan, then working for the Department of Labor, largely blamed "the self-perpetuating tangle of pathology" in African-American society on matrifocal family structures. "At the heart of the deterioration of the fabric of Negro society is the deterioration of the Negro family," Moynihan wrote, seemingly ignoring hundreds of years of slavery, Jim Crow laws, and simple, everyday racism. "It is the fundamental source of the weakness of the Negro community at the present time . . . In essence, the Negro community has been forced into a matriarchal structure which, because it is so out of line with the rest of the American society, seriously retards the progress of the group as a whole, and imposes a crushing burden on the Negro male and, in consequence, on a great many Negro women as well."[8] While Moynihan's report was met with opprobrium from both blacks and liberals, this was perhaps the founding moment of the gathering neoconservative apocalypse and, more immediately and perhaps more crucially, it succeeded in altering the terms of the racial debate. After civil rights legislation had been in place for a grand total of one year, the onus of the responsibility for the plight of Afro-America had suddenly been shifted from the structure of society to the structure of the black family. The focus of the debate became the absent black father and his tangled web of pathologies. The Black Power movement reacted by attempting to reassert the strength and pride of wounded black masculinity—unfortunately, often in the worst possible way. There was Stokely Carmichael's infamous declaration that "the proper position of women in the movement is prone" and Eldridge Cleaver's boast in *Soul on Ice* that he had raped a white woman as an act of poetic justice against white society's continual political, economic, psychological, and physical abuse of African Americans. The scabs picked open by this debate over black masculinity slowly festered, and the resentment stewed in bile until it bubbled over in the paranoid soul records of the early '70s.

But Moynihan wasn't finished in his efforts to rewrite the country's racial history. In his role as an adviser on urban and social policy to the recently elected Republican Richard Nixon, Moynihan wrote a memo to the president that would become as infamous as "The Negro Family." "The time may have come when the issue of race could benefit from a period of 'benign neglect,'" the memorandum stated. "The subject has been too much talked about. The forum has been too much taken over by hysterics, paranoids and boodlers on all sides. We may need a period in which Negro progress continues and racial rhetoric fades. The Administration can help bring this about by paying close attention to such progress—as we are doing—while seeking to avoid situations in which extremists of either race are given opportunities for martyrdom, heroics, histrionics, or whatever."[9] Granted, Moynihan was probably desperately scrambling to prevent the Nixon regime from going headlong down a path of extreme racial polarization. But, as Peter Carroll wrote, "The manipulation of language, the message implied, would diminish black expectations, allow the inertia of American institutions to absorb and soften the demands for change."[10] When it was printed in *The New York Times*, the memo, once again, was greeted by howls of protest from black leaders and liberals from Moynihan's own party. "The most significant reaction to the Moynihan letter, however, was scarcely noted," Carroll wrote. "As a historical symptom, silence is an elusive document, impossible to verify or quote. But while black leaders and liberals denounced the cynicism of administration attitudes, the mass of blacks hardly blinked at all. For them, presidential machinations simply reinforced a sense of separation, a feeling that government was a white man's game in which a handful of exceptional black leaders were permitted to participate, sometimes as equals. Few blacks, the silence indicated, were genuinely surprised by the unexpected glimpse behind the scenes."[11]

The resignation and despair, instead, were channeled into the paranoid soul of the early '70s, particularly the "smiling faces trope" that was instigated by Norman Whitfield when he wrote "Smiling Faces Sometimes" in late 1970 with his regular songwriting partner, Barrett Strong. "Smiling Faces Sometimes" first appeared on wax as a twelve-minute miniepic on the Temptations' *Sky's the Limit* album, which was released in April 1971. However, it was first recorded by a vocal trio that Whitfield formed almost as a sketchbook for his studio experimentation. When the (much better) version was finally released as a single in June 1971, the Undisputed Truth (Joe Harris, Billy Rae Calvin, and Brenda Joyce Evans) had its first and only United States Top 10 hit with its first record. Despite the uncompromising lyrics, the record's success was no surprise: With massed chorales, percussion that imitates both a ticking clock and a rattlesnake, swooping strings, the "Can you dig it?" that Isaac Hayes would borrow for "Theme From Shaft," and palpably gargantuan brass and woodwind sections, "Smiling Faces Sometimes" was the most fully realized orchestral soul production up to that point.

However, this was no Hugo & Luigi, easy-listening, crossover appeal for Sam Cooke or the Stylistics. The first four seconds let you know all you needed to to figure out what was to come. "Smiling Faces Sometimes" begins with a horn fanfare from some hyperspace where Vegas, Bob & Earl, and Charlton Heston biblical epics conjoin, only to be compounded by a heroic wah-wah echo that bounces around the sound field like a Rabelaisian Ricochet Rabbit. In the third second, the scything strings that would become blaxploitation's other signature slice the production in half, leaving a dangling guitar lick and doomy, insistent maracas. Lush arrangements straight off of Isaac Hayes's *Hot Buttered Soul* follow, but the instrumental richness is denser, thicker, more claustrophobic—the sweetening becoming ever more cloying and fulsome, like false praise. When lead singer Joe Harris comes in, he sings like a mourning Levi Stubbs: You can hear his power held in reserve as if he is subduing his hectoring tone because he has resigned himself to the fatalism the song describes.

And what a brutal vision the song relates: "Smiling faces sometimes pretend to be your friend / Smiling faces show no traces of the evil that lurks within / Smiling faces, smiling faces sometimes they don't tell the truth / Smiling faces tell lies and I've got proof . . . / Beware of the handshake that hides a snake / Beware of the pat on the back / It just might hold you back." On the surface it seems a pretty clear indictment of the white establishment that failed to deliver civil rights while promising the world and of Richard Nixon and his "Southern strategy." In an effort to reverse the century-old aversion of white Southerners to the Republican party that had freed the slaves and destroyed their way of life, Nixon appeased the Dixiecrats by shifting the focus of the racial debate from the peculiar institutions of Southern racism to the more thorny, more subtle issues of racial inequality throughout the country. While seeming to attack de facto as well as de jure segregation by bringing the race issue north of the Mason-Dixon Line, Nixon was actually aiming to destabilize the Democratic power base in the Northern unions with initiatives like the Philadelphia Plan.[12] "For Nixon, outward appearances seemed more important than substantive racial policy," Carroll said. "The President might utter rhetorical platitudes, offer sums for urban renewal and unemployment, but in secret the administration operated on different assumptions: in planning racial policy, the White House assumed that the ultimate weapon for achieving racial peace was military force."[13]

In a song written by Al Bell, the Staple Singers harped on this duplicity and saw things pretty much the same way as the Undisputed Truth. 1972's "I'll Take You There" contained the refrain, "I know a place / Ain't nobody crying / Ain't nobody worried / Ain't no smiling faces / Lying to the races." Rarely had a popular African-American record ("I'll Take You There" was #1 on the R&B chart for the entire month of May as well as being a pop #1) been so direct about its protest. However, "I'll Take You There"—along with War's "Get Down" from 1971's All Day Music ("Police and their justice laughing while they bust us")—was the least ambiguous of all the records that invoked the "smiling faces" trope, perhaps because Al Bell was a minister who had become the president of Stax Records and there was no room for equivocation in his vision of paradise. But that line about the handshake in "Smiling Faces Sometimes"—which has resonances with the Black Power movement and its numerous soul handshakes and hand signs—seems to indicate that it's not only Whitey who'll cheerfully rob you blind. It wasn't alone.

On the amazing "Don't Call Me Brother" from the O'Jays' 1973 album *Ship Ahoy*, lead singer Eddie Levert breaks into a sermon: "Just the other day, when I was hanging out down on the main drag / I went in to get me a small, teeny weeny toddy for the evening / And when I come out, I got a bad case of the blues when I saw my tires gone / I open up the door and there was my glove compartment all torn out from the dashboard / And here you come, here you come, skinnin' and grinnin', skinnin' and grinnin' / Here you come—I know you did it—with the power sign / Talkin' about, 'My man, solid on that, my brother' / I said I don't like it, how can you really, really mean it? / I know about ya, I know what you're really good for . . ."

Following the even more incredible "Back Stabbers" (more on which later), "Don't Call Me Brother" was produced by Philadelphia International's Kenny Gamble and Leon Huff, who were the main instigators of a whole series of records from that city that seemed to interrogate traditional roles of black masculinity (see also former associate Thom Bell's productions of the helium harmonies of the Delfonics and the Stylistics, who took falsetto into the realm of the castrati). Before Levert's sermon, the O'Jays took that enduring symbol of black male camaraderie, the street corner doo-wop group, and turned it into a savage indictment of black masculinity. Over some of the ripest music of Gamble and Huff's opulent career (but just as in "Smiling Faces Sometimes," the unctuous vibes and zinging strings reinforced the song's message), the O'Jays ask some ne'er-do-well, "How can you call me brother when you don't respect my woman? How can you call me brother when I can't even trust you behind my back?" But it's that sermon and its "skinnin' and grinnin'" line, "power sign" detail, and even that bit about "a small, teeny weeny toddy" that give the song its force. Given that Kenny Gamble was a Black Muslim, it seems strange that the character we're meant to identify with is drinking and criticizing at least the trappings, if not the substance, of the movement. Was this Gamble questioning his faith? Or was the sermon improvised by Levert, who was taking a camouflaged potshot at his boss? Or were the details simply coincidence?

Given the swirling paranoia of "Back Stabbers," it's hard to imagine that they were merely coincidence. Beginning with what must surely be the greatest intro of any pop song save maybe "Johnny B. Goode," "Back Stabbers" is the tale of a man whose friends want to steal his woman. The first song written by the duo of Gene McFadden and John Whitehead (with input from Leon Huff) who would later find fame with "Ain't No Stoppin' Us Now," "Back Stabbers" probably is just that: the story of a guy whose relationship is going south trying to fend off the opportunists and scavengers putting the final nail in the coffin. But those roiling piano chords that introduce the record create a drama too big to be contained by the merely personal. The heavenly strings that gradually fade in the mix, trying desperately to get the upper hand on the relentless, insistent beat only to be undone by the punchiest horns in the Philly lexicon, turn "Back Stabbers" into a huge, Shakespearean saga. "What they doin'? They smilin' in your face / All the time they want to take your place / The back stabbers." While the music speaks volumes, to really hear "Back Stabbers" as the crucial part of the smiling faces conversation, you need to listen to it as part of the album with the same title. *Back Stabbers* begins with an almost mocking James Brown horn riff before modulating into a hard funk groove called "When the World's at Peace" that borrows heavily from Sly Stone in both musical and lyrical tone. The first verse goes, "I can see the day when it's safe to walk the streets / When we'll learn to care for those lost in poverty / There'll be no need for our sons and daughters to march up and down the streets singing 'We Shall Overcome,'" and its civil rights reference places "Back Stabbers" in context. The next line is "When the world's at peace will it still be in one piece?" and the song soon slows down to a disoriented crawl.

"Back Stabbers" emerges from this percussion fog. It reached #1 on the American R&B chart on September, 9, 1972, six days before the "Plumbers" were indicted for their role in the Watergate break-in. Released at a time when the full scale of Nixon's treachery was just beginning to be revealed, at a time when the O'Jays and Gamble and Huff still believed that people needed to sing "We Shall Overcome," at a time when Moynihan was blaming the cycle of poverty on African-American men, the refrain of "Smilin' faces sometimes back stabbers" resonated with a significance that went far beyond the tale of a man whose friends were going after his lady. Coupled with the eerie piano, screeching strings, and off-kilter percussion, the air of spooks, dirty tricks, and double-crossing is unmistakable.

One year later, as John Shaft was doing his thing in Africa, former Motown lackeys the Four Tops were wailing, "There's not a street that you can walk / You gotta watch just who you're talking to / They're out to get ya / Can't turn your back on a smiling face / Next thing you know, there ain't no trace of you . . . / Gotta keep your eye on the passersby, better watch your step / 'Cause you never know where the knife will go and they ain't missed yet." Produced by Chicago soul stalwart Johnny Pate for the *Shaft in Africa* soundtrack, "Are You Man Enough" was largely pro forma blaxploitation: surging Hollywood strings, gratuitous wah-wah, hand claps, and a wonderfully cinematic intro.

For the most part, the lyrics are pretty pro forma as well. Except for two remarkable passages that add layers of meaning to the conversation, where the above lines merely reiterate the terms of the debate. If "Back Stabbers" was all suggestive metaphors and uncanny timing, "Are You Man Enough" was unquestionable intention: "There's no pretending it goes away, with every step that you take you're paying your dues / And I ain't lying / You got to struggle to see the light 'cause someone's looking to steal your right to choose / And they don't stop trying."

If Nixon was the perfect symbol of the changing same of Afro-America, then "Someone needs a friend just around the bend / Don't you think you should be there? / Are you man enough when the going's rough / Is it in your heart to care?" is a plea for new paradigms, echoing the critique implied by the O'Jays and forcefully stated by the Temptations and Norman Whitfield on "Papa Was a Rolling Stone."

Long before Harvey Ball ever dreamed up his little yellow man, America was full of even more pernicious smiling caricatures. The pickaninny was a depiction of a black child with nappy hair, bulging eyes, enormous lips, a wide mouth usually being stuffed with watermelon and, almost inevitably, a huge, stupid grin. Most scholars date the origin of the pickaninny to Harriet Beecher Stowe's Topsy character from *Uncle Tom's Cabin*, but Topsy was a solemn girl meant to symbolize the brutality of slavery. The caricatures, both literary and figurative, that followed, however, universally depicted the "good-for-nothing gator bait" pickaninny as mirthful and more than happy with his or her lot. The pickaninny was a fixture in American popular culture until very recently, with such notable examples as Little Black Sambo, Buckwheat from the *Our Gang* films, and numerous minstrelsy characters. In 1932, Cab Calloway recorded a version of the old minstrelsy number, "There's a Cabin in the Cotton": "I got a feeling so sentimental / And I see a smile so gentle / When I think of old Virginny / And my pickaninny days."

Almost forty years later, Sly Stone was slightly less sentimental when he sang, "You caught me smilin' again," on his 1971 album *There's a Riot Goin' On*. Sly & the Family Stone's early music was probably the greatest music of the '60s because it actually practiced what it preached. A mixture of rock and soul, pop and funk, whites and blacks, men and women, Sly & the Family Stone represented the words of the '60s dream made flesh. While the rock community paid lip service to tolerance and loving each other (probably only because they thought they could up their groupie quotient), the Family Stone was living it. The protest singers filled their songs with a self-righteousness that made their world a drag to live in, but the Family Stone made a joyful noise out of collectivity.

By the end of 1969, though, Sly & the Family Stone was no longer the voice of a shiny, happy, new, integrated America. "Thank You (Falettinme Be Mice Elf Agin)" of 1970 was a snarling record that intimated that Woodstock, and the group's triumph there, was a sham: "Thank you for the party, but I could never stay." The group's new album was endlessly delayed: Sly wasn't showing up for concerts, he was wrestling with drug addiction, there were rumors that black nationalist leaders were trying to force him to make his music more radical, he was getting death threats. When *There's a Riot Goin' On* finally emerged in November 1971, the joy, the gorgeous mosaic of voices, and the "different strokes for different folks" tolerance were all gone. In their places were scorn, derision, and dead spots so vast you felt like you'd just fallen off the end of the world. The deadest spot of all was the title track, which clocked in at 0:00. While Marvin Gaye was making *What's Going On* as an article of faith in the power of pop music, Sly was highlighting his pessimism by sardonically pointing out that nothing was going on.

With Sly turning to cataloging the betrayals of the '60s dream, America needed a new black icon to make it feel good about itself. Instead of someone who still believed in the possibilities of the American experiment, this new icon was an eleven-year-old boy who didn't know any better. While Michael Jackson was electrifying the world with his innocent charm, Sly was retreating into himself because he knew a lot better. "(You Caught Me) Smilin'" was a sketchy, slo-mo groove with deconstructed and incomplete JB horn charts, too wasted to try to fight their way through the narcotic haze—like Sly & the Family Stone in dub, or maybe in photonegative. Sly gurgled and wailed like a hungry baby, and sang like he was talking to his chest, railing like an incoherent drunk against the prevailing notion that ignorance is bliss. The song was a kiss-off—both to a lover and to his old constituency that didn't want him to stop smiling; he had been dragged through the wringer and he was going to take you with him.

The protagonist of the Persuaders' 1971 hit, "Thin Line Between Love & Hate," had also been left for dead. With Douglas "Smokey" Scott's overenunciated lead vocals and the old-fashioned melodrama of the arrangement, "Thin Line Between Love & Hate" is a pretty standard cautionary tale. Until the last verse, where the put-upon wife exacts her revenge and sends the cheating bastard to the hospital. As the record fades out, Scott gets on his knees and belts, "Every smiling face in a happy world . . . ," like he's got old-time religion. Unlike Willie Hutch's 1974 "Theme From Foxy Brown," which contrasts Foxy's smiles and "foxy looks" to portray a sex bomb who's not to be trifled with, it's not too much of a leap to suggest that "Thin Line Between Love & Hate" can also be seen as a warning of what lurks behind the goofy grin of "the lazy, shiftless coon."

By the summer of '75, Nixon had been pardoned, stagflation had set in, the leaders of the Black Power movement had been rounded up, exiled, or retreated into academia, and Van McCoy's "The Hustle" was heralding the disco onslaught. However, replacing "The

Hustle" at the top of the R&B charts was the last gasp for overtly political black music until the Furious Five's "The Message." "Fight the Power" was the Isley Brothers' second biggest hit, and, of course, everyone remembers it for the "all this bullshit goin' down" line. If the record company had its way, however, it would have been heard only in a bowdlerized version. Even if the DJs didn't ignore the biz's advice, however, the chorus made the point just as forcefully, so forcefully in fact that Public Enemy would borrow elements from it more than a decade later: "Time is truly wasting / There's no guarantee / Smiles in the making / Fight the powers that be." Despite the song's militancy, "Fight the Power" amply demonstrated the tricky politics of crossover, particularly when a large portion of the record-buying and dancing public seemed to have no connection to the struggle. Journalist Frank Robertson recounted a fairly common scene at discotheques all across America in 1975: "The Chinese guy in a vest, no shirt, Levi's bellbottoms and his dancing partner, a white girl with a pert steno permanent and a red hot pants suit . . . he's arched backwards on his hands and feet and she is straddling him, pumping down and up to the beat of 'Fight the Power.'"[14]

Of course, there's only so long you can stare down the barrel of a gun before you start to blink, but this is hardly to say that disco wiped the ambiguous smile off the face of black music. In 1977, a hopelessly obscure group called Smoggs released an example of that uniquely 1970s phenomenon fueled by the hysteria of the gas crisis, the comedy protest record. Produced by Joe Simon (that Joe Simon?), half of "Gotta Have a Little Talk With the Peanut Man" was taken up by a guy calling himself Willie Ray Paul Sam Robert Jones Dunlap with a low, Southern drawl trying to make a phone call to the White House, insulting the operator when she won't put him through to President Carter. The other half was an admittedly lightweight, James Brown–influenced plea for a helping hand in the face of escalating unemployment and high taxation, and it featured our pernicious little friend again: "Peanut, my life is in your hands / This ain't no time to play no games / A handshake and a grin might mean goodwill / But a handshake and a grin don't pay my bills."

In 1976, on its hit "Cherchez La Femme," Dr. Buzzard's Original Savannah Band's Cory Daye sang, "They'll tell you a lie with a Colgate smile, hey baby / Love you one second and hate you the next one / Oh ain't it crazy, yeah / All I can say, of one thing I am certain / They're all the same, the sluts and the saints," on top of music that referenced both the controversial white "King of Jazz" Paul Whiteman and camp sex kitten chanteuse Eartha Kitt. On the surface, "Cherchez La Femme" was a straightforward, if very witty, cautionary tale of the deceit that is ever-present in sexual relationships, but its intimations of class and sophistication, its odd racial dynamics, its urbane wordsmithery spoke of a profound sense of dislocation. It wasn't as wracked and wrought as "Back Stabbers" or "Smiling Faces Sometimes," or as full of extramusical connotations, but as a pop-informed examination and exorcism of everyday treachery, "Cherchez La Femme" was just as powerful, despite its flapper dress, mink stole, and caked-on makeup.

Admittedly, this was a rarity in disco. Naturally, in a genre all about pleasure, it would be hard to write songs that talked ambivalently about smiles, but pleasure itself was certainly talked about ambivalently. Disco's lifestyle was inherently perilous: Its pleasure principle was the same as its mechanism of punishment and pain; clubgoers were seemingly imprisoned by fate; its black constituency was caught between two worlds; young people were trying to make their own culture but were trampled by the oppressive weight of the '60s, by the sense that everything has been done already. Disco songs were awash in addiction and S&M metaphors (Black Ivory's "Mainline," Chic's "Can't Stand to Love You," Tamiko Jones's "Can't Live Without Your Love," Dee Dee Bridgewater's "Bad For Me," etc.) and imagery in which pleasure was as bad as pain (New York Citi Peech Boys' "Don't Make Me Wait," Inner Life's "I'm Caught Up [In a One Night Love Affair]," Loose Joints' "Is It All Over My Face").

This sense of being trapped, of being a prisoner of fate and doom, was the ghost in disco's machine, haunting the corners of the dance floors, wafting through the dry ice with every broken popper bottle. Despite disco's happy-faced exterior, the sense of chill and foreboding of the "smiling faces" songs lurked underneath every percussion break, every snazzy string arrangement, every rhinestone synth fill. This was true from the very beginning. With its strict, unwavering 4/4 drumbeat mirroring the immutability of human nature described in the song, the skipping hi-hats, the conga fills, and the hand claps, the Temptations' Norman Whitfield–produced 1973 single "Law of the Land" is perhaps the first disco single. Thematically, too, the song's dark pessimism marks the bridge between disco and soul. Dennis Edwards preaches about the impossibility of escaping your fate, that life sucks and then you die: "What goes around comes around / What goes up must come down." Soul had never been this defeatist before; it may have abandoned the church, but its language and force still came from gospel's faith that deliverance was just around the corner. This new stoicism transferred over to disco, where the theme of predestination was writ large: Teddy Pender-grass's "You Can't Hide From Yourself" ("You can't hide from your-self / Everywhere you go, there you are"), Chic's "Good Times" ("Silly fool, you can't change your fate"), Carl Bean's gay pride an-them "I Was Born This Way" ("Nature did this to me"). Even the disco denizens themselves seemed to act according to some power that was beyond their control. As Andrew Holleran described the hard-core dancers at the early New York discotheques, "They sel-dom looked happy. They passed one another without a word in the elevator, like silent shades in hell, hell-bent on their next look from a handsome stranger. Their next rush from a popper. The next song that turned their bones to jelly and left them all on the dance floor with heads back, eyes nearly closed, in the ecstasy of saints receiv-ing the stigmata. They pursued these things with such devotion that they acquired, after a few seasons, a haggard look, a look of deadly seriousness. Some wiped everything they could off their faces and reduced themselves to blanks. Yet even these, when you en-tered the hallway where they stood waiting to go in, would turn to-ward you all at once in that one unpremeditated moment (as when we see ourselves in a mirror we didn't know was there), the same look on their faces: Take me away from this."[15]

"DON'T LET THE GREEN GRASS FOOL YOU"
The Sound of Philadelphia

The inventor of the concept of the white man's burden isn't the most likely of influences for one of soul's most dramatic paradigm shifts, but then again the music that emerged from Philadelphia in the late '60s and early '70s often made for strange bedfellows. Jerry Butler, the original lead singer of the Impressions and one of the mainstays of the smooth Chicago soul sound, was in the offices of his record company sharing a corned beef sandwich with Philadelphian producers and songwriters Kenny Gamble and Leon Huff. They were talking about soul artists who had managed to sustain their careers over many years when Butler mentioned the Rudyard Kipling poem "If—" ("If you can keep your head when all about you / Are losing theirs and blaming it on you . . ."), and the lightbulb went on in Gamble's head.[16] The idea became "Only the Strong Survive," an R&B #1 and pop #4 for Butler in April 1969.

With its creamy, Wes Montgomery–style guitar licks (no chicken scratch—the definitive R&B lick—here), resonant vibraphone, prominent string section, and a kick drum that sounded like a timpani purloined from the Philadelphia Philharmonic, "Only the Strong Survive" was a unique presence on the American airwaves in 1969 (the only element that sounded secondhand was the bass line, which was lifted directly from Fontella Bass's "Rescue Me"). The record was preceded at the top of the R&B charts by the Temptations' "Runaway Child Running Wild," James Brown's "Give It Up or Turnit a Loose," and Sly & the Family Stone's "Everyday People," and immediately followed by the Isley Brothers' "It's Your Thing"— all examples of uncompromising psychedelic soul or hard funk. In comparison, "Only the Strong Survive" was like slipping on a smoking jacket and relaxing in front of the fire with a snifter of brandy. The warmth, pinpoint instrumental definition, and gently uplifting momentum of "Only the Strong Survive" heralded the Philadelphia sound as the new direction for African-American music.

Philadelphia had been a presence on the national soul scene since 1961, when the Pentagons recorded "Until Then," a tentative stab at the mix of dinner-club orchestral arrangement and storefront-church passion that would be perfected when Philadelphian Garnet Mimms recorded "Cry Baby" in New York in 1963 with fellow Philadelphian exile Jerry Ragavoy. Equally significant, though, was Philadelphia's jazz community—which boasted such titans as John Coltrane, Philly Joe Jones, Sun Ra, Jimmy McGriff, Bill Doggett, and Jimmy Heath, and their values of serpentine lines and intricate harmonic relationships—and the city's teen idol production line at the Cameo/Parkway and Chancellor labels: Frankie Avalon, Fabian, Bobby Rydell, Chubby Checker, and Dee Dee Sharp. Thanks to the close-knit nature of the City of Brotherly Love's music community, many of the musicians who spent the day working on Frankie Avalon and Chubby Checker sessions would play with Bill Doggett and Philly Joe Jones at night, and this mix of jazz style and pop vernacular would come to characterize the Philadelphia soul sound.

The song that really put Philadelphia soul on the map was Barbara Mason's "Yes, I'm Ready," a pop #5 hit in the spring of 1965. The record—a torrent of virginal teen longing—was produced by the Dyno-Dynamic Productions team: organist Johnny Styles; Luther Randolph; lead singer of the Larks, Weldon McDougal III; and local radio DJ Jimmy Bishop. They used the Larks' backing band—guitarists Norman Harris and Bobby Eli, drummer Earl Young, and bassist Ronnie Baker—as their house band, and on "Yes, I'm Ready" the backup singer was a young songwriter called Kenny Gamble. While not entirely stylistically apposite, the record established both the talent pool and the impossibly lush strings that worked with the rhythm rather than against it (on "Yes, I'm Ready," they sound as close to Bollywood's gushing string cascades as any Western recording) that would characterize the Philly sound.

Equally crucial, although not as popular, were a series of records by a vocal group called the Volcanoes, featuring the same musicians. Released a couple of months after "Yes, I'm Ready," the Volcanoes' "Storm Warning" was the first step toward the revolution of "Only the Strong Survive." While the beat and the interplay between the drums and piano were straight out of Berry Gordy's songbook (which helped it become a Northern Soul classic), the jazzy guitar that introduces the record and the vibraphone chimes throughout mark this as a significant advance on the Motown blueprint. This was where Philadelphia's jazz scene really made its mark on soul music, particularly the influence of George Shearing's legendary quintet recordings of 1949. Shearing was a British pianist who brought a vibes player, Marjorie Hyams, into his group, and the block-chord interplay between the two introduced a new sound to jazz. On "Storm Warning," it is vibist Vince Montana fleshing out the melody led by an undermixed piano. The lead being played by the piano and vibraphone would become the critical component in the Philly sound.

As Weldon McDougal said, "The Volcanoes records were really like when Philadelphia started developing their own thing. Up until then most uptempo Philly records were based on Detroit things . . . The vibes sound, the way the strings sweetened things without getting in the way of the beat, all the rhythm sounds started coming together on those records. The songs were pretty good too. Kenny and Leon wrote some of 'em."[17]

Gamble and Huff didn't write "Storm Warning," but they did write "Help Wanted!," a more straightforward Motown-styled number, for the group. "Help Wanted!" was the second song the two wrote together, and their partnership would really begin to flourish the following year, in 1966, when they formed Excel Records (soon to be renamed Gamble Records) and released a record by the local soul group the Intruders. "(We'll Be) United" was the most extravagant record yet from Philadelphia. Of course there was the characteristic vibraphone and the opulent strings that dominated the record, but there was also a harpsichord plinking away, creating a stairway to heaven for lead singer Sam "Little Sonny" Brown and his betrothed to walk up. Even though Brown was just about the most ragged vocalist in the history of soul (he's not terrible here, but listen to "Cowboys to Girls," "(Love Is Like a) Baseball Game," or "I'll Always Love My Mama," where he wanders off pitch like a drunk trying to walk a straight line), this was the first major hit of another strain of Philadelphia soul that would have a major impact on disco, "sweet soul."

According to Philadelphia soul chronicler Tony Cummings, Eddie Holman's 1966 hit, "This Can't Be True," was "unarguably the archetype on which much of Philadelphia's 'sweet soul' sound was based."[18] Holman's helium falsetto against a background of dangling guitar phrases laced with cavernous reverb, a dragging bass line that reached down to the center of the earth, a slow shuffle drumbeat

When lead singer Gene Faith left the Volcanoes for a solo career in 1969, the group changed its name to the Moods and then, in 1971, to the Trammps. Originally consisting of Earl Young (drums, lead bass voice), Ron "Have Mercy" Kersey (keyboards), Dennis Harris (guitar), Jimmy Ellis (lead tenor vocals), Stanley Wade (bass, second tenor), and John Hart (vocals), the Trammps combined the vocal interplay of groups like the Coasters with gospelish sermonizing and the driving beat of MFSB. With this blend of roots and unabashed dance floor appeal, the Trammps

TURN THE BEAT AROUND

that recalled doo-wop rhythms, and backing vocals not that far removed from the countrypolitan productions of Eddy Arnold and
Jim Reeves reinvented the sound of male vulnerability. This and
the Intruders may have been the beginning of "sweet soul," but the
sound was perfected by Thom Bell, who arranged "Only the Strong
Survive." Bell had known Gamble since high school and the two had
worked together at Cameo-Parkway in 1959, where Bell soon became the arranger for Chubby Checker. In 1968, Bell started producing the Delfonics for their manager Stan Watson's new label,
Philly Groove. The first record he did with them was "La-La Means
I Love You," a record so unctuous, soft, and squishy it sounded as if
it had been coated in laxative. Bell's Delfonics productions used as
many as forty musicians (including Baker, Young, Harris, Montana,
and guitarist Roland Chambers, with Bell himself playing keyboards
and timpani) and such utterly unsoulful instruments as flugelhorn,
oboe, bassoon, French horn, and sitar. By combining oleaginous orchestration, suave jazz licks, and teddy-bear or even castratilike male
vocals, this "softening" of the soul sound linked to dignity, noble
struggle, pride, and assertiveness in the popular imagination led inex-
orably to disco's feminizing influence and its critique of masculinity.

Bell would continue to explore this downy terrain throughout
the early '70s with ever more flocculent records by the Stylistics, the
Spinners, Ronnie Dyson, and New York City. Soon after his initial
success with the Delfonics, Bell's soft soul sound became something
of a cottage industry in Philadelphia during the late '60s and early
'70s, with numerous arrangers and producers trying their hand at it.
Vince Montana, who had first started to play the vibes at age eight
when he traded a cap gun for a friend's xylophone, was one such
chancer. The first record he arranged turned out to be a cult classic of
the genre. The Ethics' "Think About Tomorrow" was almost a carbon

---

served as the bridge between the Philly sound and the discotheque. From their earliest hit, a cover of "Zing Went the Strings of My Heart," which was originally pop-
ularized by Judy Garland and covered by the Coasters, to their mid-1970s heyday,
the Trammps replaced the tension at the heart of Gamble and Huff's signature sound
with a wholehearted embrace of the disco. With Young (the man who pretty much
invented the disco beat) at the helm, the Trammps created perhaps disco's greatest
anthems to itself: "That's Where the Happy People Go" and "Disco Inferno."

copy of "La-La Means I Love You" with Montana "us[ing] my basic sound on that: six, two and one. Six violins, two violas and a cello, plus flute and French horn,"[19] but adding a bass line that borrowed heavily from Motown's James Jamerson.

This blend of a richly upholstered musical bed and propulsive groove was writ large on "Only the Strong Survive," which had the sharpest instrumental definition of any soul record up to that point. Instead of recording the guitars through amplifiers, they were plugged directly into the soundboard, producing a deep, resonant sound that achieved almost the exact opposite effect of Motown records. Where Motown mastered its records with lots of high end, geared toward the transistor radios and car audio on which most teenagers used to listen to music, Gamble and Huff used a more naturalistic sound, perfectly in tune with the new stereo systems that were proliferating in middle-class households. Much of this was thanks to a new studio that opened in August 1968 at 212 North 12th Street in Philadelphia. Sigma Studios was built by former Cameo-Parkway engineer Joe Tarsia. Previously, Tarsia had been a researcher for Philco, one of America's largest electronics companies, where he worked on projects like early bar code readers, Sidewinder missile guidance systems, and electrostatic speakers for home stereo systems. He brought this technological nous to Sigma, which was one of the first studios to have twenty-four-track recording facilities and multitrack noise reduction capabilities. Such advanced equipment and techniques allowed Gamble and Huff to achieve their vision of soul as not so much urban music but urbane music.

On top of these arrangements and production values that once and for all left the roadhouse and chicken shack of old behind were often either raggedy voices (Jerry Butler's voice fraying at the edges, straining to reach the notes on "Only the Strong Survive," the Intruders' Little Sonny walking the tightrope of pitch, the Ebonys' tenor singer David Beasley adding a heap of gravel to the soft-soul mix on "You're the Reason Why" and "It's Forever") or defiantly patriarchal, preaching, ruggedly masculine singers like the O'Jays' Eddie Levert, Wilson Pickett, Joe Simon, and Harold Melvin and the Blue Notes' Teddy Pendergrass. While on one hand Gamble and Huff perhaps thought that such brassy and gruff singers were needed to cut through the layers of sweetening (although Thom Bell clearly didn't think so), this contrast between the cracked voice and plush appointments was also the embodiment in sound of the rise of the post–civil rights black middle class. It's a sound struggling to come to grips with itself, constantly pulling and pushing against its own edges in a vain attempt to resolve its own contradictions, a sound that is desperately trying to move forward and aspire to something greater yet at the same time trying to cling to the old familiar, to maintain a sense of rootedness. It's a sound of resolute, patriarchal masculinity and staunch classicism (the reliance on jazz licks and chords, the orchestral arrangements) wrestling with petticoat pop and vanguard technology. It's a sound of a defiant black positivity trying to piggyback on a color-blind pragmatism. As Joe Tarsia relates, "I remember going to a NATRA convention, a black broadcasters convention in DC in about 1970, '71 with the G&H roster of artists and what was to become the MFSB Orchestra. At the convention a guy came up to Gamble and asked why there were so many white musicians in the orchestra, Gamble replied, 'My color is not white or black, it's green.'"[20]

These irreconcilable differences not only made for the most fascinating music of the early '70s but also helped Gamble and Huff's Philadelphia International label to take over from Motown as the most visible and representative symbol of black capitalism (by 1978, Philadelphia International was the fifth-biggest black-owned company in the United States, with an annual gross of $25 million). The label was formed in 1971 after a distribution deal with Chess for its Neptune label (which had hits with the O'Jays' "One Night Affair" and "Looky Looky [Look at Me Girl]") collapsed when Leonard Chess died and the Chess empire fell into disarray. Gamble and Huff approached CBS president Clive Davis, who was looking for a way to gain a foothold in the black music market for his lily-white company (the only two contemporary artists of color on his roster at the time were Sly & the Family Stone and Santana). They signed a very modest independent production deal that gave them $75,000 for fifteen singles and $25,000 per album, and had some moderate success on the R&B chart with the Ebonys' "You're the Reason Why" and "Determination." In addition to his songwriting and producing duties, Kenny Gamble found himself working directly with CBS's promotions department in order to help them understand the black music world, which was completely foreign to them.

On May 11, 1972, Harvard Business School presented "A Study of the Soul Music Environment Prepared for Columbia Records Group," which had been commissioned by Columbia Records (of which CBS was a part). Costing $5,000 and prepared over the course of six months by six master's students, the study suggested that because "30 percent of the top 40 is composed of records which have 'crossed over' from soul stations," the group should end its long-standing indifference toward black music and develop a "well-planned and well-financed initiative aimed at long-term market penetration."[21] The group was encouraged to "create a cadre of black staff at the CRG; recruit successful black personnel to fill the ranks of that cadre; and develop strong links with black radio"[22] in order to strengthen the CRG's relationship with the black community, which viewed them as "an ultra-rich, ultra-white giant which has for the most part chosen to snub blacks in the business. Blacks in the trade feel that CRG has heaped upon them the ultimate insult: that of ignoring their existence."[23] Until a "Soul Product Group" could be developed, a strategy of "BUYING TIME WHILE THE REQUIRED INTERNAL SUPPORT ORGANIZATION IS STAFFED AND DEVELOPED" should be adopted, including "making custom label arrangements with 'outside product resources.'"[24] This is exactly what Davis had done with Gamble and Huff, and thus vindicated by a handful of prospective MBAs, CBS put its full promotional muscle behind Philadelphia International. Within two months, Philadelphia International had its first monster hit.

As we have seen, the O'Jays' "Back Stabbers" was an unlikely song to mark the new alliance between aspirational black capitalism and gray flannel business as usual. But, then again, so much of the record's force derives from its production values, from the vivid detail and pinpoint clarity that a new injection of cash enabled Gamble and Huff to achieve, from the tension between the candy-coated sweetening and rootsy, churchified pleading. Most of the label's other big hits—the O'Jays' "Love Train," "I Love Music," "For the Love of Money," and "Use ta Be My Girl"; Harold Melvin and the Blue Notes' "If You Don't Know Me By Now," "The Love I Lost,"

"Bad Luck," and "Wake Up Everybody"; Billy Paul's "Me and Mrs. Jones"; the Three Degrees' "When Will I See You Again"; MFSB's "TSOP"; the Intruders' "I'll Always Love My Mama"; and Lou Rawls's "You'll Never Find Another Love Like Mine"—followed a similar pattern. Where other practitioners of symphonic soul like Barry White and Van McCoy gorged on glacé strings and syrupy horn fanfares as if they had the sweet tooth of a thousand seven-year-olds, Gamble and Huff often paradoxically used the most mel-lifluous elements of the arrangement to drive the track forward. Most of the track was improvised in the studio with the musicians "jam-ming off the most skeletal of charts,"[25] meaning that even the vibes, strings, and horns were tied tightly to the prevailing rhythm. As Vince Montana said, "With Gamble & Huff, we put the vibes on with the rhythm as opposed to with the sweetening."[26] Listen to Harold Melvin and the Blue Notes' 1973 hit "The Love I Lost" to hear how they used strings to propel the music and not just soften it.

Along with the Temptations' "Law of the Land," "The Love I Lost" marks the birth of disco as a genre of music; it is the beginning of the codification of disco as a *style* rather than the *taste* of what-ever DJ happened to be playing at that time. This was hardly the fault, or the intention, of Gamble, Huff, and Harold Melvin and the Blue Notes. It was just that they had hit upon the epitome of dance music: the hissing hi-hats, the thumping bass sound, the surging momentum, the uplifting horns, the strings taking flight, lead singer Teddy Pendergrass's over-the-top gospel passion working as sandpa-per against the honeyed backing vocals. "The Love I Lost" managed the feat of providing for joyful exorcism through its tempo and Pen-dergrass's testifying while the strings and that luscious Fender Rhodes were like a sympathetic friend putting his hand on your shoulder and telling you it was all going to be okay. While drummer Earl Young basically created the next two decades of dance music with his snare pattern and hi-hat work on "The Love I Lost,"[27] it was perhaps Pendergrass taking gospel sermonizing to new levels of excess that really marked disco as a separate entity from soul. Like LaBelle's theatrics a year later, Pendergrass helped move gospelese's expressive language of grunts, wails, melisma, "Good God y'all," and punctuating shifts of emphasis away from the church and into the realm of pure stylization. While the soul singers of the '60s had already soiled the sanctity of gospel by using its language to talk about sin, they retained its faith in deliverance, even if it was only the earthly salvation provided by human, not divine, love. When disco went mainstream, however, it wasn't interested in redemption, only the pleasures of the flesh.

This is why when disco really started to hit the big time in 1975, Philadelphia International couldn't keep up with the genre that it had played such a large role in creating. It was still a huge presence on the R&B chart, but the label had fewer and fewer crossover hits and almost disappeared from the discotheques after the O'Jays' "I Love Music" toward the end of 1975. Gamble had become more concerned with writing message songs, and many of the bandwagon jumpers weren't interested in early disco's connections to positivity and didn't like being preached to. Gamble had also become preoccupied with maintaining his company's market share, and in 1976 he was fined $25,000 for his role in the payola scandal that had emerged the previous year. Most important, though, many of the key players in MFSB, who were toiling away largely anonymously for standard union day rates, gradually shifted their allegiance to an independent label based in New York.

The Salsoul label was part of the Caytronics group, which was run by three Sephardic Jewish Syrian-American brothers, Joe, Ken, and Stan Cayre. Originally a manufacturer of ladies' lingerie, Caytronics started to import Mexican records in 1966 but soon started importing records from across Latin America. With the demand for imported Latin records, New York's homegrown salsa boom propelled by the Fania label and the fact that by 1970 there were 1.4 million Puerto Ricans in the United States, 811,843 of them in New York City, Caytronics started its own label, Mericana, in 1972. One of the label's first releases was an album by Joe Bataan, an Afro-Filipino pianist and vocalist who made his name during the bugalú boom of the late '60s, called *Salsoul* in 1973. The streamlined combination of salsa and soul on album cuts like "Latin Strut" and "Aftershower Funk" made it a favorite with the influential WBLS disc jockey Frankie Crocker, who played almost the entire album on his nightly show, helping to sell twenty thousand copies of the record in New York alone. "Latin Strut" and "Aftershower Funk" became such favorites on New York dance floors that Mericana was soon renamed in honor of its biggest record.

The following year, Salsoul released Bataan's follow-up album, *Afro-Filipino*, which included "La Botella," a version of Gil Scott-Heron's "The Bottle." Further refining the combination of Latin music and soul, "La Botella" had percolating *montuño*-derived rhythms and piano passages underneath a distinctly midtown sax solo courtesy of David Sanborn and became an enormous dance floor hit and another important signpost for the direction disco was about to take. The record perfectly united both sides of the disco drive: the percussive spirituality and tribalism of its early days and the upward mobility demanded by its entrance into the mainstream. Like the syncretic blends of salsa (literally meaning "sauce," salsa mixed together the Cuban *son montuño* with Puerto Rican bombas and plenas, and jazz and rock instrumentation) and bugalú (the combination of Cuban mambo and soul) in which Bataan had previously worked, disco was essentially cross-cultural and learned its cues from these two patchwork genres.

The final piece of disco's "gorgeous mosaic" was put in place in 1975 with the first record by Salsoul Orchestra, "Salsoul Hustle." According to the label's own PR department, "The concept of blending the *Latino* sound with R&B rhythms and underscoring it all with rich Philadelphia strings was based on an idea of Joe Cayre's brother, Ken Cayre, vice president of Salsoul Records."[28] Amazingly, this seemed to jibe perfectly with a concept that Vince Montana had been harboring for a while. "I had this idea, I'd had it for years, which was the Latin feeling, the heavy soul rhythm, the lush strings, stomping brass. But I never had the money to get in and do it."[29] The two met, and Montana agreed to produce a record that fused the lush Philly soul he had been making for the past several years with the Latin funk bottom that Salsoul had made its name with. Working with MFSB's conga player Larry Washington, the great *neoyorquiño* percussionist Manny Oquendo and trumpet player Jerry Gonzalez, both from Conjunto Libre, and a bunch of New York studio musicians, Montana achieved disco perfection with his opulent, string-heavy production that floated along the waves of congas and timbals that crested with insistent wah-wah guitar.

The Latin element was distinctly played down on Salsoul Orchestra's next single, but it was sacrificed for the rhythm engine that drove that best of the Philly productions—Young, Baker, Harris—as well as a large portion of the rest of MFSB, including Bobby Eli, keyboardist Ron Kersey, string section leader Don Renaldo, and vocalists Barbara Ingram, Evette Benton, and Carla Benson. "Tangerine" was a disco reworking of the old Johnny Mercer number that was a hit for Jimmy Dorsey and featured Young reprising the beat made famous on "The Love I Lost" along with guitar comping from Harris that was somehow reminiscent of a roller-rink organ. With the mass defection of MFSB, this upstart New York label was suddenly in possession of the most sought-after studio musicians in the world and very quickly became the most important disco label on the New York scene with Double Exposure's "Ten Percent" (the first commercially available twelve-inch single),[30] Silvetti's "Spring Rain," Ripple's "The Beat Goes On and On," Anthony White's "Block Party," First Choice's "Let No Man Put Asunder," and "Dr. Love," Gary Criss's "Rio De Janeiro," Judy Cheeks's "Mellow Lovin'," and Salsoul Orchestra's "You're Just the Right Size," "Nice 'n' Naasty," and "Magic Bird of Fire" in its first couple of years.

Montana's arrangements for Salsoul Orchestra were, well, more orchestral than most of the MFSB records. Perhaps because he had anticipated the arrangements that would characterize disco—particularly the string stabs and the way the strings, wah-wah guitar, and vibes all interacted—in 1969 when he arranged a bubblegum funk record called *Keem-O-Sabe* made by a group of Philadelphia studio stalwarts (including Eli, Len Barry, Jon Madara, and a certain Daryl Hall) under the name the Electric Indian, strings were given a more prominent role in Salsoul Orchestra. It was hardly as if the records were drowning in saccharine orchestration (certainly less than almost all of the Thom Bell productions), but the records attracted scorn from people accusing them of denuding black music of its thrust and vigor. "The same players who performed with such fire on 'Bad Luck' and the anthemic 'I Love Music' made, recording as the Ritchie Family and Salsoul Orchestra, a series of incredibly insipid records, eventually helping drown the Philly sound in clichés," wrote R&B historian Nelson George. "The sales of . . . the fake Philly sound of Salsoul Records—with a stamp of approval by prominent deejays [who, notes George, are mostly gay, and he castigates them for championing female vocalists over male singers]—made the majors believe that these musical technologies would accelerate the black crossover process. So the new dance music inspired by the inventions of Gamble and Huff, came to celebrate a hedonism and androgyny that contradicted their patriarchal philosophy."[31]

Yes, Salsoul Orchestra used female voices to utter single entendres that wouldn't be out of place in a *Carry On* movie, but to say that a few tongue-in-cheek references to sexuality defiled Gamble and Huff's vision of racial uplift, particularly since the MFSB recordings were primarily instrumental, is preposterous. Furthermore, the soft soul sound of Gamble and Huff associate Thom Bell was certainly as androgynous and antipatriarchal (or at least apatriarchal) as anything released on Salsoul, or any other pure disco label, for that matter. What George really seems to miss, though, is that Salsoul Orchestra records are quite simply hotter than the MFSB records. Perhaps George thinks that the fiercer rhythm section of Salsoul Orchestra is somehow more hedonistic than the penthouse jazz of MFSB. Sure, Salsoul Orchestra recorded medleys of Christmas songs and backed Charo, but regardless of the chintz it had to work with, Montana shined the spotlight on Young and Baker. "Basically, I'm a percussionist, and I like to hear my drums," Montana said. "They're what people dance to . . . I know what my vibes sound like one foot from my ear, and that's what I expect it to sound like coming out of the speaker. And I think that's what the people want too, the real sound. They're buying *sounds* today."[32] Using a grainbrain, an electronic gate that cuts out certain frequencies, on each different percussion sound, Montana was able to achieve even more instrumental definition than Gamble and Huff, particularly on the bottom end. As journalist Davitt Sigerson said at the time, "Unlike the masters Gamble & Huff, whose MFSB productions are often frankly vapid, drowned in slick and unimaginative strings and horns, Salsoul keeps the rhythm tracks as hot as Wick Fowler's Three-Alarm Texas Chili, and brings up Earl Young's fine and usually undermixed snare drum . . . Wah wah guitar, clavinet, bongo and conga cook with exceptional clarity."[33]

"DON'T LET ME CROSS OVER"
Disco, the Black Middle Class, and the Politics of Crossover

Philadelphia International's inability or refusal to wholeheartedly embrace disco caused the label to fade from the mainstream after 1976. While the label continued to have R&B hits with the O'Jays, the Jones Girls, and Teddy Pendergrass, its last significant pop hit was perhaps unsurprisingly the record that most unequivocally espoused the disco aesthetic—McFadden & Whitehead's "Ain't No Stoppin' Us Now" in 1979. Written and performed by the pair behind the O'Jays' "Back Stabbers," who claimed that the song was simply a celebration of the fact that Gamble and Huff had finally let the pair into the studio as performers in their own right, "Ain't No Stoppin' Us Now" was one of those all-purpose cheerleading disco anthems like Sister Sledge's "We Are Family" (which followed it at the top of the R&B charts) that seemed to fit any circumstance and any cause. Less plush, less preachy, less bluesy than most Philadelphia International records, "Ain't No Stoppin' Us Now" ditched the ambivalence of old in favor of firmly buying in. The music was positively triumphant—more like Bill Conti's version of the Philly sound on the *Rocky* soundtrack than Gamble and Huff—while John Whitehead dispensed NAACP platitudes like a hip guidance counselor: "There's been so many things that's held us down / But now it looks like things are finally comin' around / I know we've got a long way to go / And where we'll end up I don't know / But we won't let nothing hold us back / We're puttin' ourselves together / We're polishin' up our act / And if you've ever been held down before / I know you refuse to be held down anymore."

This vision of upward mobility disguised as an assertive statement of black pride fit in perfectly not only in the discotheque but on black radio as well. By 1979, black radio in the United States had changed its complexion from a more grassroots, community-oriented medium to one that more closely resembled the mainstream American dream. The instigator of this trend was one of the most iconic DJs in the history of American radio, Frankie Crocker. In the mid-1970s Crocker was the afternoon/evening drive-time DJ and, more important, the program director at New York's biggest black-owned radio station, WBLS. Instead of waiting for the promotion men to come to him to pitch records, Crocker went out on the disco circuit—frequenting places like the aspirational black disco Leviticus at 45 West 33rd Street, Studio 54 and, most famously, the Paradise Garage—to discover his own, and the playlist changed accordingly. Crocker's mix of music was elegant, suave, sophisticated and, most important, color-blind. Crocker played off-the-wall (for black radio) stuff like Led Zeppelin and Bob Dylan's "Gotta Serve Somebody" and long album cuts as well as singles. Under his stewardship, WBLS changed from "the total black experience in sound" to "the world's best looking sound." When he went on air, Crocker locked the studio door, turned off the studio lights, and lit a candle in order to create the right mood for his chic style. At the time Crocker called himself "Hollywood," and he envisioned a post–civil rights world of cocktail parties full of urbane chatter around swimming pools and debonair brothers in earth-tone suits making business connections. "Hollyw-o-o-o-d! . . . is not in California; it's the main thought stream of the new disco scene, a seductive freeway straight to the heart of all hard partyers," was how journalist Mark Jacobson described Crocker's world. "It's got nothing to do with drugs, although one might bring some along for the ride. Hollyw-o-o-o-d! is a suspension of reality, not an escape from it. It's modulated blues and browns, not flashy pimp oranges. It's Walt Frazier dribbling through all hostile hands, playing ah-fense and dee-fense so smoothly you can't tell which team has the ball. It's Superfly and Shaft, not Martin Luther King and Malcolm X . . . Frankie [Crocker] says, 'Hollyw-o-o-o-d! is just something good, very good . . . it's just another dream . . . we all need to dream.'"[34]

Just like Philadelphia International's, Crocker's fantasy of the good life was fueled by technology as well as the music itself. "None of the FM radio stations were really utilizing stereo back then; WBLS were the first to really bring that home," remembers Danny Krivit, a budding disco DJ at the time. "Even with their announcements, they would go [mimics stereo panning] 'W-B-L-S' and really make you understand it. They were starting to play records that other stations weren't; radio was still a 3:45 maximum-length medium, very formatted. BLS was breaking out of that, playing album cuts, the album versions of hit records. 'Love Is the Message'—a long album-only instrumental that's also kind of disco, basically it just isn't radio—became kind of popular, and BLS jumped all over it to show how different they were."[35]

WBLS's plush stereo sound demanded a new kind of music. Of course, the sumptuous arrangements of Philadelphia International and the lavish orchestrations of Barry White fit the bill perfectly, but even relatively straightforward R&B that didn't have symphonic pretensions started to become more "refined," more "Hollywood." "The result has been a new genre of black rhythm-and-blues music that is totally different from the driving, maximum pentration of 'danceable' 60s R&B," Jacobson wrote. "The new songs are like big barroom fans that sweep the air around you as you dance. They make you want to roller-skate. They're softer, more playful, almost approaching mirth. The lyrics have little to do with the blues . . . The singing, in the Smokey Robinson tradition, is lilting, spacey, filled with otherworldly falsettos. Very few tunes have bedrock, gravelly blues voices. Horn parts aren't low-life and King Curtis–Jr. Walker things; they're brassy and up."[36]

This new sound was epitomized by a vocal group from Los Angeles, the Hues Corporation. St. Clair Lee, Fleming Williams, and H. Ann Kelley first got together in 1969 and named themselves after the company owned by billionaire recluse Howard Hughes. They released a couple of flops in the early '70s before appearing on three tracks on the soundtrack of 1972's *Blacula*. In 1973, they went into the studio with the Crusaders as their backing band and re-corded *Freedom for the Stallion*. The album went nowhere, but one track, "Rock the Boat," was popular at discotheques and generated enough buzz to propel the track onto radio playlists and, almost a year after it was released, to the top of the American pop charts. The song was a tortuous extended metaphor about a love affair on the rocks, but the title phrase, which was repeated ad nauseam, seemed to echo the message of upward mobility that stations like WBLS were projecting: "Don't rock the boat." The music—gently lilting bass line, trade-wind string washes, breezy ersatz gospelisms straight out of the supper club—certainly wouldn't have done any damage to any seafaring vessel as it lapped against the hull like the tide going out.

Crocker and disco musicians like the Hues Corporation, Barry White, George McCrae, the Joneses, the Originals, Van McCoy, Jimmy Ruffin, and Carol Douglas supplanted soul's roadhouse with the penthouse and the church with the discotheque. In many ways disco represented the ideal of integration as laid out by the civil rights legislation of the '60s. "Disco, unlike many other entertainment mediums, has exhibited an extraordinary ability to bring together people of varying colors, races, ideologies, sexual preferences and social financial levels, in an ecumenical dialog of music and dance which transcends many of the limitations of petty everyday prejudices," wrote *Billboard*'s Radcliffe Joe.[37] Even during the heyday of the '60s, it was still remarkable that Otis Redding, Richie Havens, and Sly Stone would appear on the same stage as rock artists. As *Rolling Stone*'s Abe Peck said, by the mid-1970s, "black style [was] more accessible to whites than it was during the Smoldering Sixties."[38]

This accessibility paralleled the rise of the black middle class; it signified the transformation of Afro-America from underclass to full participation in the American dream. The percentage of black families below the low-income level shrank from 48.1 percent in 1959 to 27.8 percent in 1974.[39] "From 1965–69, the percentage of blacks making less than $3,000 decreased, while the percentage of blacks earning over $10,000 increased to 28%. In 1965, ten percent of all young blacks were in college; six years later that figure was 18%. By 1972, 2,264 blacks served as elected officials, the highest number in American history at that time. The total annual income of black America was $100 billion."[40]

The problem with this economic and political miracle, though, was that civil rights legislation largely delivered what it promised: the equation of racial liberation with entrée into corporate America. It was a vision of success and salvation that had nothing to do with uplifting the African-American community as a whole, but rather sought to encourage individual achievement and to promote equality and justice as the attainment of white standards of excellence. As a result, Nelson George wrote, "the amount of [black] income invested in black communities was minuscule, and most of that college-trained talent became workers in established white businesses, not independent entrepreneurs. Moreover, many of the economic gains were created by government intervention and monitoring. Blacks were not, then, growing into an independent economic force, but were becoming an increasingly lucrative market for white-provided commodities."[41]

But even this imperfect position was perilous and difficult to maintain. As journalist Ellis Cose wrote, citing the research of sociologist Sharon Collins, "For blacks, middle-class status was largely a 'politically dependent condition.' A disproportionate number of blacks worked for the government, often in 'black-related' agencies, others owed their jobs to 'legislation that forced employers to hire blacks.' Still others were in positions that 'depended on money being funneled from the government into the private sector in all sorts of ways,' from job-training programs to minority set asides. If the government had not been looming in the background, 'these people would not have been hired for the most part.'"[42]

The fragility of status and the sacrifices of assimilation have long been conditions suffered by immigrant groups throughout the world. Of course, the vast majority of African Americans weren't recent or voluntary immigrants, and it took them hundreds of years to attain a position that most ethnicities reach within two or three generations. Although disco mostly championed assimilation, the tensions and resentment of the new black middle class were articulated in two extraordinary records by one of the original prophets of the integrationist aesthetic.

As one of the principal songwriters at Motown, Lamont Dozier had been one of the architects of the "sound of young America," applying Fordist production methods to the gospel tradition. Dozier left Motown, along with songwriting partners Brian and Eddie Holland, in 1968 and started writing more political material that would have never made it past Quality Control under Berry Gordy's regime. "Fish Ain't Bitin'" (1974), Dozier's second single as a solo artist, begins like a standard early '70s "times are bad, woe is me" complaint before turning into one of the few records to openly attack Nixon's racial policies head-on: "Tricky Dick is trying to be slick / And the short end of the stick / Is all I'm gonna get / Tricky Dick, please quit . . . lord, when will I overcome or am I just destined, destined to be a bum? . . . can't afford to be lazy when the cost of living's gone crazy." Where other soul records that explicitly critiqued Nixon—the Honeydrippers' "Impeach the President," Weldon Irvine's "Watergate," the JB's' "You Can Have Watergate Just Gimme Some Bucks and I'll Be Straight"—were aimed more at Watergate and his duplicity, the lyric referencing "We Shall Overcome" gave "Fish Ain't Bitin'" a different dimension. The flip side was "Breaking Out All Over," which smushed together a model stunted funk groove (short, really clipped guitar riff and under-mixed horn exclamations) in one channel and more sophisticated chord changes and instrumentation (flutes, soaring strings, a piano somewhere between the church, supper club, and Keith Jarrett's *Köln Concert*) in the other—a near-perfect exposition of the "Hollywood" style even if the lyrics about the after-effects of trying to kick an addictive love affair were darker than the norm.

On 1975's "Going Back to My Roots," Dozier sought to resolve this double consciousness: "Zippin' up my boots / Going back to my roots / To the place of my birth / Back to down earth . . . / I've been living in a world of fantasy / I'm going back to reality / I've been searching for riches I had all the time / And finding out that happiness was just a state of mind / I'm going back home, back where I belong . . . / I've been standing in the rain / Drenched and soaked with pain / Tired of short time benefits / And being exposed to the elements / Picking up the pieces of what's left of me / Going back to nest in my family tree." The arrangement shifts almost imperceptibly from a standard, but admittedly very funky, disco-era Crusaders (both keyboardist Joe Sample and reeds player Wilton Felder played on the session) groove—the big, blocky piano chords, the lush guitar effects, the stringlike synth fills, Paulinho da Costa's run-of-the-mill percussion runs and, most important, the very straight-ahead main rhythm—to, all of a sudden, at about the five-minute mark, percussion and the tightly coiled (very African sounding) guitar riffs. Then the breakdown (all Brazilian percussion and vocal whoops and a massed African chorale) just builds and builds, but never resolves itself—it just fades out. The song was covered in 1981 by Odyssey, but that version begins with part of the African chant and a guitar riff and a bass line that are distinctly more African than at the beginning of Dozier's version. In other words, there is no journey in Odyssey's version, whereas Dozier's original reenacts the restlessness and strains at the heart of the new black middle-class dream.

Dozier's notion of going back to one's roots is escapism as surely as Crocker's cocktail-party paradise, but it was escapism based on betrayal rather than a desire to buy in. Although "Going Back to My Roots" was a smallish disco hit, its message ran counter to disco's prevailing discourse. The problem was that disco was championing a view of the world that was being dismantled as it was being celebrated. The economic crises of the 1970s disproportionately affected African Americans largely because their economic gains were heavily dependent on government intervention. As sociologist Bart Landry declared, "Without prosperity, the civil rights laws lost much of their impact." Indeed, Landry found that the recession in the early '70s resulted not only in a slowdown in the expansion of the black middle class but also a rollback: "Close examination of the data from the 1973–75 and 1980–82 recessions reveals that middle-class blacks not only fared worse than whites during these periods but they actually *lost ground relative to whites.*"[43]

While disco's view of the world was faltering in the black suburbs, it was positively collapsing in America's urban ghettos. Even the growth of black political power (or, at least, representation) couldn't help the condition of the inner city. "The dilemma for urban blacks is that they are gaining political influence in large urban areas (in 1975 blacks were mayors of 11 large metropolitan cities with populations of 100,000 or more) at the very time when the political power and influence of the cities are on the wane," wrote sociologist William Julius Wilson. "The growth of corporate manufacturing, of retail and wholesale trade on the metropolitan periphery; the steady migration of impoverished minorities to the central city; the continuous exodus of the more affluent families to the suburbs; and, consequently, the relative decline of the central-city tax base have made urban politicians increasingly dependent on state and federal sources of funding in order to maintain properly the services that are vital for community health and stability. Whereas state and federal funds contributed about 25% to major-city revenues a decade ago, their contribution today amounts to about 50%. Thus, America's metropolises are increasingly controlled by politicians whose constituencies do not necessarily live in those cities. It is this *politics of dependency* that changes the meaning and reduces the significance of the greater black participation in urban political processes."[44]

This trend was repeated in the music industry. Disco held out the promise of crossover success on a mass scale. It never materialized. In fact, the exact opposite was true. As Radcliffe Joe wrote, "It is one of the great ironies of the multi-billion dollar discotheque phenomenon that while the whole concept has its roots in black music and black lifestyles, it has emerged as something of a mixed blessing for blacks."[45] According to Joe, in 1973 (just before the disco boom took off), black artists accounted for thirty-six of the one hundred best-selling singles in the United States; by 1978, the number was down to twenty-one. Nelson George expressed the same trend slightly differently: From 1967 to 1973, the average R&B number one would reach #9 on the pop charts; between 1974 and 1976, the average fell to #15; and in 1978, it was down to #22. While this average roller-coastered up and down, it hit a low in 1981 of #30. As Joe concluded, "A survey of the leading charts shows that disco has not, as had originally been anticipated, made it easier for black artists to enjoy crossover . . . to the pop charts."[46]

This sense of betrayal, shattered hopes, and fear was the dark heart behind disco's glossy veneer. Disco was a party, but it was celebrating a world that was slipping away; it was movin' on up at the same time as it was imprisoned by fate. Salvation, whether by the grace of God or the power of the dollar, was no longer something to believe in or hold out for. The only solidity was provided by the "changing same": No matter what they promise, they just find another way to pull out the rug from under your feet. While this theme popped up from time to time on many of disco's finest records—"Going Back to My Roots," the Temptations' "Law of the Land," Harold Melvin and the Blue Notes' "Bad Luck"—it would become writ large by disco's greatest group.

"DON'T BE A DRAG, PARTICIPATE"
Chic

It's New Year's Eve 1977. Bassist Bernard Edwards and guitarist Nile Rodgers have had the year of their lives. The two studio musicians abandoned a lifetime of anonymous session work to make a name for themselves by wholeheartedly embracing the disco boom. Working with a few other musicians and singers as Chic, the two have scored two of the year's biggest dance floor hits, "Dance, Dance, Dance" and "Everybody Dance," and released an album with the giant Atlantic label. To top it all off, singer/model/actress/New York nightlife queen Grace Jones wants to work with them on her next record and has invited them to her gig at Studio 54.

Edwards and Rodgers are dressed to the nines. "That night both Bernard and I were in black ties," Rodgers told journalist Anthony Haden-Guest. "I had a Cerutti dinner jacket and Bernard had an Armani. We were killin'. I probably had a wing-collar shirt, with a decorative front, but not lacy. Pleated, with studs. The whole bit. Spectator shoes. You know, two-tone . . . You know, Grace Jones! And we were Chic. We wanted to look Chic. We wanted to *smell* Chic!"[47] However, it's snowing and the slush is ruining their threads. They make their way around back and tell the doorman that they're on the guest list. He doesn't find their names. After pleading their case to no avail, Edwards and Rodgers go to the main entrance to join the throngs desperately hoping that the doorman, Marc Benecke, would deem them worthy for entrance into the hallowed confines of Steve Rubell's pleasure palace.

Rodgers's girlfriend at the time knew Benecke, who would frequently get him into the club. "I'm waving and jumping," Rodgers said. "But Marc totally disregarded us. He didn't give us a second look."[48] They stayed around till one in the morning, hoping that Jones would realize what was happening and make an effort to get them inside. She didn't, and Rodgers's precious Spectators were ruined.

Frustrated and dejected, they made their way a few blocks through the snow to Rodgers's apartment on Fifty-second Street between Eighth and Ninth avenues. On the way, they bought marijuana, cocaine, and a bottle of champagne and had their own party. "We resorted to using music therapeutically, which is what we had always done up until that point," Rodgers said. "Bernard and I started jamming, just guitar and bass. We were just yelling obscenities: 'Fuck Studio 54 . . . Fuck 'em . . . Fuck off . . . Fuck those scumbags . . . Fuck them!' And we were laughing, entertaining the hell out of ourselves. We had a blast. And it finally hit Bernard. He said, 'Hey Nile, what you're playing sounds really good!'"[49]

After working with Rodgers's guitar part for a little while, Edwards came up with a bass line and then a chorus. "We said, 'Damn, that sounds like a song,'" Rodgers said. "And we wrote a whole obscene song about fucking Studio 54 and those assholes. But it had melody and texture and form. And we said, 'This is hysterical.' So we recorded it. We made a little demo. And after we laughed, we said, 'You know, this is really catchy!'

"We changed 'Fuck Off' to 'Freak Off,'" Rodgers continues. "But that sounded lame. Then we realized that the biggest dance in America at the time was called the Freak ... We changed one word, 'Off' to 'Out,' and the floodgates opened up."[50] They used Chubby Checker's version of Hank Ballard's "The Twist" as a template, reworked the lyrics, finally changed the title to "Le Freak," and those floodgates opened to the tune of six million copies sold. "Within 25 to 30 minutes we had the biggest hit record of our lives. It's still the biggest hit single in Warner Brothers' history. And as far as copyrights are concerned, it's the third largest in the history of music, after 'White Christmas' by Irving Berlin and 'Rudolph, the Red-Nosed Reindeer' by Johnny Marks."[51]

So the biggest non-Christmas record ever and disco's most popular anthem started life as a snarling guitar vamp that married funk groove with punk attitude. For most musicians, particularly disco musicians, this would merely be an amusing anecdote, a story rehashed and retold time and again on nostalgia television programs. However, for ex-art rockers Nile Rodgers and Bernard Edwards, the story of "Le Freak" is emblematic of a career spent caught between different worlds, daring to peer beneath disco's glittering surface and chronicling the heights and depths of the disco dream.

Rock fans talked about disco denizens as if they were lemmings marching to the cliffs, while soul patrons lampooned them as robots who were faking the funk. They criticized Chic for being escapist music when pop music is meant to be all about escape in the first place. (Why these same people didn't say the same thing about Marvin Gaye and Tammi Terrell singing "If I Could Build My

Whole World Around You" while Detroit was burning around them is a mystery.) Regardless, the mid- to late '70s demanded that kind of music, particularly in New York. In a climate of stagflation, when the country at large was being held hostage by OPEC, when New York City owed fealty to the bond-issuing robber barons who bailed the city out of bankruptcy, when the mercenary laissez-faire capitalism of the '80s was just starting to take hold, when Reagan and the rollback of civil rights legislation was just around the corner, and without the moral consensus of the '60s, the only possible reaction was escapism. But Chic wasn't just about escape. While they enjoyed shaking their groove thing as much as anybody, they also recognized hedonism's limitations and saw its dangers.

Nile Rodgers and Bernard Edwards were both twenty years old when they met in 1972 as members of the Big Apple Band backing the vocal group New York City, which had a big hit in 1973 with "I'm Doin' Fine Now." Breaking off from New York City, the Big Apple Band—when it wasn't backing up Luther Vandross's group—began to play a ferociously metallic brand of Miles Davis–esque jazz-fusion that would have cleared the floor at Studio 54 in the blink of an eye, but even that was nothing compared to the black rock maelstrom that Rodgers and Edwards concocted in their other group, Allah and the Knife-Wielding Punks. It was a long way indeed from Rodgers's days as a guitarist in a *Sesame Street* touring band.

Before laying down some tasty licks over which Big Bird and the Cookie Monster would drop science, however, Rodgers had played guitar on original Last Poet Kain's *Blue Guerrilla* album in 1971. The album's psychedelic soul and lounge-jazz arrangements and surreal black arts–inspired poetry hinted at Rodgers's adolescence as an acid freak and member of the Black Panthers. "The very first time I took acid was with Timothy Leary, and I didn't even know who he was," Rodgers claims. "I was just this little black kid in Los Angeles who wanted to be a pimp or the Temptations because that's what the music stars looked like to me—they were all pimped out with the suits and the ruffled shirts and the wraparound cuff links and the white shoes. At thirteen years old, that's what I wanted to be like. Then one day I went out to this thing called the Teenage Fair and it was all of these hippies, and I had never seen hippies, never seen white guys with long hair like that. They really looked like they had come from another planet, but they looked so cool to me . . . These hippies said to me, 'Hey, wow, you guys want to take a trip?' We thought they meant to like go someplace, so we were like, 'Sure.' We're thirteen, we don't care about anything, let's go, 'Where you guys want to go?' 'Oh man, we're gonna go take a trip.' We're like, 'Great, let's go take a trip.' And they took us up to the house in the Hollywood Hills and Timothy Leary was there and we took LSD. We couldn't believe anything so small could do anything: 'Oh, yeah, we're gonna get high on that.' Meanwhile to us, we used to drink quarts of vodka and entire bottles of wine and vomit and all that stuff. 'Okay, this little piece of paper's gonna get us high. Yeah, sure, no problem.' Two days later I show up back at my house. My grandmother's got the cops looking for me and everything. So I went from Motown to totally into the Doors in *one* day. I went from 'Don't Mess With Bill' and 'Hunter Gets Captured by the Game' and 'Ain't That Peculiar' to, the very next day, 'This is the end / Beautiful friend / Mother, I want to [he screams].' So needless to say, my grandmother thought I was psychotic. And then what happened was that the music also affects your social scene. Now if you start to gravitate to other kids who listen to that type of music, there's usually a certain philosophy that goes along with it all. Then you get political, then you get radical, then you get old, right? [laughs] So I got political and we're all 'Peace now,' and the cops and National Guard would beat us up. So you take that for a few years, and then you go, 'Wait a minute. Let's try to fight back.' Politics in America got very radical, people got killed at Kent State and stuff. I joined the Black Panther Party when I was a senior in high school."[52]

While for many, the disco era was the death of politics and struggle and meaning in popular culture, Rodgers views disco as almost the inevitable result of the Black Panthers and the Black Power movement. "We were tricked," he says. "The music was the reflection of society. We were tricked into believing that we had really made all these leaps and bounds. In other words, the Vietnam War stopped. When the Vietnam War stopped, it made us feel empowered—we made that happen, it was all the protesters. The protesters joined forces: It was the Black Power movement with the gay power movement with the women power movement. We were all out there protesting together. And when that ended, it masqueraded as liberation for everybody. It masqueraded as 'Whoah, we did it. Guess what, we're equal.' And then they stopped the draft. So there's no more draft, it's a volunteer army, so black people aren't gonna be pulled into the service unfairly and in unfair numbers and blah blah blah. And gay rights and women and everybody—wow, this is great! So what happens? You celebrate. And that's all that happened. In the middle seventies, we started celebrating the victories."[53]

In 1976, with disco celebrating at full force, Rodgers and Edwards recruited drummer Tony Thompson and vocalists Alfa Anderson and Norma Jean Wright to produce a record called "Dance, Dance, Dance." After toying with the names Boyz and Orange Julius, Edwards suggested the name Chic to the new group. "Tony and I thought it was the most absurd name we'd heard," Rodgers remembers. "Tony and I were rock guys, we wanted to be, you know, the Punks and the blah blah blah. 'Hey, we could be the Chic Punks, the punks who dress up in whatever.' But Bernard explained to us why it made sense. We were big Kiss fans, and Bernard was like, 'Check this out: Kiss is a *k*, an *i*, and two *s*'s, and Chic has an *h*, an *i*, and two *c*'s.' In the world of rock-and-roll logic, that was as clear as a bell to me and Tony . . . 'Wow, hey, 'Nard, you're on to something here. This is cool.' And in the other band we loved, Roxy Music, Roxy's got four letters. 'Wait a minute, we got four letters—Roxy, Kiss, Chic— phhh, done. Done. We got it. You're on the money here. We understand. Bernard, our fearless leader, you've got it.' That's it, that's the beginning of Chic."[54]

The newly christened group proceeded to shop the demo, and after a string of rejections, the record was finally picked up by Buddah and then by Atlantic. Why anyone passed on the record is an absolute mystery: A more perfect club record has yet to be devised. Tales of music causing speaker damage are routinely bandied about regarding all sorts of records, but when you play them at home they barely tax your subwoofer. In the mid-1970s, however, "Dance, Dance, Dance" destroyed many a cabinet: It was the first record to feature subbass. Before "Dance, Dance, Dance," bass tones below a frequency of 60 Hz were taken out in the process of mastering a record, but Rodgers and Edwards realized the effect that these shuddering tones had in a club and insisted that they be kept in. Combine these bass quakes with Tony Thompson's punishing, metronomic drum technique (as Rodgers has said, "He hits the drums harder than anyone I've ever seen"), and you have a record that practically bludgeoned you into submission on the dance floor.

Over this galloping rhythm that sounded like, well, lemmings marching over a cliff, Anderson and Wright intoned the title phrase like deers caught in the headlights. To drive the point home, they borrowed Gig Young's catchphrase "Yowsah, yowsah, yowsah" from *They Shoot Horses, Don't They?*, Sydney Pollack's filmic attack on the American psyche that uses a dance marathon as its setting. "When you talk about 'Dance, Dance, Dance,' after we had seen that film, we realized that it was about these people who were trying to survive during the Depression," Rodgers declares. "It was spectacle entertainment, it was like being in the Colosseum in Rome. People were going to watch these people, and a lot of them died from sheer exhaustion, so they were entertained 'cause they could hear the music and all that stuff, but it was torture, it was physical torture. It was interesting that it was so popular to watch people endure that kind of stuff."[55] Typical of the mind-set that these art-rockers at heart were lampooning, no one got it, and "Dance, Dance, Dance" reached #6 on the American charts in 1977.

The million-selling success of "Dance, Dance, Dance" landed the group an album deal with Atlantic. Their self-titled debut album contained the first disco song that Edwards and Rodgers wrote together, "Everybody Dance." As with "Dance, Dance, Dance," the song was based around a couple of outlandish concepts; this time, though, they were a bit closer to the heart of the disco denizens. "Everybody Dance" clocked in at around ten minutes. While the extended twelve-inch single had just been invented to satisfy the needs of the disco DJs, Rodgers and Edwards were trying to satisfy a rather different imperative. For decades, the first rule of the pop song was that it last no more than three minutes. Of course, the "progressive" late '60s temporarily changed that, but that was only for "mind-expansion." Chic's idea was "pleasure-expansion": Why hold someone you like close for three minutes when you could dance cheek to cheek for ten minutes?

More important, the success of "Everybody Dance" at Chic's earliest gigs provided the group with its overarching concept and signature style. "'Everybody Dance' . . . was the perfect Chic kind of song," Rodgers told Marc Taylor, giving another version of the Chic creation myth. "The chord changes were real sophisticated, very jazzy, the bass playing was phenomenal, the groove infectious, and we used to play this record over and over again at this black after-work club in New York. Our song 'Everybody Dance' became one of the hottest cuts in New York but no one could buy it because we just recorded it in our little studio. We realized that the people who were dancing to our music had a certain look. They were all wearing suits and the girls were fine and made up. We looked at them and it was like, 'Damn, what if we looked like that?' 'Everybody Dance' was pumping in this club for three or four months. At the time Bernard and I were still musicians, working with other people. We would go to this club every night and see the black urban professionals dancing to our music and we decided, 'What if we started to look like the people who were relating to our music?' That's how we came up with the idea for Chic. We didn't have any name, we were just doing music. When we looked at the people we said, 'Damn, there's the concept right in front of our faces.'"[56]

The concept wasn't just mirroring the new class of black urban professionals but also providing a grounding for a group of people that were torn from their roots and thrust into mainstream white society. "Everything about Chic is based on the black musicians from the Depression Era, the black musicians who were allowed to entertain for whites but couldn't stay in the same hotel that they were performing in," Rodgers says. "The thing is, though, they emulated the people they were working for. So they had royalty, *Duke* Ellington, *Count* Basie; they were emulating, they were trying to assimilate. A person doesn't want to think of themselves as beneath somebody, they want to think of themselves as an equivalent. So in that era, that's when the black jazz musicians were really coming out, like, 'I'm royalty. I'm special. I'm this, I'm that.' Sophisticated, high society, that's what they wanted to be like. They wanted to live on Park Avenue, they wanted to have private clubs because they were playing at those places, they knew that they existed. Like they say, 'How are you gonna keep 'em on the farm once they've seen Paris?' Once you've been exposed, you want it. Everything about Chic was trying to achieve that kind of class struggle for recognition based on who you were and who you've become as a human being, and we wanted to be proud; we were proud of other people who wanted to be proud. And that's what Chic is *all* about, to this very day. That's why our lyrics seem braggadocious, but they're not braggadocious, they're hopeful, they're ambitious."[57]

No matter how chic Chic was, however, Edwards and Rogers still couldn't get into Studio 54 that fateful New Year's Eve. And, while they may have changed the words to the snarling, popping funk vamp that even James Brown wouldn't have touched, the attitude was still there. With Luci Martin replacing Wright, the disembodied vocalists who served as narrators once again could not be trusted, and they seemed to mock the disco-as-liberation ethic with odd, stilted language sung in a deadpan that had no place in a record about a dance craze: "Night and days, uhhh, stomping at the Savoy / Now we freak, oh what a joy"; "Big fun to be had by everyone / It's up to you, surely it can be done." Although that characteristic Chic vocal style seemed to ooze ambivalence and alienation, Rodgers claims that it was purely functional. "That was the Chic robotic thing," he says. "We did that so they would get out of the way of the band [laughs] . . . Chic is about the music. The vocals and the hooks and the arrangements are just part of an overall musical experience. It's not a group where the singing is the star, so to speak. That's our philosophy. Cab Calloway, Count Basie, those guys were musicians. They would hire singers, but it was those musicians that made those things happen. If the singer went up there and sang a cappella, the club would empty out. That's our philosophy, it's about what we play . . . When we talk about the early days, 'stomping at the Savoy,' and the big bands and the struggles they went through and the dignity that they still felt within, that's the glorious period in black music to us. Those people are glamorous and wonderful to us . . . When we talk about stuff like that, we're not protesting as much as we're acknowledging and understanding that in the midst of struggle, in the midst of being a second-class citizen, in the midst of slavery, in the midst of being an entertainer for rich white people—but you have come in through the servants' entrance—you still feel good. Cab Calloway loved being up on that stage, that was the time when you were equal. Maybe, at the point, you might even be considered above. At that point, they were look-ing at you with awe. That's what we mean: 'Like the days of stomp-ing at the Savoy, now we freak.' It's exactly the same. In those days you used to do the jitterbug or the black bottom or whatever, but now we do this dance called the freak. In those days you were second-class citizens, but you did these things to release yourself and feel good about who you were. Now we do the freak. It's sexual, just like in those days, those guys got criticized for those dances, which they said were too sexual . . . That's what we talk about. We say times haven't changed. I'm not criticizing as much as I'm being observant."[58]

"Le Freak" was the most obvious example of Edwards and Rodgers's ingenious songwriting technique. Where most pop songs are structured strictly according to the verse-chorus-verse blueprint, Chic picked up on the standard jazz pattern of intro-theme-solos-theme but reworked for the pop market. They would begin with an intro, then go straight into the chorus, then the verses and the bridge/solos. As they had intuited, disco wasn't about deferring pleasure for the one big payoff; it wanted to keep it up all night. By putting the chorus up front, Chic's records hit you right off the bat; there was no build, no rising tension, just forward momentum the whole way.

"Le Freak" anchored *C'est Chic*, but, as if to prove once and for all that they weren't a real disco group, the conceptual genius and impossible grooves continued through the entire record. Like the Roxy Music fans they were, Rodgers and Edwards dressed the band up in Halston, Gucci, Fiorucci, and laid the ambiguity/distance schtick on thick. "At Last I Am Free" continued where "Le Freak" left off, only with a crawling tempo and Anderson and Martin, sounding alternately like zombies and angels, chanting the mantra, "At last I am free / I can hardly see in front of me." Even more of an incantation and just as caustic was "Chic Cheer," a five-minute vamp with fake crowd noise, the most heavily miked cymbals ever, and the cheerleaders at Disco High exhorting the crowd, "If you're fans of Chic / Consider yourself unique." Chic's great theme would be the disco lifestyle's inherent fatalism, and "I Want Your Love" was one of their finest love-as-addiction tales, complete with gloomy bells and an itching guitar part that never gets relieved.

For all their smarts and oddball touches, though, it was the grooves that everyone listened to. Rodgers is quite possibly the greatest rhythm guitar player ever and Bernard Edwards was certainly one of the five most creative bassists to have slapped some round wounds in anger. With Tony Thompson, "the human metronome," behind them, the two distilled and updated Motown, James Brown, Stax, and Miles Davis into the most lethal rhythmic attack of the last quarter century.

The group's third album, *Risqué*, led off with disco's crowning achievement, "Good Times." Not only a brilliant single and one of the most influential records of the era (it helped kick off hip-hop when it was sampled on Sugarhill Gang's "Rapper's Delight" and Grandmaster Flash's "The Adventures of Grandmaster Flash on the Wheels of Steel" and was ripped off almost note for note by Queen's "Another One Bites the Dust"), it worked perfectly in the context of the album. Like all of their best work, Chic had it both ways on "Good Times." With Bernard Edwards's stunning bass line and Nile Rodgers's seething guitar work, the record bumped like a motherfucker. However, the scything strings and ghostly piano gave the game away. With vocalists Alfa Anderson and Luci Martin intoning catchphrases like they were in a Valium haze, the pep rally that "Good Times" seemed at first became harder and harder to believe. Its evocation of the good life ("Clams on the half shell and rollerskates, rollerskates") was so absurd that not even Carly Simon would have sung the lyrics seriously. Then, when they repeat the second chorus, the song's sense of impending doom becomes clear: "A rumor has it that it's getting late / Time marches on, just can't wait / The clock keeps turning, why hesitate? / You silly fool, you can't change your fate."

During the disc's second half, sadism keeps cropping up in the lyrics ("Love is pain and pain could be pleasure"; "The way you treated me, you'd think I were into S&M"; "Used me, abused me / Knocked down and walked all over me"). Perhaps even more revealing are the lines, sounding like slogans at a political rally or from the transcripts of the Iran-contra trial, that leap out fully formed from the disembodied vocals: "Now you've got yours, what about me?"; "That sinister appearance and the lies / Whew, those alibis." Even the seemingly celebratory "My Feet Keep Dancing" revolved around a riff on the old racist chestnut that black people's brains are in their feet.

The filler fluff of "Warm Summer Night" is the only breath of fresh air on the album, the rest deals with the impossibility of changing your fate and railing against sadistic lovers—a more perfect metaphor for the Thatcher-Reagan era was never found. "We were thinking about all those old mystery movies—Charlie Chan, the whole 40s thing—the Agatha Christie books," Bernard Edwards told *Blues & Soul* magazine in 1979. "So the essence of what *Risqué* is about is 'who done it?'"[59] Accompanied by strings that sound like the stabs in Bernard Herrmann's score for *Psycho*, Anderson and Martin sing the title phrase of "My Feet Keep Dancing" over and over again, either like they were hypnotized or like a mantra to keep the bogeyman away. Maybe they were right about the lemmings.

After Chic had basically bankrolled Atlantic for the next few years with 1978's "Le Freak," Edwards and Rodgers were offered the choice of producing anyone on Atlantic's roster. They could have chosen Aretha Franklin, the Spinners, Donny Hathaway, Roberta Flack, heck, even Crosby, Stills & Nash. Like the iconoclasts they were, however, Chic picked a journeywoman girl group that barely had a hint of a hit during its five years at the label. Chic wanted to work with a group that didn't have an identity yet, but with Sister Sledge they didn't quite get a blank slate.

Kathie, Joni, Debra, and Kim Sledge were the granddaughters of opera singer Viola Williams, who started recording as Sisters Sledge as teenagers in 1971. Based in Philadelphia, they released some material on the Money Back label and worked as backup singers for Gamble and Huff's Philadelphia International operation. As Sister Sledge, they signed to Atlantic in 1973 and had a small amount of success with "Love Don't You Go Through No Changes on Me" in 1975, but for the most part they toiled in the background for half a decade until Chic rescued them from terminal obscurity. Based on an impression of the group given to them by Atlantic president Jerry Greenberg, Rodgers and Edwards subtly changed the standard Chic formula. Instead of crafting the strangely cryptic, ambivalent songs they did for Alfa Anderson and Luci Martin, Rodgers and Edwards gave Sister Sledge undeniably anthemic songs that downplayed Chic's disembodiment in favor of full-blooded disco-gospel release. "[Greenberg] talked about them in the most celebratory, uplifting kind of way," Rodgers remembers. "That's why we came up with 'We Are Family.' He talked about when these girls come, they're sisters and they're just so much fun; if one walks down the hall, they all walk down the hall. Which was how we thought of 'And we flock just like birds of a feather,' stuff like that. Everything he said about them gave us a picture of them. You've got to remember, we never even met them. When we met them it was like, 'Okay, here's how the song goes.' They just had to walk into the studio and hear these two strangers define the rest of their lives . . . All of the content on that record came from that one day with the president. It may have happened in an hour or half an hour, I'm not sure. But to us that was our picture of Sister Sledge. Think about it. 'Lost in Music,' 'Thinking of You,' these are all about this group of girls that we thought had this incredible, musical, wonderful, loving life. They're religious girls, blah blah blah, which is very unlike me. I'm mister party guy, stay out all the time, so I was fascinated and enthralled by the concept of people who loved music who could be 'nice girls' in the midst of the whole disco era. It was fabulous to me. It was the greatest experiment to me because the kind of women I was used to were like Grace Jones [laughs]."[60]

The first single from *We Are Family* was "He's the Greatest Dancer." Led by an amazing, popping, almost slap-bass-sounding guitar figure from Rodgers, "He's the Greatest Dancer" became the group's first major hit, reaching the pop Top 10 and #1 on the R&B chart. The record featured some of the Chic Organization's best playing—Rodgers's guitar, Edwards's fluid if horribly undermixed bass line, Tony Thompson banging the skins harder than anyone this side of John Bonham, Raymond Jones's best Fender Rhodes lines, impeccable stuff from concert master Gene Orloff's Chic Strings, and one of the great disco breakdowns—but it also highlighted Rodgers and Edwards's songwriting prowess. Lines like "Arrogance, but not conceit / As a man he's complete" and the immortal internal rhyme, "Halston, Gucci, Fiorucci," were evidence of their gift for absurdist, plain speech lyrics. Despite all this, the song almost didn't make the record. "We had a huge fight in the studio over the lyrics to 'He's the Greatest Dancer,'" Rodgers recalls, "and we refused to change them because we knew the world that we were writing about obviously more than they did because they had never even been in a disco. There's a lyric that says, 'My crème de la crème please take me home,' and they were *furious* because to them that made them seem like loose women. To this very day, when you see Sister Sledge sing that song live, they say what they had suggested to me in the studio, which was, 'My crème de la crème, please don't go home.' I said, 'That's lame, what do you mean, "Please don't go home"? He ain't going to go home because he's the greatest dancer and it doesn't make any sense. Why would he go home?' [laughs] I said, 'Guys, you're making this song about you. It ain't about you, it's about him. "My crème de la crème, please don't go home"— what are you talking about? You just nullified the whole meaning. He wears the finest clothes, he's the greatest dancer, he's gonna stay there longer than you.' They just didn't want to sing it because all they kept thinking about was them. I said, 'Guys, listen to the song, you're telling a story. It's "*He's* the Greatest Dancer," *he's* the subject matter, not you.' No matter how much I kept explaining it to them, they kept saying, 'My God, my mother's gonna think we're whores.' For me, songs are important, lyrics, everything. There's not one word that's not very, very important to me. And it has to be a complete story to me: a beginning, a middle, and an end. If the logic is all of a sudden thrown away, I can't appreciate that."[61]

The album's best writing, however, was to be found on "Lost in Music." One of the few songs about music to live up to its claims, "Lost in Music" may not have been released as a single, but it struck such a universal chord that it was covered fifteen years later by the cantankerous, Mancunian postpunk band the Fall, which joined Robert Wyatt (who covered Chic's "At Last I Am Free") as the group's most unlikely fans. Where Chic would have emphasized the "Caught in a trap / No turning back" part of the lyric with haunted vocals and deep spaces in the groove, Sister Sledge embodies the "I feel so alive / I quit my nine to five" refrain with Kathie's swoops and curlicues and Rodgers's surging, uplifting chicken-scratch riffing.

For all of the brilliance of "Lost in Music," the album's biggest song was the title track. Based on a riff stolen from, of all people, Children of God, a group that Rodgers used to dig when he was a hippie, "We Are Family" might have been a gospelesque get-happy tune about the joys of sisterhood, but it quickly became an all-purpose anthem that was used by everyone from feminists to gay rights activists marching on Washington, D.C., to NAACP conventions to the Pittsburgh Pirates baseball team. Its almost universal appeal was largely due to Kathie Sledge's infectious, utterly delightful lead vocals. "Whatever I write, the musicians make it better," Rodgers says. "In other words, yeah, when I wrote 'We Are Family' it was a pretty great song to begin with, but when Kathie Sledge came in and heard it for the first time, she got so inspired that her first take was the one that we know and love. All that ad-libbing and stuff, it's just because she was so overwhelmed by the track: 'Come on, Bernard, wooo!' She was just reacting. She wasn't doing ad-libs necessarily, she was listening and hearing it for the first time."[62] There are other gems on *We Are Family*, like the very fine disco love songs "You're a Friend to Me" and "Thinking of You," but it was the Pirates, who won the World Series with "We Are Family" as their theme song, who offered proof of Chic's greatness.

As the across-the-board appeal of "We Are Family" intimated, "Disco has been the one source of music where everyone is equal, where you can have a good white disco group and a good black disco group and people that come to see you couldn't care less," Rodgers told journalist Geoff Brown in 1979. "*All* of the black people in America had the Bee Gees record. *Everybody* buys Chic records, everybody buys Donna Summer. Disco has almost given us the opportunity to just be normal. It's the product that's important. And I like that . . . it's difficult for me to talk about it because it means a lot to me inside, but it just really gives us the chance to be the same as everybody else and it's a really fantastic feeling to actually compare our record sales with Foreigner and the Rolling Stones and Firefall and the Beatles. We never would have had this opportunity with an R&B record . . . Before disco you couldn't really be like that. You could be like Otis Redding, and that's great. But if he were around today I doubt if he could compete with the Bee Gees doing just regular soul music because it's too alienating."[63]

By 1980, though, Chic was apparently too alienating. Disco was dead in the water as far as the mainstream was concerned, and Chic was thrown out with the bathwater. *Real People* was bitter and sniping, but this time it wasn't disguised by elegance or pop hooks. The music is an astringent kind of funk, sour and sharp—Rodgers almost sounds like punk guitarist Robert Quine at times. Anderson and Martin's robotic vocals are largely absent; instead, they sound more assertive, even straining. The veneer had been sanded down and stripped away. The record is at once a plea for help, succor, and shelter ("I wanna be with some real people"; "You can't do it alone"; "I got protection from your infection") and a lashing out. The remarkable "Chip Off the Old Block" would have fitted in perfectly alongside records like "Papa Was a Rolling Stone" and "Don't Call Me Brother" in its interrogation of masculinity: "Just like a robot he'll do / What he's programmed to . . . Some of us think these qualities are grim / To be just like the one before him." Rodgers and Edwards even used some of the language that the "disco sucks" brigade used to denigrate disco: "A plan to make humans act synthesized / I think we've homogenized." "That was the downfall of Chic," Rodgers says of the album. "That was the first time in our lives that we made records listening to other people. In the beginning, no one cared who we were, but now that we're selling millions of records, everyone had an opinion. All of a sudden, we're forced to do stuff that we don't really want to do. The powers that be at the record company were changing, and the next thing we knew there were new people involved in our lives telling us what to do and how to do it. And we're like, 'What are you talking about? We never listened to the record company.' We wanted to say, 'You're the same geniuses that when we played "Le Freak" everybody in the conference got up and walked out and told our attorney, "Oh, my God. What else do they have on the record?" Ummm, it's only the biggest-selling record in the history of Warner Brothers, but still you guys now want to start telling us what to do. Where are your credentials to back that up?' At least if we fail, we fail on our own. But now, that was the downfall. Now they could play the divide-and-conquer game, and they

TURN THE BEAT AROUND

could say to Bernard, 'Man, Nile's not listening to us.' And then they could say to me, 'I don't know what Bernard is up to, man.' We started listening, and we were confused. That's why in 'Real People' we said, 'Real people, man I want to live my life with some real people.' It was really out of character for us because we were really protesting. And that was something I always promised Bernard that we would never do because he knew my whole Black Panther past and we made a pact that we were going to do celebratory music. But if you listen to the lyrics of 'Real People,' it's uncomfortable for us to say that shit. We even say, 'Rebels are we, we are the rebels baby.' We tried to make it funny because I stole that from Woody Allen. If you see *Bananas*, they say, 'Now let us sing the song of the rebels: "Rebels are we / Born to be free / Just like the fish in the sea."' I kept thinking, 'Man, Woody Allen is cool. He never sued us, he never went, "Hey, wait a minute, those are my lyrics."' It was a joke to us, but at that point we were angry and bitter and it was real, but we weren't real, we weren't being rebellious, we were going along with the bullshit. So now we were listening to people who didn't know. They were afraid and 'disco sucks,' so they were trying to make us not disco."[64]

"STRANDED ON THE ISLAND OF RACE MUSIC"
August Darnell

What a row the brute makes!   —Joseph Conrad, *Heart of Darkness*

In America during the '70s there was only one thing that could compete with the disco juggernaut on the cultural front: nostalgia for the 1950s. *American Graffiti* and *Grease* cleaned up at the box office, while *Happy Days* was a constant presence in the top five of the Nielsen ratings from 1975 until the end of the decade. Heck, even duck-tailed greaser throwbacks Sha Na Na managed to get a nationally syndicated TV show. America was trying to put the chaos of the '60s behind it and hark back to a more innocent, less divisive time in its history, a time when father still knew best and the good guys always wore white. The '50s may have been the era of rock and roll and doo-wop, *Brown v. Board of Education*, and Governor Orval Faubus's stand at the door of Little Rock Central High School to prevent desegregation, but conflict (other than gentle generational) and black faces were scarce in any of the '70s representations of the '50s. As we have seen with Chic, though, African Americans too were looking back to the past, but not to the strife of the '50s, and they certainly weren't doing it to rescue some mythical golden age. Instead, such remembrance was done in order to bring historical experience to bear on the present, to wrestle with tradition, and to poke holes in its often suffocating fabric. Cloaking themselves in the suavity, élan, and romanticorealist style of the age of Cab Calloway and Lorenz Hart, disco's most extraordinary revivalists, if you can call them that, were Dr. Buzzard's Original Savannah Band.

The group was the brainchild of two mixed-race half brothers from the Bronx hung up on George Raft and James Cagney movies. Pianist/vocalist Stony Browder Jr. was the musical mastermind, while bassist/vocalist Tommy (aka August Darnell) Browder, fresh from drama school, was the wordsmith. Allegedly inspired by one Dr. Carrash Buzzard, an itinerant musician who had a minstrel show in the '40s, and the multiculturalism of their house (a French-Canadian mother and Dominican father) and environs, the two started toying with the conventions of "race music" and formed Dr. Buzzard's Original Savannah Band with singer Cory Daye, percussionist Andy Hernandez, and drummer Mickey Sevilla in 1974 to explore it further. At the time, there were plenty of hapless artists attempting to mix disco dazzle with Jazz Age pizzazz—Tuxedo Junction's "Chattanooga Choo Choo," Wing & a Prayer Fife and Drum Corps's "Baby Face," Salsoul Orchestra's "Tangerine," New York Rubber Rock Band's "Disco Lucy," Ethel Merman's disco album, Taco's "Puttin' on the Ritz"—but as Browder told *Black Music* magazine in 1977, "I thought of the Dr. Buzzard project as being a High School thing, a Dead End Kids thing, not tails and Manhattan Transfer . . . We aren't interested in nostalgia."[65] Instead, the fraternal coconspirators constructed a fantasy world in which show tunes actually swing, the ghetto is filled with Golden Age Hollywood glamour (or the glitz of 1940s Hollywood is tempered by hardened ghetto realism), and heartbreak can be exorcised with a witty turn of phrase. Granted, on paper it sounds like the most regressive, retrograde, revisionist kind of record, but on the turntable their self-titled debut album was one of the most fully realized, dazzling artifacts from the black bohemian intelligentsia.

The first words that you hear on Dr. *Buzzard's Original Savannah Band* are "zoot suit city"; the first couplet rhymes "if that would get me ovah" with "equivalency diploma"; the first sounds are the *rum-tum-tum* of the tom-tom and some Glenn Miller (not even Count Basie) brass razzle-dazzle. Stony Browder lays the penguin-suited–big-band schmaltz on thick, with help from veteran 4 Seasons arranger Charlie Calello.[66] Daye displays a winning combination of Great White Way razzmatazz and uptown soul: She rolls her tongue à la Billy Stewart and Jackie Wilson, gives the lyrics some Rita Moreno sass, and oo-poo-pah-doos like Betty Boop. So far, so tacky. No wonder the album went gold.

After you get used to the Cotton Club shtick, though, you start to notice the Latin rhythms, realize how great the bass is throughout the record, and discover that beneath the children's chorus on "Sunshower" is a skeletal Nigerian juju track complete with Hawaiian guitar and talking drums. You remember that the phrase "zoot suit city" doesn't refer just to some idealized beau monde, but that it recalls the Zoot Suit Riots in Los Angeles in 1942–43 when military personnel clashed frequently with Mexican-American youths. Instead of wallowing in rhinestone kitsch or indulging in disco escapism like their contemporaries, the brothers Browder use the Busby Berkeley glitz both to interrogate the present and rehabilitate the past. This was glamour as fashion pose and archness, to be sure, but when Stony Browder told *Black Music's* Davitt Sigerson that "Lyrically . . . there used to be wit. People could say things without getting flustered. There was none of the pure aggression of more recent music,"[67] it became clear that the pose was just a deflection mechanism. This was glamour as defiance. Browder and Darnell were daring to dream of a world that they were locked out of as a matter of course (unless they wanted to be Butterfly McQueen or Stepin Fetchit), but they were equally locked out of the world traditionally ascribed to them because of their mixed race and light skin. Caught in between two worlds, they chose the path that would alienate both.

Darnell may fetishize the glory days of Tin Pan Alley, but there's nothing approaching *moon-June-spoon* here: Darnell has Daye singing lines like "I'll grow a tail or two for you / Spend the rest of my days locked up in a zoo"; "They're all the same, the sluts and the saints"; and "Now the sun must rise / With her bag of tricks and cheats and dirty lies." But it's not just the wordplay that zings. Aspiring to and self-consciously aping the cultured bons mots of Cole Porter is about as radical a gesture as a black songwriter can make. Of course, if Darnell merely staked a claim on that world of yacht clubs, Central Park West cocktail parties, and frolicking around gaily on a crisp autumn afternoon in the Connecticut woods, it would be a mark of unseemly aspiration and the false consciousness of class. However, Darnell wasn't writing whoop-de-do songs to be sung in Gramercy Park penthouses. He was dragging Porter away from the confines of Yale and the Astor Bar and into the ghetto; he was elevating an equivalency diploma—that symbol of substandard education—to something with the transcendent power and ennobling force of the *Mona Lisa* or the Colosseum in Rome. But he's also realist enough to know that love can't transcend the material world, that there's always "Lemon in the Honey," that "the sun must rise / With her bag of tricks and cheats and dirty lies."

Of course, Browder's music helps. The strings swirl, swoop, and swoon like Veronica Lake has just walked on camera when Daye sings, "She's sick and tired of living in debt / Tired of roaches and tired of rats." On tracks like "Sour & Sweet / Lemon in the Honey" and "Cherchez La Femme," his synthesis is so perfect that, just like Chic (with different conclusions), Browder sees no difference between stomping at the Savoy and bumping at Studio 54. To Browder and Darnell, miscegenation was not something that merely diluted the gene pool, but something that offered endless possibilities. Rejecting such hoary old stereotypes as the "tragic mulatto" and the "wild half-caste," these half-breeds asserted that fusion was strength, not adulteration, and refused to have their fates defined by pity or revulsion. Their version of the disco beat recognizes all the rhythms of the New York melting pot that simmered down to create it: rumba, mambo, funk, tango, compas, calypso, cha-cha-cha, merengue. "To me, the beauty of music is its possibilities for mutation," Darnell told *The New York Times* in 1981. "And that mutation represents a larger ideal: global coexistence."[68]

After two more Dr. Buzzard's Original Savannah Band albums

that went way over the heads of just about every audience with their sharp, acerbic lyrics, brittle sarcasm, occasionally discordant jazz arrangements, and oblique Spanish-language non sequiturs, Darnell, fired up by sibling rivalry, pursued this larger ideal as a songwriter, as the in-house producer for Ze Records and in his own postdisco project, Kid Creole & the Coconuts. Working with the fairly nondescript disco/R&B group Machine in 1979, Darnell cowrote (with Kevin Nance) disco's finest morality play, "There But for the Grace of God Go I." On top of hysterical, urgent keyboards that are halfway between the Isley Brothers and Hi-NRG, Darnell weaves the tale of Carlos and Carmen Vidal, who move from the Bronx in order to raise their child somewhere safe. Inevitably, their move backfires and their daughter "turns out to be a natural freak" who runs away from home at sixteen, leaving her mother to bang her head against the wall and wail that "Too much love is worse than none at all." Darnell would continue to write and produce artfully crafted, deceptively airy pop baubles for artists like Aural Exciters, Cristina, Gichy Dan's Beachwood #9, and Don Armando's 2nd Ave. Rhumba Band, but it would be as his alter ego Kid Creole that he would gain most attention.

When Darnell joined Ze Records, most of their roster was taken up by acts from the postpunk scene: Suicide, Lydia Lunch, James Chance & the Contortions, Mars, Lizzy Mercier Descloux, and Les Garçons. While he was too much of a craftsman to incorporate their anything-goes approach to music, their championing of the "nonsinger" and their abrasiveness appealed to this born cynic, and Kid Creole became a mixture of Ziegfeld Follies fabulousness and Johnny Rotten scrape 'n' grate. With Andy "Coati Mundi" Hernandez (from Dr. Buzzard's) and three European ice queens in tow, Darnell created a three-ring zoot suit circus that oozed glib erudition, gently poked fun at sexual pathology, viewed Manhattan as the northernmost Caribbean island, read from Bobby Short's supper club lexicon, and played confidence games with racial stereotypes. Darnell's debonair but roguish sophisticate was teased and mocked every step of the way by Coati Mundi and the Coconuts, never letting the rakish mountebank get the upper hand. Darnell constructed epic travelogues in order to revive archetypal images from the recesses of American cultural memory—Carmen Miranda, Fay Wray, the pith-helmeted explorer—and unmoor (and un-Moor) them from their traditional associations to speak for themselves.

By using these archetypes, dance music, comic scenarios, and the language of Broadway and Hollywood, Darnell attempted to universalize the plight of the mulatto misfit. Darnell's two great themes—being out of place and everyday human cruelty—essentially made all of his characters into half-castes, all of them wrestling with the cost of selling out, all of them resigned to the fact they're doomed to be fish out of water no matter what path they choose. Darnell explored these themes most effectively on his two masterpieces, *Fresh Fruit in Foreign Places* and *Wise Guy* (aka *Tropical Gangsters*, apparently named after the Rhode Island store that provided him with his zoot suit wardrobe).

Fresh Fruit ostensibly told the tale of the Kid sailing the seven seas in search of his elusive paramour, Mimi, who had absconded in uncertain circumstances to some tropical locale. It was a Homerian epic that, while populated with sirens and sorceresses, was concerned more with nebbishes and cads than heroes and monsters. Instead of cyclopes and lotus-eaters, the putative protagonist had to outwit fast-talking natives, cope with difficult Latin music and strange customs, and fend off predatory Swiss ski instructors. Of course, our hero probably never even leaves Manhattan, and Darnell designed the scenario so that he could explore alienation while trading barbs with Joseph Conrad on the set of *The Road to Zanzibar*.

After beginning his travelogue with "Goin' Places"—a song that echoes Saul Steinberg's famous *New Yorker* cartoon, "View of the World from 9th Avenue," which depicts the Manhattanite's worldview as pretty much ending at the Hudson River ("Believe me I know that when you leave New York you go nowhere")—Darnell imagines New York as a primeval rain forest teeming with weird biomass, dense mist, restless natives banging their war drums, and spooky creepy-crawlies skittering and slithering underfoot. With its didgeridoo undertow, blocky piano chords, rain dance percussion, and monkey chants, "In the Jungle" is a dark, dank place harboring all sorts of demons both real and psychic—you half expect Mr. Kurtz suddenly to emerge from the overgrowth, clasping a knife between his teeth. "I don't believe in integration just to achieve miscegenation," the song's narrator sings. "Don't offer me remuneration / I don't believe in acclimation . . . I don't believe in propagation / Just to achieve cafe au laition / Don't offer me emasculation / I don't believe in deprivation."

The reggae feel of "Animal Crackers" follows with a riff on the Tokens' "The Lion Sleeps Tonight" at the beginning. The lyrics continue the tone of poking fun at exoticists and square white guys with a character halfway between *Fantasy Island*'s Mr. Roarke and Daniel Defoe's Friday telling our fearless hero, "You've got no reason to be dangling from up here / You'll disembark and find there's nothing here to fear / We've got no history of human sacrifice / We welcome you, your children and your wives / But Frosted Flakes and coffee cakes ["painted eggs" after the second verse] customs will deny / And your bag of Animal Crackers . . ." When the square peg protagonist dares to set foot on foreign soil, he's set adrift in a land full of "Latin music" that he can neither comprehend nor countenance: "I'm so confused / This Latin music's got me so, so bemused / The accent's worse than Cockney / I'm not amused, it's killing me . . . Frazzled and floored / This Latin music's mayhem / I won't endure / There's too much syncopation / Where's the two and four?" Later, the air of displacement and preposterousness is heightened by one reggae song that's half in German and another about a woman who runs off with a Swiss ski instructor.

Like *Fresh Fruit in Foreign Places*, *Wise Guy* was a mock travelogue in which the band is "washed up on the shore of B'Dilli Bay—an island of sinners ruled by outcasts where crime is the only passport and RACE MUSIC the only way out!" However, unlike *Fresh Fruit*, dislocation and orientalism were not the main concerns of *Wise Guy*, and while the pan-Caribbean vibe of *Fresh Fruit* reappeared in the ersatz soca/salsa of "Annie, I'm Not Your Daddy," the tradewind lilt of "No Fish Today," and the synthesized steel drum and timbal fills of "I'm Corrupt," *Wise Guy* was mostly straight-ahead, if slightly astringent, R&B. Well, as straight-ahead as a guy who calls his backing musicians "the Pond Life Orchestra" can be. *Wise Guy*'s deceptively simple light funk bottom effectively streamlined the band's sound, reining in the big-band arrangements and the pan-American references without neutering their effectiveness, and created a sharp-focus background for Darnell's tales of quotidian inhumanity. Here, the savages weren't the fetish objects of "race music" but the seemingly normal people you take for granted every day as you walk past them on the street.

"No Fish Today" was everything Steely Dan wanted to be but couldn't: With the siren harps and sea-mist strings, the music evokes a tropical paradise that is undercut by one of the harshest dialogues this side of Harold Pinter, in which a fishmonger refuses to sell a woman any fish during a shortage because "the authorities agree that if anyone should eat, it should be the upper class." Of course, the merchant was "neither right nor wrong, just another pawn" who "got to be this old because [he does] what [he's] told." Crueler still was the amazing "Annie, I'm Not Your Daddy." Over the most detailed music of his career and the Coconuts singing "onomatopoeia" in the background, Darnell didn't break it to her gently: "If I was in your blood, you wouldn't be so ugly." Elsewhere, there was the breakup invective of "Loving You Made a Fool Out of Me," in which both parties get in some choice insults, and the Ellingtonian razzle-dazzle of "Stool Pigeon" ("The FBI rewarded him because they like a guy who will stab a friend"). Even the seemingly balmy Bali Hai of "The Love We Have" was the plaint of a man suffering the slings and arrows of a lover who blows hot and cold.

Like most of the best disco music (Chic's "Good Times," Inner Life's "I'm Caught Up [In a One Night Love Affair]," New York Citi Peech Boys' "Don't Make Me Wait"), Darnell's records both celebrated and damned disco's glitterball sophistry. Instead of feeling trapped by disco's rock-and-a-hard-place position between two worlds, Darnell reveled in it. Darnell's characters were guys desperately searching for someone real, someone who wouldn't sell them down the river, yet in his forties street hood getup, Kid Creole was the most hyperstylized character around. He replaced the gospel salvation of the African-American tradition with the flashy resplendence of show tunes—in Darnell's world the material trumps the promises of the future every time—but, driven by sarcasm, there was no redemption, only endless mutation.

ABOVE: Mixing it up at Arthur before the dawn of disco. (Corbis)

Vegetable shortening: it's not just for cherry pie anymore. Dancers at Crisco Disco. (Bill Bernstein, Retna Ltd.)

THANKS FOR YOUR CONTINUED SUPPORT

A TOM MOULTON MIX

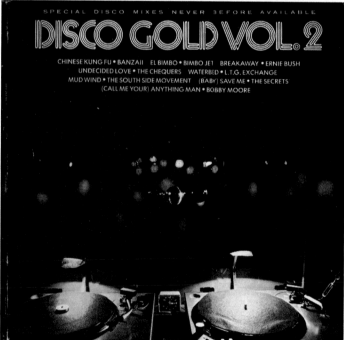

SPECIAL DISCO MIXES NEVER BEFORE AVAILABLE

DISCO GOLD VOL. 2

CHINESE KUNG FU • BANZAII   EL BIMBO • BIMBO JET   BREAKAWAY • ERNIE BUSH
UNDECIDED LOVE • THE CHEQUERS   WATERBED • L.T.G. EXCHANGE
MUD WIND • THE SOUTH SIDE MOVEMENT   (BABY) SAVE ME • THE SECRETS
(CALL ME YOUR) ANYTHING MAN • BOBBY MOORE

Two turntables and a glitterball: disco bliss.

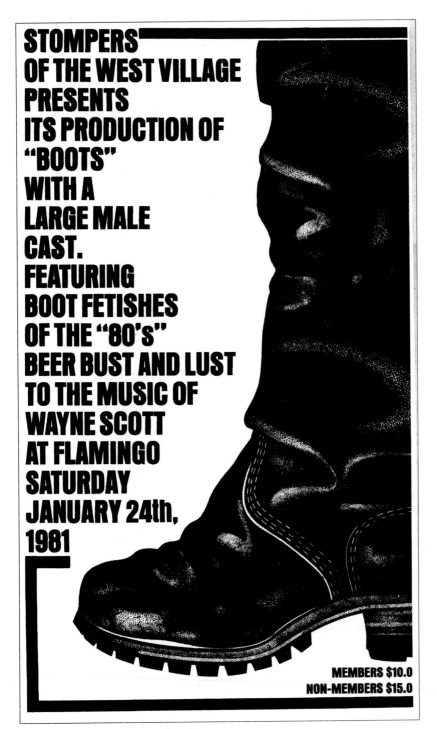

STOMPERS
OF THE WEST VILLAGE
PRESENTS
ITS PRODUCTION OF
"BOOTS"
WITH A
LARGE MALE
CAST.
FEATURING
BOOT FETISHES
OF THE "80's"
BEER BUST AND LUST
TO THE MUSIC OF
WAYNE SCOTT
AT FLAMINGO
SATURDAY
JANUARY 24th,
1981

MEMBERS $10.0
NON-MEMBERS $15.0

Flyer for the Boot party at the Flamingo.

LAND OF MAKE BELIEVE

Come Play With Us

The Saint
Saturday Night, April 10, 1982

Live:
Esther Satterfield
singing "Land of Make Believe"

Music: Howard Merritt
Lights: Mark Ackerman

Time: Midnight

Members: $20
Guests: $30

Easter Sunday, April 11, 1982
Free Tea to Members   Guests $10

Movie: "The Wizard of Oz"

Screening time: 9:50 P.M.
Doors open at 9:00 P.M.

Dancing after the movie

Music: Roy Thode
Lights: Jim Hicks

LEFT: Flyer for the Land of Make Believe party at The Saint.

ABOVE: Le Jardin when it was still "a gala affaire for monsieurs." (Allan Tannenbaum)

Cruisin' the streets with Bill Motley's Boys Town Gang.

The popper and coke-fueled glamour of Studio 54. (Bill Bernstein, Retna Ltd.)

Actor Ben Vereen and skate-dancing troupe The Goodskates roller-boogeying at Xenon. (Corbis)

He-man Patrick Juvet
wants to play hockey
with you.

Andy Warhol is "hell on
wheels." (Allan Tannenbaum)

The night that disco died: the Disco Demolition Derby at Comiskey Park, Chicago, July 12, 1979. (Corbis)

Disco Sucks patch.

D.R.E.A.D.
CODE OF CONDUCT

I will never wear platform shoes.
I will never wear zodiac jewelry.
I will never listen to disco records
and/or disco radio stations.
Silk dresses and three piece suits
are extremely suspect.
A violation of any of these
conditions is punishable by . . .

"THE CHAIR"

Saturday
Night Cleaver

George Swell
George Swell

Jim Johnson
Jim Johnson

Richard T. Bruiser
Richard T. Bruiser

D.R.E.A.D. Executive Board

Detroit Rockers Engaged
in the Abolition of Disco
membership card.

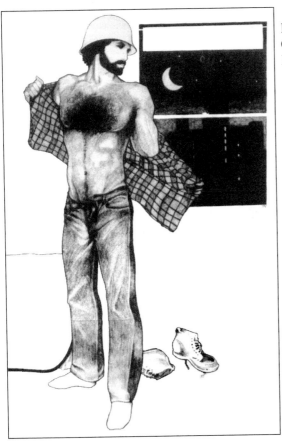

Flyer for one of the Paradise Garage's famous Construction Parties.

BELOW: The infamous Soul Night at the Mudd Club. (Allan Tannenbaum)

PRI/ONER/ OF THE NIGHT

The Di/co Craze

There will be disco dancing at the inaugural ball for President Carter on January 20. In the first ever disco show at a presidential inauguration, the Portable Peach mobile disco outfit of Scott Woodside and Barry Chase of Atlanta will travel to Washington for the ceremonies at the invitation of the Carter fundraising committee. In addition to disco dancing, the show will also feature two disco dancers in peanut costumes dancing to the music of the *Bicentennial Disco Mix* released last year by Private Stock Records.
—*Billboard*, January 22, 1977

I'm not sure if it was heaven or hell. But it was wonderful.
—Jimmy Carter's mother, Lillian, on her visit to Studio 54

I'll keep you hot when the fuel runs out.   —Executive Suite

In the summer of 1973, the bop apocalypse occurring at the Loft, Tenth Floor, and Third World Gallery started to become big news. The lure of the discotheque was rapidly spreading from its main constituency and ensnaring everyone caught in New York's web of despair and desolation. As an estimated one hundred thousand New Yorkers were boogying away the blues in the Big Apple's discos every Saturday night, Vince Aletti, in an article for *Rolling Stone* in September, was the first to mark out disco music as its own particular genre separate from R&B and soul; two weeks later, *Billboard* noted the discotheques' growing influence in creating pop hits.[1] The remarkable success of the discotheques "began to suggest an entertainment formula for the secretive 70s: take people out of their own neighborhoods, let them wander around in the desolation of the warehouse district with a scribbled address they've gotten from a friend; give them a rush of quadrophonic input and the stimulus of satin blouses under strobes; add a taste of kinkiness; limit the membership to a chosen few—and they'll show up in droves."[2] Cheap, functional, stark, seedy, and somewhat exclusionary, the modern discotheque was an entertainment formula that was keenly in touch with the realities of New York City.

But as much as disco wallowed in squalor, it also soared to the heavens. It offered communion and ecstasy, fantasy and release. After all, one hundred thousand people don't gather together every weekend to be miserable together. The stratospheric rise of the disco scene paralleled New York's own upsurge. Under banner headlines like "City Will Turn Tide of 'Urban Sickness'" and "Rebirth of Lower Manhattan," architect Minoru Yamasaki's World Trade Center (which opened on April 4, 1973[3]) was hailed as signaling New York's phoenixlike ascent from the ashes of urban turmoil and fiscal mismanagement. While Yamasaki had envisioned his two 110-story towers as utopian symbols of world peace, New York's Port Authority, which had funded the project, had rather different aims in mind. Even though New York had definitively become the global financial capital after World War II, lower Manhattan (where New York's financial district was located) was largely a derelict, desolate place that was left behind by both the industries that had fled the city's tax code and the commercial real estate boom that was transforming midtown.[4] The Port Authority and its allies, like David and Nelson Rockefeller, tried to remedy this situation with "a massive and fully tax-exempt public intervention in the private real estate market through the development of the world's largest office building."[5] The WTC's ten million square feet of office space (the equivalent of seven Empire State Buildings) was meant to revitalize an area often called "Hell's Hundred Acres" seemingly by sheer force of will. These soaring, gleaming rectangular spires rising from a sinkhole that resembled some third world outpost much more than it resembled capitalism's capital city were meant to act as beacons signaling to the money-worshipping flock that New York had changed its ways. "If you build it they will come" was the logic—the architectural equivalent of Horatio Alger's pick yourself up by your bootstraps philosophy.

In the midst of the city's crippling financial crisis, as its infrastructure was crumbling, as gasoline prices in the United States were quadrupling as the result of an embargo called by Middle Eastern members of OPEC on all crude oil shipments to Western nations that supported Israel during the Yom Kippur War, New York City had constructed potentially the largest white elephant the world had ever seen. Instead of acting responsibly and saving its pennies for the rainy days that long ago arrived, Gotham was saving up all its money for Saturday night, when it could put on its gaudiest platform shoes and step out in style—damn the consequences. Despite itself, the plan worked. Slowly, companies moved into the WTC and into lower Manhattan. Ironically, it was in reaction to the megalomania of projects like the World Trade Center that in October, New York's Landmarks Preservation Commission recognized the SoHo–Cast Iron Historic district (an area bounded by West Broadway to the west, Crosby Street to the east, Houston Street to the north, and Canal Street to the south) as an area of architectural importance and deemed its old warehouses and sweatshops worthy of preservation. Thanks to the work done by the artists, musicians, DJs, and party-goers who initially transformed these dead areas of the city under the very noses of the Port Authority, conservative preservationists, real estate agents, and stockbrokers "discovered" that the lofts of SoHo and TriBeCa, the neighborhoods immediately to the north of the World Trade Center, made ideal upscale living spaces. It wouldn't be long before the formerly derelict buildings of lower Manhattan became the most fashionable addresses in the world. As Deep Throat told Bernstein and Woodward around this time, "Just follow the money." Just as money transformed the sites of disco's birth, the influx of capital into the disco industry would remake disco into something largely unrecognizable to its earliest practitioners.

In early 1975, Van McCoy, a longtime presence on the soul/R&B scene (having previously worked with everyone from the Shirelles and Jackie Wilson to Faith, Hope & Charity and the Stylistics), was working overtime in order to finish recording an album of instrumentals for producers Hugo Peretti and Luigi Creatore's Avco label. David Todd, the DJ at Manhattan nightspot Adam's Apple, had been pestering him for several weeks to come to the club to check out a new dance that was creating a stir. McCoy was too busy to go to a nightclub, so he sent his friend and business partner, Charles Kipps Jr., in his place. What Kipps saw at Adam's Apple excited him so much that at around midnight he left the club and brought two dancers with him back to Mediasound Studios where McCoy was working. "When he came back, he showed me this very strange dance," McCoy told *Essence* magazine. "It was something completely different from the you-do-your-thing-and-I-do-mine dances; it was people dancing together again. The hustle reminded me of ballroom dancing, and I love graceful dancing."[6] McCoy wrote "The Hustle" right there on the spot, and he recorded it the next day during the one hour of studio time he had remaining for his session with the Soul City Symphony (drummers Steve Gadd and Rick Marotta, bassist Gordon Edwards, keyboardist Richard Tee, guitarist Eric Gale, a horn section, and concertmaster Gene Orloff's strings).[7] This afterthought became not only McCoy's solitary Top 40, let alone #1, single as an artist, but also, thanks to its accompanying dance craze, the record that truly catapaulted disco from an underground phenomenon to worldwide furor.[8]

At first blush, "The Hustle" is hardly the kind of record that you normally associate with a dance craze. After its great, almost mysterious intro, it devolves into the strangely rhythmless, inane, singsong, prim and prissy instrumental equivalent of Starland Vocal Band's "Afternoon Delight"—not exactly the fire and blood or blatant, unrepentant hucksterism that marks a great dance craze disc. But thanks to that infernal flute line boring into your skull with the savage ferocity that only elevator music can muster, "The Hustle" was inescapable and inevitable, the kind of record that crawls under your skin, subliminally taking root to the point where you find yourself whistling it while masturbating. It was the perfect record for the novocaine bliss of Nixon and Ford's America: Brush years of stress and strife under an ornate carpet of strings and woodwinds, mollify the rage with a cheap come-on from a breathy bird, and placate the masses with tooth fairy promises and doe-eyed innocence.

On the week that "The Hustle" had fallen out of the top spot in the American charts, former Nixon speechwriter and *New York Times* op-ed columnist William Safire hailed the hustle as a return to self-discipline and decorum on the dance floor after years of "frantic self-expression" and "personal isolation."[9] "Unlike their older brothers and sisters who took pride in a pair of dungarees, free-flowing, unkempt hair and 'hang-loose' dances, today's young people value sleek clothes, fancy high-heeled shoes and a more stylized, structured form of dancing," Safire's *New York Times* colleague Dena Kleiman had announced a month earlier. "It's no longer 'anything goes' but what looks good . . . Unlike the more vigorous, inner-directed dances of the 1960s in which contact between couples was to be avoided and shaking, jumping, and turning at whim was the mode, the hustle is a dance of posture, rigor, and coordination."[10] This wasn't an instance of conservative commentators donning flares and open-necked Kiana shirts in an effort to jump on a passing bandwagon and look like they're with it. No, they were hailing the hustle as the return of the purity of American culture, a homecoming of innocence and safety, as the reaffirmation of "standards." "The political fact is that the absolute-freedom days of the dance are over," Safire trumpeted. "When you are committed to considering what your partner will do next, and must signal your own intentions so that the 'team' of which you are a part can stay in step, then you have embraced not only a dance partner, but responsibility."[11]

This wasn't just rejoicing over the return of the repression and Victorian courtship rites of ballroom dancing and the reaffirmation of traditional gender roles where a man leads a woman around the dance floor, or even the triumph of "personal communication" over the ghastly and unseemly self-absorption of the freeform dancing that had been the rage since the twist and the filth and loose mores that characterized the '60s. The hustle was the harbinger of a conservative revolution. "After a terpsichorean era of confrontation, we are entering an era of negotiation," Safire asserted. "The geopolitician who fails to see this social phenomenon is out of touch with his time. As dancing requires instruction, genuine standards become the fashion; as eyes focus on and arms enfold a partner, responsibility and humanity come into vogue."[12] Seemingly, it wasn't just Safire, with his conservative agenda and baggage, who was interpreting the hustle as a decisive break with the Age of Aquarius. "The '60s was so solipsistic, so narcissistic: look at the way people dance!" a friend of journalist Andrew Kopkind exclaimed. "Disco is just as exhibitionist, but you create it with someone else, with another person on the dance floor. It's a retreat from that scary chaos into patterns."[13]

On the surface, the hustle seemed so regressive and sterile: the familiar old box steps of ballroom dancing, the man taking the lead, the well-groomed men in suits and the women in frilly dresses—there was something frightfully *Stepford Wives* about it all. Yet, the hustle's origins were anything but anodyne. The word *hustle* (which comes from the Dutch word for "shake") had long had currency in the underworld, where it was used as a term for describing the work of pickpocketers, scam artists, and prostitutes. The hustle was born in the Latino sections of the Bronx, where it was a vision of romance floating gracefully out of the squalor and decay of Fort Apache. It was men and women dressed to the nines, spending whatever they could afford in order to attain that one minute of ecstasy that dancing on the rubble could provide. "The first time I saw the Hustle was probably in 1972," says Michael "Lucky Strike" Corral, who grew up on 181st Street in the Bronx and joined the Puerto Rican gang the Savage Skulls at the

DISCO AND THE "ME DECADE"

While Safire and Kopkind's friends were praising disco for liberating society from the self-admiration of the '60s, other commentators were bemoaning disco for its own brand of solipsism. "[T]he real thrust of disco culture," Albert Goldman wrote, "is not toward love of another person but toward love of self—the principal object of desire in this age of closed-circuit, masturbatory vibrator sex. Outside the entrance to every discotheque should be erected a statue of the presiding deity: Narcissus."[14] As if to prove this, "the Mad Hatter [discotheque] in Tampa, Florida will offer the TV generation the ultimate audiovisual experience in the 'I-want-to-be-in-pictures' syndrome. It is installing video-dish systems that will record the action on the dance floor and then project it onto the walls of the disco in pictures sixteen feet wide and ten feet high. That way, the disco dancers can simultaneously watch— and star in—their own disco movie."[15] In his best seller *The Culture of Narcissism: American Life in an Age of Diminishing Expectations*, Christopher Lasch wrote that after the turmoil of the 1960s, Americans retreated into the "purely personal." "The contemporary climate is therapeutic, not religious," he wrote. "People today hunger not for personal salvation but for the feeling, the momentary illusion, of

age of thirteen after connecting with them through pigeon flying.[16] "I used to see them [the older members of the Savage Skulls] and the Javelins [a gang allied to the Skulls] dance on the rooftops . . . They started bringing radios to our coops while we were flying birds, so I got more into the music. And that's how I got down [with the Skulls]."[17] In order to become a full-fledged member of the gang, he had to run "the Apache line" (walk down the middle of two lines of ten people each who were throwing punches and elbows) and, finally, survive a game of Russian roulette ("losers" were unceremoniously dumped in abandoned buildings, where they would eventually be found by the police, who took them to be suicides). This probably wasn't the return to civility and "standards" that William Safire had in mind.

According to Corral, in the early days, the biggest hustle record was Barry White's "Can't Get Enough of Your Love, Babe." Van McCoy somehow must have intuited this because, with its string fanfaronade, cooing vocals, and jazzy guitar licks, "The Hustle" is almost a carbon copy of White's arrangements for "Can't Get Enough of Your Love, Babe" and Love Unlimited Orchestra's "Love's Theme." While the hustle started in the barrio in the early '70s, eventually worked its way through the outer borough Latin clubs

---

personal well-being, health, and psychic security."[18] Disco as shallow, self-centered quasi culture or as a regressive retreat back to safety from the anarchic free-for-all of the 1960s: Either way it looked like the death of politics, meaning and the Left.

Of course, on one hand the '70s *were* all about "self-actualization," "plugging in," and *Looking Out for #1*—it was, as Tom Wolfe dubbed it, the "Me Decade." When they found that it was easier to raise capital on the markets than it was to raze the Capitol, most of the '60s radicals folded up their tents and dungarees in favor of BMWs and three-piece suits. However, as both Lasch and futurist Alvin Toffler noted, the distinction that separated people coming of age in the '70s and after from previous generations was the lack of a sense of permanence and solidity brought on by postindustrialization and a feeling of severe rootlessness. The sense of time, too, had collapsed, where the past no longer informed the present. While this led to nostalgia (for the 1950s, disco's fetishization of the 1930s and '40s), this was also at the very root of disco's liberationist impulse. As a form of trance, the most ritualistic aspects of disco culture viewed time as cyclical, unshackling it from Western teleology and returning to a pre-Christian notion of "salvation as liberation from time."[19]

until it arrived at the Manhattan discotheques in early 1975, and then exploded internationally with McCoy's "The Hustle," its roots can be traced back to the *guaguancó*, a 4/4 rhythm that was developed in the late nineteenth century when European-style marching bands attempted to play the more syncopated *son* and *rumba* rhythms native to Cuba. When these rhythms made their way to the United States with waves of immigration from Puerto Rico and Cuba, they merged with jazz to create the cha-cha and the mambo. This meeting with jazz caused the music to be further harnessed by the 4/4, and at New York clubs like the Palladium, the Cheetah, and the Corso, the mambo developed into a slot dance, a standard format of ballroom dancing in which the action of the dance, especially the woman's, is defined by an imaginary line drawn on the dance floor. As Latin music in New York mutated into salsa (a mixture of Cuban, Puerto Rican, and American elements), the tempo increased and the dance, too, changed. "What [the Savage Skulls] were dancing was a mixture of salsa, that street salsa mixed with the hustle type of thing," Corral remembers. "It wasn't like your typical ballroom stuff." To all intents and purposes, the hustle is a slightly faster version of salsa with a few more flourishes. "The hustle was more competitive," Corral explains. "You could do aerial moves, which in the salsa they don't really do that. We would do these incredible aerial moves. The salsa is just a little bit more conservative. It's similar, but it's not as well put together with strategy and acrobatic stuff. We was doing a lot of acrobatic stuff."[20]

Corral was part of the Hustle Kings, an informal dance troupe whose members tried to earn money by competing in every hustle contest they could possibly attend. "We used to go to all the clubs, and I'm talking *all* the clubs all over New York, like three clubs a night, even the gay clubs, the Ice Palace, Crisco Disco," Corral reveals. "I used to have to pencil in a mustache lightly so I could get in [laughs]. I was young and I had a baby face." With his gang background, he wasn't the kind of guy you'd expect to be hanging around Manhattan's queer discos wearing flashy, skintight clothes. "I remember myself and little Lourdes, who was my partner, and Eddie Vega [leader of the Hustle Kings and future choreographer who taught Patrick Swayze everything he knew in *Dirty Dancing*], we entered *Dance Fever* [a televised weekly dance contest] and, well, I was one of the winners of the $1,000, which was like a national thing, and Eddie won the $25,000, which was the first place," Corral recalls. "I should try to get the footage of all that. The way we used to dress was incredible. I was wearing an electric blue type of body suit. It was just how you dressed."[21]

By this time, the hustle had mutated into myriad different styles and substyles. There was the New York hustle, Latin hustle, L.A. hustle, Bay Area hustle, Continental hustle, West Coast hustle, tango hustle, rope hustle, American hustle, street hustle, sling hustle, etc. "The music had progressed a bit and it got a little faster," Corral says. "Then it was Cerrone, 'Love in "C" Minor' type of thing."[22] The popularity of the king of disco soft porn suggests that the hustle's return to touch dancing had absolutely nothing to do with civility and everything to do with why dancing is so central to youth culture to begin with. For white folks the '60s were all about "turning on, tuning in, and dropping out." Unlike the dolly birds who danced in London's Ad-Lib club in the mid-1960s without so much as a glance from the men, discogoers danced as if they had been coated in Spanish fly. The hustle marked the return of dancing as a surrogate for, or prelude to, sex. The sexual revolution may have happened during the '60s, when chemists unleashed the birth control pill and LSD at the same time, but disco dancing was the clarion call of sexual liberation.

But it was more than just the sexual body that disco was concerned with. The dance floor is nothing if not communal, and this group body was a polymorphous, polyracial, polysexual mass affirming its bonds in a space beyond the reach of church, state, or family. At the discotheque, the rigid boundaries imposed by such institutions were thrown out with the careless disregard of someone tossing a spent popper bottle. In this, the experience of Michael Corral—a Savage Skull member who felt more comfortable in the miniature Sodom of Crisco Disco than in the more racially and socioeconomically homogeneous clubs of his neighborhood[23]—was typical. As long as you strutted your stuff on the floor, disco was essentially democratic (once you got into the club, that is). Even that bible of the '60s dream, Rolling Stone, declared that "Because it is so democratic—on the boards, the dancer is the ultimate star—disco is probably the most compelling, artful and popular dance movement in generations."[24]

In a sense, in the discotheque the '70s practiced what the '60s preached: The communion offered by the dance floor was the embodiment of the vision of peace that the '60s yearned for. The naïve utopianism may have been ditched, but the radically different attitudes to race, gender, and sexuality born in the '60s remained and flourished most evidently on the disco dance floor. As Le Jardin DJ Steve D'Aquisto enthused to the *New York Post* about the club, "even Saturday night 'is like a little Woodstock, all races and creeds becoming one.'"[25] On the dance floor, the politics is one of the body, not of rhetoric—it's an internalized politics, a politics of gesture, perhaps reminiscent of the stance of many of the hard-line Leftist groups of the early '70s for whom even the most mundane daily activity was imbued with political significance. "Back in my hippie days, we talked about freedom and individuality, and it was all bullshit," declares Chic's Nile Rodgers. "The fact is, you could tell a hippie a mile away. We conformed to our nonconformity. As the celebratory phase of the struggle, disco really *was* about individuality. And the freakier, the better."[26]

In June 1974, Truman Capote was a guest on the *Tonight Show* and was regaling the talk show's host, Johnny Carson, with tales of his freaky adventures on the New York nightlife circuit. Capote, with his bizarre Big Easy lisp, big floppy hat and dark glasses, and nonexistent posture, looked like he had just beamed in from Mars, so Carson, who played the relaxed, affable, Middle American straightman when interviewing his guests, could only smirk and wink knowingly at the TV audience as Capote described his favorite club in New York. "[Le Jardin] has these Art Deco couches all along the room, these palm fronds drooping down everywhere," Capote drawled, "and out on the dance floor, this terrible churning, the whole place churning like a buttermilk machine."[27]

The spume whipped up by the agitated dancing at Le Jardin was the first wave of the disco craze. While disco *records* had topped the charts before, the *culture* of disco was largely invisible to mainstream America until the mini–media frenzy that surrounded Le Jardin in 1974–75. Opened by former South African model John Addison in June 1973 as "a total gay experience. A gala affaire for monsieurs,"[28]

Le Jardin was a perplexing bilevel club that occupied both the basement and the penthouse of the past-its-prime Diplomat Hotel at 110 West 43rd Street. Strangely for a club whose elevator was described as having a "housing-project urine odor,"[29] Le Jardin blended the belle epoque feel of the jet-set clubs like Le Club with the wild abandon of the Sanctuary. Unlike most of his predecessors, Addison was willing to spend money—not just on the banquettes, palm trees, and pretty-boy waitstaff, but, most crucially, on the lighting and sound systems. The club's combination of hard-core gay partiers and celebrity glamour (Capote, Diana Ross, David Bowie, New York Dolls singer David Johansen, and Warhol superstar/punk pinup Cyrinda Foxe) made for an atmosphere that was pretty much unique in the history of clubbing anywhere in the world at the time. Le Jardin was the first truly mixed discotheque in New York, if not the world, and its combination of gay abandon and fashion with hip heterosexuals created disco's myth and allure.

Another reason it was unique was that it wasn't purely a discotheque—the club's upstairs ballroom was where Kiss got its start and where Patti Smith launched her legendary *Horses* album. However, it was the dance floor that attracted the most attention, and the man responsible was Bobby DJ Guttadaro, who had been poached from the Continental Baths. Guttadaro was one of the best mixers around, and along with the Loft's David Mancuso, he was early disco's prime tastemaker. Thanks to his position at the most famous club in New York, Guttadaro had the ability to turn records like Love Unlimited Orchestra's "Love's Theme," Carl Douglas's "Kung Fu Fighting," and Disco Tex & His Sex-O-Lettes' "Get Dancin'" into bona fide pop hits, and he got gold records in recognition of his contribution to their success.

Inevitably, because of its image and above-ground notoriety, after two years "the people who pride themselves on being one dance ahead had moved on to the private clubs . . . leaving Le Jardin to the people."[30] According to *Rolling Stone*'s Ed McCormack, this new crowd was still pretty freaky: "At Le Jardin, the music commands a snaking daisy chain of dancers through pelvic puppet paces as the atmosphere grows heady with the adrenaline incense of Brut cologne and a thousand amyl nitrate poppers, each lending its queasy aphrodisiac crush to the whole mind-boggling, switch-hitting group grope going on out there on the floor. After all, this is the place where the gamut of dress runs from Pierre Cardin suits to silver costume clothing, from Halston originals to backless halters, through all the shades, cycles and fetishes of chic, camp and queer, until it culminates in the truly bizarre ensemble of one muscular young madman who sports a leather aviator's cap, smoked Captain Midnight goggles and red plastic clothespins clamped onto his bare nipples, squeezing them out into two little ouch-drops of excruciating S&M ecstasy while he goes limpidly gazonkers out on the dance floor."[31] Soon enough, though, the remaining scenesters and pansexuals left for good, and Le Jardin was almost exclusively populated by square Long Islanders and secretaries from New Jersey in Zodiac T-shirts and Jordache jeans. The club had been taken over by the dreaded bridge-and-tunnel crowd.

Le Jardin may have been disco's first truly mixed club, but maintaining the right social mixture is a precarious balancing act: Let in too many of the "wrong" people and the vibe is destroyed; let the "right" people dominate the club and the spirit of communion becomes nothing but an incestuous love-in. Underground dance cultures have always had a problematic relationship with the mainstream, and even though it didn't really have any utopian dreams to protect, this was particularly true of disco because of its roots as a refuge for the pariahs of straight society. The tug-of-war between exclusivity and inclusivity reached its peak in 1977 when "The head of the New York State Liquor Authority here has again warned disco owners and operators that some of their admission policies may infringe on the constituional rights of patrons and could, as a result, lead to revocation of their license . . . Laurence J. Gedda's new warning comes in the wake of reports that many New York clubs still scrutinize their patrons, and make admission difficult if not impossible. The practice, according to officials of the Authority, continues in spite of recent stepped-up action against such clubs."[32] Yet again, here was disco's essential tension: the urge to merge versus the desire to remain separate but equal. The problem for disco was that, unlike many underground dance cultures, the music was quintessentially mainstream; it didn't have to make any concessions to the tastes of Middle America. Its vision was nearly universally intoxicating and it was instantly apprehended by even middle-management types from Lima, Ohio.

When the tourists started coming en masse to Le Jardin, however, Bobby DJ jumped ship to a new club being opened by Addison's cousin, Maurice Brahms, where he would alternate with Jim Burgess. Infinity, at 653 Broadway in a former envelope factory, was a huge space (the dance floor was a block long) that featured a big pink neon penis right by the entrance. Naturally, when it opened in November 1975 it was intended to be a gay club, but Guttadaro by now had such a big reputation that he was the focus of a lot of press attention, and the unmarked door between Bleecker and Third streets was soon set upon by scene makers, mink-clad ladies and celebrities like Paul Newman, Gloria Vanderbilt, and Jack Nicholson. While there were still plenty of people like the guy in saddle shoes who "strapped a life-size female doll to his ankles and wrists and . . . moved lightly across the dance floor with her,"[33] the "scurve" ("singles who live with roommates on the Upper East Side or in the middle-class neighborhoods of New Jersey and Long Island, people drifting around and trying to get picked up"[34]) had set in. "Now middle-class young men cruise the banquettes each weekend, but the tone of the place is sufficiently gay that a woman can protect herself by adopting a fierce glare to indicate dykishness, or by staring fixedly at herself in the mirror, for self-absorption is respected here."[35] In fact, Infinity was so popular that the vibration on the dance floor caused the stylus on Bobby DJ's turntables to cut across his records, forcing him regularly to use his reel-to-reel backup tapes. Inspired by the suspension of a 1947 Packard, soundman Bob Casey solved the problem by suspending the turntables using rubber bands—a solution so successful that it became the industry standard for the next twenty years.

But Infinity was important for more than just its ingenious DJ setup. The interior of this enormous loft space was either left industrial or painted black and featured two-story art deco mirrors running along the side of the dance floor and one of the most expensive lighting systems ever installed in a nightclub. Infinity was the bridge between the loft aesthetic of the Gallery, Tenth Floor and, naturally, the Loft and the glitzy nostalgia that would soon characterize disco design during the boom. And the boom certainly took root at Infinity, so much so that even the wealth-porn rag *Forbes* ran a glowing feature on the club and Brahms. The music and the vibe, though, were every bit the equals of the staggering surroundings. "I was hit by the sight of all these lasers and guys dancing with their shirts off and these huge metallic fans catching the light," Ian Levine reminisces about his first visit to the club in 1977. "I can always remember, I walked in and they were playing Cerrone's 'Give Me Love,' which was a very 'me' record—you know, it had the strings and stuff. The thing about 'Give Me Love' is that it's a whole side of an album with three songs. Each one leads into the other one, and it stops at one point and the beat stops completely and nothing happens but just the strings, not even the hi-hat, just the strings going *dun-dun-dun-dun-dun-dun-dun d-d-dun-dun-dun-dun*, and when that happened the place went wild and there were two thousand hands in the air and screaming. I was sort of caught—it was like a photo catching a moment in time. I can still picture it today. It was quite magically electrifying . . . In all the years later and all the New York discos I went to—and I went to all of them— I never saw that moment re-created in quite the same way. That one moment of magic with Jim Burgess DJing at the Infinity really was quite special."[36]

After Le Jardin and Infinity came the deluge. By the end of 1975 there were an estimated five hundred discos in New York City alone and some ten thousand nationwide.[37] Part of the reason for the boom was simply that discos were extremely lucrative. As *Forbes* magazine explained, at Tramp's Discotheque in Washington, D.C., the owners spent $100,000 on renovating and converting the banquet room of the Carriage House restaurant. The club averaged two hundred to five hundred customers every night of the week, making an average gross of $900,000 a year. Of that gross, 20 percent was spent an alcohol and 35 percent on payroll and upkeep, leaving a cool profit margin of 45 percent, or $400,000. The discotheque business was so profitable that Mike O'Harro, one of the owners of Tramp's, talked about another of his ventures as becoming "the McDonald's of disco."[38]

Of course, disco was about more than just the economics. Disco was the first genre of music that was inextricably linked to the night-

TURN THE BEAT AROUND

club environment, so disco became more than just music, more than just something in the background, more than just a facilitator to sexual relationships. Disco became people's entire social lives. In Manhattan, some discotheques opened at lunchtime so that office workers chained to a nine-to-five regime could frolic for an hour in the disco environment without threatening their work performance with late nights and substance binges. La Martinique, a predominantly black disco at 57 West 57th Street, held lunchtime sessions every Friday from noon until 3 p.m., where junior executives in well-tailored polyester suits danced with women in pantsuits and six-inch platform shoes and enjoyed a buffet of cold cuts, salad, and fruit. Meanwhile, across the Hudson, "[a]t dawn in New Jersey, the disco scene is cranking into high gear. If you still want to dance after the bars close, if you need a disco booster shot to carry you into the next day, there are the disco breakfast clubs, places like the Second Half in Clifton, the Last Resort in Bloomfield and Long Branch both. These places will pound Barry White into your synapses right while you're chowing down on your bacon and eggs."[39] In other cities the disco not only fulfilled a social role but also acted as a hub for business networking. "In a pace-setting Sun Belt city like Atlanta, the disco functions as a multimedia melting pot," Newsweek magazine proclaimed. "At predominantly black and swinging Cisco's disco, leading figures in the local news come in once a week to answer questions. 'Here,' says Jim Wright, publisher of Lovely Atlanta magazine, 'discos have been the most viable means politicians and businessmen have found to meet the necessary people they need to make their businesses go.'"[40]

The rise of the discotheque paralleled the growth of the service economy in the 1970s. With America making its shockingly rapid transition from a manufacturing to a postindustrial society (particularly in New York City with the decimation of its industrial base in the '60s and '70s), discotheques, many of which were situated in abandoned factories and warehouses, were recolonizing the dead industrial space, replacing the production of goods with the production of illusions. The economy was in tatters and people wanted to do what they did during the Great Depression—dance. Just as the Depression saw the heyday of grand pleasure palaces like the Savoy Ballroom in Harlem and Midtown's Roseland Ballroom, the postindustrial, inflationary '70s spawned their own fantasy factories, combining nostalgia and extravagance with a devil-may-care attitude that not only perfectly summed up the times, but also foreshadowed the bleakness of what was on the horizon. Inflation had turned America from the land of prim, gray, thrifty, virtuous savers into a land of profligate thrill seekers, betting on both the past and the future with the right now.[41] In *The Culture of Narcissism*, Christopher Lasch wrote that America had become detached from a sense of time, that the past was no longer informing people's actions or their understanding of events. "Instead," he wrote, "we had only nostalgia, a past built of symbol and sentiment, and readily exploited as marketable commodity. Bourgeois values, on the other hand, had so eroded (an inflationary economy abetted the cultural shift) that we lived without a sense of the future as well. Indefinite hedonism thus came to dominate the modern psyche. 'Restless, perpetually unsatisfied desire' moved mass society on its rudderless course."[42]

By November 1974, discotheques like Le Jardin, the Gallery, and Hollywood (located on the site of the old Peppermint Lounge) were such a force that they were influencing not only what was being played on radio but also how the records were being played. In response to the growing popularity of the nightclubs, New York FM station WPIX started the world's first disco radio program that month. Disco 102 was hosted by Steve Andrews every Saturday night from 8 p.m. to midnight and aired songs that were being played in the city's discos. While Andrews didn't blend or mix like the club DJs, he didn't play any jingles and his between-song patter was kept to a minimum to better replicate a club atmosphere. This format was soon exported to Boston and then rapidly throughout the country, with varying degrees of success.

Although the disco bug was spreading across the country at an alarming rate, with hotel chains like Ramada trying out discotheques in far-flung locales like Fargo, North Dakota (with three phones to the DJ booth placed througout the lounge so that people could make requests), in an effort to boost revenue,[43] New York (and even then only a small fraction of the Big Apple's vast clubbing scene) was still calling all the shots. "In New York, the gay discos still influence the sound," Tom Moulton reported in *Billboard*. "You'll find the gay discos are much more into things they're not familiar with, whereas in the straight discos, people still feel they have to hear something they're familiar with."[44] Even in major music cities like Los Angeles, Chicago, San Francisco, and Boston (with the exception of DJs John Luongo and Jimmy Stuard), the clubs' music programming was nowhere near as sophisticated or up-to-the-minute as New York and was largely dependent on the audiences' familiarity with the music to generate any dance floor atmosphere.[45] The one major exception was Miami. Part of the problem for DJs outside of the Big Apple was the difficulty in obtaining promotional copies of new records in order to keep right up-to-date. DJs in Miami, though, were very well served by the city's dominant independent distributor and label complex, Henry Stone's T.K. Records empire.[46]

Henry Stone was born in 1921 in the Bronx, and when his father died in 1929 he was sent to an orphanage. As a kid he fell in love with the sound of Louis Armstrong and started playing the trumpet. While in basic training in New Jersey, he played trumpet in the army's first integrated band. When he was discharged after World War II, he became a traveling salesman for the L.A.-based Modern Records. Settling in south Florida, he set up his own Rockin' and Glory labels in the early 1950s and started producing records as well, including early sessions with Ray Charles and the vocal group the Charms. After setting up Tone Distribution at the end of the decade, he started the Dade and Glades labels and recruited Steve Alaimo and Brad Shapiro to work as producers/A&R men for his various labels. Like Stone, Alaimo and Shapiro were both white fans of black music, and the integrated studio followed the pattern set by other Southern soul studios like Stax and Fame in Memphis and Muscle Shoals in Alabama.

In the late '60s, a singer called Terry Kane built an eight-track studio above the Tone Distribution offices in the run-down Miami suburb of Hialeah, and Stone would let some of the young employees who worked in his warehouse use the studio at night during downtime. Two of these kids were Richard Finch and Harry Wayne Casey. Casey had heard the Bahamian Carnival music, junkanoo (similar to the music made by New Orleans's Mardi Gras Indians with its cowbell percussion, whistles, and goat-skin goombay drums), and had the idea to integrate it with more straightforward R&B rhythms. Calling themselves KC and the Sunshine Junkanoo Band, in 1973 Casey (KC), Finch, and members of the multiracial studio band recorded what would become the first release on Stone's new T.K. label. "Blow Your Whistle" was a slightly strange mixture of an out-of-date soul bass line and drums with jingling percussion roiling underneath until the dams burst during the whistle-blowing breaks. Despite its awkwardness, the record's Carnival vibes worked perfectly in a disco context, and thanks to this exposure the record reached #15 on the R&B chart. Its similarly styled but funkier follow-ups (released as KC and the Sunshine Band), "Sound Your Funky Horn" and "Queen of Clubs," were also big hits in the United Kingdom.

While their band was boosting R&B with heavily syncopated Caribbean percussion, Casey and Finch went the other direction with a song they wrote in 1974 called "Rock Your Baby." Gone was the party vibe of the KC and the Sunshine Band records and in its place was the proto–drum machine beat familiar from Timmy Thomas's "Why Can't We Live Together?" The song was originally intended for KC and the Sunshine Band, but it was in too high a pitch for KC to sing, so they offered it to Betty Wright and Gwen McCrae, two female singers with T.K.-associated labels, but they both turned it down. McCrae's husband, George, was then offered the song. While its simplicity was the diametric opposite of the lush records from Philadelphia and Barry White, "Rock Your Baby" wasn't exactly straightahead soul/R&B either. McCrae sang it as if in a reverie, his dreamy vocals playing off perfectly against the cotton-ball keyboards. This strangely novel articulation of ecstasy and its faint trade-wind lilt made "Rock Your Baby" a huge hit not only among disco tastemakers always on the lookout for visions of pleasure outside of the straight and narrow but also among the general public, who made it the third American pop number one in less than a year (after Love Unlimited Orchestra's "Love's Theme" and the Hues Corporation's "Rock the Boat") whose success was directly attributable to the discotheques.

McCrae's chart success paved the way for the mainstream breakthrough of KC and the Sunshine Band. And what a breakthrough it was. Until *Saturday Night Fever* made the Bee Gees superstars, KC and the Sunshine Band were the undisputed kings of disco. "Get Down Tonight," "That's the Way (I Like It)," "(Shake, Shake, Shake) Shake Your Booty," and "I'm Your Boogie Man" were all pop

#1s between 1975 and 1977, and "Keep It Comin' Love" reached #2. KC and the Sunshine Band's bouncy, bubble-headed enthusiasm and slightly square approach (those horns!) to black slang were two things that gave disco its bad name. While KC's background in the Pentecostal church perhaps had something to do with the band's singles bar straightness, it also gave him some honest-to-goodness vocal chops, and it was clear that the members were not some Johnny-come-latelies capitalizing on a trend. They loved the music, and their enthusiasm, however ungainly, was infectious.

T.K. had more dance floor success with the Caribbean vibe started by KC and the Sunshine Band in the form of records like Ralph McDonald's "Calypso Breakdown," but the label had all disco bases covered with funky disco from Jimmy "Bo" Horne (also produced by Casey) and T-Connection, straight-ahead disco from Celi Bee & the Buzzy Bunch, Peter Brown, Foxy, Anita Ward, and Joe Thomas, and Eurodisco from Kebekelektrik, USA-European Connection, and Voyage. While T.K. was one of the disco era's biggest success stories, it was also one of the most spectacular failures. When the antidisco backlash reached critical mass in 1979, T.K. sank seemingly without a trace and declared bankruptcy in 1981.

With Stone's forty-year presence on the R&B scene, T.K. maintained connections with the soul world, recording James Brown and providing homes for the side projects of MFSB/Salsoul Orchestra players Ron Kersey (Wild Honey) and Bobby Eli (Eli's Second Coming). However, this was a rarity among primarily disco-oriented organizations. In the spring of 1973, MFSB's Norman Harris produced a single for a new singer named Gloria Gaynor for Columbia Records. "Honeybee" was a strange mix of trademark Philly soul and a buzzing fuzz guitar, imitating the title's insect, that sounded like it was played by a '60s garage band. It was an uncomfortable meeting and the record tanked. After the disc's failure, the rights reverted to Gaynor's manager, Jay Ellis, who had discovered Gaynor earlier that year while she was working at the Wagon Wheel Club on Forty-fifth Street in Manhattan. Ellis had recently set up DCA (Disco Corporation of America) with former Tommy James and the Shondells producer Meco Monardo and Motown engineer Tony Bongiovi, and the production team had hit immediately with Don Downing's "Lonely Nights, Lonely Days." DCA decided to tinker with "Honeybee" and kept the buzzing guitar (but placed way down in the mix), the strings, and Earl Young's drums, but changed the bass line, added new instruments, and generally smoothed out the record. The record was rereleased (as "Honey Bee") in April 1974 on MGM, and it became a modest R&B hit and an enormous disco hit. While the sound of Philadelphia was revered among the early disco pioneers, the newcomers felt they knew better and brought in Broadway arrangers to give dance music a classic pop makeover. The result was the ersatz showbiz of variety shows and Eurovision telecasts with Earl Young's Philly drums reduced to nothing but that hissing hi-hat sound and Norman Harris's jazzy guitar licks remade as "single muffled note" riffs that Monardo called "bubble" guitar.[47] While this formula paid dividends on the pop charts and on more mainstream dance floors with records like Gaynor's "Never Can Say Goodbye," Carol Douglas's "Doctor's Orders," and Don Downing's "Dreamworld," a bunch of white guys weaned on classical music and making their living churning out bubblegum pop hits scribbling over one of the sacrosanct soul forms alienated both the R&B community and the more hard-core disco scene.

From the time disco entered the mainstream, such racial tension became commonplace. The ruptures of disco's racial politics were personified by Vicki Sue Robinson. Robinson was born in Philadelphia in 1955 to a folk singer mother who was a Russian Jew of French-Canadian descent and an actor father who was black with Scots blood. When she was ten, the family moved to Harlem, where she studied acting and dancing at the radical theater school, the Neighborhood Playhouse, while occasionally singing alongside such folk

---

"WHOOP! WHOOP!"

As the Beastie Boys said, "'Whoop! Whoop!' is the disco call." While an exaggerated "paarrtaayy" was early disco's most recognizable sonic hallmark, the high-pitched "Whoop! Whoop!" was undoubtedly the disco craze's signature sound. Ironically, the sound (albeit at a lower pitch than what would become the norm) was first used by the jazz-funk band the Blackbyrds on "Party Land" from their 1976 album *Unfinished Business* and was something that they probably picked up from the crowd at one of their gigs. Mastermind's "Hustle Bus Stop" from 1977 was the next record to use the sound, but, as Davitt Sigerson notes, "The fad only really got going in the spring of 1978 with two pop/disco hits: 'The Groove Line'

legends as Pete Seeger and Woody Guthrie. She soon appeared in the original Broadway productions of *Hair* and *Jesus Christ Superstar*, and went to Japan to model but found herself singing with Japanese Prog rockers Sadistic Mika Band instead. On her return to New York she was discovered by journeyman producer Warren Schatz, and they hit immediately with the peerless "Turn the Beat Around." The record was the culmination of everything that had been coalescing as "disco" since it went above ground in 1973: the quasi-Latin percussion runs (courtesy of Carlos Martin), the soaring strings, the hi-hat sound created by Earl Young, the thumping bass, the pop arrangement colliding with soul imperatives, the mixture of Broadway phrasing with churchy inflections, the showbiz razzmatazz somehow adding something to the "authentic" melisma. How could something so obviously informed by Andrew Lloyd Webber be so damn funky, so uplifting? "I've had some weird happenings behind that color thing, people not knowing how to deal with it, thinking it's a white girl trying to sing black," Robinson told journalist Denise Hall in 1976. "As far as I'm concerned, I'm just doing what I'm doing."[48] What she was doing was laying out in the plainest terms possible disco's poetics and intimating that, even during a period of intense corporatization, where the bean counters who run the music biz held sway, disco could transcend even the hollowest of motives amd the thorniest of contradictions as long as the drummer hit that *rat-tat-tat-tat* on the drum.

Records like "The Hustle," "Turn the Beat Around," "Get Down Tonight," Thelma Houston's "Don't Leave Me This Way," Diana Ross's "Love Hangover," Johnnie Taylor's "Disco Lady," and the

---

by Heatwave, and 'Let's All Chant' by the Michael Zager Band."[49] After these two records managed to connote dance floor revelry with this simple sonic phrase, copycat records flooded the market: Foxy's "Get Off," Teddy Pendergrass's "Get Up, Get Down, Get Funky, Get Loose," Kleer's "Keep Your Body Workin'," Sun's "Sun Is Here," and Rick James's "Be My Lady," to name a few. The "Whoop! Whoop!" led directly to that other late disco hallmark, the high-pitched "Boo!" of the synth toms used on records like Anita Ward's "Ring My Bell," Flakes' "Sugar Frosted Lover," Debbie Jacobs's "Hot Hot (Give It All You Got)," Kelly Marie's "Feels Like I'm in Love," Love Deluxe's "Here Comes That Sound Again," and Arpeggio's "Love and Desire."

Miracles' "Love Machine" staked disco's claim on the pop charts, and by 1976 it was a big enough genre to have recognized subgenres: East Coast funk (Brass Construction, Mass Production, T-Connection, Slave, Brainstorm), which fused disco's galloping drums and thumping bass lines with the vocal chants, horn blares, and off-beat rhythm guitar and keyboard riffs of funk; East Coast disco (Gloria Gaynor), described by Tom Moulton as, "It's like traffic, fast with sudden jerks, and the lights changing quickly. You could walk down the street to those records in New York. But anywhere else, you'd have to *run*"[50]; sophisto soul (Love Unlimited, Gene Page, Van McCoy); the Miami sound (KC and the Sunshine Band); and West Coast disco (the Originals), which combined Philly touches with more traditional R&B-styled horn charts and arrangements. However, it wouldn't be until 1977 that disco would make the full-on transformation into discomania.

The biggest disco artifact of them all was *Saturday Night Fever*, and it was a lie. Released in December 1977, *Saturday Night Fever* told the story of Tony Manero (played by John Travolta), a Brooklyn kid caught in a dead-end life whose only joy is going to the disco on the weekend and dancing away his blues. The movie was a tough and unforgiving look at the constrictions of working-class life, and Travolta was electric as Manero. The film's opening shots of Travolta strutting down Ridge Boulevard in tight trousers to the undeniable groove of the Bee Gees' "Stayin' Alive" ensured that *Saturday Night Fever* would have more popular culture impact than any movie since *Gone With the Wind*. The soundtrack, which was dominated by the Bee Gees' helium falsettos and producer Arif Mardin's pop polish, tempered director John Badham's rugged, masculine movie, allowing a younger, female audience into an otherwise forbidding film world. With its timeless story line and broad-based appeal, *Saturday Night Fever* was a "disco movie" made for a decidedly nondisco audience; change the soundtrack and the setting and it could have been virtually any teen movie from *Rebel Without a Cause* to *Save the Last Dance*. *Saturday Night Fever* grossed over $100 million at U.S. box offices, and by end of 1978 the soundtrack had sold thirty million albums and become the biggest-selling record of all time (until Michael Jackson's *Thriller* knocked it out of the top spot). Like the movie, the *Saturday Night Fever* soundtrack was "disco" only in quotation marks. The music had most of the hallmarks of disco—the bouncy bass lines, the cod-Latin percussion, unmacho male singers, etc.—but it was really the kind of pure pop that works in any era given a rhinestone spit shine. The combination of the Bee Gees' (and Mardin's) pop perfection, Travolta's iconic performance, and the commercial synergy between film and soundtrack made not only *Saturday Night Fever* inescapable but also disco, which became the subject of hi-beam media focus like never before, unavoidable as a whole.

The movie, which was produced by Robert Stigwood's RSO (it's no small irony that RSO also released Rick Dees and His Cast of Idiots' infernal novelty record "Disco Duck" in 1976), was based on an article that had appeared in *New York* magazine in June 1976. "Tribal Rites of the New Saturday Night" was written by Nik Cohn, a British journalist originally from Northern Ireland who had only recently moved to New York. The article allegedly chronicled the rising discotheque culture of New York's outer boroughs, but anyone with even a passing knowledge of British youth culture would have smelled a rat from the very first sentence.

"Vincent was the very best dancer in Bay Ridge—the ultimate Face," Cohn began. "He owned 14 floral shirts, eight pairs of shoes, three overcoats, and had appeared on *American Bandstand*." Becoming a "Face" was, of course, tantamount to becoming a saint in British Mod culture; that this, or Vincent's impressive wardrobe, had anything to do with Bay Ridge, Brooklyn, was nothing but pure fantasy. Cohn continues: "Purity. A sacrament. In their own style, the Faces were true ascetics: stern, devoted, incorruptible."[51] Again, Cohn betrays his frame of reference with the use of "incorruptible," long a term in the Mod/football hooligan lexicon. Cohn was essentially transplanting British youth culture to New York, merely trading a Cockney accent for heavy Brooklynese. The story's Mod aspects were retained in the film, right down to Tony Manero's dancing, which seemed to be taken from Northern Soul. Northern Soul dancing was all about individuality, with dancers performing athletic spins and leaps; disco dancing was fundamentally communal, not the grandstanding displayed by Manero.

Of course, frameworks are inescapable in journalism or writing screenplays: All knowledge must be processed according to some ground rules. If that's all "Tribal Rites of the New Saturday Night" was, it would be merely another event in the long history of Britons misinterpreting American popular culture and making a fortune out of it. However, the story was a bold-faced lie. "My story was a fraud," Cohn finally admitted two decades later. "I'd only recently arrived in New York. Far from being steeped in Brooklyn street life, I hardly knew the place. As for Vincent, my story's hero, he was largely inspired by a Shepherd's Bush mod whom I'd known in the Sixties, a one-time king of the Goldhawk Road."[52]

Unsurprisingly, for a movie whose origins are so contested, *Saturday Night Fever* generated a wide range of interpretations. "In *Saturday Night Fever*, John Travolta decides that the only way that he can transcend his boring life is to become the best dancer in the city," wrote journalist Jon Savage. "To achieve this individuality, however, he has to negate his own personality: the dancing steps required of a Disco champion are so formulaic that to excel he must become an automaton. This was the true blankness to which Punks never came close. The hedonism propagated by Disco was more immediately subversive of established morality."[53] On the other hand, historian Peter Carroll stated that "*Saturday Night Fever* reinforced a conservative message of conformity, expensive dress, and self-discipline. Only by embracing these traditional American values could the youthful ethnic hero, played by John Travolta, hope to attain the upward mobility implied in leaving his working-class origins in Brooklyn for a new life in Mahattan."[54] Still further, Chic's Nile Rodgers proclaims, "I just think *Saturday Night Fever* is genius. It's about a very racist kind of community, and he just deals with it in such a simplistic, wonderful way. He doesn't change and become an intellectual. He changes and becomes an open-minded human being by saying something like, 'That's what it's all about: Because my father gets dumped on, he gets home and dumps on my mother, then she's gotta dump on me, then we gotta dump on the Spics because we gotta dump on somebody, and then they dump on the blacks,' or whatever. It was just a very simplistic but accurate way of saying that racism exists and unfairness exists: 'How could you give the trophy to us when we're not nearly on the level of the Puerto Ricans, but you just gave it to me because I'm a homeboy, I'm like you, I'm white, I'm Italian, I'm from the neighborhood, but these Puerto Rican guys come in and venture into our community and are better than we are and we can't acknowledge the fact that they're better.' And that was so powerful. Very few people go home with that message, but that's the message of the film. That's what the movie was all about. In New York, we used to call these Italian guys 'hitters,' so this hitter becomes an open-minded, broad-thinking human being who has contradictions in his world and in his life, but through music and dance he's transformed. It's easy to say it's super-fluous because it's disco, but that's just not true. Those songs are powerful; they tell the story. When they use 'More Than a Woman' and 'You Should Be Dancing' and 'Disco Inferno,' that's serious stuff. That's just as relevant and as valid—and I know people don't like to hear stuff like this—as when the Sex Pistols are delivering a message or when Pink Floyd is delivering a message or when the Beatles are delivering a message. This is politically, socially relevant stuff, and it's just a reflection of the times."[55]

Despite its perfidious heart, *Saturday Night Fever* nailed one of disco's most perplexing conundrums. While Cohn's story was a fake, the truth was that disco was spreading like wildfire in the white ethnic communities of New York's outer boroughs. These were the children and younger brothers of the construction workers who had only a few years earlier gone on a rampage against most of disco's main constituents during the Hard Hat Riots. Now Staten Islander Tony Pagano was telling Ed McCormack, "What my old man doesn't understand is that you don't have to be a fag to be into this scene . . . My old man doesn't understand that dancing is not a tight-assed, uptight sex role scene. It's just a way of communicating with people you might not have anything to say to if you sat down to talk."[56]

"Broadly speaking, the typical New York discotheque DJ is young (between 18 and 30), Italian, and gay," journalist Vince Aletti declared in 1975. "The prime variable is 'Italian,' because there are a large number of black and Latin DJs; 'gay' is less variable, but here it's more a description of sensibility than sexual preference."[57] Remarkably, almost all of the important early disco DJs were of Italian extraction: Francis Grasso, David Mancuso, Nicky Siano, Michael Cappello, Steve D'Aquisto, Tom Savarese, Bobby DJ Guttadaro, Frankie Strivelli, and Hippopotamus's Richard Pampianelli. For whatever reason, Italian Americans have played a significant role in America's dance music culture from the teen-pop dance crazes that came out of the Philadelphia hit machines in the early '60s (Frankie Avalon, Fabian, etc.) through the disco and freestyle scenes of the '70s and '80s to the House and Techno records from New York's Tommy Musto, Frankie Bones, and Joey Beltram. While Italian Americans mostly from Brooklyn largely created disco from scratch, the two men most responsible for putting disco over the top in every sense of the phrase were Jews from Queens.

> The atmosphere inside starts to take you over
> Music and fantasy
> I'm just inside the door at 54
> Faces in the crowd
> Fashions are too chic
> Music playing loud at 54.
>
> —Bob McGilpin, "54"

> At Studio 54, waiting at the door
> Can't get in, just can't win.
>
> —Dennis Parker, "New York By Night"

In November 1977, *New York Times* journalist Anna Quindlen described a typical Saturday night on the block of West Fifty-fourth Street between Broadway and Eighth Avenue as club owner Steve Rubell was performing the nightworld rite of social engineering that he called "tossing a salad." "[H]undreds crowd the street, whining the name of Mr. Rubell," she wrote. "With index fingers raised in a gesture of reluctant supplication usually reserved for cab drivers on rainy nights and waiters in over-priced French restaurants, they repeat over and over again, 'Steven . . . Steve . . .' while staff members, resembling well-groomed guard dogs, push the overanxious back and a huge man named Big George stands by, a huge disincentive to violence."[58] The throng was desperate to be anointed with Rubell's decree of grace and be allowed past the fabled velvet ropes into the world's most famous pleasure dome where there was a possibility that they might snort coke off of Truman Capote's monocle or watch someone pleasure the wife of the prime minister of Canada. "'I'll let in anyone who looks like they'll make things fun,' [Rubell] says, standing behind the ropes and ignoring the repeated sound of his own name. 'We like some guys with guys because it makes the dance floor hot, you know? There are certain people who come that we know are good. But I'll tell you something—I wouldn't let my best friend in if he looked like an East Side singles guy.'"[59] This Shangri-la, of course, was Studio 54.

Discotheques started off as places where the elite could hide themselves from the rest of the world and confront on their own terms the youth culture of rock and roll that would help destroy their olde worlde. But as the discotheque concept was translated into a language that long-suffering New Yorkers could understand, the discotheque became more egalitarian and less stuffy, and people actually danced. It was only a matter of time, though, before the world of privilege would have its revenge on the hoi polloi. It came in the shape of the most famous discotheque of 'em all, and from two men who would have even excluded themselves from the club.[60]

Steve Rubell and Ian Schrager were two fairly small-time restaurant owners from deepest, darkest Brooklyn who dreamed of the big time and were desperate to escape what they saw as their lowly origins. In other words, they were quintessential bridge and tunnelers out for revenge on the world that excluded them—except that the only revenge they ever exacted was on the world that they came from. Their first entry into New York's nightworld was the Enchanted Garden, a discotheque housed in an eleven-room mansion situated on city-owned land bordering the golf course in Douglaston, Queens (an area often disparagingly referred to as "the gateway to Great Neck"), which opened in 1975. The club was popular for its theme nights ("Island of Paradise" with a luau, hula dancers, palm trees, and fire dancers; "Arabian Nights" with llamas, camels, and a snake charmer) and its "love-nest room," which had couches the size of beds and a gazebo filled with stuffed birds—"installed after $4,000 worth of live ones died from the constantly changing temperatures."[61] Aside from the fact that the club was about as far east as you could go in New York City without actually setting foot in suburban Long Island, the Enchanted Garden had the further drawback of being directly below the flight path into JFK International Airport. Nevertheless, the Enchanted Garden attracted a fair bit of notoriety and, in Paul Casella, it had one of the finest DJs in the city. However, it wasn't only the 747s passing over the club that were giving Rubell and Schrager headaches. The wannabe suburbanites of Douglaston hated the club and launched a sustained campaign aimed at shutting it down. Eventually, the city's Parks Department decided to threaten Rubell and Schrager with eviction, and the duo were soon searching around for a place in Manhattan itself.

They were introduced by club promoter Carmen D'Alessio to a consortium trying to buy an old theater/television studio at 254 West 54th Street in order to turn it into a nightclub. Rubell and Schrager loved the space, and when that group lost most of its financing, Rubell and Schrager outmaneuvered the remaining member (paying him off with a finder's fee of $1,000) and took over the project that was already called Studio 54. The project was unprecedented in terms of both scale and symbolism. Studio 54 dwarfed Infinity not only in size and money lavished on its design but also in ambition. Previously, discotheques had recolonized the dead spaces left by deindustrialization and recession; they breathed new life into abandoned warehouses and decrepit hotels. But Studio 54 was a bold display of disco's ascendancy over New York's most famous entertainment industries: Broadway and television. With the opening of Studio 54, the discotheque had established itself definitively as New York's principal manufacturer of dreams. Disco had become theater.

And what an extraordinary dream Studio 54 proffered. As the chairman of the Federal Reserve Board Paul Volcker was announcing that "the standard of living for the average American has got to decline,"[62] Studio 54 was boldly and defiantly declaring the exact opposite. Studio 54 was excess as triumphalism, glitz for glitz's sake: Why have one set when you can change it every other week? More than anyone else, Rubell and Schrager understood disco's perverse economic imperative—you need to spend money in order to make money. The club's design was largely overseen by D'Alessio, and the work was carried out by theater professionals and environmental lighting engineers rather than nightclub experts, giving it a dazzle and pop baroqueness that nightworld's mostly functional spaces could only dream of. The first thing you saw as you entered Studio 54's hallowed doors and its burgundy-carpeted lobby was a 1950s camera boom left over from the old days—this was disco as showbiz, after all. Hovering over the dance floor was a wooden rendering of the man in the moon; at midnight, it would be lowered toward the crowd as a coke spoon shoveled flake into its nose while a string of lights fired up from its nostril to its eye. On the opposite side of the parqueted floor was a metal Aztec sun god that would spew smoke from the sides of its face. The dance floor was broken up by columns of multicolored lights that would flash throughout the night. There was a waterfall at the back of the dance floor, confetti guns that shot brightly colored paper over the club at peak times, and lavish flower arrangements throughout the club. The bartenders and busboys (including, in 1978, a twenty-one-year-old Alec Baldwin) all wore gray satin gym shorts and sleeveless T-shirts. D'Alessio was also responsible for booking the parties, and it was largely her fashion and celebrity contacts that made the guest list glitter with the same intensity as the club's interior. It was more than just the design and the A-list roster, though, that made Studio 54 special. The club's sound system was designed by disco's preeminent soundman, Richard Long, and Rubell and Schrager managed to lure Paul Casella's former spinning partner at Hollywood, Ritchie Kaczor, to the new club. Kaczor (who by 1979 was earning $50,000 a year and was the world's best-paid DJ) was generally acknowledged as one of the best beat mixers around, and his technical skills initially gave Studio 54 cachet among New York's clubbing cognoscenti, which was only reinforced when Rubell hired Nicky Siano as his alternate.

However, Rubell and Schrager were never particularly precious about the music; they simply wanted someone to play what effectively was background music that kept people dancing but wouldn't get in the way of the "scene." And if that someone had a great reputation, so much the better. Their vision was Le Jardin dressed to the nines, Infinity to the nth degree. When Kaczor dropped the needle on C.J. & Co.'s "Devil's Gun" on the evening of Tuesday, April 26, 1977, they achieved it tenfold. The nondescript block on the fringes of the theater district that had been largely left to the prostitutes and pimps prowling the area was suddenly overrun with limos and paparazzi. Cher, Brooke Shields, Donald Trump, Margaux Hemingway, and Bianca Jagger all showed up, but the chaos was so great that not only could neither Mick Jagger nor Frank Sinatra get inside, but even Carmen D'Alessio had trouble getting into her own party. The thousands of lesser luminaries stranded on the wrong side of the velvet ropes decided that they didn't need Rubell or Schrager's blessing to have their own party and promptly reenacted Sodom and Gomorrah by having an orgy on West Fifty-fourth Street.

Despite all the hoopla, the next few days at Studio 54 were dead, and Rubell and Schrager were getting anxious. That would all change on May 2, when the club held a birthday party for Bianca Jagger. The club—which was filled with white balloons and on one wall featured a light bulb display that spelled out "BIANCA" in huge letters—was fairly empty, with Mick Jagger gaily cavorting with Halston and Liza Minnelli (who had already become Studio regulars). As soon as Siano dropped the needle on the Rolling Stones' "Sympathy for the Devil," Bianca Jagger rode in on a white horse that Rubell had hired for the occasion led by a naked man "wearing" a body-painted tuxedo. The handful of paparazzi who had bothered to turn up went berserk, and the photo of Bianca on the white horse became one of the iconic images of the disco era. The photos appeared in the tabloid press across the world, and in a flash Studio 54's reputation was sealed. It had suddenly become the most talked-about disco in the world, the home of the outrageous, the place where everyone wanted to go, the center of the glitterball universe.

While Quindlen observed that, "Unlike the elegant La Folie, where the clientele sometimes seems moneyed and staid, or Hurrah's, where they seem merely idiosyncratic, or Regine's, whose ubiquitous celebrities and selectivity have given the impression of dancing right out of the common man's market, Studio 54 combines public figures with the wealthy and the unusual and throws in a good measure of the average to set them all off,"[63] Studio 54 was nevertheless the celebrity hotspot to end all celebrity hotspots. Rubell, in particular, was enamored of the new crowd he suddenly found himself traveling in, and with cloying enthusiasm somewhere between stalker and tireless self-publicist, he ceaselessly courted celebrities. Rubell set up the notorious downstairs VIP room, where anything and everything was readliy available; he made sure that celebs had a ready supply of their drugs of choice and ensured that alcohol was available to them even when Studio's liquor license was revoked; he would change the club's decor if a favored patron had a whim for a special party. Of course, nightclubs have always treated special customers well and bent over backward in order to accommodate celebrities, but there was something qualitatively different about Rubell's relentless pursuit of the famous, something bordering on blind worship. As Studio 54 historian Anthony Haden-Guest wrote, "It was the preliminary tremor of a social upheaval that would prove much more enduring than the populist revolution of the sixties: the coming of the Celebrity Culture."[64] Three years earlier *People* magazine had been launched as a mainstream, nonconfrontational version of supermarket tabloid tittle-tattle; Liz Smith's influential gossip column in the *Daily News* began in 1976; and Andy Warhol's *Interview* had been masquerading celebrity worship as art since 1969: This was the beginning of a ravenous, insatiable press desperate for stories to sell papers and magazines in a world oversaturated with media. Of course, gossip had been a part of journalism ever since Daniel Defoe started writing his column in *The Review* in 1704, but this was the beginning of gossip and celebrity running on its own momentum, the beginning of being famous just for being famous. For the previous 270 years, gossip had been principally about the social set and its "events," with the odd mention of film stars, but paralleling the course of nightclub history, gossip had become focused almost exclusively on the popocracy, and the Studio crowd fit the bill perfectly: Liza, Bianca, Halston, Andy, Truman—people whose best work was well behind them and were now just simply names. The antiestablishment hellions of the 1960s were now safely ensconced as members of a new aristocracy.

With such a unique environment, Studio 54 wasn't merely a playground for established celebs; it had the power to create its own: the septuagenarian dance floor diva Disco Sally and Rollerena, by day a Wall Street employee, by night a cross-dressing roller queen who skated around the floor in a wedding dress that sported a button reading, "How Dare You Presume I'm Heterosexual." Inevitably, even Studio's doorman, Marc Benecke, became a minor celebrity in his own right, starring in a short-lived Broadway production (Benecke's stand-in, Al Corley, became a star years later when he joined the cast of *Dynasty*). Of course, Rubell, a combination of genial host and overeager puppy, became the biggest star of all. The constant media attention went to his head, and very quickly his doorway judgments on who was to be let into his kingdom became something a bit more pernicious than merely "tossing a salad." Rubell acted with the hauteur of a member of the nobility, either completely ignoring or lashing out at the crowd with cynical comments. But disco (at least not this version) was never really about celebrity; it was about the comforting anonymity of belonging to a community, the freedom of having a shared identity that could now be shouted across a crowded dance floor. Nevertheless, the opulent fantasyscapes of places like Studio 54 were playgrounds of sexuality and identity. As journalist Sally Helgesen wrote of René, a makeup artist at the quintessential disco boutique Fiorucci, "René is only 21, but he says he's been going to discos four nights a week for eight years, before the straight crowd picked up on the scene. He likes only the fanciest places, where he can wear the most outrageous costumes and live out whatever fantasy might strike him on a particular evening."[65]

However, it was impossible for anyone to reconcile disco's liberationist aspects with the fact that these disco "revolutionaries" were partying with people like Imelda Marcos, Roy Cohn, and Betty Ford. It was easier just to run a picture of Margaret Trudeau, the scandalously young wife of Canadian Prime Minister Pierre Trudeau, who was photographed at Studio 54 sans underwear on May 22, 1979, the night before her husband lost a reelection bid. Maybe this was the conservative revolution that William Safire had predicted

---

THE STORY OF "I WILL SURVIVE"

Studio 54 will always be remembered for cocaine in the back room with Liza, Andy, and Halston, but it wasn't merely about excess and decadence. On occasion, it was actually about the music, and none more important than the night in 1978 when Ritchie Kaczor decided to play (with a little encouragement from Polydor A&R man Rick Stevens) the B side of Gloria Gaynor's most recent single, a cover of Clout's "Substitute." When he played it, nearly everyone left the dance floor, but Kaczor persisted, and within a few more spins "I Will Survive" was the biggest record at Studio. The buzz was such that soon every disco in New York was playing it, and the record company rereleased the single with "I Will Survive" as the A side. It eventually went to #1 in just about every country in the world. Its association with Studio 54 may have been why it initially became a dance floor hit, but the record had everything a great disco record is supposed to have: full-throated gospel release

when he first saw the hustle in 1975. As Charles Kaiser wrote, "Everything about the ambience of Studio 54 made it the antithesis of the spirit of the sixties. There was certainly nothing democratic about it. Frank Rich remembered that 'to be there as a peon, as I was on a few occasions, was to feel that the Continental Baths crowd had finally turned nasty toward the intruding straights and was determined to make them pay (with overpriced drinks and condescending treatment). Even as everyone was telling you that this was where the action was, you felt that the real action, not all of it appetizing, was somewhere in the dark periphery, out of view—and kept there, to make you feel left out.'"[66]

The real action at Studio 54 was money, and it was in the dark periphery, out of view, tucked into Hefty bags hidden in the walls, in crawlspaces, and in between plumbing pipes. At 9:30 a.m. on December 14, 1978, acting on a tip from a disgruntled employee, officers of the IRS and the Organized Crime Strike Force raided Studio 54 and found the Hefty bags, which contained almost $1 million in cash. Not content with hobnobbing with the rich and famous, Rubell and Schrager were taking their money—skimming $5 million a year, 80 percent of the club's gross by one estimate. The authorities also found evidence that Rubell and Schrager were paying off Mob loansharker Sam Jacobson, but instead of agreeing to the plea bargain deal offered to them if they turned over evidence on Jacobson, Rubell and Schrager said that they had information

---

complemented by the surging bass line, dramatic strings, hissing hi-hats, and a hint of Broadway razzmatazz. Although Gaynor was crowned the "Queen of Disco" after dance floor favorites like "Honey Bee," "Never Can Say Goodbye," and "Casanova Brown," "I Will Survive" was one of those exceedingly rare records that are more like forces of nature than pop hits. While the song has become something of a feminist anthem, Gaynor says that "When I sang 'I Will Survive' I was relating it to my recovery from spine surgery [after a fall while performing on stage in 1978]. And because the word was going around after my accident that the 'Queen of Disco is dead,' one of my main thoughts was that my career would survive! And in a funny way it was also, for me, to do with surviving the death of my mother. I know for most people the song is about abusive relationships and women asserting their independence of men and all that sort of thing and of course I have suffered in that way myself, but for some reason I was never thinking of that when I sang it."[67]

on narcotics use by White House chief of staff Hamilton Jordan. Ironically, the case against Jacobson collapsed, but by turning on the federal government, Rubell and Schrager doomed themselves to face the full force of the law on their income tax evasion charges. On January 18, 1980, they were each sentenced to three and a half years, fined $20,000, and received the opprobrium of the judge, who criticized their "tremendous arrogance."[68] Despite his protestations that he was "sorry," at his farewell party in March, Rubell serenaded his well-wishers with an out-of-tune rendition of "My Way."

Unwilling to be pushed aside by the outer borough interlopers, Maurice Brahms and John Addison decided to join forces on a club called New York New York. Located at 33 West 52nd Street between Fifth and Sixth avenues, the club was designed by Angelo Donghia, who created a space of cool white and gray elegance, with color provided by red lacquer tabletops and palm trees both real and neon. The club opened a few weeks after Studio 54 and was conceived of as its high-class rival; or, as one employee put it, the club's "motif was clean taste."[69] Where Studio 54 merely occupied an old television studio, New York New York was "'the primetime slickly produced television variety show special' of discos."[70] The nightspot's opening night on May 18, 1977, was every bit the success that Studio's launch was, with throngs of celebrities both inside and left out in the cold. "In the middle of a number someone, somewhere, pushes a button and a cloud of smoke, scented with Fabergé perfume, rises to the waists of the assembled dancers," Anna Quindlen wrote of her visit to the club.[71] Unfortunately, this "fog" was as humid as its name implied, and it took the creases out of men's trousers. More successful was New York New York's light show: minnows of magenta, blue, white, and green light that darted around the club; a curtain of tiny beads of light that hung over the dance floor and reflected in the mirrors to create the club's vaunted "infinity effect." Like most variety show specials, however, New York New York's magic wore off almost immediately. Perhaps it was because Brahms and Addison were already established presences in Manhattan's nightworld and felt that they didn't need to bend over backward for celebrities the way

Rubell and Schrager did, or maybe it was that the overly conceptualized interior was too bright, too out in the open to allow the rich and famous to get up to nefarious activities the way they could in the relative darkness of Studio 54, or maybe it was that Studio really did have that je ne sais quoi that made it truly special. Whatever the reason, New York New York became the place that people who couldn't get into Studio 54 went to instead. "A great many of the men wear sport coats with shirts open at the collar and medallions hanging in the resulting hairy V's," Anna Quindlen wrote. "They outnumber the women substantially."[72] As if becoming the bridge and tunnelers' favorite nightspot wasn't enough of an indignity, New York New York failed to get the after-party for Martin Scorsese's film of the same name, and Liza Minnelli, one of the movie's stars, spent the night at Studio 54 much to Brahms and Addison's chagrin and the delight of the tabloids' gossip pages.

A similar fate almost befell the Times Square discotheque Xenon when it opened in June 1978. Located in the old Henry Miller Theater (the dance floor was where the stage used to be and the seats were replaced by leather banquettes) at 124 West 43rd Street, Xenon boasted a sixteen-channel sound system, the most expensive ever put in a club in New York, a spectacular light show, and a spaceship designed by Douglas Trumbull (who created the special effects in *Close Encounters of the Third Kind*) that was to descend from the ceiling and hover just above the dancers' heads. Xenon's first mission was aborted, however, when the spaceship didn't work and the light show was something less than advertised, and owners rock promoter Howard Stein and former European disco impresario Peppo Vanini decided to lick their wounds and start over. When it reopened in the autumn, Xenon became Studio's main rival in the celeb stakes, hosting parties for the likes of Warren Beatty, Pelé, Gregory Peck, Lauren Bacall, and Richard Avedon. Xenon even managed to lure away Disco Sally from Studio 54. Like Studio, Xenon was disco as theater. As one of the club's doormen told journalist Vita Miezitis, "If we have a number of celebrities or rich people inside, I will look for people who will entertain this group both in the way they are dressed and the show I think they will put on inside the club."[73] The proscenium of this disco theater was formed by two columns of light designed to look literally like pinball machines, while the stage setting was a number of garish neon frescoes surrounding the dance floor that depicted the New York skyline with a cowboy straddling the Brooklyn Bridge and King Kong beating his chest.

With the amount of attention generated by places like Xenon and Studio 54, by 1979 discotheques were spreading like the plague throughout the United States, each hoping that some of the sparkle would rub off on it. One thousand of these nightclubs were in the New York metropolitan area, but this isn't to say that the Big Apple had a monopoly on discotheque outrageousness. Perhaps inevitably, Tinseltown was New York's match in terms of over-the-top design: the DJ at L.A. discotheque Dillon's was fitted with a special harness so that he could fly over the crowd on the dance floor, while *Billboard* magazine described the decor of Hard Times Charlies as "an antiques collector's delight. Costing in excess of $150,000, it includes a DJ booth converted from an early 18th Century French elevator. A colorful carnival carousel hangs suspended over the dance floor. The seating features pews from old English churches, and there's an original marble and brass shoeshine parlor salvaged from Chicago's colorful past."[74]

Across the pond, however, clubs were much more sedate despite the tremendous influence the United Kingdom exerted over disco music. London's disco scene was shackled to its gentlemen's/workingmen's club roots thanks to the country's restrictive licensing laws and to the DJs, who couldn't respond to American disco culture because they were too busy fighting the musicians' union, which aggressively targeted DJs as job killers. The Big Smoke's most famous discotheques were the hopelessly staid aristo watering hole Annabel's in Berkeley Square and the Embassy in Old Bond Street. Although the Embassy was owned by Jeremy Norman, who published *Burke's Peerage*, it wasn't all old colonels reminiscing about the Raj and braying, horsey Sloanes, although they were there in abundance. It was essentially a smallish ballroom with a sunken dance floor surrounded by palm trees decorated with white mannequins. Après Studio 54, the club's busboys wore silk briefs and maybe shoes. "There are no particular dance steps in vogue," Andy Blackford wrote of a visit there. "The Hustle and the Bump were New York inventions and there's an implicit understanding among the London elite that New York is so far ahead in everything disco that to import its dances would be a transparent admission of failure."[75]

What the Embassy did have, though, was a DJ who could mix records. This was quite a rarity at the time—as late as 1979, there were only a few DJs in Britain who mixed, and most of those were American imports. "DJs were very primitive, you know, they would announce the records and have no concept of mixing and what disco's about," remembers Ian Levine, one of the only mixers in the country, who took over at Angels in Burnley when the Blackpool Mecca closed down in 1979. "The London DJs, in particular, were so entrenched in funk."[76] At places like Lacey Lady in Ilford, the Royalty in Southgate, the Goldmine in Canvey Island, Frenchie's in Camberley, Surrey, and Crackers in the West End, the music was almost exclusively soul-boy funk and jazz funk, records like Norman Connors's "Captain Connors," Bob James's "Westchester Lady," and Side Effect's "Always There." To further distance themselves from the more populist British disco scene, many of the DJs on the jazz-funk scene (Chris Hill, Greg Edwards, Robbie Vincent, Bob Jones, Tom Holland, etc.) banded together as the "soul mafia."

Meanwhile, on the Continent, the influence of the olde worlde discotheques still reigned. Although the European aristocracy had to spend the decade dodging the Red Brigade and Baader-Meinhof gang, the European discos of the '70s were no longer the basement hovels of old. They were pleasure palaces to compete with the most luxuriant of New York's beau monde nightclubs. The most splendid of these dolce vita dance halls was undoubtedly Rituel on the Costa Smeralda, the section of the Sardinian coast that the Aga Khan turned into a millionaire's playground in the '60s. Rituel was "a glistening white cave shaped like an amphitheatre, with successive tiers etched into the rock walls and strewn with hundreds of white pillows, upon which the rich recline in splendiferous near nudity. A slowly turning light machine fills the cave with vivid colored images, and at the lowest level of the cavern, on a tiny dance floor of ebony marble, gorgeous people move ever so slightly . . . If, God forbid, they should perspire, there is a rustic terrace reached through a hole in the cave's ceiling. From that lofty perch they can turn their brows toward sea breezes while they watch the moon over the calm Mediterranean."[77]

I'm hell on wheels, let's roll.   —Cher, "Hell on Wheels"

Can you do it on skates?   —Citi, "Can You Do It on Skates?"

Disco may have been fabulously glamorous and resplendently decadent, but it was also downright silly. And no aspect of disco culture was more ludicrous than roller disco. Perhaps because it was more proletarian than the high falutin world of Studio 54, more tailored for teenagers than twentysomething sophisticates, roller disco encapsulated the worst of the fadishness and velour-shirted mindlessness (with elbow and knee pads) of the 1970s. When it hit the mainstream thanks to the new polyurethane wheels that replaced the scraping and bumpiness of the old metal ones, the legend of Rollerena, the beloved blond bimbos of Venice Beach, the bizarre popularity of roller derby and Cher's "Hell on Wheels," roller disco spread across the world with the unrelenting fury of the pet rock. Suddenly, everywhere from Hixon, Tennessee (site of Skateland, which had one of the country's most expensive light shows), to Dunstable (home of the United Kingdom's first roller disco, the California, DJed by Peter Preston), there were pockmarked teens with Goody combs sticking out of the back pockets of their Toughskins and gamine women wearing rainbow-colored boob tubes, hot pants, and matching leg warmers trying to do the roll and rock or the coffee bean without dropping their glowsticks. Celebs the world over were boogying on wheels (Jack Nicholson had black boot skates with green neon tubing, and Cher had skates whose wheels lowered like the landing gear of an airplane); games manufacturer Gottlieb made a very popular "Roller Disco" pinball machine; there were at least three movies made and rush-released to capitalize on the trend, all of them nominees for the worst films ever made—*Roller Boogie* (starring Linda Blair), *Skatetown, U.S.A.* (featuring a stellar cast including Scott Baio, Flip Wilson, Ruth Buzzi, Maureen McCormick, Ron Palillo, Billy Barty [playing Flip Wilson's son!] and, in his first role on the silver screen, Patrick Swayze as Ace Johnson), and *Xanadu* (producer Alan Carr's car-crash of a musical with Olivia Newton-John and Gene Kelly)— and the legendary "Roller Disco" double episode of *CHiPs* (with guest stars like Leif Garrett, Jim Brown, Fred Williamson, *F-Troop's*

Larry Storch, and M*A*S*H's Larry Linville). The dark side of the roller-skating craze was conjured by movies like *The Warriors*, which featured gangs of roller-skating toughs terrorizing the Bronx, and an ad for Hostess Fruit Pies in which the Incredible Hulk rescues a town from the pillaging "Roller Disco Devils."

Inevitably, many of disco's early devotees hated roller disco and everything that it represented. As the disco scene was becoming ever more commercialized, a character in Andrew Holleran's *Dancer From the Dance* laments, "The music was atrocious: that roller-skating music they're turning out now that discos are big business."[78] Very few of the roller discos had liquor licenses and so attracted a much younger, teeny-bopper crowd than the standard discos. But the truth is that, like disco itself, roller disco had a history deeper and richer than its mainstream face would indicate. Roller skating was first developed in the Netherlands in the eighteenth century as a way for the Dutch to practice their national sport, ice skating, during the summer months. Dancing on roller skates (to brass bands and pipe organs) began in the parks and promenades of Victorian England in the 1880s, and roller rinks throughout the world employed organists (think of the music of Dave "Baby" Cortez) as a matter of course until the 1970s. In the mid- to late 1960s, Hector and Henry Abrami, owners of the Empire Rollerdrome on 200 Empire Boulevard in the Crown Heights section of Brooklyn, decided to hire a DJ to replace the organist as a cost-cutting measure, and the seeds of roller disco were sown. The Abrami brothers opened the Empire in the 1930s, when Crown Heights was an area almost exclusively inhabited by Eastern European immigrants. The neighborhood started to change in the 1960s with an influx of Afro-Caribbean immigrants, and the DJ started to tailor his set toward their musical tastes. The result was the most famous roller disco in the world. In the mid-1970s, a technique called the "Brooklyn Bounce"—based on varying stride patterns and frequent stops—was developed by skaters Bill Butler and Pat the Cat, and the roller disco craze was born. Soon, busloads of tourists (including JFK Jr. and Cher) would visit the thirty-thousand-square-foot rollerama decorated with brightly colored rainbow murals on Wednesday night, which became known as "white night" (at almost every other roller disco in the country

Wednesday night was "black night") to gawk at the dancers who were universally acknowledged as the best roller boogiers on the planet. It was a spectacle of speed, improvised choreography, and athleticism that no regular disco could hope to match.

Despite its Crown Heights location (which could have been in Mississippi as far as most Manhattanites were concerned), the Empire was one of the true crucibles of disco in New York—legendary DJ Larry Levan (see Chapter 6) even worked there as a skate guard (in the early '80s, Mike Tyson had his job). The Empire's preeminence was in no small part due to its DJ in the mid-1970s, Peter Brown. He played a combination of disco classics (Eddie Kendricks's "Girl You Need a Change of Mind"), funk standards (the O'Jays' "For the Love of Money" and Kool & the Gang's "Hollywood Swinging"), and obscure club favorites like Cymande's "Bra."[79] Brown was also involved in record promotion, and in 1975 he helped get a record by the vocal group Four Below Zero, "My Baby's Got E.S.P.," signed to Morris Levy's Roulette label.[80] The producer of "My Baby's Got E.S.P." was Patrick Adams, the former head of A&R at the Perception / Today labels and producer and arranger for the cult vocal group Black Ivory, and he and Brown quickly formed a partnership. The two used Brown's old P&P label[81] as a vehicle for Brown's own productions and for Adams's more experimental records.[82] The label's first twelve-inch release was Adams's own DIY project, "Atmosphere Strutt," made under the name of Johnny Copeland (Cloud One) Orchestra in 1976. The record set out the label's house style, which would be duplicated on the pair's other labels (Heavenly Star, Queen Constance, Land of Hits, Golden Flamingo, and Sound of New York,

---

THE OTHER PETER BROWN

The name "Peter Brown" is the source of much confusion in disco lore. The Peter Brown who worked with Patrick Adams is *not* the Peter Brown who had a megahit with "Do Ya Wanna Get Funky With Me" in 1977. That Peter Brown was from the Chicago suburbs and recorded the single on a four-track recorder in his bedroom and played all of the instruments. He secured a release on the T.K. subsidiary Drive, and it became the first twelve-inch single to sell a million copies. Its B side, "Burning Love Breakdown," essentially a dubbier, instrumen-

USA): a deep, spacey bass sound, syncopated rhythms that felt like anything but 4/4, askew vocals, strangely tinkly keyboard melodies, and wild Minimoog flourishes. It sounded nothing like the cookie-cutter synth gallop that was starting to dominate disco, and "Atmosphere Strutt" quickly became an underground disco classic, as did other releases like Clyde Alexander's "Got to Have Your Love," Licky's "African Rock," the Ahzz's "New York Moving," and Cloud One's "Disco Juice."

While the P&P releases expressed Adams's more experimental instincts, he was also one of the greatest of the commercial disco producers. Not that he ever achieved sales commensurate with his skills, just that his productions were some of the most nuanced, well-crafted, and that worst of all musical phrases, "soulful" of the disco era. Although his previous work with the Universal Robot Band, Bumble Bee Unlimited, and Black Ivory gained him notoriety among the cognoscenti, Adams really came to widespread attention in 1978 with Musique, a studio project based around vocalists Jocelyn Brown, Christine Wiltshire, Mary Seymour, and Gina Tharps. On Musique's two big hits, "In the Bush" and "Keep on Jumpin'," Adams replaced the oblique vocal mumblings and synth weirdness of his P&P releases with great-big diva vocals, chirpy horn charts, and scything strings—the big-budget production values didn't hurt either. He also ratcheted the pace up several notches to ensure spins at peak times when the dance floors were packed. Along with Adams's two great underground records from the same year, Sine's "Just Let Me Do My Thing" and Phreek's "Weekend," "In the Bush" and "Keep on Jumpin'" were unabashedly "disco"—reveling in its garish textures

---

tal remake, is a certified underground disco classic and one of the precursors of House music. Brown went to record an even more successful follow-up, "Dance With Me" (featuring Betty Wright on vocals), and eventually cowrote "Material Girl" for Madonna. There is also plenty of confusion surrounding Brown and Adams's Sound of New York, USA label. This is *not* the Sound of New York label that was a subsidiary of Beckett and released late disco classics like Indeep's "Last Night a D.J. Saved My Life," Kinky Foxx's "So Different," or Stone's "Crazy."

and tempos—but they also pointed a way out of the lamé morass of clodhopping bass lines, unctuous orchestration, and cocaine decadence that characterized mainstream disco. Their bounciness and rapprochement with funk's "boom-slap" laid the groundwork for the R&B-flavored "street music" and "boogie" that replaced disco at the turn of the '80s, the similarly styled roller-skating music popular at clubs like the Roxy at the same time (Vaughan Mason's "Bounce, Skate, Rock, Roll," Rose Royce's "Pop Your Fingers"), and the Garage sound that would soon emerge from New York's Paradise Garage and New Jersey's Zanzibar.

However, Adams kept on making straight-ahead disco records in the form of his two biggest chart successes—Herbie Mann's "Superman" and Narada Michael Walden's "I Don't Want Nobody Else (To Dance With You)"—and his two masterpieces, both made with Jocelyn Brown. Brown's cover of Marvin Gaye and Tammi Terrell's "Ain't No Mountain High Enough" (especially Larry Levan's remix) and Inner Life's "I'm Caught Up (In a One Night Love Affair)" are absolute disco perfection: that unique combination of catharsis and seduction, the bittersweetness of lost love summed up in one larger-than-life wail set against pillow-soft strings and surging, upful bass and guitar figures, while the chorus sassily urges you to wash that man right out of your hair.

With the changes that Adams inadvertently wrought on disco, though, his form of dance music gradually fell out of favor, and after Wish featuring Fonda Rae's great "Touch Me (All Night Long)" in 1984 and Skipworth & Turner's equally marvelous "Thinking About Your Love" in 1985, Adams largely vanished from the production scene. However, Adams's studio chops meant that he wouldn't disappear altogether. During what is almost universally acknowledged as hip-hop's "golden age" (1987–91), Adams was one of the most sought-after engineers in New York. As well as engineering records for Salt-N-Pepa and Teddy Riley, Adams worked on Eric B. & Rakim's first three albums and developed the technique of using a bass drum microphone to record Rakim's voice, helping him become one of hip-hop's most lauded rappers. This was hardly an isolated instance of the merger of disco and hip-hop, but such coupling was rare given the animosity and mistrust that the two genres' principal constituencies shared for each other.

Funky music is music with so much to share
I love America.

—Patrick Juvet, "I Love America"

The fashions, the mores, the dance steps made roller disco pretty goofy and laughable, but if disco had a nadir it was unquestionably the Village People. The Village People represented everything un-cool about disco: the stale beats seemingly phoned in by studio hacks, the dunderheaded English-as-a-foreign-language lyrics, the complete lack of subtlety, all delivered by guys wearing a Native American headdress and a loincloth, a construction worker's clothes, a police uniform, and leather biker gear. Then, there was the group's cinematic fiasco *Can't Stop the Music*, a movie so resplendently aw-ful (even if it is Steve Guttenberg's finest moment) that it's been turned into a drinking game. To top it all off, they were the product of the imaginations of the French.

Henri Belolo grew up in Morocco and was turned on to music by American soldiers stationed there after World War II. He eventually worked for Barclay and Polydor, and discovered disco and the Philadelphia International sound on a trip to the United States in 1973. Two years later he met Jacques Morali, a budding producer who wanted to make a disco version of the old standard "Brazil (Aquarela do Brasil)." Belolo thought it was a fantastic idea, and the two went to Philadelphia to work on the project with members of MFSB, including drummer Earl Young. They recruited three singers—Cheryl Jacks, Cassandra Wooten, and Gwendolyn Oliver—to be-come the voices and faces of the group that was called the Ritchie Family after the arranger, Ritchie Rome. Although it was a pretty pale imitation of the Philly sound, "Brazil" reached #11 on the Amer-ican charts and was followed by other overorchestrated and ever more ridiculous travelogues like "Peanut Vendor," "African Queens," "In a Persian Market," "Quiet Village," and the medley "The Best Disco in Town." Jacks, Wooten, and Oliver laid the schtick on thick with their theatrical overenunciation, Morali's lyrics were the cheapest fantasies imaginable ("I am fire / I am sex / I am brown and I'm beautiful / A gyrating, vibrating, heartbreaking sister"), and Rome arranged as if he was scoring a Busby Berkeley movie, but the ab-surdist nature of the project was highlighted by their album covers, which were even kitschier than the lyrics and featured the group decked out as Egyptian royalty and football players.

Morali and Belolo went from the high camp of the Ritchie Family to what may be the most subversive group in the history of popular music. Of course it wasn't intentional—just the deliciously bad taste of men raised on Johnny Hallyday and Charles Aznavour—but to explode Kenneth Anger camp into hypertrophic cartoon characters so absurd that only children and grannies from Arkansas could possibly like them was probably the most effective weapon in the battle of assimilating gay culture into mainstream America this side of the pill and *Queer Eye for the Straight Guy*. But everything Belolo and Morali did—from their imagery, which was so flagrant it was positively rococo, to the feigned innocence of their interviews—made it seem like this was the greatest in-joke, the greatest media prank ever perpetrated on the American public.

It all started innocently enough, with Belolo and Morali walking through New York's West Village when they spotted someone sporting a full Native American costume and were entranced by his presence and his foot bells. They followed him into a bar, where he worked as a tabletop dancer. A customer wearing a cowboy hat was watching him intently, and the concept for the Village People was born right there in the Anvil. Morali's concept was to portray the "gorgeous mosaic" that was the American male, and since they were in Greenwich Village with all its fabulous characters, the group became the Village People. With this macho drag notion in mind, Belolo and Morali held open auditions for the group and secured the services of songwriters Phil Hurtt (who had previously written for the O'Jays, Joe Simon, and the Spinners) and Peter Whitehead, who helped the Francophone Belolo write some thematically appropriate songs. With Morali's befeathered muse, Felipe Rose, already recruited, Broadway extra Victor Willis became the policeman; former backup singer for Bobbi Humphrey, Alex Briley, became the soldier; Randy Jones, a member of Agnes de Mille's dance company, became the cowboy; out-of-work Broadway actor David Hodo "joined the group because he needed a week's work to qualify for unemployment"[83] and became the construction worker; and former toll collector in the Brooklyn Battery Tunnel, Glenn Hughes, transformed himself into the leather biker.

The first, self-titled album (largely recorded with just Willis and the backup band Gypsy Lane) extended the Village People concept with the gay travelogue of "Fire Island" (featuring such kitsch-as-can-be lyrics as "Don't go in the bushes / Something might grab ya!"), "San Francisco (You've Got Me)," and "In Hollywood (Everybody Is a Star)"—they left off "Key West" and "Sodom and Gomorrah" until the second album. The cartoonish subversion, though, didn't really start until 1978's "Macho Man," an undeniably catchy tongue-in-cheek ode to the Muscle Marys who were beginning to dominate the gay disco scene. The locker-room muskiness of "Macho Man" may have been utterly ridiculous, but its camp esprit de corps was somehow universal enough for the record to reach #25 on the American pop charts. This hypermasculinity quickly became the Village People's stock-in-trade: the mustachioed lumberjack chorale of "Go West," the homoerotic military fetish of "In the Navy," the towel-snapping bathhouse bonhomie of "Y.M.C.A." While such unabashed celebrations of masculinity would normally be the preserve of Tom of Finland fans, the irony was that the Village People were practically persona non grata in the gay clubs. Instead, the Village People got most of their play at aerobics classes for senior citizens who could form the letters Y, M, C, and A with their arms without taxing their bodies too much, at barbecues by car mechanics who thought "Y.M.C.A." was about playing basketball, at straitlaced high school proms in Kansas, and at children's playgroups. It was Middle America that took the Village People close to its bosom, so much so that "In the Navy" was *this* close to becoming the recruiting song for the United States Navy until someone thought better of it. Whether they realized it or not, Belolo and Morali had achieved what George Clinton had with his Parliafunkadelicment Thang—forcing an unprepared, unknowing audience to groove to a message that they would ordinarily find singularly unpalatable through sheer force of the stupidity (or stoopidity, as Clinton would put it) of their music.

After churning out four albums in less than two years, and releasing *Can't Stop the Music*, the Village People had largely run their course. However, Belolo and Morali had only just started their mission to take Middle America for all it was worth. After parting company with erstwhile collaborator Jean-Michel Jarre, Patrick Juvet, a Swiss singer with flowing blond locks and unfeasible cheekbones, hooked up with Belolo and Morali for a series of records that redefined disco risibility. Juvet sang with a falsetto so fey that it was the diametric opposite of the Village People's he-man oratorio, so when paired with Belolo and Morali's insipid production the effect was like an abstract watercolor. Juvet's biggest hit was 1978's "I Love America," an unintentionally comic fourteen-minute love letter to American music with such bons mots as, "When I first learned how to Latin / I had so much fun / The salsa sound was so different / Than any sound around / The demanding music / From the people of Puerto Rico / I love to watch them play / Their music is so great." Belolo and Morali's Can't Stop Productions continued to crank out disco product in the form of such ill-advised records as Phylicia Allen's (Victor Willis's wife and the future Mrs. Huxtable on *The Cosby Show*) Josephine Baker concept album, *Josephine Superstar*; Dennis Parker's (aka porn star Wade Nichols) rather shocking "New York by Night" and "Fly Like an Eagle"—he sang about as well as adult film stars act; Gloria Gaynor's gay-lib-by-numbers version of "I Am What I Am" (from *La Cage aux Folles*); and Eartha Kitt's monotonal "Where Is My Man."

None of this is to say, however, that the mainstream disco experience was pure, unadulterated crap, or that art and commerce didn't exist side by side during the disco era. Only the most sourpussed curmudgeon or hard-core disco aesthete could deny the goofy pleasure of the Village People, the sing-along catharsis of "I Will Survive," KC and the Sunshine Band's whistle-stomp booty quake, or the precision-tooled craftsmanship of the *Saturday Night Fever* soundtrack. Studio 54 is still one of the nightclubs that all others are measured against and was undoubtedly a pretty special place even if you did have to suffer Rubell and his band of cretins. Even when it was purveyed by chancers and formulaic followers of fashion, disco was a remarkable moment in American cultural history, a time when female voices (even if they were singing the words of mostly male songwriters and producers) temporarily drowned out the beefy bluster that usually characterizes American discourse. Not since Noël Coward's reinvention of Tin Pan Alley had articulations of gay pleasure and style been so acceptable and so popular. It wouldn't be long, though, before it all became a bit too much and even the grannies from Kansas started to get the joke. The camping of America had got out of hand.

"WHERE WERE YOU WHEN THE LIGHTS WENT OUT?"

Disco is like a great porno film. If the characters and filming techniques are interesting, it's great for five minutes.   —Herbie Mann

Disco is as identifiable a commodity as *Smile* buttons and just as vital.
                                                              —Lester Bangs

Death to Disco Shit! Long Live The Rock! Kill yourself. Jump off a fuckin' cliff. Drive nails into your head. Become a robot and join the staff at Disneyland. OD. Anything. Just don't listen to disco shit. I've seen that canned crap take real live people and turn them into dogs! And vice versa. The epitome of all that's wrong with civilization is disco. Eddjicate yourself.   —John Holmstrom, *Punk*

For all the glamor of Studio 54, the taboo shattering of New York's urban demimonde, the radical production techniques of the remixers and synth whizzes, and the derring-do of the DJs, the quintessential mainstream disco experience was more prosaic. Disco wasn't getting swept off your feet by John Travolta or Donna Summer having twenty-three orgasms in one session; it was hearing "Y.M.C.A." six times in one night at the Rainbow Room of the Holiday Inn in Cedar Rapids, Iowa, while doing line dances with a bunch of traveling salesmen. Outside of its original contexts, disco was anything but what it promised, and it was this stupefying mundanity that finally punctured disco's veneer of splendor and dazzle.

In his book *Noise: The Political Economy of Music*, Jacques Attali, the onetime head of the European Bank for Reconstruction and Development, wrote that music heralds changes in society more quickly than other art forms or social organizations.[84] Mainstream disco's abandoning of its original constituency and its values, its unseemly greed, its whitewashing of race and, to a certain degree, gender, its legions of two-bit hacks hoping that some of the musical wealth of the genre's true geniuses would trickle down to them by merely imitating their opulence made it the perfect bridge from the liberalism that largely dominated the '50s and '60s to the neoconservatism that has shaped the Anglo-American axis since the 1980s. Journalist David Toop wrote that Casablanca, the quintessential label of the disco craze, "anticipated the junk bond scandals of the 80s with a boom-to-bust trajectory driven by hot air, hype and invisible, ultimately non-existent money."[85] Casablanca head Neil Bogart was the man who almost single-handedly invented the disco bubble. One of his chief business tactics was shipping records platinum, even those by unknown artists, and counting the shipped records as sales. With such a high-risk business strategy, Casablanca required a hype machine that operated in a similar overdrive. Puffing up no-talent acts with a load of hot air became the norm for the record industry during the disco boom, and it was during this time that companies started to pass the burden of the cost of promotion on to the artists themselves, saddling them with huge recoupable expenses that ensured that a record would have to go gold before the artist would start earning any money. Bogart's most Ivan Boesky–like moment, though, occurred when launching Donna Summer's career in the United States. For her American debut, Bogart "had Hansen's of Los Angeles sculpt a life-size cake in her image. The cake was flown to New York in two first-class airline seats, met by a freezer ambulance, and taken to the Penta discotheque for Summer's performance there."[86]

"More, More, More" was how former porn star Andrea True presciently described disco's insatiable appetite in 1975, and in 1979 it ultimately gorged itself to death. At the beginning of the year there was a critical mass of twenty thousand discos operating in the United States. "Boogie Fever" was a virus, and it never met a host it didn't like: There were disco versions of everything from "Beer Barrel Polka" to "Jingle Bells"; advertising jingles, Broadway musicals (Jerry Brandt's Got Tu Go Disco, a retelling of Cinderella set in a Manhattan nightspot starring Studio 54's doorman, Marc Benecke), wedding ceremonies (a club in Dubuque, Iowa, offered a "disco wedding" package complete with lighting effects and a smoke machine), pinball machines, even the Jewish liturgical tradition (Sol Zim, "the disco cantor") were all colonized by the disco bug. Not even children were safe: The beloved TV show Sesame Street released not one but two disco albums (Sesame Street Fever and Sesame Disco!); cereals like Count Chocula, Frankenberry, and Boo Berry, which were aimed at kids, gave away the truly monstrous "Monsters Go Disco" record with every box; there were Winnie the Pooh "disco players,"

"Disco Mickey Mouse" watches and pillowcases, and rhinestone "disco suits" for toddlers. Addled by the potent combination of Hai Karate fumes and disorienting strobe lighting, disco denizens appeared to be George Romero zombies boogying ever-onward, but toward what no one was very sure. They were just hypnotized and swept along by the relentless surge of disco's 4/4 death march ("Even in Jonestown, children wrote the names of recent disco hits in their notebooks," noted reporter Jesse Kornbluth[87]). The existential crisis wrought by disco was perhaps best exemplified by a club at Eleventh Avenue and Twenty-sixth Street in Manhattan. It was named Les Mouches after Jean-Paul Sartre's play that critiqued the notion of religious guilt. And, even more perfectly, it was Imelda Marcos's favorite New York haunt.

Rock bad boys like Kiss, the Rolling Stones, and Rod Stewart also succumbed to the disease. While it was perhaps inevitable for Kiss (which was signed to Casablanca) and the Rolling Stones (because of the group's abiding love for black music and refusal to be seen as the keepers of last year's blues) to go disco, Rod the Mod's "interpolation" of Jorge Ben's "Taj Mahal," "Do Ya Think I'm Sexy?," was about as sexy as a eunuch in a posing pouch and was a particular disgrace to the rock community (even worse was former Yes keyboardist Rick Wakeman's "Rhapsody in Blue," but luckily almost no one heard it). Old showbiz stalwarts like Frank Sinatra, Ethel Merman, Andy Williams, and Burt Bacharach went disco in a vain effort to shift product. Aside from the truly shocking music most of these recordings featured, the problem with these attempts to go disco was the superstar billing. The disco scene may have had its hyperarrogant DJs and gossip-column fodder celebrities, but disco music was never about superstars. It was about behind-the-scenes producers and anonymous session musicians, vocalists who were plucked from obscurity and then went right back there—think, for example, of Evelyn "Champagne" King, discovered singing in the bathroom of Philly's Sigma Sound Studios, whose enduring "Shame" is one of disco's greatest moments, or of Cheryl "Got to Be Real" Lynn, discovered on *The Gong Show*. Disco dancers had little use for the gargantuan ego of Mick Jagger or Frank Sinatra—the records should be about the groove and the exorcism of the demons of lost love, not the persona of the performer. For a culture born of the manumission from the shackles of repression and surveillance and pathologizing, the anonymity of disco is one of its most subversive and liberating aspects. While disco began with Francis Grasso blending Led Zeppelin and Chicago Transit Authority, disco had no use for rock and roll when it abandoned its connections to dancing and celebration in favor of offshore tax shelters and corporate sponsorship. Of course, this perfectly suited the bankers who ran the major labels, and so the dancing public was bombarded with thousands of beat-by-numbers records in the hope that one or two of them might catch on.

Even the centuries-old establishment of "high culture" was defenseless against the marauding leisure suit barbarians. Alec R. Costandinos remade Shakespeare's *Romeo and Juliet* and Victor Hugo's *The Hunchback of Notre Dame* as soft-porn schmaltz epics positively dripping with sickly string swoops and crass horn fanfares. Already reeling from the blasphemy of Walter Murphy & the Big Apple Band's "A Fifth of Beethoven," classical music suffered a further humiliation when, in a desperate bid to increase the shrinking attendance at its concerts, on January 6, 1979, the Rochester Philharmonic shared the stage at the Dome Arena in Henrietta, New York, with a DJ from the local discotheque, Club 747.[88] Perhaps disco's greatest indignity to the edifice of Western culture, though, was Costandinos's Sphinx project, an overripe dance floor passion play that made *Ben-Hur* look cheap and restrained. When *Rolling Stone*'s Mikal Gilmore expressed his doubts about the project to the label's publicist, she remarked, "It's the first time in Christian history that we can dance to the Stations of the Cross. Some people might find that blasphemous or pagan, but when you're out there on that floor with a lot of other people, sharing the grief of the Lord's betrayal, I dunno, it seems sort of . . . *uplifting*."[89]

Of course, America's biggest religion is money, and on that front disco was certainly not committing heresy. In February 1979, journalist Andrew Kopkind wrote, "Today, the disco industry is a mammoth $4 billion enterprise—bigger than television, movies, or professional sports in America."[90] From the time Chic's "Le Freak" replaced Barbra Streisand and Neil Diamond's "You Don't Bring Me Flowers" at the top of the American pop charts in December 1978, every American #1 single (with the possible exception of the Doobie Brothers' one-week reign with "What a Fool Believes") was a disco record until the Knack's "My Sharona" replaced Chic's "Good Times" on August 25, 1979. Then, as DJ Danny Krivit jokes, "Disco died in a week. One week."[91] He was barely exaggerating. After the Knack reintroduced rock to the American charts, there were only a handful of disco records that topped the charts—Herb Alpert's "Rise," Barbra Streisand and Donna Summer's "No More Tears (Enough Is Enough)," and Diana Ross's "Upside Down"—and these were all by well-established artists, not by musicians who made their names during the disco craze. Seemingly as suddenly as it emerged, disco vanished from the landscape of American popular culture. Kopkind had unwittingly provided a clue as to why.

As a country heavily invested in myths of masculinity, achievement, and its own uniqueness, America reserves a special place in its psyche for professional sport. No sport is more crucial to American fable than baseball, where every pitch is invested with cosmic significance and every home run is chronicled as if it were a labor of Hercules. Baseball is as much about American wholesomeness as *Father Knows Best* or *The Waltons*, as much about American masculinity as John Wayne or Gary Cooper, so it was inevitable that the camp disco beast would be slaughtered on the national pastime's fields of dreams. No other sport in the world, not even cricket, is so mired in a golden-age nostalgia of the past, so obsessed with making its past greats into mythic heroes. Despite the fact that there are nine players on a team, baseball is all about the individual—a gallant twentieth-century version of Davy Crockett who no longer kills bears with a switch but swats balls into orbit with a thirty-six-ounce bat. At times it feels like the entire bulwark of American exceptionalism would crumble without baseball.

Disco, then, with its problematic relationship with masculinity, and baseball, where "heterosexual performance off the field is naturalized as an extension of athletic prowess,"[92] always had an ambivalent relationship in the arena of popular culture. As *The Washington Post's* Bill Straub writes, "Of course, baseball in the mid-1970s was the only thing worth believing in. At a time when the nation was embroiled in Watergate and the after-effects of the Vietnam War, civil strife and the . . . disco scare, baseball represented at the time all things Americans are supposed to hold dear. It was pure, everyone started out on an even basis, excellence was rewarded and, in an increasingly cynical age, it was always there for you."[93]

The most obvious harbinger of disco's doom came from Chicago's Comiskey Park on July 12, 1979, in between games of a scheduled twi-night doubleheader between the Chicago White Sox and the Detroit Tigers. It was already scheduled to be "Teen Night," where kids under the age of twenty got a gift for attending the game, but with the White Sox having a lousy season and attendance dwindling, the team's promotions manager, Michael Veeck, thought that something else was needed to lure fans to the ballpark. Veeck was no stranger to outlandish promotional schemes: He was the son of the team's owner, the legendary Bill Veeck, the man who dreamed up the concept of the promotional giveaway (including live pigs and cases of beer), not to mention exploding scoreboards, weddings at home plate, and sending in a midget to pinch-hit during a game. The younger Veeck came up with the idea of staging a "Disco Demolition Derby" during the between-game intermission, and any fan showing up with a disco record to be demolished got into the stadium for 98 cents.

Veeck's coconspirator was a twenty-four-year-old morning drive-time disc jockey for radio station WLUP named Steve Dahl. In March of that year, Dahl had been fired from his job at station WDAI, which had switched from a rock format to an all-disco one, and he began his antidisco campaign when he retook the airwaves later that month. Following in the footsteps of "shock jock" Don Imus, Dahl attracted a sizable audience for antics, like forcibly taking over a teen disco, destroying a copy of Van McCoy's "The Hustle" on the day McCoy died of a heart attack, and offering free tickets to a Village People concert if the winners would pelt the group with marshmallows emblazoned in Magic Marker with "Disco Sucks." He also released a parody record set to the tune of Rod Stewart's "Do Ya Think I'm Sexy?" called "Do You Think I'm Disco" that featured such lyrics as "I like to dance with girls in sleazy dresses / Lipstick, nail charms and make-up in excesses / Buy them a drink and try and get their number / Usually they're as cold as a cucumber / Do ya think I'm disco / Am I superficial / Looking hip's my only goal" sung in a voice somewhere between Sean Penn's in *Fast Times at Ridgemont High* and "Weird Al" Yankovic's. Dahl even recruited his own "Disco Army," the Insane Coho Lips (named after the coho salmon, a species introduced into the Great Lakes in order to eliminate the lamprey eel, a parasite that had almost wiped out the lakes' fish population), which was "dedicated to the eradication and elimination of the dreaded musical disease known as DISCO."[94]

Dahl heavily promoted the "Disco Demolition Derby" for weeks on his radio show, and by the time July 12 rolled around, Dahl's audience of Middle American burnouts was worked up into a frenzy. The game was a sell-out, with an attendance of fifty thousand. There were another estimated fifteen thousand people without tickets or disco records hanging around outside (many of whom paid the turnstile attendants to let them in or simply scampered up the drainage pipes to get inside) and an unknown number stuck in a traffic jam on the Dan Ryan Expressway. If you didn't have a car, the main means of transportation to the stadium was the Archer bus, which was filled with teenagers drinking beer, passing around bottles of peppermint schnapps and joints, chanting "Disco sucks! Disco sucks!"

The atmosphere inside Comiskey was equally crazy. Fireworks were being set off and being thrown indiscriminately into the crowd. Inevitably, many fans had brought more than the one record to be sacrificed on Dahl's pyre, and records were being tossed like Frisbees at Tigers center fielder Ron LeFlore during the first game. Beer vendors were selling around three times their average amount. By the end of the first game, most of the crowd was totally loaded and braying for blood like Romans at the Colosseum awaiting the Christians and the lions.

After the White Sox lost the first game, Dahl, dressed in army fatigues and helmet, took the field in a jeep, accompanied by Lorelei, a blond bombshell who was one of Dahl's sidekicks, and proceeded to set off a number of explosives inside a box containing ten thousand disco records. Immediately after the explosion, fans started to jump over the outfield walls from the bleachers. Soon, there were hundreds of fans on the field, setting bonfires in the outfield, tearing up the grass, stealing the bases, destroying the batting cage and the pitcher's mound, and enagaging in oral sex on home plate. White Sox broadcaster Harry Caray took to the stadium's PA system to beg people to return to their seats; some of the fans who had remained in their seats began chanting (to the tune of Steam's "Na Na Hey

Hey Kiss Him Goodbye"), "Na na na na, na na na na, hey assholes, sit down!"; and, finally, a shaken Bill Veeck went out to home plate with a microphone to calm the crowd, but to no avail. Only the appearance of police on horseback quelled the riot. The field was so damaged that the White Sox had to forfeit the second game.[95]

Dahl's campaign was hardly an isolated instance of masculine energy run amok against the feminizing influence of disco. Detroit, that other crumbling icon of the Rust Belt and home to thousands of disaffected teenage rock-and-roll burnouts incensed that Bianca Jagger had superseded Mick as a cultural symbol, had its own anti-disco campaign. DREAD (Detroit Rockers Engaged in the Abolition of Disco), whose logo was a meat cleaver smashing a record with the inscription "Saturday Night Cleaver" below it, was an organization sponsored by rock radio station WRIF.[96] Card-carrying members— who had to swear that they would never wear platform shoes, zodiac jewelry, silk dresses, or three-piece suits—would be entitled to discounts on Styx and Boston records at local music chain Harmony House and to half-price entry to the Cranbrook Planetarium, which staged "Laser Pink Floyd" every weekend. The trend for destroying disco records was probably started in the summer of 1978 by a DJ in San Jose, California, calling himself Dennis Erectus. His show, Erectus Wrecks a Record, for radio station KOME (with promotional ads like "the KOME spot on your dial" and "Have you KOME today?") featured Erectus playing a couple of bars of a disco record, "then crank[ing] the turntable up to 78 rpm (especially effective on 'Macho Man'), grind[ing] the needle into the vinyl, play[ing] sound effects of toilets flushing or people throwing up, and follow[ing] it up with the searing guitar chords of Van Halen or AC/DC."[97] New York's WPIX, the station that had the world's first disco program, soon followed suit when it introduced its new all-rock format in January 1979 with "record-breaking weekends." Then, the deluge: In Los Angeles, KROQ DJ "Insane" Darrell Wayne buried disco albums in the sand as part of a disco funeral at Ventura Beach; in Portland, Oregon, KGON DJ Bob Anchetta destroyed stacks of disco records with a chain saw; Seattle station KISW had a nightly show called "Disco Destruction"; on the weekend of April 13–15, 1979, DJs Sue O'Neil and Glen Morgan of New York Top 40 station WXLO staged a "No Disco Weekend"; ads in the back of *Rolling Stone* for "Death to Disco" and "Shoot the Bee-Gees" T-shirts started appearing as early as 1978; in Oklahoma, J. B. Bennett ran (unsuccessfully) for a state senate seat on an antidisco platform, calling it a "corrupting influence on our young citizens."[98] Nor was the rage of the angry white man confined to America. A 1979 edition of the ultra-right-wing British National party's *The Young Nationalist* warned, "Disco and its melting pot pseudo-philosophy must be fought or Britain's streets will be full of black-worshipping soul boys."[99] Meanwhile, scientists at the University of Ankara in Turkey "proved that listening to disco turned pigs deaf and made mice homosexual."[100]

Nevertheless, it was the melee at Comiskey Park that became "the shot heard round the world" in the antidisco campaign. While America had a long history of moral panics over dance crazes—from Reverend Billy Sunday calling the tango "the rottenest, most putrid, stinkingest dance that ever wriggled out of the pot of perdition"[101] in 1915 to Southern preachers condemning rock and roll as "jungle music"—the Comiskey Park riot, as well as most of the flare-ups of antidisco sentiment, seemed to spring up spontaneously out of the will of people who just couldn't take it anymore. However, the "disco sucks" movement had all the hallmarks of a Nazi Kulturkampf—of the collaborationists in Paris rounding up Les Zazous—or at least the coordinated record burnings that accompanied John Lennon's pronouncement that the Beatles were bigger than God, and a large part of it was actually carefully orchestrated from afar. Lee Abrams of the radio-consulting firm Burkhart-Abrams Associates was a consultant for WLUP when Dahl began his campaign, and in May 1979 he advised his other clients that Dahl had found remarkable success with it.[102] Abrams also based his antidisco advice on the findings of independent media consultant John Parikhal, who set up focus groups of, and sent out questionnaires to, fifteen- to twenty-five-year-olds in Canada. "They thought disco was superficial, boring, repetitive, and short on 'balls' . . . They were also intimidated by the lifestyle—partly by its emphasis on physical and sartorial perfection, partly because its atmosphere is so charged with sex . . . Rock fans' disparaging characterization of disco as music for gay people seemed linked to their perception that it hasn't got balls . . .

At the same time they resented it for pressuring them to be sexual . . . Obviously, some people dislike disco for being black and gay. It's an exclusionary assertion of sophistication and confidence by the same two groups whose most recent attempts at economic and political self-assertion met with the notorious backlash responses of Allan Bakke [who effectively started the anti–affirmative action movement in the United States by contesting the University of California medical school's minority-admissions quota] and Dan White [a disgruntled former San Francisco supervisor who murdered openly gay Supervisor Harvey Milk and Mayor George Moscone in 1978]."[103]

Coming from Chicago—a place that poet Carl Sandburg once dubbed the "City of the Big Shoulders" and whose character is largely defined by the substantial population of white ethnics that Nixon turned into his silent majority—Dahl's disco riot was emblematic of the politics of resentment of the white everyman that would enable the 1980s conservative revolution. The disco riot was a weird tangent to the skirmishes—beginning with Nixon's vice president Spiro Agnew assailing the liberal media as the "nattering nabobs of negativism" in 1970 and the 1974 battle over the presence of books by black power activist Eldridge Cleaver and Beat poet Lawrence Ferlinghetti in a school library in West Virginia—that finally escalated into a full-fledged culture war when Reverend Jerry Falwell founded the Moral Majority in 1979. That same year, the "pro-God, pro-family" former beauty queen and orange juice shill Anita Bryant fought to have gay rights ordinances repealed in Miami, Florida, St. Paul, Minnesota, Wichita, Kansas, and Eugene, Oregon. She called her campaign "Save Our Children," and one of her refrains was, "If homosexuality were the normal way, God would have made Adam and Bruce."[104] Despite her efforts, it was Steve Dahl and his foot soldiers—even though they were the ones who desecrated the altar— who managed to have the most visible flowering of gay liberation excommunicated from the church of American popular culture.

It wasn't just deviant sexuality, though, that rankled the straight white male of the Midwest. It was something far worse: impotence. Detroit had once been the shining industrial beacon of the American economic miracle. Its massive car factories provided high-paid blue-collar jobs to just about everyone, and the images of third-generation Germans, Jews, recent Polish immigrants, and newly arrived African Americans from the Deep South working side by side on the shop floor were enduring symbols of both the might and beneficence of American capitalism. In the face of the gasoline crises of 1973 and 1979, and with a tsunami of cheap Japanese cars flooding the country, Motor City was in deep trouble. In the freezing winter of 1976–77, the electric company was forced to cut voltage throughout the state of Michigan, "dimming lights and darkening moods," as historian Bruce Schulman put it.[105] The beacon was shining no more.

Not only was America overly dependent on foreign oil, but the dollar was now hitting all-time lows against the German mark and Japanese yen. Inflation was running rampant, exacerbated by OPEC price increases, and President Jimmy Carter seemed powerless to do anything about it. As interest rates rose to unprecedented levels, Paul Volcker, the chairman of the Federal Reserve Board, announced that Americans' standard of living would decline for the first time in living memory. The ultimate humiliation, though, occurred on November 4, 1979, when Fundamentalist Muslim students stormed the American embassy in Tehran, Iran, and took its sixty-six occupants hostage. America's might had not only been questioned but openly mocked by a country that had escaped feudalism a mere twenty-five years earlier. With its mincing campness, airbrushed superficiality, limp rhythms, flaccid guitars, fey strings, and overproduced sterility, disco seemed emblematic of America's dwindling power. The high falsettos of disco stars like the Bee Gees and Sylvester sounded the death knell for the virility of the American male. Disco came from New York, "Sodom on the Hudson," the home of both namby-pamby knee-jerk liberals and Spiro Agnew's "Northeast liberal media elite." Viewed in this context, Dahl's military pomp makes a bit of sense: He was waging a war on the enemy within that was draining America of its life force.

Dahl's shenanigans wouldn't be the last we would hear from disco in the sacred confines of the ballpark, though. In fact, that very same year, Sister Sledge's "We Are Family" was the theme song of the Pittsburgh Pirates. The song, which quickly became an anthem for feminists and gay rights activists, was put back in the hands of the patriarchy at Pittsburgh's Three Rivers Stadium. The team was nicknamed "The Family" and its captain was thirty-nine-year-old Willie "Pops" Stargell, who would often lead the fans in singing the song's chorus during games. Even though the Pirates went on to win the World Series that year with the song as their soundtrack, the sanitization of disco had begun. It was now safe to be used as fodder for car advertisements and highlight reels: The graffiti were on the wall and disco was dead.

However, for those really paying attention, the first alarm bell that signaled disco's death—and the birth of something new—in the mainstream was set off in October 1977 during the World Series between the New York Yankees and the Los Angeles Dodgers. Yankee Stadium is situated at 161st Street and River Avenue on the west end of the South Bronx, at the time probably the most notorious urban area on earth. During game one of the series, which took place in the evening, the sky surrounding the stadium was noticeably orange, and ABC, the network televising the game, frequently cut to aerial shots provided by the ever-present Goodyear blimp of buildings on Charlotte Street, a couple of miles to the northeast of the stadium, burning to the ground. During one of these shots, the sportscaster Howard Cosell announced to the nation, "There it is again, ladies and gentlemen. The Bronx is burning."

During the mid-1970s, the South Bronx had an average of twelve thousand fires a year; it lost 40 percent of its housing stock and 57 percent of its population.[106] The infant mortality rate in this twelve-square-mile area was twenty-nine per one thousand births (the national average was thirteen per one thousand), and 25 percent of the city's malnutrition cases occurred here.[107] The reasons for this degeneration were numerous: the building of the Cross-Bronx Expressway, completed in 1963, had destroyed many previously tight-knit, middle-class neighborhoods, creating "instant slums"[108] in their place; high city taxes had forced many of the borough's manufacturing businesses to relocate to the suburbs or out of state altogether; in the late 1950s, the city began a policy whereby a substantial number of welfare recipients were essentially "dumped" in the South Bronx by offering landlords above-market rents to house them; Housing Preservation and Development Administrator Roger Starr's policy of "planned shrinkage," which advocated that many essential services be removed from "sick" neighborhoods in order to concentrate diminishing resources elsewhere;[109] and, most crucially of all, building owners realized that they could recoup some of their failing investments through fire insurance payments. "Some of the fires were accidents, the inevitable result of decaying electrical systems," wrote journalist Robert Worth. "Many were set by landlords who would then collect the insurance money. Often they would sell the building—whether it was still inhabited or not—to 'finishers' who would strip out the electrical wiring, plumbing fixtures, and anything else that could be sold for a profit before torching it. 'Sometimes there'd be a note delivered telling you the place would burn that night,' one man who lived through the period told me. 'Sometimes not.' People got used to sleeping with their shoes on, so that they could escape if the building began to burn."[110]

While the residents of "Fort Apache" were suffering with a median income of $5,200 (around half the New York City average), the absentee landlords were making out like bandits: In 1975 alone, they earned $10 million in insurance payouts.[111] Decimated by such neglect and horrible planning decisions, faced with a crime rate spiraling out of control, and with no reason for civic pride, the Bronx became a brutal place to live. The first generation of 1970s children and teenagers in the Bronx was the first group to try to piece together bits from this urban scrap heap. Like carrion crows and hunter-gatherers, they picked through the debris to create their own sense of community, finding vehicles for self-expression from cultural ready-mades, throw-aways, and aerosol cans. If disco's clubgoers, DJs, musicians, and producers were fiddling while New York burned, these kids from the Bronx were trying to make sculptures from the cinders. What rose from the ashes was hip-hop, and mainstream America first caught sight of its milieu in the fires outside of Yankee Stadium on that crisp October night in 1977.

Autumn couldn't come soon enough for most New Yorkers that year. It was one of the hottest summers on record: In the middle of July, it was over 100° for eight straight days. The Puerto Rican nationalist group FALN (Fuerzas Armadas de Liberación Nacional) continued its three-year-old terrorist campaign by exploding bombs in the Chrysler Building, the Manhattan offices of Gulf & Western and Mobil Oil, the American Bank Note Company, the New York headquarters of the FBI, a Madison Avenue building used by the Defense Department, and three Manhattan department stores. The city was further terrorized by David Berkowitz, the "Son of Sam" serial killer, who had murdered his tenth, eleventh, twelfth, and thirteenth victims in June and July after several months of inactivity. And right in the middle of that July heatwave, on July 13, lightning struck an electrical transmission line in upstate New York, and by 9:35 p.m. the entire city was plunged into darkness. Unlike the blackout of November 1965 (or, indeed, that of August 2003) which saw quiet and orderly streets and a solidarity among complete strangers who helped each other out, looting and arson broke out all over the city within minutes of the 1977 power failure. By the time power was restored the next evening, there had been 1,037 fires, the city had suffered $300 million worth of damage, and the police had arrested more than three thousand people.[112]

The looters were variously described by commentators as "urban insect life," "vultures," and "a jackal pack."[113] Historian Herbert Gutman wrote an op-ed piece in *The New York Times* decrying such characterizations and comparing them to the way Jewish women had been described as "animals" and "beasts" during a meat riot in 1902.[114] The reaction to Gutman's article was just as fierce as the reaction to the looters themselves. Historian Joshua Freeman described the outpouring of hostility in the Letters to the Editor section of *The Times*: "Over and over, the letter writers proclaimed how different their impoverished forebearers had been from the current poor, how the 1902 rioters were engaged in legitimate protest, while the blackout looters 'sought only selfish gain.' A *Times* editorial characterized the letters as raising 'the "my grandfather" question: "My grandfather pushed a pushcart all over the Lower East Side to earn enough to feed and raise his family. He worked to make it. Why can't *they*?"' It left unaddressed the utter lack of empathy among the letter writers for New York's poor, the meanness and self-satisfaction that pervaded their outrage at Gutman's linkage of their ancestors with contemporary rioters in his effort to show that the animal metaphor always 'separates the *behavior* of the discontented poor from the *conditions* that shape their discontent.'"[115]

New Yorkers may have lampooned the tax revolts of California and the born-again morality of the Bible Belt, but the failure of liberalism had instilled its own version of that mind-set in what was once liberalism's capital city. "Bring me your tired, your poor, your huddled masses" had turned into "Round up the tired, the poor, and the huddled masses and get 'em off the streets—they're stinking up the joint." Even though it was never explicitly stated, the root of this shifting attitude was race: The looters were by and large black, the shopkeepers were mostly white. The dehumanized pack animals roared back by wallowing in the "go for yourself" greed and smoldering spite and projected it right back at white society.

If the dream of the 1960s was finally incinerated with the 1977 blackout, a new dream, a new set of values, a new way of seeing the world was born on that same day. Hip-hop had been slowly gaining popularity across the Bronx since Kool DJ Herc unwittingly created the aesthetic at his parties at 1520 Sedgwick Avenue in 1973. Crews centered on a new breed of DJs like Afrika Bambaataa, Grandmaster Flash, Grand Wizard Theodore, and DJ Breakout were proliferating throughout the borough. Two of these DJs, DJ Disco Wiz and DJ Casanova Fly (soon to become known as Grandmaster Caz), had brought their sound system to the park on 183rd Street and Valentine Avenue on July 13, 1977. Caz had just dropped the needle on DC LaRue's "Indiscreet" (a disco record that appealed to him because of the long break highlighting the kick drum pattern, making it perfect to rap over) when two lights in the park blew out. "And then the streetlights started goin' out one at a time, all the way up the block, like 'poof, poof, poof, poof, poof,'" Caz told filmmaker Charlie Ahearn. "We looked at each other. I go, 'Oh shit,' 'cause we're plugged into one of the streetlights, and I thought we blew out the whole street! The whole neighborhood went dark . . . People are like, 'What's happening?' Then one person screams, 'Blackout! Hit the stores!' . . . Everybody stole turntables and stuff. Every electronic store imaginable got hit for stuff. Every record store. Everything. That sprung a whole new set of DJs. It's funny, 'cause I have a theory," Wiz continues. "You know what? Before that blackout, you had maybe five legitimate crews of DJs. After the blackout, you had a DJ on every block . . . That blackout made a big spark in the hip-hop revolution."[116]

While the nascent hip-hop nation was going for itself by any means necessary, disco's revelers kept the party going by any means necessary and evoked a rather different "nation." "The night of the blackout, people stayed over all night," the Loft's David Mancuso told journalist Vince Aletti. "We had candles and played radios and people were sleeping over, camping out. It was very peaceful, a little Woodstockish. The party still went on."[117] Disco may have traded the campfire sing-along of the '60s counterculture for glitterballs and strobe lights, but underneath all the medallion-clad bravado and feathered airheadedness was a longing for community, a desire to belong. Disco may have had a hard gloss and an icy, metallic sheen, but it could still be warm and fuzzy when it needed to.

You could never say that about hip-hop. Hip-hop's raison d'être was the "battle"—a ferocious display of one-upmanship among DJs, MCs, b-boys, and graffiti artists where each participant would try to come up with the most outlandish flourish, the most original stylization, or the most damning insult. Its fierce competitive nature—its echoes of Clint Eastwood and Lee Van Cleef meeting face to face at the big gundown—was precisely why it appealed to kids left to fend for themselves in the lawlessness of the ghost towns of the Bronx. The outlaw vibe was reinforced by the only community that hip-hop seemed to recognize, the "posse": a group of DJs, MCs, bodyguards, friends from the block, and hangers-on affiliated to one another by bonds of loyalty, honor, and money. Hip-hop's only pleasure principle seemed to be the art of survival. The musicians who were (and are) celebrated were the ones left standing after the microphone wars and turntable crossfire. Listen to tapes of the early parties and it's all shout-outs to people in the crowd, "All the Scorpios in the house, make some noise!"; "Everyone from the boogie-down Bronx, I wanna hear you scream!"—as if acknowledging one's very existence was reason enough to have a party.

Disco, too, was "born to be alive." Like hip-hop, it was originally a sort of naming ritual: the declaration of the existence, rights, and pleasures of a group of pariahs. Through their use of much the same techniques, disco and hip-hop were in many ways the flip side of the same coin: one keeping the *groove* going in order to foster a communitarian, celebratory spirit, the other splitting and chopping the *beat* to highlight the virtuosic abilities of its participants. Both were after a sense of empowerment: one by the force of numbers, the other by individual heroics. It's little wonder, then, that at the very beginnings of hip-hop, it and disco were hard to separate: DC LaRue and disco obscurity "Pussy Footer" by Jackie Robinson at the park jams; according to legend, Afrika Bambaataa attended some of the Loft parties; Grandmaster Flash was an original member of the Record Pool; the Sugarhill Gang rapping over Chic's "Good Times"; the bulk of the Sugarhill house band being made up of members of Wood, Brass & Steel, a jazz fusion group that had a disco hit with "Funkanova"; early rap star Kurtis Blow opening up for Chic on one of its tours and playing at the legendary disco club Paradise Garage shortly after his first single, "Christmas Rappin'," was released.

Of course, both disco and hip-hop were originally figments of the DJs' imaginations and fingertips: In the early days, it was the respective DJs' taste that determined what was or wasn't a disco or hip-hop record. Like all twins (it's up to you which one sports the pencil mustache and wears the black leather jumpsuit à la Michael Knight's evil twin in everyone's favorite episode of Knight Rider), hip-hop and disco share the same DNA—the break, the short section of a record where most of the instrumentalists drop out to "give the drummer some." The archetypal disco breaks are the ones on Titanic's "Sultana" and Eddie Kendricks's "Girl You Need a Change of Mind." The Norwegian rock group's "Sultana" is the blueprint for Eurodisco: cod-Latin percussion to connote summertime on a beach in Ibiza and an unchanging "groove" that resides in some strange netherworld between rock and funk where uptight librarians thrust and shake their hips in an unconvincing manner. Spacious and spacey, with congas twisting around Kendricks's short vocal interjections like a reggae dub mix, the break on "Girl You Need a Change of Mind" was like an old-fashioned gospel breakdown, slowing the pace, giving the dancers or worshippers time to relax, put their hands in the air, whoop and shout hosannas to the DJ or the Lord before the main thrust of the record comes back in for a rousing finale. The hip-hop break was just the opposite: It was the most intense part of the record, the part that the dancers waited for to showcase their most devastating moves. As Danny Krivit, one of the few DJs who spun for both crowds in the '70s and '80s, says, "A lot of that [hip-hop] stuff was a lot livelier. If you played Titanic and Tribe [another early disco prototype] next to that, it came off very straight and disco. They really had a consistency and straightness to it, and the style of dancing didn't lend itself to that, they didn't explode on records like that. These other records that they focused on were a lot harder, and when you saw the style that they danced, you could tell right away that something like Titanic was too straightforward."[118]

The hip-hop DJs were after a kind of low-end militancy, and the records they chose were full of drum tattoos, black holes of bass, scorched-earth screams, and searing guitars. The two archetypal hip-hop breaks were Jimmy Castor's "It's Just Begun," in which a roiling bass line and insistent flanged guitars built a manic intensity that was brought to boiling point by the Latin percussion and scything guitar solo, and the Incredible Bongo Band's "Apache," which sounded like a drum phalanx marching on the bandits in a spaghetti western flick. It's not just coincidence that most of the titles of the classic hip-hop breaks are imperatives ("Get Into Something," "Listen to Me," "Give It Up or Turnit a Loose," "Dance to the Drummer's Beat") or filled with warlike images ("Apache," "Theme From S.W.A.T."). Marking a break from the gospel-inspired soul continuum, hip-hop wasn't turning the other cheek; it was staking a claim and asserting itself.

However ridiculous the imagery may have been, disco was fixated on a romantic vision of the good life—the syrupy strings and lush chorales were the aural equivalent of soft-focus boudoir photography. Hip-hop, on the other hand, was about the here and now and self-determination; there was no time to waste on romance. Just as the DJs didn't bother with the niceties of buildup, tension, or contextualization and went straight for the climactic break beat, hip-hop culture couldn't be bothered with foreplay either. Echoing Steve Dahl's complaints about disco's alleged superficiality, Grandmaster Flash derided the Trammps, Donna Summer, and the Bee Gees as "sterile music."[119] The sexual metaphor couldn't have been more apt. While there was some class resentment in both disco critiques, the main focus of the "disco sucks" brigade and the hip-hop crews was disco's questionable sexuality. In the mass consciousness, hip-hop began with the Sugarhill Gang's 1979 single "Rapper's Delight," which featured "Big Bank Hank" Jackson rapping, "She said, 'I go by the name Lois Lane / And you can be my boyfriend, you surely can / Just let me quit my boyfriend called Superman' / I said, 'He's a fairy I do suppose / Flying through the air in pantyhose / He may be very sexy or even cute / But he looks like a sucker in a blue and red suit . . . He can't satisfy you with his little worm / But I can bust you out with my super sperm.'" It may have been fairly harmless, but this was only the beginning of literally hundreds of antigay rhymes in hip-hop, most of which are a lot less funny.

However, it would take hip-hop several more years before it would become a constant presence in the mainstream. Instead, disco's hustle to the top of the charts was largely hogtied by hip-hop's racial inverse, country music. In the late '70s and early '80s, the American Top 40 was filled with ditties by Dolly Parton, Crystal Gayle, Kenny Rogers, the Oak Ridge Boys, Johnny Paycheck, Alabama, and Eddie Rabbitt. Perhaps the most significant of these hits was "The Devil Went Down to Georgia" by the Charlie Daniels Band, which hit #3 in the summer of 1979. Hardly your archetypal country song about Mom and the good old days or crying in your beer because your woman left you, "The Devil Went Down to Georgia" told the tale of Satan challenging a cocky good ol' boy named Johnny to a fiddling duel. The devil was joined by a "band of demons" who played a pretty mean disco-funk vamp over the top of which Beelzebub improvised some evil *Psycho*-style string gashes. Johnny, on the other hand, played it strictly traditional, like you could hear on any Appalachian back porch. Despite the protests of millions of people who knew nothing about the eternal verities of old-timey string band music and thought that Johnny was cut by Mephistopheles, Johnny won the duel and saved his soul. While the record would never have crossed over to the pop charts without its disco touches, the implicit antidisco message of the song couldn't have been clearer either. The South's reaction to disco was perhaps most succinctly summed up by an album by Arizonan Western Swing group Chuck Wagon & the Wheels titled *Country Swings, Disco Sucks*.

The Charlie Daniels Band had first come to attention in 1975 with "The South Is Gonna Do It," a pugnacious assertion of regional pride that fitted neatly alongside songs like Merle Haggard's "Okie From Muskogee," Loretta Lynn's "Coal Miner's Daughter,"

Lynyrd Skynyrd's "Sweet Home Alabama," John Denver's "Thank God I'm a Country Boy," Tanya Tucker's "I Believe the South's Gonna Rise Again," and Hank Williams Jr.'s "The South's Gonna Rattle Again." This veritable litany of redneck anthems voiced Dixie's defiance after the shame of segregation and the defeat of Jim Crow by the "second war of Northern aggression." The good ol' boys below the Mason-Dixon Line weren't going to have pencil-necked geeks from up north tell them how to run things anymore; they were going to don their cowboy boots, get into their flatbed Fords, kick some in-tell-ect-chools' asses, and raise a little hell.

Since the end of the Civil War, the South had been the "sick man of America," the racist, bucktoothed simpleton that the rest of the country tried to hide in its room to spare their embarrassment. But a funny thing happened on the way home from the civil rights march—the South reinvented itself. With the dawn of the 1970s, the South changed almost overnight from the poor, rural backwater presided over by a tobacco-chompin' cracker sheriff who lynched first and asked questions later to a region that boasted the largest concentration of high-tech industries in the country.[120] Much of this growth was at the expense of what was, since the Industrial Revolution, America's industrial heartland—the Rust Belt, which ran roughly from Duluth, Minnesota, to Boston, Massachusetts. While the Rust Belt was indeed rusting, people and businesses moved down south at a rate that effectively reversed "the great migration" that occurred during the first half of the century. New York governor Hugh Carey warned that the Northern industrial region was in danger of becoming "'a great national museum' where tourists would see 'industrial plants as artifacts' and visit 'the great railroad stations where the trains used to run.'"[121] The response from the booming Sun Belt, where there was virtually no public transport and everyone drove across the sprawl of the world's largest metropolitan areas, was a bumper sticker that read, "Let 'Em Shiver in the Dark."[122]

Blackouts, gasoline shortages, a faltering currency—these were striking symbols of the waning of American power. But while the Northern states moaned, the Sun Belt took the bull by the horns and fought back. The South's newfound pride ran against the prevailing mood of a nation that was facing what Bruce Schulman called a "crisis of confidence."[123] The perilous state of the United

States in the '70s had taught many Americans that they could no longer rely on the government and liberalism, and had to rely on themselves instead. In declaring its self-confidence, the Sun Belt delved deep into the country's soul and reconfigured America's most cherished icon, the cowboy. Cowboy chic was everywhere in the late '70s and early '80s in an attempt to heal the wounded psyche of the American male. The real American man was not someone who pranced about in a leisure suit (let alone sequined hot pants and makeup) and was a lady killer on the dance floor, but someone who wore jeans and a Resistol hat and could kill his own supper. While the new man of the new South was certainly no rhinestone cowboy, he wasn't the same man who had conquered the West, nor was he the ign'rant poor white trash who spent his days at the fishing hole and his nights at the whiskey still. The new Southern male still had a gun rack on his pickup truck, but he was an engineer at a company in North Carolina's Research Triangle; he still attended church every Sunday, but he worked for NASA; he was a banker in Atlanta but rejected the Brooks-Brothers-suit-and-yacht-club conservatism of the Northeast Republicans in favor of a populist brand of conservatism that was first articulated by the Sun Belt's Barry Goldwater in 1964.[124] Instead of lassoing steers and bucking broncos, the cowboy now tamed the market. America's mythical rugged individualism had been replaced by entrepreneurial zeal.

The biggest change in the new Southerner, though, was that his views on race had moved into the mainstream. As soon as the most vile aspects of the Jim Crow South had been eliminated by the bus boycotts, voter drives, marches, and civil rights legislation, the focus of America's race problem shifted to the Northern metropolitan areas. In cities like Denver and Boston, there was massive resistance to school busing and other court-ordered remedies for de facto segregation, there was widespread dissatisfaction with the country's welfare program, and efforts at urban renewal were stymied at every level. The South's distrust of big government and the welfare state, and the racial dynamic of that hatred, had come to dominate America's political discourse.

Disco, in a sense, was liberalism's last hurrah, the final party before the neocon apocalypse. Disco's own last hurrah was Chic's "Good Times," a song that seemed to know exactly what was on the horizon. Here were those George Romero zombies again, only now they were articulating the sense of impending doom that lay behind their death march: "A rumor has it that it's getting late / Time marches on, just can't wait / The clock keeps turning, why hesitate? / You silly fool, you can't change your fate." Two years later, before Reagan made jingoism fashionable again, country singer Merle Haggard recorded his own eulogy for the good times, "Are the Good Times Really Over? (I Wish a Buck Was Still Silver)." Unlike Chic, Haggard believed that he could turn back the clock. Disco's fatalism was replaced by nostalgia; its lapsed utopianism replaced by a mean-ness that was camouflaged by a homespun simplicity: "I wish a buck was still silver / And it was back when the country was strong / Back before Elvis and before the Vietnam War came along / Before The Beatles and 'Yesterday' / When a man could still work and still would . . . / It was back before Nixon lied to us all on TV / Before microwave ovens, when a girl could still cook and still would / Is the best of the free life behind us now? / And are the good times really over for good?" While Haggard believed that if we all "[Stood] up for the flag and [rang] the Liberty Bell, the best of the free life [was] still yet to come," for disco the good times were really over for good.

"*J*O WHY *J*HOULD I BE A*J*HAMED?"

Di*r*co Goe*r* Underground

In March 1982, Studio 54, once the epicenter of fabulous, was converted into a low-key "salon." "The music will be soft and classical," an invitation to an after-work "party" read, "and serve only as a background to encourage lively conversation and business interactions. There will be no dancing music or flashing lights."[1] These quiet gatherings, which took place on Wednesdays between five and ten in the evening, were networking sessions for businessmen and stockbrokers who paid $8 for the privilege. They were so successful that they were soon held on Sunday evenings as well. Presiding over the exchanges of business cards and hush-hush stock tips was former '60s radical turned free-market apologist Jerry Rubin. The yippie had turned yuppie, and Studio 54 was now awash in the preppies and Upper East Side single guys that Steve Rubell was once so hell-bent on preventing from entering his pleasure dome. The '80s had definitely arrived.

The '80s may have been dreadfully drab and frightfully conservative compared to the rhinestone radiance of the '70s, but disco's eclipse by Reagan's "morning in America" wasn't just the result of Steve Dahl's pogrom or the South rising again. Like all subcultures and artistic movements, disco sowed the seeds of its own destruction. Not in the sense that disco gorged itself to death on its own decadence, but that sprouting within its very essence was the kernel of the generation that followed. Nowhere was this more apparent than in the celebrities who abandoned the discotheque as their clubhouse when the next big thing appeared on the horizon. And at the dawn of the '80s that big thing was a return to "American values"—no more European extravagance and social welfare programs, just plain, homespun truths, hard work, and John Wayne riding in on his white horse.

While the look of the Reagan era did away with the polyester, wide ties, and even wider lapels of the '70s, much of its sensibility was born in the disco era. Along with Ralph Lauren, Calvin Klein was the prime mover of '80s fashion in America; his minimally elegant clothing set the tone for a country that was going back to basics and pursuing the American dream with a renewed vigor. While Klein cannily rode the zeitgeist, what was really remarkable about him was not his clothes but his marketing, which was an outgrowth of the style of the clubs he used to hang out in during the '70s. As journalist Michael Gross suggested, Klein was obsessed with attaining the mystique of fellow Studio 54 habitué Halston and pulled no punches when it came to pursuing celebrity—even if that meant putting your name on the ass of every woman in America.[2] More important, though, Klein's advertisements, with the help of photographer Bruce Weber, promulgated a style that had its roots in the Fire Island Pines (where Klein shared a house with fellow designer Giorgio di Sant'Angelo) and in his favorite haunts: 12 West, the Flamingo, and Studio 54.

Klein's ads utilized sexual innuendo and fetishized the male body in a way never seen before in mainstream American culture. Of course, if you had ever seen a Flamingo flyer or cruised the busboys at Studio, the ads were nothing new. As Frank Rich wrote of the Calvin Klein aesthetic, "The Klein style excluded unpretty men, zaftig women, the imperfect, the overweight, the square . . . As had also been true of the discos that restricted entry to the gay and the pretty, there was a scent of fascistic decadence to the Klein ads."[3] What was strange, though, was how this taboo iconography, this imagery from a group that was damned to hell by most of Reagan's main constituency, fit in so well with the prevailing culture. As Rich concluded about Klein's gay-derived ads, "The new body worship was nothing if not in tune with the moneyed, selfish culture of the Reagan years."[4]

Sure, most of disco's celebs, hucksters, and lucky chancers cut their hair, put on some jeans and penny loafers, and slid easily into the Brie and chardonnay parties ushered in by Reaganomics. But what rose from disco's ashes wasn't a glorious phoenix, but a two-headed beast that was just as contradictory as disco during its heyday. While disco was never about anything other than sensual gratification of the most extreme kind, it was never simply mindless escapism either. As journalist Vince Aletti wrote, "A good case could be made for it as a tribal rite, an affirmation of high spirits and shared delight, a coming together to let loose that in no way ignores the problems of everyday life . . . but relieves them."[5] Although disco helped define the narcissism and rapaciousness of the Reagan-era mainstream, the other side of disco—its communitarian spirit and challenge to puritan constrictions—was kept alive by both revelers and theorists in the underground.

> Drugs brought money back and Reagan was elected president and shit went on. In fact that's the sad part: hippies survived Nixon, but punk caved in to Ronald Reagan, know what I'm saying? Punk couldn't actually take a good challenge.   —Mick Farren

When punk rock exploded out of the dingy clubs of New York and London in the mid-1970s, it was hailed as the most exciting thing to happen to popular music since the Beatles. Punk's champions praised the new sound as a kick in the butt to a stagnating, self-important music scene and as a burst of liberating energy that cut through the Valium haze of the '70s. As the liner notes to *Streets*, a compilation of punk singles, declared, "1977 was the year that the music came out of the concert halls and onto the streets; when independent labels sprang out of the woodwork to feed new tastes; when rock music once again became about energy and fun; when the majors' boardrooms lost control. Suddenly we could do anything."[6]

Although punk and disco were often seen as sworn enemies, the truth was that, despite John Holmstrom's editorial in the inaugural issue of *Punk* magazine (see Chapter 5), in many ways they were actually allies. Both the mainstream white rock community and the black community alienated, and were alienated by, disco and punk. In different ways, both genres celebrated and openly mocked the spectacle of rock's bloated, rotting corpse. "I never really cared much for rock music of that time," says engineer/producer Bob Blank, who worked with both disco divas Musique and punk priestess Lydia Lunch, reflecting punk's critique of the rock scene. "It was very self-important. Dance music seemed a lot earthier and fun."[7] Disco's questioning of the sanctity of the work of art with DJ mixes and making the clubbers themselves the stars was essentially the same strategy, and just as much of a challenge to rock's cult of personality, as that of punk. As punk chronicler Jon Savage said, "Many of the qualities of Disco that were so derided were mirror images of those qualities that were celebrated in Punk: an annihilating insistence on sex as opposed to puritan disgust; a delight in a technology as opposed to a Luddite reliance on the standard Rock group format; acceptance of mass production as opposed to individuality. It was the difference between *1984* and *Brave New World*, between a social realist dystopia, and a nightmare all the more realistic because accomplished through seduction."[8]

Despite disco's acceptance into the mainstream and its resulting commercial imperatives, the glitter ball exerted a strange fascination over punks and avantists, and not only because they shared rock and roll business as usual as a common enemy. While everyone in the '70s was mesmerized and narcotized by Farrah's hair, Donny's teeth, and the streaking craze, an incredibly profound shift in Anglo-American society was occurring: the erosion of the public sphere by the Me Decade's tidal wave of tax revolt and EST retreats. Reagan and Thatcher were merely the final nails in the coffin, even if they were useful figureheads to rally against. While disco culture's hedonism was certainly part of the new solipsism, it was also the last gasp of the integrationist instinct before it dissolved in a blur of identity politics and special interest groups. On the dance floor, at least, disco represented a community, albeit without the utopian naïveté of the '60s. This sense of being trapped in the headlights of the oncoming cultural paradigm shift—not quite dancing through the apocalypse, but something similar—undoubtedly attracted the punks, avant culture vultures, and outsiders who started venturing into the disco at the end of the decade.

The trickle became a stampede as the Thatcher and Reagan era and AIDS reared their ugly heads and freedoms of all kinds were being curtailed. In such a climate, talking positively about sex and pleasure was as radical and provocative a gesture as declaring yourself the antichrist was in 1977. Since the body became the prime political battleground (not only over AIDS but also, in the United States at least, over abortion rights in the face of an escalating conservative and evangelical backlash) in the early '80s, disco had lots to offer punk. Punk was largely an abnegation of sex and the body—consider Johnny Rotten's famous comment about love being "two minutes and 52 seconds of squelching noises," or that punk's dance was not a rite of courtship and touching but either pogoing (i.e., jumping up and down) or hurling yourself violently around the room and bashing into your fellow "dancers"—but disco was often nothing but sex and one long body high, and the blending of punk's more expressly political ambitions with disco's pleasure principle was more than just a marriage of convenience.

Of course, punk had plenty to teach disco too. While disco certainly had more than its fair share of divas, women were largely absent from the production and decision-making processes. There were very few female DJs of note during the disco era: Kathy Dorritie, Ann Henry, and Bert Lockett from the early days; Sharon White of lesbian disco Sahara and the Saint, and Lizzz Kritzer at La Folie during its heyday; and Susan Moribito, Wendy Hunt, and Jenny Costa during the later stages. Punk opened up space for people whose voices were too shrill or too deep for the pop status quo or were just plain unruly and weird, and its DIY spirit allowed women to take greater roles, to form bands, to become more than just eye candy. Since women generally have fewer aesthetic hangups than more tribal young men, the merger of grate and groove, of feedback and fatback was often done in their hands.

That said, the first proof of punk and disco's empathy[9] was made by a mixed gender group, New York's James White & the Blacks. James White (né Siegfried) also went by the name James Chance, and with his group the Contortions he made jazz and funk snarl with the same intensity as punk rock. As James White, he did the same thing to disco. "I've always been interested in disco," he told the *SoHo News*. "I mean, disco is *disgusting*, but there's something in it that's always interested me—*monotony*. It's sort of jungle music, but whitened and perverted. On this album I'm trying to restore it to what it *could* be. Really primitive."[10] "Contort Yourself" was released in late 1978 and it was really primitive. Robert Quine's main guitar riff was a twitchier take on the archetypal Nile Rodgers riff, and it was less sympathetic to the rhythm. The secondary guitar riff had more than a slight similarity to Cymande's great Brit funk one-off, "Bra." White's skronky sax bleats were similarly abrasive, while the hand claps and cod-Latin percussion fills could have been lifted off a Gloria Gaynor record.

While groups like Blondie followed James White & the Blacks by making ironic disco records ("Heart of Glass"), others remade disco in their own image. Public Image Limited's "Death Disco," which reached #20 on the British pop charts in July 1979, was perhaps the most uncompromising record ever to make a Top 20 chart. While only a thoroughly miserable bastard like John Lydon would come up with a title like "Death Disco" or even conceive of writing a disco song about his mother dying, "Death Disco" revealed the darker truth about disco: It was a culture that was just as much on the brink as punk; its participants were equally trapped; it attempted to suggest answers to questions posed by a society in the process of abandoning a universalist communitarian model for a vision based on cutthroat individualism; disco's glitter queens and escapist working-class teens were kicking against the pricks the only way they knew how. Part Kaddish, part Lydon throwing himself on his mother's funeral pyre, part fiddling while Rome burns, the seething funk guitar inferno arabesque of "Death Disco" remains postpunk's finest, most defiant, most radical moment. Nevertheless, even though guitarist Keith Levene largely based the music on a rather different form of dance music (Tchaikovsky's *Swan Lake*), the only part of the record that prevented "Death Disco" from being played at New York's more adventurous discotheques like Paradise Garage or the Loft was Lydon's infernal wailing.

"Death Disco" was, however, played at many of the new breed of nightclubs that were opening up in New York, not as Studio 54's less glamorous stepsisters but as Studio's bitter and twisted evil twins. These clubs were certainly reacting against what they perceived to be disco's snobbishness (even though they often replicated it, just with a different dress code), but they were also borrowing from disco and reaching back to the early '70s when disco and punk developed side by side, reacting against the same things.

TURN THE BEAT AROUND

The connection between punk and disco goes back to Aux Puce DJ Kathy Dorritie, who would transform into Warhol superstar, David Bowie publicist, and punk singer Cherry Vanilla in the early '70s. One of her regular haunts was the legendary Max's Kansas City, a bar at 213 Park Avenue South that was opened in 1965 by Mickey Ruskin. Max's crowd was a who's who of American bohemia: in the front room macho artists like Carl Andre, Donald Judd, Dan Flavin, John Chamberlain, Robert Rauschenberg, Brice Marden, and Frosty Myers cavorted with fashion photographers like John Ford, Richard Davis, and Izzy Valaris, who brought along models like Jean Shrimpton and Twiggy; while in the backroom, Andy Warhol held court with his Warhol Superstars, receiving supplicants like Lou Reed, Patti Smith, Alice Cooper, David Bowie, and even Terry Noel. They were served by Debbie Harry, who was a waitress at Max's in the very early '70s. The crowd of regulars may have been glittering, but most of them went to Max's because if you came during cocktail hour and bought one drink you could eat yourself sick on the famous chickpeas.

In 1969, Ruskin opened a disco upstairs from the bar with Criss Cross as the DJ and slide shows by Tiger Morse. As the disco started to attract regular visitors like Rauschenberg and New York Knicks great Walt Frazier, Cross was replaced by Paul Eden (who was particularly fond of playing "Monkey Man" by the Rolling Stones) and Claude Pervis, and then by Wayne (later Jayne) County, who would wear a Dusty Springfield wig and wield a dildo while spinning. The last record of the night was always the Stones' "Gimme Shelter." The disco also hosted live shows, including a famous performance by Elephant's Memory (of "Mongoose" fame), who got the gig because they were friends with Jerry Rubin. It was more famous, however, for being one of the crucibles of punk thanks to performances by the Velvet Underground, New York Dolls, Iggy & the Stooges, the Ramones, Suicide, and Patti Smith.[11]

Based on the traditional rock band format with a raison d'être of pure confrontation, punk was pretty much exclusively a performance-based genre. However, punk's nihilism and its reliance on the tools of the enemy meant that it was an aesthetic dead end doomed to burn out almost as quickly as it began. Punk survived by adapting disco groove and reggae skank (largely thanks to Don Letts, who noticed the millennial fervor of both genres and spun reggae during intermissions between punk bands at the Roxy in London, and to Lydon himself, who played reggae alongside Krautrock and Van Der Graf Generator on his radio show on London's Capital Radio) to its own ends and, as it did so, the punk discotheque started to take shape. Hurrah, at 36 West 62nd Street, was opened by New York nightlife mainstay Arthur Weinstein as a pre–Studio 54 celeb joint. It lasted for a little while, but when Studio stole its fire, it turned more bizarre in order to carve out its own niche rather than struggle on as a place that people went to if they couldn't get into Studio. In the summer of 1978, Jim Fouratt was made the manager, and he brought in a British DJ who played synth-punk records by the Normal ("Warm Leatherette") and Cabaret Voltaire ("Nag Nag Nag"). Soon, Hurrah started to call itself "The Rock Disco," and it quickly became the preeminent postpunk club in New York, stealing the thunder of CBGB by becoming one of the first clubs to show videos and by following the clues in the music and combining DJing with live performances from groups like Liquid Liquid and ESG.

These two New York groups represented the most experimental end of the punk-disco fusion. ESG was a quartet of sisters (with a little help from their friend Tito Libran) from the South Bronx projects who named themselves after emerald, sapphire, and gold, and expressed an admiration for Barry Manilow and Christopher Cross, but somehow still managed to open up for both the Clash and PiL. From their creation myth (Rene, Marie, Valerie, and Deborah Scroggins's mother bought them their first instruments to keep them off the streets), which says everything you need to know about the redemptive power of music to the universes contained within the stark lines of their masterpiece—their self-titled EP containing "Moody," "UFO," and "You're No Good," which was recorded at Hurrah—ESG perfectly summed up the times. As Rene told journalist Steven Harvey, "I don't feel like a disco group, I don't feel like a punk group. I feel like a funk group, maybe like Rick James says, punk-funk. I feel we're right here, in between, we've got something for everybody."[12]

Liquid Liquid (bassist Richard McGuire, drummer Scott Hartley, vocalist Salvatore Principato, and percussionist Dennis Young), meanwhile, started off life as a punk band from New Jersey called

Liquid Idiot. After getting turned on by Can, Fela Kuti, and dub reggae, the renamed Liquid Liquid became rock deconstructionists with a ferocious but minimal groove. Its 1983 track "Cavern" was huge in discos throughout the Big Apple, got airplay on WBLS (New York's main black radio station), and even reached the mid '50s on *Billboard*'s disco chart. As a further example of the rare synergy that existed between not only punk and disco, but also hip-hop at the time, "Cavern" was used as the basis for Grandmaster Flash & Melle Mel's "White Lines (Don't Do It)." Unfortunately, Liquid Liquid was never credited, and the ensuing lawsuit bankrupted its label, 99 Records, and split the band apart.

Not too long after Fouratt took over Hurrah, Steve Maas, who used to work with maverick filmmaker Jack Smith, opened the Mudd Club at 77 White Street on October 31, 1978, with the B-52's playing. Instead of the hundreds of thousands lavished on Studio 54, Xenon, and their ilk, the interior of the Mudd Club cost a grand total of $15,000—sound system included—with much of the decor coming from the surplus stores around the corner on Canal Street. While the Mudd Club presented itself as the alternative to Studio 54, it was still exclusive—it just had a steel chain instead of a velvet rope. David Bowie, Mariel Hemingway, Diane von Furstenberg, and Dan Aykroyd were regular visitors. *People* magazine even reported that "Andy Warhol is happy to have found a place, he says, 'where people will go to bed with anyone—man, woman or child.'"[13]

While the club remains a legend in New York nightlife for its blaxploitation parties, its erotic Twister nights, and its Mother's Day party in 1979 where half the people came dressed as Joan Crawford and the other half "wore pinafores and Band-Aids as Mommie's battered dearests,"[14] the club's music policy was often less festive. Although DJ Glenn O'Brien would typically play Lipps, Inc.'s "Funkytown" and the Trammps' "Disco Inferno" with an ironic wink, the Mudd Club was known for a more arty blend of disco camp and punk sneer. Painter Jean-Michel Basquiat frequently played there with his band Gray (Michael Holman, Nicholas Taylor, and Justin Thyme). Unlike the bold colors and information overload of Basquiat's canvases, Gray's music was minimalist disco noir. Another Mudd Club regular was Stuart Argabright, whose group Ike Yard specialized in industrial desolation, but as Dominatrix he created the perfect blend of punk and disco sexuality with "The Dominatrix Sleeps Tonight."

While groups like Spandau Ballet, Haircut 100, and Duran Duran (whose stated ambition was to combine Chic with the Sex Pistols) and clubs like Blitz and Club for Heroes were the public faces of the punk-disco merger in Britain, plenty of other groups followed PiL's twisted route toward a more "serious" music that belied both disco's tacky surface and punk's pleasure-denying sneer, and provided some of the most satisfying resolutions of popular music's eternal mind-body problem.

London may be the United Kingdom's metropole, but much of the best multicultural genre bending was occurring in provincial cities like Manchester and Bristol. Most of Bristol's mutant disco action centered on Dick O'Dell and his Y label. O'Dell was a recovering hippie who had previously worked the lights and sound for Pink Floyd and the Sensational Alex Harvey Band. In 1978 he started managing the Pop Group, a Bristol band that blended punk dissonance, disco grooves, dub bass, and dislocation, and lyrics that read like headlines from *Socialist Worker*. Y began in 1980 with releases from the Pop Group and the Slits (an all-female band working in the same territory) but had its biggest hit with Pigbag's "Papa's Got a Brand New Pigbag." Great dance music and Cheltenham somehow don't go together, but then again the early '80s were all about strange combinations. Streamlining the Pop Group's aural anarcho-syndicalism (and with former Pop Group bassist Simon Underwood on board), Roger Freeman, Chris Hamlyn, Chris Lee, and James Johnstone came up with punk disco's biggest hit with their cowabunga rendering of the old *Tarzan* theme. And, more important, they were the only disco interlopers to understand the power of the party whistle and the synth chirp. While O'Dell would release very undisco records from Diamanda Galás and Sun Ra, Y would continue to twist the dance floor into new shapes with records from New York's Pulsallama (an all-female group that sounded like Pigbag combined with Julie Brown), Leeds's Shriekback (who formed from the ashes of Gang of Four) and Bristol's Glaxo Babies and Maximum Joy, whose "Stretch" was the perfect blend of funk intensity and claw-your-eyes-out skronk even though the rap was so bad that it paled next to George Michael blessing the mike on "Wham! Rap."

Manchester's A Certain Ratio was a mixed-race band that idolized Parliament-Funkadelic and saw itself as part of the United Kingdom's rare groove scene. The problem was that on early records like *The Graveyard and the Ballroom*, the group's brand of funk was as dour and desolate as its northern surroundings. However, its sprightly 1981 cover of Banbarra's "Shack Up" was a hit in many New York clubs, and the group went to the United States to soak up the influence of the clubs and to record (with Martin Hannett, who also recorded ESG) its first studio album.

A Certain Ratio's labelmates Section 25 were largely a Xerox copy of miserablists Joy Division, but they had one moment of dance floor transcendence. "Looking From a Hilltop (Megamix)," mixed by New Order's Bernard Sumner and A Certain Ratio's Donald Johnson, was a big club hit in New York, Chicago, and Detroit—the three titans of America's Rust Belt who, amid the great population and cultural shift to the Sun Belt, were looking for solace in the United Kingdom's abandoned industrial heartland. But "Hilltop" was no pumping piston, Kling Klang, metal-on-metal behemoth; despite all the electronics, it was almost pastoral with little-girl-lost vocalist Jenny Ross giving it a kind of wind-sweeping-across-the-moors mystery.

It was probably New Order, though, that made the biggest impression on disco dance floors. The group formed from what was left of Joy Division after lead singer Ian Curtis committed suicide in 1980. They decided to pursue a synthesizer-based direction, and although they initially were as bleak as their previous incarnation, they soon took on board the influence of Giorgio Moroder, particularly the chill of tracks like "E =MC^2," and Kraftwerk's *Radio-Activity* album. The real turning point in their career, though, was when they heard Afrika Bambaataa & the Soul Sonic Force's "Planet Rock." The electro hip-hop remake of Kraftwerk's "Trans-Europe Express" and "Numbers" was largely crafted by producer Arthur Baker. New Order were so enamored with the record that they sent him a tape of their first album. He was particularly impressed with one track, "5 8 6," a brief downtempo, largely beatless synthscape, and told them that they should expand it into a full-fledged song. The result was "Blue Monday"—a combination of the melody from "5 8 6," the disembodied chorus sound from Kraftwerk's "Uranium," and synth lines from the Moroder and Patrick Cowley songbooks—which became the biggest-selling twelve-inch single in history. The record was so popular in the clubs that Bobby Orlando paid New Order the ultimate tribute: He ripped them off hook, line, and sinker on his production of Divine's "Love Reaction."

With disco as a specific musical genre (rather than a state of mind) in sharp decline in the United States by late 1979, the only clubs that kept afloat in New York were ones that encouraged quirkiness and experimentation. A Certain Ratio's first gig in New York said pretty much everything you needed to know about the bizarre combinations that were being concocted in the Big Apple in the early '80s. In December 1982, a certain Madonna opened up for A Certain Ratio's performance at the ultimate breeding ground among the disco, punk, and art scenes, Danceteria. The Danceteria was started by Jim Fouratt and his partner, Rudolf Pieper, in March 1980 at 252 West 37th Street. The club was short-lived but eventually reopened in 1982 at 30 West 21st Street. In its new incarnation, Danceteria was a three-floor space with a performance area and dance floor downstairs, another dance floor on the second floor, and a video lounge and restaurant on the third floor. Fouratt and Pieper had a staggeringly open-minded booking policy—everyone from salsa artists like Tito Puente and Típica '73 to Sun Ra to Eric Bogosian perfomed there.

DJs like Bill Bahlman, Johnny Dynell, Anita Sarko, and Mark Kamins connected the dots among postpunk, disco, hip-hop, salsa, and New Wave. Fouratt, meanwhile, explored the commonalities between disco's tawdry fleshpot and the rarefied world of modern composition—i.e., that nothing can violate the supremacy of the rhythm or pulse and a fixation on repetition—with a series of ambitious programs that brought composers like Philip Glass and Glenn Branca into the nightclub environment. "It's all about mixing up these different kinds of people," Fouratt told *The New York Times*. "We deliberately try to present serious music in a 'vulgar' format, to use the original connotation of the word. At places like The Kitchen [a high-brow experimental art venue], this work is perceived in a serious, reverential way. At Danceteria, if they like something, they cheer; if they don't, they just move on to another floor."[15]

If there was one artist, though, who truly characterized this peripatetic genre bending by spanning both the Kitchen and Studio 54 in a single bound, it was an avant-garde cello player by the name of Arthur Russell. Charles Arthur Russell Jr. was born and raised in landlocked Oskaloosa, Iowa, where, as the son of a former naval officer, he became obsessed with the ocean. In 1968, Russell moved to San Francisco to join a Buddhist commune. He was forbidden to play his cello, so he played in his closet. Russell then studied Indian music with Ali Akbar Khan and played cello on several Allen Ginsberg recordings. In 1973, he moved to New York and played drums with Laurie Anderson and worked with Talking Heads, Peter Gordon, and David Van Tiegham before going on to curate the music program at the Kitchen. Sometime in the mid-1970s, Russell went to the Gallery to see Nicky Siano spin. After his disco baptism, Russell immediately connected the dots between Hamilton Bohannon and the minimalism of Steve Reich, between a marathon DJ set and the sustained, subtly shifting harmonic clusters of Phill Niblock.

Working together as Dinosaur, Russell and Siano released "Kiss Me Again" in 1978. Talking Heads' David Byrne played one of the most clipped guitar phrases in history, while Russell's background cello was partially responsible for the record's perplexing bass sound. "Kiss Me Again" was recognizable as disco, but it was also bafflingly weird: the muffled bass line that never resolved itself, the guitar solo during the break not unlike the skronk being played by Arto Lindsay in the No Wave group DNA, and the electronic sounds that acted as a shield during the chorus, preventing any sense of release from developing, creating the sense of longing and unfulfilled desire that marked many of the best disco records.

As bizarre as it was, "Kiss Me Again" worked within established disco parameters and became a fairly substantial club hit. Russell, however, would largely abandon dance music's recognizable shapes in favor of a vision of disco as drift, as floating through and across waves and dimensions of sound. "He loved out-there stuff," says engineer Bob Blank, who was a frequent collaborator with Russell.

"He was a real artiste, and we seemed to work well together—he believed in first takes, and I was a fast engineer. We had similar musical sensibilities . . . Arthur walked in one day to make music, right after 'Kiss Me Again' came out, and we hit it off right away. He was always coming in saying that he had gotten three hundred dollars as a grant and could we do an LP—pretty wild. He once traded a 1951 Chevy that was his dad's old car for some studio time!"[16]

In 1980, Russell hooked up with another early DJ, Steve D'Aquisto, and went to Blank's studio to work on an album for West End Records, originally under the name the Little All-Stars, but they soon changed their name to Loose Joints. With an array of studio musicians and three vocalists they recruited from the dance floor of the Loft, the duo recorded countless hours of tape, but only three releases ever resulted. "Is It All Over My Face?" was originally released with a male vocal, but it didn't do much, so label head Mel Cheren asked Larry Levan to do a remix. Levan got a friend to let him into a studio when the boss wasn't around to work on the remix, but he was only three hours into it when the boss returned and Levan had to stop working. The unfinished quality of the remix perfectly suited both the track's mantralike aspects and the spacey instrumentation. "Pop Your Funk" and "Tell You Today" were both even weirder than "Is It All Over My Face?" and didn't have a Larry Levan mix to bring them back to earth—they were just left to float off on their own.

Russell's greatest dance floor achievement, however, is probably Dinosaur L's "Go Bang! #5," released on the label he founded with Will Socolov, Sleeping Bag. "Go Bang!" originally appeared on the 1981 album *24-24 Music* as "#5 (Go Bang)." The music was recorded in June 1979 with a lineup including Peter Gordon, Peter Zummo, Julius Eastman, the Ingrams, and Wilbur Bascomb, and existed in some bizarre nether region between Herbie Hancock, the Love of Life Orchestra, and D. C. LaRue. For the single release, the track was remixed by François Kevorkian, who, while restraining John Ingram's hyper and sibilant drumming into a manageable shape for the dance floor, made it even weirder by stretching the space and focusing on Eastman and Jimmy Ingram's *Phantom of the Opera* keyboards.

Indian Ocean's "School Bell / Tree House" was Russell with Zummo and Walter Gibbons, and, if anything, is more dislocated and more disjointed than "Go Bang!" The track is largely Russell mumbling ethereally (if that's possible) over some percussion loops (one conga loop and a nagging hi-hat) and a whisper of his cello in the background. As *The New York Times*'s Robert Palmer wrote about one of his performances, it conjures the image of "Russell alone on a sailboat, singing into the wind."[17] More conventionally club-friendly was Lola's "Wax the Van," a record Russell made with Bob Blank, his wife, former James Brown associate Lola, and their six-year-old son, Kenny. The enormous bass sound, water drop percussion, and windswept vocals continued Russell's fascination with oceanic sounds. Both "Schoolbell/Tree House" and "Wax the Van" can be heard, even more buffeted by wind and salt, on Russell's startlingly stark solo album of processed cello, vocals, and percussion, *World of Echo*.

Russell was a true original, but he was by no means disco's only explorer of psychedelic caverns of low-end flux. François Kevorkian was a DJ from France (where he played Yes, King Crimson, and Mahavishnu Orchestra to hippies), who moved to New York in 1975 to study with jazz drummer Tony Williams after he was booted out of university in Lyon for starting a general strike. In February 1976, Kevorkian was hired by Galaxy 21 to play drums and percussion alongside DJ Walter Gibbons. Kevorkian had little knowledge of the music being played at New York's after-hours clubs when he was hired, but being thrown in at the deep end forced him quickly to gain an intimate knowledge of disco structure. When Galaxy 21 closed, Kevorkian worked as a kitchen porter and toilet cleaner at Experiment Four, where John "Jellybean" Benitez spun before he made his name at the Funhouse. Jellybean gave Kevorkian access to his home studio, where he would experiment with tape edits, initially imitating the homemade edits that Gibbons used. After he got a feel for the equipment and the format, Kevorkian started to add effects to his edits—something that no one else in New York was doing at the time—an idea that he got from reggae. "The psychedelic multidimensional planetary Reggae that the people like Black Uhuru was doing with that one album 'Black Uhuru in Dub' [a dub of the *Love Crisis* album] really changed my whole way of thinking," Kevorkian told writer Jonathan Fleming. "After I heard that album, it was like my life had changed. I saw landscapes that I had never knew existed before as far as the way to use effects in the studio or the way to use effects as music."[18]

Kevorkian soon landed a gig at Sesame Street, a black gay after-hours club that used the Flamingo's space while it was closed during the summer, and then at Studio 54 challenger New York New York. While playing at New York New York, Kevorkian was approached by former Scepter/Wand A&R man Marvin Schlachter, who had just started a disco label called Prelude, and asked if he would do remixes for the new label. Kevorkian agreed, and his first mix for the label was Musique's "In the Bush," which he did in conjunction with engineer Bob Blank. "François came in and was given three hours by Prelude to remix 'Bush,'" Blank remembers. "I basically did my thing and he directed. He later was a very hands-on pro-ducer, but at the time he had never done a remix and actually did not know what to call the 4/4 beat that the bass drum provided—he kept saying, 'Give me more *poom poom poom*.' The sounds, dy-namic, etc., was all me, but François created the intro progression from bass drum up."[19]

Kevorkian did dozens of mixes for Prelude and was a constant presence in Blank's Blank Tapes Studios. "I was passionate about the fact that we were working in a new medium," Blank says of his time working with Kevorkian on remixes. "Previous to that, records were very dense, with three minutes of tightly integrated music. We were changing that by dropping out parts, adding loops of rhythm, mak-ing it sound more like we heard it."[20] Despite Kevorkian's early edits, his love of Jamaican dub, and the example of Walter Gibbons's mix of Bettye Lavette's "Doin' the Best That I Can," most of his Prelude mixes were extensions and boosts rather than full-on restructuring work. It wasn't until a British obscurity, the dub mix of "Love Money" by TW Funkmasters, became a huge club hit in New York that he fully realized the power that dub effects had over a dance floor.[21] "Love Money" propelled Kevorkian to explore the farthest reaches of outer space on his remixes of Jimmy Cliff's "Treat the Youths Right" and "D" Train's "Keep On." Kevorkian's ultimate dub excur-sion, though, was a journey he took with former PiL bassist Jah Wobble, Can's keyboardist and tape manipulator Holger Czukay, and U2 guitarist The Edge. "Snake Charmer" was egghead disco at its very best, a merger of Kraftwerk-style drum programming (from Kevorkian himself), dub bass lines, and tape collages reminiscent of David Byrne and Brian Eno's *My Life in the Bush of Ghosts*, also an early '80s club favorite.

In the hands of people like Arthur Russell and François Kevorkian, disco wasn't the oversexed, airheaded clotheshorse that it became in the mainstream. It was no longer music for the belle of the ball, but for the wallflowers who danced to their own drummer. If this moment in dance music history can be seen as the revenge of the nerd, the class valedictorians were undoubtedly Was (Not Was). The group was formed in 1980 by Donald Fagenson and David Weiss, childhood friends from Detroit who had spent their adolescence locked in each other's basements listening to MC5, Frank Zappa, John Coltrane, and Firesign Theater. Such listening habits inevitably led to a surfeit of ideas that came tumbling out every which way on their records: reggae skank guitar, Robert Quine–style solos courtesy of MC5's Wayne Kramer, surreal, sarcastic lyrics via Dylan and Lenny Bruce, James Brown/Nile Rodgers chicken scratch, rudimentary synth riffs, bass lines that alternated between Jah Wobble's work with PiL and Terry Lewis's Minneapolis sound, paranoia that seemed to come straight from a 1950s public service announcement. It was all wrapped up in the brittle production values that marked the '80s—the eggshell sound lending a piquancy to the rueful observations of Reagan and Thatcher age facades.

Of course, the goal of the best dance music is to get you to think with your entire body, and that's exactly what Was (Not Was) succeeded in doing. It wasn't merely the détourned words of Ronald Reagan that let you know that "Tell Me That I'm Dreaming" was not your ordinary hands-in-the-air disco stomper; it was the astringent guitar riff, the dub alienation, the comedic voices, the sibilant hi-hat that would soon become the hallmark of house music. "Wheel Me Out," produced and mixed by Don Was and longtime partner in crime Jack Tann (who was in Was's early punk bands the Traitors and President Eisenhower), represented everything great about the merging of postpunk, dub, and dance music in the early '80s. It was cathartic yet eerie and uncomfortable, cryptically political, full of nuance and intrigue. "A few people, myself included, had started to listen to Jamaican dub reggae," Was told Anthony Haden-Guest.

"The result was a different kind of disco. It wasn't this happy kind of thing. I think maybe the drugs changed. The first time I went to the Paradise Garage I was high on mushrooms. Which is distinctly different from going to Studio and doing a bunch of blow. It's a very different kind of experience. It was enormous. *Man, it felt like the speakers were five stories high!* The place took on a really dark monolithic feel. And it wasn't like . . . happy."[22]

> I went down to Paradise Garage
> I took my place in line
> The cashier said, "Are you alright?"
> I said, "I'm feeling fine"
> I'm a stranger to nirvana
> I don't box outside my weight
> But when I stepped outside the taxi, I did not anticipate this feeling
> —Tim Curry, "Paradise Garage"

When disco put on its loincloth and face paint in 1978 and went, frankly, a bit moronic, there was one club that upheld the early ideal of disco as a "Saturday night mass." When disco was beaten up, stripped, and left for dead by the side of the road two years later, there was one club that kept the faith, refused to let it die, and nursed it back to health. That was the Paradise Garage, and although it doesn't have the name recognition of Studio 54, both nightlife and dance music cognoscenti venerate it with the same devotion as a supplicant has for a saint.

On the surface, there was nothing particularly special about the Paradise Garage. As its name indicates, it was housed in a nondescript parking garage at 84 King Street in SoHo. There was a neon version of the club's logo (a curly haired guy hiding behind his massive biceps holding a tambourine) at the end of a long ramp that led you from the garage to the club itself, but no spectacular lighting effects inside. The front and rear rooms where dancers went to cool off were covered in sawdust and sometimes showed movies like *Midnight Cowboy* and *Altered States*, but there was no lavish VIP room stocked with endless supplies of coke, blow jobs, or champagne (there was, in fact, no alcohol served at the club at all). The club's centerpiece was the dance floor, not because it had multicolored lights or special wood imported from Sumatra, but because it was huge and people came to dance. "It was a different kind of dance floor," writes Mel Cheren, who lent money to the club's owner, Michael Brody, to help finance it, "in part because the people on it were so different from those at every other major disco at that time. For one thing, they were without question the city's most serious dancers. There was no attitude here, no cliques defined by their muscles, no fashion victims, no A-list. These people were dancers."[23]

While the Paradise Garage is shrouded in myth and mystique and held up as the pinnacle by people who never went there, one thing is certain: It is considered by many people to be the greatest discotheque ever because it was a temple to the music. The sermons to the flock were delivered by a sound system that has never been equaled. Designed by Richard Long, the system mimicked the qualities of David Mancuso's setup at the Loft, but for a dance floor packed with a couple of thousand people rather than a living room with a couple of hundred. It was ferociously loud (some people say it was too loud) and, unlike the Graebar systems at places like 12 West and the Saint, the bass made your bowels quake, but it was also crystal clear and capable of remarkable detail. The leader of the congregation was the DJ, Larry Levan, who would spend hours fine-tuning the system and deploying little tricks like gradually upgrading the cartridges on his turntables throughout the night so that the peak would be overwhelming in its effect. With the amazing sound system at his disposal, Levan became a master at manipulating the EQ levels and teasing new nuances out of a record.

Levan is almost universally revered as the greatest DJ of all time. This is not because Levan was a great mixer (he was actually pretty lousy) or was a technological or virtuosic innovator, but because he was a master at creating a mood and had that trait of which most DJing legends are made: He had a telepathic relationship with his dancers. Stories abound of Levan's "dance floor evangelism": people he knew claiming that they felt certain records talking to them specifically and then looking up at the DJ booth to see Levan glaring at them or blowing them kisses depending on the message the song was conveying. Levan would drop ballads and a cappellas at peak times, leave seconds of dead air in the midst of a set, and let two records run together, creating a grating cacophony, but he also created an intensity on the dance floor that has yet to be replicated. Levan took risks—not only by restructuring records like Loleatta Holloway's "Runaway" on the fly or by playing a single record for an hour as he did in 1984 with Colonel Abrams's "Music Is the Answer," but by constantly searching for records from outside of "dance music" that fit his aesthetic. He championed records like the Clash's "Magnificent Dance," Jah Wobble's "Snakecharmer," Manuel Göttsching's E2-E4, and Marianne Faithfull's "Why d'Ya Do It?"

To Levan, DJing wasn't about mixing, skills, or taste. It was about feeling and, strangely enough, narrative. Levan often told stories or made comments through his song selection. "Out of all the records you have, maybe five or six of them actually make sense together," Levan told Steven Harvey in 1983. "There is actually a message in the dance, the way you feel, the muscles you use, but only certain records have that. Say I was playing songs about music—"I Love Music" by The O'Jays, "Music" by Al Hudson—and the next record is "Weekend" [by Phreek or Class Action]. That's about getting laid, a whole other thing. If I was dancing and truly into the words and the feeling and it came on, it might be a good record, but it makes no sense because it doesn't have anything to do with the others. So, a slight pause, a sound effect, something else to let you know it's a new paragraph rather than one continuous sentence."[24]

While on one hand Levan attempted to become if not the Homer of the turntables at least the O. Henry, he was also aiming for wild abandon, trying to create epiphanic bursts of energy that shattered structures like narrative. Some of his signature tics—like cutting off a record midflow or his car-crash mixes—seemed almost like the DJing equivalent of punk rock dissonance or feedback. He was after what Roland Barthes defined as "punctum": that moment of explosive insight where everything suddenly becomes clear, the crack of the Zen master's cane across the back of your head, the divine contact that comes after a whirling dervish ritual.

As a teenager, Levan had frequented the Loft and the Gallery when they first opened, and got his first DJing gig at age eighteen at the Continental Baths in 1973. "I was doing lights and the DJ walked out," he recalled to Harvey. "The manager who was like, a six foot three inches, Cuban guy, said, 'You're going to play records tonight!' I told him that I didn't have any records. 'You've got five hours!'"[25] Well, Levan managed to find some records and ended up playing the Baths for about a year.

Levan left the Baths in 1974 to play at Richard Long's after-hours loft club, SoHo Place, at 452 Broadway. While Levan's growing following ensured that the place was packed, the club was in Long's workshop and was essentially a showcase for Long's recently started sound equipment business. Unfortunately, the club's booming bass ensured that it wouldn't stay open for very long. As soon as SoHo Place closed, Levan was asked by Michael Brody to DJ at his newly opened club at 143 Reade Street in what is now known as TriBeCa. The club was situated in an old meat locker and still had the temperature control switch, which Levan would play with along with the DJ crossover that allowed him to manipulate specific frequencies of a record. It was at Reade Street that Levan would develop the techniques as well as the sound—the deep, dark bass, the queasy, dubby emotion that he would extract from records—that would make him a legend.

With an unsympathetic landlord and space issues, Reade Street was never going to be the right space for Levan's rising star, so Brody closed the club in 1976 and asked Levan not to play anywhere else until he found a new place. The new place was the Paradise Garage and it was built explicitly for Levan—probably the only nightclub ever constructed for a specific DJ. The Garage unofficially opened in January 1977 with the "Construction Parties" that were held in the club's small nine-hundred-square-foot Grey Room in order to raise money for the rest of the club's construction. When the full club (with the second largest dance floor in New York) finally officially opened in February 1978, it was a disaster. There was a hitch with the sound system, and even though it was in the middle of a snowstorm, no one was allowed inside until it was fixed. Once they got inside, it was practically as cold as it was outside. Almost all of the A-list Flamingo crowd that Brody had invited left, vowing never to return.

It's debatable whether the pretty boys would have stayed at the Paradise Garage even if they had stuck around to hear Levan spin. Their environment was the Flamingo, which specialized in relentlessly chipper music; Levan played darker, more bottom-heavy records that retained their connection to the gospel continuum. As time went on and "disco" became less and less popular, Levan's music got darker, weirder, more disjointed, particularly the remixes that he made specifically for his own dance floor. Levan was one of disco's true dub champions, and his mix of Instant Funk's "I Got My Mind Made Up" and his production of New York Citi Peech Boys' "Don't Make Me Wait" are classics of dub technique used in the service of dance floor imperatives: delaying climax while building tension and stretching the beat, and as an impressionistic canvas to depict the club life dystopia of constant, but unfulfilled, temptation and unrequited desire. His most radical remix, however, just may be his dub mix of Smokey Robinson's minor R&B hit "And I Don't Love You." One of the most famous voices in the history of popular music becomes nothing but a ghost, and a devastatingly haunting one at that, only mournfully intoning the title phrase a couple of times from behind a fog of echo and distended guitar. Levan uses echo to double the prevailing beat over itself and inserts a cascade of synth-toms, subverting a rather ham-fisted '80s funk-lite groove to create an opiated palette of dance floor colors that gives the lie to naysayers who claim that disco is capable of only one, skweaming emotional timbre.

The Garage's heyday was in the early '80s, after disco had supposedly been banished into exile. "In the early '80s no one seemed to have any direction. The [DJs] were all scattered around trying to find the new thing because disco was dead," Paradise Garage regular Danny Krivit says about the Garage's ability to continue to attract huge crowds. "They were really playing a lot of stuff that they didn't feel . . . [Levan] was completely unaffected by this. He was playing stuff that he thought was good music. The club had a clear direction. Maybe the name disco or the trash disco was easy to throw away, but you couldn't lump all this music together as bad music. There was a lot of good music there. The Garage got people back to that—this is just good dance music."[26]

The gospel of the Paradise Garage spread quickly, particularly to a club in New Jersey. The Zanzibar opened in Newark in August 1979 after the club's owner, Miles Berger, inspired by a visit to the Paradise Garage, got Richard Long to design a system in his club at the Lincoln Motel. Hippie Torales was the club's original DJ, but he was replaced in 1981 by Tony Humphries and Tee Scott. While clubs like Zanzibar and later the Shelter in New York ensured that "Garage music" would become ossified, enshrined in the mausoleum of genre, they weren't the only culprits. Even Levan's own crowd got protective of what it thought Garage music was. Krivit remembers that when hip-hop first came out "quickly, people were like, 'I don't like this, don't push rap on me.' Certain people were getting a little standoffish, like, 'This is Garage music, that doesn't belong here.' That used to bother Larry whenever anyone said that. He was like, 'Good music is good music, so when I hear something that's rap and it's good, I'm going to play it here.'"[27] Nevertheless, out of Levan's hands and outside of its original environment, Garage came to mean only soulful New York dance music, especially with a jazzy feel; gone were the weird records, the messianic intensity, the messy mistakes. Garage soon was characterized by the same rigid beat and lack of inspiration that doomed disco—albeit on a smaller scale.

As the Paradise Garage was reinstating the spirituality and communion of early disco after its fall from grace, another enormously influential nightclub was propelling disco into the future by remaking it as a kind of doo-wop, one not to be sung on the corner or a stoop under a streetlight, but in the arcade by the glare of a video game screen and mostly by girls. Blending the innocence of the early girl groups and doo-wop singers with disco's fractured sense of melody and a percussion sensibility halfway between disco and hip-hop, the music that emerged from the Funhouse was called freestyle. While many of the aural hallmarks of disco were no longer in evidence, this new music was still very much a tribal rite, a declaration of often forbidden sexuality and an expression of the ambivalence about crossing over.

Situated in one of many of Manhattan's warehouse districts at 526 West 26 Street, the Funhouse opened on March 30, 1979, with Jim Burgess and Bobby DJ. They were soon replaced by Jonathan Fearing, who played a sort of classicist disco at a time when traditional disco was dying and was mutating into new forms. Fearing was replaced in 1981 by young hotshot John "Jellybean" Benitez, who had his finger on the pulse of the changing dance scene in New York. Benitez drew a fanatical following of Hispanic and Italian-American teenagers from the Bronx and the outlying areas of Brooklyn and Queens like Canarsie and Ozone Park. The dancers at the club were called "buggas," and their uniform (for both boys and girls) consisted of short, sleeveless cutoff T-shirts (often with the name of their neighborhood printed on it) that showed generous amounts of midriff, sweatpants, bandanas rolled as thin as possible and tied around the forehead, and Chinese slippers.

The vibe was a combination of hip-hop and disco: The crowd would bark if they liked a song that Jellybean was playing and boo if they didn't; the boys would be prowling the dance floor looking for people to battle with (both with dance moves and with fists) while the girls would be singing along to the cathartic songs of heartbreak. Jellybean, whose DJ booth was situated inside a twelve-foot-high clown face, played a combination of electro (Man Parrish's "Hip-Hop Be-Bop"), disco (Jimmy "Bo" Horne's "Spank"), weird disco (Martin Circus's "Disco Circus"), Italo-disco (Harry Thumann's "Underwater"), British New Wave (New Order's "Confusion" and Wide Boy Awake's "Slang Teacher"), and classic break beats (Jimmy Castor's "It's Just Begun").

The sound the club was most known for, though, was the hard electroboogie of Arthur Baker and John Robie, especially records like Jenny Burton's "Remember What You Like," Freez's "I.O.U.," Planet Patrol's "Play at Your Own Risk," and Slack's "Slack." Robie was one of the most important keyboard players since World War II, largely because of his mastery of the Emulator sampling keyboard, a more affordable version of the Fairlight without any sequencing capabilities, which was released in 1982, ushering in the era of sampladelia. While sampling is most associated with hip-hop, its first use on record was on former Main Ingredient vocalist Cuba Gooding's 1983 version of his old group's "Happiness Is Just Around The Bend" (a cover of the Brian Auger song). Robie concocted an entire chorus out of one syllable, Gooding singing "bop." The sampling on "Happiness" was fairly discreet: You had to be part of the cognoscenti to notice it. However, later that year Robie made unmistakable use of the Emulator on C-Bank's stunning disco *concrète* classic "One More Shot," which used a snippet of the sound of breaking glass as a percussion device and all manner of weird synth striations and nasty scratches to give a grim edge to vocalist Jenny Burton's tale of heartbreak and lover's paranoia.

Records like these were the flip side of the music popular in late gay discos like the Saint and Trocadero Transfer: Where Patrick Cowley used the new technology to imagine a brave new world of sexuality, Robie and Baker's harsh drum machines, piercing synthesizers, and non sequitur sound effects made perfect sense to alienated kids raised on video games; where Cowley et al. were celebrating the fact that it was raining men, these records were asking that age-old question of teen love—will you still love me tomorrow? Somewhere in this mechanical matrix, New York Latinos heard ancestral echoes of salsa piano lines and *montuño* rhythms. In the hands of producers like the Latin Rascals, Paul Robb, Omar Santana, and Andy "Panda" Tripoli, the Pac-Man bleeps, synth stabs, and Roland TR-808 claves became a robotic Latin jam session called freestyle.

Freestyle's ground zero was Shannon's 1983 single "Let the Music Play." Although it didn't have the hi-hat sound that would come to characterize freestyle percussion, the song's electro-woodblock-and-cowbell percussion and kick drum/snare drum interaction sounded like a cross between Gary Numan and Tito Puente, and provided the blueprint for freestyle's street-smart tales of innocence and experience. "Please Don't Go," by sixteen-year-old Nayobe and produced by Andy Panda, further Latinized the "Let the Music Play" formula by featuring keyboard patterns stolen from both Eddie Palmieri and Patrice Rushen on top of synthesized timbal beats. With these records taking off in his club, Jellybean attempted to reclaim the old break beat classic "The Mexican" for Latinos from both Ennio Morricone and British prog rock group Babe Ruth.

However, as freestyle was starting to take off, Jellybean's interest was elsewhere. According to legend, one night in 1983 a Funhouse regular had sneaked into the DJ booth and managed to play her demo over the club's sound system when Jellybean wasn't paying attention. The crowd loved what they heard, and the clubgoer persuaded Jellybean to produce a track for her. Her name, of course, was Madonna. Although she had previously sung backup for Patrick "Born to Be Alive" Hernandez, and Jellybean's production of "Holiday" was significantly more melodic and more streamlined than most of what he played at the Funhouse, Madonna's early style owed a huge debt to the freestyle sound.

Jellybean quit the Funhouse in June 1984 to pursue his own recording and production career, but freestyle continued to dominate the club thanks to Jellybean's replacement, Lil' Louie Vega, who would later go on to fame as one half of Masters At Work. Meanwhile, former Funhouse dancer Lisa Velez was discovered by production team Full Force and, as Lisa Lisa, became freestyle's biggest early star. With a dubby synth effect stolen from Robie's Emulator and a Roland woodblock pattern, Lisa Lisa and Cult Jam's debut record, "I Wonder If I Take You Home," became the first freestyle record to dent the American Top 40 in 1985.

Records like Shannon's "Let the Music Play" were also big on Friday "Wheels of Steel" nights at the Roxy, an enormous club at 515 West 18th Street. Freestyle was also called "Latin hip-hop," and its drum machine beats fit in with the electro sound that was being developed at this club by DJs like D.ST and Afrika Bambaataa. While the uptown hip-hop kids were turning downtown technology to their own ends at the "Wheels of Steel" nights, there was a similar reclamation effort going on with disco the rest of the week.

The Roxy was conceived of as a roller rink, and "initially, they wanted to be Studio 54 but with roller skates—the red ropes, celebrities, everything," claims Danny Krivit, who was the original DJ there. "A couple years into it, the [original] owners sold it to another guy. The new owner really wanted to open the club up and fill it. Roller skating, they'd consider three, four hundred people a good night. I remember that I started doing Monday nights because that was the only night of the week he wasn't there trying to tell me what to play. It was only about thirty or fifty people that night—he didn't care about that night. Very quickly I got the numbers up to twelve hundred, which for roller skating is very crowded. And it dwarfed any of his other nights. It was only because I was playing what they needed to hear rather than what he thought they needed to hear—real roller-skating music."[28]

Developing from more R&B-flavored disco, like Patrick Adams's productions, Brass Construction, and the Mizell brothers' work on A Taste of Honey's "Boogie Oogie Oogie," this "real roller-skating music" was more downtempo and less strictly 4/4 than classic disco because you just can't skate to high-tempo music. Krivit was playing records like Shalamar's "Take That to the Bank" and "The Second Time Around," the Whispers' "And the Beat Goes On," Lakeside's "Fantastic Voyage" (all released on Los Angeles's Solar label), Rufus's "Do You Love What You Feel," and Vaughan Mason's "Bounce, Rock, Skate, Roll." While maintaining much of disco's groove, these records also marked a return of what dance music historian Brian Chin calls "an upbeat-and-downbeat, one-two feel to dance."[29]

Away from the roller rink, this "funkier" groove came to be known as "boogie" or "street music," "to distinguish it from Hi-NRG and the styles of '80s dance music in Europe."[30] Many of the early records in this style—the Fantastic Aleems' "Get Down Friday Night," Logg's "I Know You Will," Convertion's "Let's Do It" (all featuring LeRoy Burgess on vocals), Central Line's "Walking Into Sunshine"—were hits at the Paradise Garage, and pop trinkets like Indeep's "Last Night a DJ Saved My Life" had an across-the-board appeal. Soon enough, though, records like Young & Company's "I Like What You're Doin' to Me," Goldie Alexander's "Show You My Love," Major Harris's "Gotta Make Up Your Mind," Kinky Foxx's "So Different," and Ceela's "I'm in Love" began to articulate a more defiantly R&B sensibility and broke away from the rainbow coalition that defined New York in the immediate postdisco era, feeding into R&B styles like the Minneapolis funk of Jam & Lewis and the New Jack Swing of Teddy Riley that severed any connection to disco or "white" music.

"YOU MUST FEEL THE DRIVE"
Italo-Disco

Disco may have been tarred and feathered, drawn and quartered, and flayed in the United States, but disco never died in Europe. It was never even dragged through the mud or had its name used in vain. Instead, disco became part, if not the basis, of the continent's pop framework. Perhaps it was because disco maintained a connection to old-fashioned Tin Pan Alley melodies or because in Europe pop is treasured for its frivolity or because Europeans saw disco as their last chance to maintain a foothold on a pop landscape that was fast mutating into the primary vehicle for American cultural imperialism. But whatever the reason, disco was perhaps even bigger in Europe after its 1979 death in America than before. Part of this was due to laws in many European countries that mandated that a certain proportion of records played on pop radio had to be homegrown, but it is also undeniable that disco flourished in the hands of European producers in the 1980s, under protectionism or not, and nowhere more so than in Italy.

Italy had plenty of jet-set discos in the late '60s/early '70s, including the regular Roman haunt of the Onassises, Number One (two blocks from the Via Veneto), where a drug investigation in 1972 quickly turned to stolen art trafficking, forcing many members "to [leave] hurriedly for safaris in East Africa and for the sun in Acapulco."[31] However, typical of the fractured history of disco, the story of Italo-disco really begins in France.[32] The Peppers were a poppy prog rock quintet featuring synth player Mat Camison and drummer Pierre Alain Dahan, who, inspired by the success of Chicory Tip's cover of Giorgio Moroder's "Son of My Father" and Hot Butter's "Popcorn," decided to put out their own goofy synth novelty number. With its bouncy clavinet bass line, hand claps, "bop-bop-bop-bop bop-bop-a-da-da" vocals, and whiny synth melody, "Pepper Box" was a huge hit across Europe in 1973 and was an early disco hit in the United States the following year. A few years later, Dahan was recruited to be part of a group to flesh out a TV theme song for widespread commercial release. The group was called Space, and "Magic Fly" ushered in synth disco along with Donna Summer's "I Feel Love" in 1977. But where "I Feel Love" used the Moog throb for distinctly erotic purposes, "Magic Fly" was not Spanish fly and used synth pulses and sequencer rhythms to sail topographic oceans and explore the dark side of the moon. This obsession with space and the prog rock tendencies would come to characterize Italo-disco.[33]

Disco music had arrived in Italy in the mid-1970s wearing more typical clothing. "From 1974 to 1976, there was this club [Baia Degli Angeli in Gabicce, near Rimini on the Adriatic coast] with two American DJs, Bob Day and Tom Sison," says Italian DJ Daniele Baldelli. "They had beautiful records that Italian DJs never listened to before because there was no import-export in that period. We received records from America maybe six months later. So when these two boys came, it was very good to listen to this music."[34] The beautiful records that Day and Sison were playing were examples of the Philadelphia sound that would soon set Europe alight with its mixture of soaring melodies and driving rhythms.

In 1977, Day headed back to the States and asked Baldelli, who had been DJing since 1969 in nearby Cattolica, to replace him. Baldelli agreed and, along with Claudio Rispoli, carried on playing Day and Sison's mixture of Philly, disco, and funk. "At Baia Degli Angeli they had something very nice for the DJ," Baldelli remembers. "I was playing in a glass elevator, so I could go up and down from the ground floor to the first floor and see all the dance floors in the club—the three inside and the two outside near the pool."[35]

Baldelli left Baia Degli Angeli in 1978, and in April 1979 he became the DJ at the Cosmic club in Lazise, a small town on Lake Garda.[36] The club, which had a capacity of one thousand people, was based on famous American discotheques: The dance floor had the same multicolored lights as Odyssey 2001, where *Saturday Night Fever* was filmed, and the club had columns of light similar to those at Studio 54. However, the Cosmic was much more egalitarian than its models. "The people that came to Cosmic . . . were Italian people from eighteen to twenty-eight, all the same style," Baldelli says. "They dressed with jeans, T-shirts, the girls were like hippies in Woodstock, many flowers and so on. At Cosmic there was no door selector."[37]

The clubbers themselves may have been down to earth, but the music that Baldelli played lived up to the club's name. "In 1979 I was playing the same music I was at Baia Degli Angelli, then from 1980 until 1984 it started something in me," Baldelli says. "I was looking in every kind of music . . . On one record I used to play, *Bolero* by Ravel, and on this record I played African sound of Africa Djolé [a Guinean percussion troupe], or maybe the electronic sound of Steve Reich over which I mix Malinke sound of Guinea [probably ethnographic recordings], or I mix T-Connection with Moebius and Roedelius, or maybe Cat Stevens and Lee Ritenour, or maybe Depeche Mode at thirty-three instead of forty-five, or I play Yellowman forty-five instead of thirty-three. I mix twenty African songs with one pattern of Korg electronic drum. I play one Brazilian batucada with a song of Kraftwerk. I was using synthesizer effect on the voice of Miriam Makeba, Jorge Ben, or Fela Kuti. Or I play Indian [sic] melody of Ofra Haza or Sheila Chandra with the electronic sound of German label Sky [late-period Krautrock like Cluster, Michael Rother, and Streetmark]."[38]

This combination of spaced-out rock and tribal percussion became known as Cosmic music in honor of the club. Crank up the speed a bit (Baldelli says that most of the music he played was between 90 and 105 bpm) and this was the same formula as Italo-disco. While the Cosmic club is often seen as the crucible of the Italo sound, most of the ingredients were already in place prior to Baldelli's epiphany, no matter how unique his music was. In fact, Baldelli himself dismisses most Italo-disco as too mainstream. "Claudio Simonetti, Gazebo, Mario Boncaldo—all this, for me the Italian music I didn't like, I think it was too much commercial," he declares. "The only songs I played in Cosmic was Koto [responsible for "Chinese Revenge"], Hipnosis [Italo band that covered both Jean-Michel Jarre and Vangelis] and Mario Boncaldo [the man behind the pinnacle of the Italo sound, Klein & MBO's "Dirty Talk"], all the other production was really commercial. I preferred to play the electronic music that came from Germany, especially the Sky label."[39]

Claudio Simonetti, keyboardist for the Italian prog rock group Goblin, came up with a similar formula to Baldelli in 1978 after being turned on to disco at Rome's Easy Going club by DJ Paolo Micioni. Simonetti's early productions for Easy Going ("Baby I Love You" and "Fear") and Vivien Vee ("Give Me a Break") were Giorgio Moroder–style disco but seen through the refraction of Alan Parsons Project's "I, Robot" and his experience at Cinecittà studios soundtracking countless films and absorbing ideas from film/TV composers like Nino Nardini, Piero Piccioni, Giampiero Boneschi, Mario Nascimbene, and Ennio Morricone himself. Easy Going's "Fear," in particular, was essentially Pink Floyd remixed by Moroder and Silver Convention.

Another important early influence on the Italo sound was the husband-wife duo Krisma. Maurizio and Christina Arcieri lived in London in the late '70s and combined punk antics and fashion, New Wave melodies and guitar lines with Vangelis-style electronics on records like "Chinese Restaurant" and "Many Kisses." Soon enough, though, the Italo sound would be influencing London's New Wave scene. Klein & MBO's "Dirty Talk" was the perfect Italo package: a prog rock sense of exploration and portentousness, the sangfroid of British synth pop, really cheap-sounding synthesizers, a very Moroder hi-hat shuffle, and although the percussion never really gets going, the multiple oscillating bass lines give it a sort of syncopated feel. "Dirty Talk" was an enormous hit on dance floors across the world and became an acknowledged influence on New Order's "Blue Monday."

"Dirty Talk" was also a big hit at the Paradise Garage and at the Warehouse in Chicago, where Levan's friend and former DJing partner at the Continental Baths, Frankie Knuckles, DJed. Knuckles had moved to Chicago from New York in 1977 when he was recruited by the owners of the Warehouse. Knuckles initially played mostly Salsoul and Philly records and gospel-influenced message records, but by the late '70s the crowd started to respond more and more to the weird, dubby records that Levan was spinning back in New York. In response, Knuckles started to augment his old disco records with the more rigid beats of a cheap drum machine and reedited them to make them either punchier or dubbier. Legend has it that this combination of disco with drum machines and reel-to-reel tape edits became known as House music after people kept asking record stores for "the records they played at the Warehouse."

Another way of expressing the formula was Salsoul + Italo = House. Records like "Dirty Talk," with its electronic minimalism and its simultaneously warm and eerie sound, fit in perfectly at the Warehouse and at rival club the Music Box, where Ron Hardy DJed in a similar style. Italo records were huge in Chicago, largely thanks to Paul Weisburg's Imports Etc. record shop,[40] and provided much of the blueprint for House music, which would distill the excess of disco into a drum machine beat and a synthesized bass line. The influence of records like "Dirty Talk" and Gaz Nevada's "I.C. Love Affair" on deep House auteur Larry Heard and Capricorn's "I Need Love" on producer Farley Jackmaster Funk is obvious.

Equally apparent is Italo-disco's influence on the other crystallization of the disco sound to emerge from the American Midwest, techno. Techno was born in Detroit—well, actually in Belleville, a fishing village about twenty-five miles outside the city—as the sound of profound postindustrial alienation. Although often described as

Parliament-Funkadelic meets Kraftwerk, the earliest techno records bear at least as big a stamp of Italo as that of George Clinton or Düsseldorf's showroom dummies. One of the first techno-style records to emerge from Detroit was A Number of Names' "Share-vari," which lifted its hook directly from Kano's early Italo record "Holly Dolly" even if its prime influence was arch British synth-pop. Alexander Robotnick's (a pseudonym for ex–jazz musician Maurizio Dami) "Problèmes d'Amour" was another Italo record that found its way to Detroit from Canada (where the Italo sound was enormously popular) and into the hearts and sequencers of Juan Atkins, Derrick May, Kevin Saunderson, and Carl Craig, the producers who would largely create techno. For its American release, "Problèmes d'Amour" was remixed by François Kevorkian, providing a further link be-tween disco and the dance music that it melted into.

"STAYIN' ALIVE"

Disco Today

There's something which very few people write about or understand—but it's probably one of the most important processes of popular culture—and that is a generation recognising itself in music.　　—Colin Newman

I was thinking that what happened in the 1970s had much more impact on modern culture than what happened in the 1960s. As far as I can tell, the way they act, the way they look . . . It's not about what happened in the 1960s, it's really about what happened in the 1970s.　—Clem Burke

June 29, 1999, was "'70s Night" at Chicago's Wrigley Field. Before that night's game between the Chicago Cubs and the Milwaukee Brewers, the Village People performed a miniconcert. Standing at home plate, the group sang their hits "Y.M.C.A.," which had become a standard between-innings song at most of the country's ballparks, and "In the Navy." Nearly twenty years to the day after Chicago's disco riot, and only a few miles up the road from Comiskey Park, the Village People, the most iconic symbol of everything that was wrong with disco in the eyes of Middle America, not only escaped a baseball stadium with their lives and no field invasion, but they were given a standing ovation.

Almost five months later, on November 17, the United States Postal Service unveiled its disco stamp as part of the Celebrate the Century series of commemorative stamps. The stamp, which depicted a man and a woman dressed like John Travolta and Karen Lynn Gorney in *Saturday Night Fever* dancing under a mirror ball, garnered 365,221 votes in a nationwide ballot to choose fifteen images that best represented the 1970s from a choice of thirty. Disco was outranked by only the smiley face, *Sesame Street*, and Earth Day; it outpolled VCRs, the nation's bicentennial, *Monday Night Football*, the Pittsburgh Steelers winning four Super Bowls, the women's rights movement, the *Pioneer 10* spacecraft, and *All in the Family*.

Twenty-five years after the fact, "disco" is no longer a five-letter word that can't be uttered in polite company; it's no longer the guilty pleasure hidden in the closet along with your macramé wall hangings and lava lamp. Disco is now even enshrined as part of the establishment; it has the imprimatur of the federal government. A year before the stamp and the Village People's triumphant appearance at Wrigley, disco was the subject of two feature films—*54* and *The Last Days of Disco*—and had a costarring role in a third, *Boogie Nights*. While *Boogie Nights* did attempt to replicate the wild sexual abandon of the era (being about the porn industry, it could hardly not), the movies were all marked by the almost complete absence of gay or black characters. It was a whitewash comparable to the hosing down of the balconies at Studio 54 and the Saint: Effacing both the unrepentant, orgiastic stink that made disco so subversive in the first place and the holding out for false promises that gave it its weight and tension, these movies left behind nothing but the after-trail of revisionist kitsch. Imprisoning disco in the gloss of nostalgia—with its little inconveniences swept under the cover of a twenty-inch bell-bottom—these acts of preservation have forced disco to be seen through the rose-tinted mirror shades of irony. Reduced to nothing but stockbrokers in leisure suits and good-time girls in tube tops, the contemporary memory of disco serves only to camouflage the pain of one of the most difficult decades in American history with an afro wig and rainbow-colored stockings.

On the other hand, disco's cheery image is a reminder that it belongs to everyone: from drunk guys at the ballpark to members of a drag revue, from revivalist bores and "quality music" snobs to girls ready to go out on the town—all can claim disco as their own. Despite the media's focus on the elitism of Studio 54, it was and is populist music par excellence. Its willingness to be all things to all people—born from the alienation at the core of its soul—marks it as the perfect American music despite what its detractors claimed. The only thing un-American about disco was its derision of authenticity, that crutch used to prop up the fragile ego of an upstart nation. But from a contemporary perspective, maybe even that's not so true.

Disco was the last gasp for integration in America, and its pluralist aesthetic has acted as a beacon for producers reacting against today's musical apartheid. "I think in the past twenty years or so America has become a lot more stratified," says Daniel Wang, a dance music producer whose work explicitly references disco. "In the mid- to late '60s there was the civil rights era, and in the '70s there was a certain remnant idealism about having cultures mix. And you hear that very explicitly in disco music. You hear it when Vince Montana talks about Salsoul: 'Hey, we got the white jazz xylophone player, the blues guitar player . . .' In Patrick Juvet's 'I Love America' you literally hear for thirteen minutes, 'Here's the Latin New York. Here's the rock New York. This is why I love America, because you got all of all these mixes.' Nowadays, I think there are all these enclaves. The gay sound has a very specific sound because it wants to be separatist and *gay*; it's about white men who take a lot of steroids and K and crystal meth, and they only want to be with their own kind. Black people, too, R&B: It's a very canned drum-machine beat, but that beat becomes nothing more than the empty signifier—it signifies nothing more than the fact that this is black music. Although in itself it's not funky anymore; it's canned, it comes from some drum machine or some MPC and it's the same beat. Every R&B song is exactly the same beat. The only thing that makes it black is a black voice talking on top, but of course it's all processed. The same thing with rock music. They signify only their own ethnic or sexual enclave. That idealism has been replaced by commercial marketing to the correct socioeconomic or racial group. Maybe that's the disappointment we hear in music nowadays."[1]

On a series of EPs released on his own Balihu label, as well as on records for likeminded labels such as Environ and Ghostly International, Wang exorcised his disillusionment by refracting the warm techno of the '90s through the prism of the mirror ball. He seriously freaked the François Kevorkian drum sound, rubbery Shep Pettibone keyboards, and Walter Gibson percussion that ruled New York in the early '80s. Every leftover synth and sound effect from labels like Prelude, West End, Streetwise, Cutting, Sleeping Bag, Tommy Boy, and Next Plateau made an appearance on his records. On his *Silver Trophies* EP, Wang harked back to Japan's Yellow Magic Orchestra with a sly, electronic wink at Western stereotypes of "the Orient."

Wang was born in California but spent most of his formative years in Taiwan. "I used to watch this show called *Dance Fever*, and they would have all these hustle dancers on," he recalls. "They'd play [Dan Hartman's] 'Instant Replay' and Patrick Hernandez 'Born to Be Alive,' and I'd get really into it and repeat the moves in front of a mirror. In '82 and '83 I started to listen to Madonna, like 'Burning Up,' and the early Hi-NRG, Evelyn Thomas, Hazell Dean, Freez 'IOU,' early freestyle . . . I spent a small fortune on a Vidal Sassoon haircut, and the other boys in the school thought I was a total fruit, which I was."[2]

While sexuality undoubtedly played an important role in his initial identification with disco, he cites a different conversion experience. "I was DJing gay college parties at Yale in about '89, '90, and then about '91, '92, I started to hear the Strictly Rhythm records, all the early House records. Then in about '94 I would come to the city and go to these parties at this place called House Nation at Fareta Dance Music Studios on Broadway at Bleecker . . . François Kevorkian was in the side room playing *Seven Deadly Sins* by Rinder & Lewis, Eddy Grant, but this Rinder & Lewis thing hit me like a ton of bricks and made me realize that disco was not all this loop-based whatever and that there were people who made these very complex structures and interesting arrangements . . . Then there was hearing Danny Krivit and Tee Scott play 'Evolution' by Giorgio Moroder, which is probably the most sonically evolved record ever made—it's a virtual catalog of what one can do with synth effects with a great sort of orchestral composition on top . . .

"The single sentence that sums up why we—every person in this generation—keep going back to that period was that music was relatively innocent," he continues. "It wasn't based on genre—of course there was money it, it was a huge industry and completely commercialized—yet on the musical level the entire disco and dance music industry was trying out every timbral and orchestral possibility that could happen over a 4/4 or funk beat. In other words, everything was brought into play: Latin music, classical music, this is a cliché but it's true. You had the best string session players who were playing at Lincoln Center on the weekdays and on weekends they were moon-lighting for disco orchestras. There hasn't been anything really like that since. The last time that was happening in pop music was in the '30s and '40s when you had huge orchestras—Glenn Miller, Duke Ellington, Benny Goodman—hiring that number of people. I like to think that it's not really nostalgia, that if one listens to so-called pure music in an absolute sense, richness of composition and tim-brality, the late '70s are just *the* golden period."[3]

On one hand, Wang's defense of disco as "quality music" bril-liantly undercuts everyone who derides disco as nothing but escapist pap and lily-livered nelly music. On the other, however, it falls into the same trap and uses the same arguments that were used to denigrate disco in its heyday. Disco is "real music" with real live musicianship, it has flesh and blood unlike the "plastic" and "canned" synthesizer music of today. With this new authenticity comes connoisseurship (even though disco has always had this aspect because of the DJs' role in creating it). Disco now has its own canon to separate the masterworks (read: obscure rarities played by Larry Levan and David Mancuso) from the "cheese" (i.e., the popular records).[4]

While the VH1 crowd is gorging themselves silly on "Gee, Dad, is that you with the feathered hair?" nostalgia of Studio 54 and the Bee Gees, the underground is finding solace in rescuing rare twelve-inch singles from history's dustbin, and, of course, raising the value of their own record collections in the process. But nostalgia is nostal-gia no matter how cool it is, and even if it's dressed up as lunatic scholarship it is just the hipper flip side of "I love the '70s" syn-drome. Although none of the perpetrators would deny the music's gay roots, there's also an aspect to this scene that's nearly as perni-cious as the filmic rewrites of disco history. As Wang says of fellow travelers like Metro Area (Morgan Geist and Darshan Jesrani), DJ Harvey, Idjut Boys, DJ Thomas (aka the Mammal), and Eric Duncan, "They're all completely straight. They're big white guys with big beards, and the aesthetic they're proposing is rock and get drunk and get high and have fun to this music. It's much more decadent than gay people are now."[5]

That decadence is the key component of the disco nostalgia. Any contemporary look at disco views it through the filter of what was initially known as "the Saint's disease." The disco era was the last period of truly unbridled hedonism that existed and probably will exist in our lifetimes. The planets truly aligned in the 1970s—the pill, civil rights, gay rights, cheap cocaine, economic recession—for a party of epic proportions. That combination of consequence-free sex (give or take a herpes outbreak or two) and political enfranchisement will never be duplicated. Wang and his peers all came of age sexually at the exact moment that AIDS was beginning to cast its dreadful shadow across nightlife, and this was the original sin, the moment of being banished from the Garden of Eden. The collector's instinct is to return to the garden and tend to it, making sure that no weeds emerge to spoil what's left of it now that its prime is long past.

Art critic Philip Gefter told gay historian Charles Kaiser that in the mid-1970s, "Sex was like a handshake," but a decade later "the novelist David Leavitt recalled the mid-1980s as 'a time when the streets were filled with an almost palpable sense of mourning and panic.'"[6] As Andrew Holleran, who had chronicled the early days of disco, put it, sex had become the Siamese twin of death. "The bars, the discotheques that are still open seem pointless in a way," he wrote. "The social contract, the assumptions, that gave them their meaning, is gone."[7] Perhaps in response, disco's extravagance was replaced by the severe minimalism of Chicago house music while Detroit's techno producers were toying with the man-machine interface as a way of escaping their prisons of flesh.

"The personal is political" was always implicit in disco culture, but AIDS and the initial reaction to it by the government and health-care industry necessarily brought that to the fore. The body became the main political battleground in the '80s, and whether it was still managing to generate the will to dance, thumbing your nose at the puritans by advocating safe sex practices, or confronting the religious right at the doorstep of an abortion clinic, pleasure, desire, and sex all became struggle—it was something you had to fight for. This was why punks and intellectuals joined forces with disco in the '80s, and why this sound is being revisited again today.

Groups like the Rapture, Radio 4, LCD Soundsystem, Chicks on Speed, and the whole electroclash crew are raiding the early '80s rapprochement among punk, disco, funk, and reggae for ideas, inspiration, and sound, for a way of making sense of a world where the body is now a battleground between science and "nature," where trickle-down economics and rampant privatization have replaced the contract between government and its citizens. The music offered a seductive vision of the world where style collided with substance, where deconstruction made a reconciliation with melody and hooks, where groove embraced distortion, where punk's outcast geek was transformed by the fairy godmother of disco into a "Halston, Gucci . . . Fiorucci"–clad suavecito with a social conscience and a brain. The punk-dance sound resonates now because of its sharp, acidic, left-wing cynicism. It's a voice that almost the entirety of today's popular music has silenced. Unlike the bedazzled groove of Timbaland or the Neptunes embracing money, glitz, and technology with equal verve, early '80s punk-disco was dance music as a way of shaking off the heebie-jeebies, shedding the skin of the daytime daze, jolting you out of your nightmares, only for you to realize that you weren't imagining anything. As Was (Not Was) once pleaded, "Tell me that I'm dreaming."

In 1994, a rather bizarre sound echoed around the terraces of Europe's football stadiums and crisscrossed the continent. It was the sound of thousands of testosterone-fueled young men chanting the tune of "Go West," a hit for the Pet Shop Boys the preceding autumn and originally a hit for the Village People in 1979. Granted, they were often singing stuff like "Stand up if you're a Schalke fan" or "One-nil to the Arsenal" and were using the song simply because it has a simple, very-easy-to-remember melody, but the massed chorale of unswervingly straight voices expressing tribal violence to the tune of one of the campest visions of earthly paradise was a breathtaking spectacle.

No one is very sure where it started—different accounts place its genesis in Italy, Turkey, and West Bromwich Albion in the British Midlands—but what is certain is that it is emblematic of the very different relationship that Europe has with disco, and pop music as a whole, as compared to the United States. While the Village People are now accepted at American athletic contests as intermission entertainment where fathers are permitted to be goofy with their young children whom they've dragged along to the game, using disco as a vehicle for displaying macho pride is unthinkable. In European pop culture, on the other hand, flamboyant frippery and violence often go hand in hand—just think of the teddy boy subculture, groups of working-class toughs dressed up in Elizabethan finery who scandalized Britain in the 1950s.

Not only did disco music not die in Europe, it wasn't even a blip on the chart the way it was stateside; it was simply business as usual. Perhaps this was because pop music has never been anything other than a collection of disposable baubles and trinkets in Europe; with the possible exception of French chanson, it's never been a question of it expressing the heart and soul of a culture. Compare, for example, the way the United Kingdom and the United States bemoan the state of popular music: In Britain it's always that no one in America is buying the music, it's always a matter of commerce; whereas in the United States it's a matter of declining morals and the erosion of the character of its young people.

Another reason for disco's unremarkableness in Europe is perhaps how important the gay aesthetic has been to its pop scene. "It was fascinating, from the sixties onwards, to see how often gays and their lifestyle had cropped up in the history of British music business," wrote Simon Napier-Bell, a gay man who is one of Britain's most prominent music managers. "The number of gay people in major record companies has been negligible. Even the number of gay artists has been very small. Yet their importance seems to outweigh their numbers. In one form or another, the influence of gays on the British industry has been on a par with the influence of blacks and black music on the American industry."[8]

So it's hardly surprising, then, that ever since groups like Duran Duran and ABC made the links between Chic and Roxy Music even more apparent in the early '80s and Stock, Aitken & Waterman pilfered the Hi-NRG formula for their run of British pop hits in the late '80s, disco has never been very far from the top of the European pop charts. In the early '90s Ian Levine emerged as the producer of the most influential pop group of the decade, Take That. Initially conceived as Britain's answer to New Kids on the Block, Take That redefined the boy band formula by combining Elton John earnestness with disco dazzle. The dazzle initially came from Levine, who produced covers of Tavares's "It Only Takes a Minute" and Barry Manilow's "Could It Be Magic" for the group. When Levine was bumped from the group in 1993, producer Dave Lee (aka Joey Negro, one of the world's biggest disco trainspotters and advocates) was hired to produce a version of Dan Hartman's "Relight My Fire" for the group. Ever since, disco has dominated the European charts in the shape of covers (All Saints' "Lady Marmalade") and samples (Alcazar's "Cryin' at the Discoteque").

When America decided to put its own spin on the boy band format, the basis wasn't disco, but hip-hop. Rather than injecting Botox into disco's jowls, Backstreet Boys and 'N Sync, America's two biggest boy bands, bleached R&B that was about five years out of date, used hip-hop slang that was almost as old, and dusted off some hoary "running man" dance routines to melt the hearts of Midwestern girls. Hip-hop has become the lingua franca of American pop music, and unless you're on a reality television show it's practically impossible to break the Top 10 without someone rapping on your single.

The old chestnut about the United States and the United Kingdom being two countries separated by a common language has never been more appropriate. Hip-hop is wholly about individuality, about distinguishing oneself from the crowd with the dopest lyrics, the flyest threads, the freshest kicks; it's a culture solely concerned with competition and, at times, a brazen, mercenary, go-for-mine capitalism. Hip-hop came of age at the exact time America was abandoning whatever pretenses it had of being a social democracy— it was the soundtrack to the birth of the corporate state.

Like hip-hop, disco may have started in New York, but these days it's as European as social welfare programs and high-carb diets. Disco may have been trapped between two visions of the world— between a utopian, communitarian dream and a hard-bitten cynical view where nothing moves but the money—but, ultimately, disco was and is about inclusivity and community, about pleasure and leisure rather than labor, about the democracy of the dance floor rather than the false idols of the stage. It was, as Danny Wang suggests, a time when anything and everything could be united under the banner of the 4/4, when music was still about fun and not about survival.

TIMELINE

Spring 1939. The Swing-Jugend (Swing Kids), a small middle-class youth movement dedicated to jazz and outrageous fashion as a reaction to Nazi discipline, starts gathering momentum in Hamburg, Germany. Their underground parties, where people danced to records chosen by a "disc jockey" for a specific crowd, were the origins of the disco aesthetic.

1942–43. According to writer Albert Goldman, La Discothèque, a basement nightclub with only a turntable for entertainment, opens in Paris.

1947–48. Paul Pacine opens the Whisky à Go Go on the Rue de Beaujolais in Paris and sets in motion the discotheque as the main form of European nightlife, particularly for the jet set.

1961. The Twist takes off among the celeb crowd as they gather at a Times Square dive called the Peppermint Lounge.

December 1963. Graphic artist Harvey Ball designs the first smiley face.

July 2, 1964. The Civil Rights Act, prohibiting discrimination in employment and public places, is passed.

July 18, 1964. "Race riot" in Harlem and Bedford-Stuyvesant neighborhoods of New York.

1965. Roger Eagle starts DJing at the Twisted Wheel in Manchester and helps create the foundation for the Northern Soul scene, which would have an enormous impact on disco.

May 1965. The ultratrendy Arthur opens in New York. It was here that DJ Terry Noel became the first DJ to mix records.

1966. The multiracial band from north London, the Equals, release their first single, "Hold Me Closer." The following year, the flip, "Baby Come Back," becomes a huge hit across Europe, setting in motion Europop and soon Eurodisco.

September 1968. The Continental Baths, an over-the-top and overground gay pleasure palace, opens in New York.

November 1968. Richard Nixon wins the presidential election by appealing to "America's silent majority."

1969. The Church, later called the Sanctuary, opens in an old church in New York's theater district. Francis Grasso, one of the crafters of the disco aesthetic, is the club's DJ.

1969. *Time* magazine declares the "Middle American" as the "Man and Woman of the Year."

February 1969. Jerry Butler's "Only the Strong Survive" is released. The record would help define the sound of Philadelphia International, which would become the most important component of the disco sound.

June 27, 1969. The Stonewall Inn, a dingy gay bar on Christopher Street in Manhattan, is raided by police. Fed up with constant harassment by the cops, the bar's patrons protest, and the gay pride movement is born.

December 31, 1969. The Cockettes, a cross-dressing theater troupe featuring Sylvester, debut in San Francisco.

February 14, 1970. David Mancuso holds his "Love Saves the Day" party at his loft space on Broadway. His weekly parties take off and become the most crucial crucible of disco.

May 8–20, 1970. The "Hard Hat Riots" explode in lower Manhattan when construction workers attack an antiwar demonstration.

May 27, 1970. The Ice Palace, an important gay discotheque, opens on Fire Island.

December 1972. Fire Island habitués open the Tenth Floor in an abandoned warehouse in New York's garment district.

Late 1972 / early 1973. Two Motown records, Eddie Kendricks's "Girl You Need a Change of Mind" and the Temptations' "Law of the Land," become the prototype disco records.

1973. Latin record label Mericana changes its name to Salsoul after its most successful record, and will soon become the most important disco label.

1973. Kool DJ Herc throws his first party at the community center at 1520 Sedgwick Avenue, in the Bronx, and hip-hop is born.

June 1973. Manu Dibango's "Soul Makossa" enters the American pop charts after it becomes a favorite record at the Loft and other New York nightclubs.

September 1973. Featuring the drumming of Earl Young, whose hissing hi-hat sound would come to define the disco beat, Harold Melvin & the Blue Notes' "The Love I Lost" is released.

1974. Tom Moulton does the first of his extended mixes on Don Downing's "Dream World."

February 9, 1974. Love Unlimited Orchestra's "Love's Theme" hits #1 on the American pop charts. It's the first #1 whose popularity was credited to discos.

June 1974. Disco's "national anthem," MFSB's "Love Is the Message," is released.

November 1974. New York radio station WPIX starts the world's first disco radio show.

December 1974. The Flamingo, perhaps the most legendary of New York's gay clubs, opens in SoHo.

January 1975. Silver Convention's "Save Me," the calling card of Eurodisco, is released.

Spring 1975. Moulton's extended mix of Moment of Truth's "So Much for Love" becomes the first twelve-inch single.

May 1975. New York City faces meltdown when financial institutions refuse to lend it money any longer.

June 1975. The Jackson 5's "Forever Came Today," featuring the first example of what would become the quintessential disco bassline, is released.

Summer 1975. The Hustle craze is in full flight, leading to disco seemingly taking over the music industry.

December 1975. There are an estimated ten thousand discos across the United States.

May 1976. Double Exposure's "Ten Percent," mixed by Walter Gibbons, becomes the first commercially available twelve-inch single.

1977. The Warehouse opens in Chicago with Frankie Knuckles at the helm. The club would become the crucible of House music, into which disco eventually dissolved.

April 26, 1977. Studio 54 opens.

July 1977. Disco's ultimate synthesizer record, Donna Summer's "I Feel Love," is released and creates not only the template for Hi-NRG but also for the mechanized, dehumanized feel that disco detractors hated.

December 1977. Saturday Night Fever is released.

February 1978. The Paradise Garage, the club presided over by the person nearly everyone calls the world's greatest DJ, Larry Levan, officially opens.

November 1978. James White & the Blacks release "Contort Yourself," the first merger of punk and disco.

February 1979. America's disco industry is valued at $4 billion.

July 12, 1979. Chicago DJ Steve Dahl explodes ten thousand disco records in between games of a double-header at Comiskey Park, setting off a riot that destroyed not only the outfield but disco as a mainstream genre.

December 6, 1979. Europe's most famous gay discotheque, Heaven, opens in London.

September 20, 1980. The gay discotheque to end all gay discotheques, the Saint, opens in New York's East Village.

1981. John "Jellybean" Benitez takes over as the DJ at the New York club the Funhouse, and presides over the rise of freestyle, one of the many forms into which disco mutated.

1983. Ian Levine produces Miquel Brown's "So Many Men, So Little Time," and Hi-NRG is born.

1994. Terrace chants to the tune of the Village People's "Go West" echo across European football/soccer stadiums.

November 17, 1999. Disco is enshrined by the U.S. Postal Service with a disco stamp.

DIJCOGRAPHY

1. THE ROTTEN APPLE

Abaco Dream. "Life and Death in G & A," 1969, A&M 1081.

Ace Spectrum. "Keep Holding On," 1975, Atlantic DSKO60.

Afrique. "Soul Makossa," 1973, Mainstream 5542.

All Directions. "Soul Makossa," 1973, Buddah 362.

Anderson Brothers. "I Can See Him Loving You," 1974, GSF GS003.

Hank Ballard and the Midnighters. "The Twist," 1960, King 5171.

Darrell Banks. "Open the Door to Your Heart," 1966, Revilot RV201.

Barrabas. *Barrabas*, 1972, RCA APL10219.

——. "Mellow Blow," 1975, Atlantic DSKO56.

J. J. Barnes. "Our Love Is in the Pocket," 1969, Revilot RV222.

Rose Batiste. "Hit & Run," 1966, Revilot RV204.

Biddu Orchestra. "Summer of '42," 1975, Epic 50139.

——. "Blue Eyed Soul" from *Blue Eyed Soul*, 1975, Epic 80836.

——. "I Could Have Danced All Night"/"Jump For Joy," 1976, Epic 50173.

——. "Rain Forest," 1976, Epic 4084.

Black Blood. "AIE (A'Mwana)" from *Chicano*, 1975, Biram 6325634.

Genie Brown. "I Can't Stop Talking" from *A Woman Alone*, 1973, Dunhill/ABC DSX50155.

James Brown. "Night Train," 1962, King 5614.

——. "(Get Up I Feel Like Being a) Sex Machine," 1970, King 6318.

——. "Hot Pants (She Got to Use What She Got to Get What She Wants)," 1971, People 2501.

Polly Brown. "Up in a Puff of Smoke," 1975, GTO 1002.

B.T. Express. "Do It ('Til You're Satisfied)," 1974, Scepter 12395.

Buari. "Advice from Father" from *Buari*, 1975, RCA APL11045.

John Cage. *Imaginary Landscape No. 1* from *Early Modulations: Vintage Volts*, 1997, Caipirinha CAI2027.

Calhoon. "(Do You Wanna) Dance Dance Dance," 1975, Warner Bros. PRO601.

Carstairs, The. "It Really Hurts Me Girl," 1973, Red Coach 802.

Ralph Carter. "When You're Young and in Love," 1975, Mercury 73695.

Cat Mother and the All Night Newsboys. "Track in 'A' (Nebraska Nights)" from *The Street Giveth . . . and the Street Taketh Away*, 1969, Polydor 244001.

Tina Charles. "I Love to Love (But My Baby Loves to Dance)," 1976, CBS 3937.

Chubby Checker. "The Twist," 1960, Parkway 811.

————. "(At the) Discotheque," 1965, Parkway 949.

Chicago Transit Authority. "I'm a Man" from *Chicago Transit Authority*, 1969, Columbia GP8.

Cooley High, 1975, Motown 7840.

Joey Dee & the Starliters. "Peppermint Twist," 1961, Roulette 4401.

Detroit Emeralds. "Feel the Need in Me," 1972, Westbound 209.

Manu Dibango. "Soul Makossa," 1973, Atlantic 2971.

Diga Rhythm Band. "Sweet Sixteen" from *Diga Rhythm Band*, 1976, Round Records RX110.

Disco Par-r-r-ty, 1974, Spring SPR6705.

Disco Tex & His Sex-O-Lettes. "Get Dancin'," 1974, Chelsea 3004.

Doobie Brothers, The. "Long Train Runnin'," 1973, Warner Bros. 7698.

Doors, The. "The End" from *The Doors*, 1967, Elektra EKS74007.

Double Exposure. "Ten Percent," 1976, Salsoul 12D2008.

Carl Douglas. "Kung Fu Fighting," 1974, 20th Century 2140.

Al Downing. "I'll Be Holding On," 1975, Chess 2158.

Don Downing. "Dream World," 1974, Scepter 12397.

Elephant's Memory. "Mongoose" from *Take It to the Streets*, Metromedia 182, 1970.

Equals, The. "Baby, Come Back"/"Hold Me Closer," RCA Victor 9583, 1968.

————. "Black Skin Blue-Eyed Boys," 1970, President PT325.

————. "Funky Like a Train," 1976, Mercury 6007106.

Exuma. "Exuma, the Obeah Man," 1970, Mercury 73084.

First Choice. "This Is the House (Where Love Died)," 1972, Scepter 12347.

5000 Volts. "I'm on Fire," 1975, Philips 40801.

Flamingos, The. "The Boogaloo Party," 1966, Philips 40347.

Foundations, The. "Baby, Now That I've Found You," 1967, Uni 55038.

————. "Build Me Up Buttercup," 1969, Uni 55101.

James Fountain. "Seven Day Lover," 1976, Cream CRM5002.

Four Tops. "What Is a Man"/"Don't Bring Back Memories," 1969, Motown 1147.

————. "Still Water (Love)/Still Water (Peace)," 1970, Motown 1170.

Boris Gardiner Happening, The. "Melting Pot" from *Is What's Happening*, 1973, Dynamic Sounds DYLP3330.

Gloria Gaynor. *Never Can Say Goodbye*, 1975, MGM 2315.

Gaytones, The. "Soul Makossa," 1973, Action 4610.

J. Geils Band, The. "Give It to Me," 1973, Atlantic 2953.

Merle Haggard. "Okie From Muskogee," 1969, Capitol 26260.

Brenda Holloway. "Just Look What You've Done," 1967, Tamla 54148.

Loleatta Holloway. "Hit and Run," 1977, Gold Mind 12G4006.

Marvin Holmes & Justice. "You Better Keep Her," 1974, Brown Door 6576.

Iron Butterfly. "In-A-Gadda-Da-Vida" from *In-A-Gadda-Da-Vida*, 1968, Atco SD33250.

Johnny Johnson & the Bandwagon. "Breakin' Down the Walls of Heartache," 1968, Epic 24657.

————. "(Blame it on the) Pony Express," 1970, Bell 1128.

Syl Johnson. "We Did It," 1973, Hi 2229.

Eddie Kendricks. "Girl You Need a Change of Mind" from *People . . . Hold On*, 1973, Motown 11213.

Simon Kenyatta Troupe. "Soul Makossa," 1973, Avco 4620.

Fela Kuti. "Shakara" from *Shakara*, 1974, Editions Makossa EM2305.

———. "Expensive Shit" from *Expensive Shit*, 1975, Editions Makossa EM2315.

Bettye Lavette. "Doin' the Best That I Can," 1978, West End WES12113.

Led Zeppelin. "Whole Lotta Love" from *Led Zeppelin II*, 1969, Atlantic ATL 40037.

Pat Lewis. "No One to Love," 1967, Solid Hit SH109.

Little Sister. "You're the One," 1970, Stone Flower S 9000.

Love Unlimited Orchestra. "Love's Theme," 1973, 20th Century 2069.

Mahogany, 1975, Motown 858.

Mandre. "Solar Flight (Opus I)," 1977, Motown 1429.

Herbie Mann. "Waterbed," 1975, Atlantic DSKO 58.

The Marketts. "Out of Limits," 1963, Warner Bros. 5391.

Martha & the Vandellas. "Come and Get These Memories," 1963, Gordy 7014.

MFSB. "Love Is the Message" from *TSOP*, 1974, Philadelphia International 80154.

Mighty Tomcats, The. "Soul Makossa," 1973, Winley 1103.

Moment of Truth. "Your Love," 1974, Roulette 7158.

———. "Helplessly," 1976, Salsoul 12D2009.

Montclairs, The. "Hung Up on Your Love," 1974, Paula 390.

Bobby Moore. "(Call Me Your) Anything Man," 1975, Scepter SDT12405.

Nairobi Afro Band. "Soul Makossa," 1973, Town Hall TH777.

Ken Nordine. *Colors*, 1966, Philips PHM200224.

Babatunde Olatunji. "Jin-Go-Lo-Ba (Drums of Passion)" from *Drums of Passion*, 1959, Columbia CS8210.

———. "Soul Makossa" from *Soul Makossa*, 1973, Paramount PAS6061.

Osibisa. "Music for Gong Gong," 1971, MCA 5079.

Ozo. *Listen to the Buddha*, 1976, DJM 4.

Ann Peebles. "I'm Going to Tear Your Playhouse Down," 1972, Hi 2232.

Barbara Pennington. "Twenty-Four Hours a Day," 1977, United Artists UADW928.

Pointer Sisters. "Yes We Can Can," 1973, Blue Thumb 229.

Rare Earth. "Happy Song" from *Back to Earth*, 1975, Rare Earth 548.

Mitch Ryder. *The Detroit-Memphis Experiment*, 1969, Dot DLP25963.

Salsoul Orchestra. "Nice 'n' Naasty," 1976, Salsoul 12D2011.

Sapphires, The. "Gotta Have Your Love," 1965, ABC-Paramount 10639.

Sessomatto. "Sessomatto," 1976, West End WES12100.

Sly & the Family Stone. "Everybody Is a Star" from *Greatest Hits*, 1970, Epic 10555.

Kenny Smith. "Lord, What's Happening to Your People," 1972, General American GAR 317.

Gloria Spencer. "I Got It / Stay Jesus Stay," 1971, Jay-Walking JW016.

Amii Stewart. "Knock on Wood," 1979, Ariola 7736.

"Superstar" from *Jesus Christ Superstar*, 1971, Decca DXSSA7206.

Taste of Honey, A. "Boogie Oogie Oogie," 1978, Capitol 4565.

Timebox. "Beggin'," 1968, Deram DM194.

Titanic. "Sultana," 1971, CBS 5365.

———. "Rain 2000," 1972, CBS 8185.

Trammps, The. "Hooked For Love," 1975, Atlantic DSKO59.

Troubadours du Roi Baudoin, Les. *Missa Luba*, 1963, Philips PCC206.

Earl Van Dyke & Motown Brass. "Six by Six," 1967, Soul 35028.

Ventures, The. "Soul Makossa" from *Only Hits*, 1973, United Artists LA147G.
War. "City Country City" from *The World Is a Ghetto*, 1972, United Artists UAS5652.
James Wells. "My Claim to Fame," 1978, AVI 6045.
Anthony White. "Block Party," 1976, Salsoul 12D2030.
Betty Wright. "If You Love Me Like You Say You Love Me," 1972, Alston 4609.
Zulema. "Giving Up" from *Ms. Z*, 1974, Sussex SF8419.

2. "I'M JUST AN OUTLAW, MY NAME IS DESIRE": Disco and Sexuality
Area Code 615. "Stone Fox Chase," 1973, Polydor PD14215.
Roy Ayers. "Running Away," 1977, Polydor PD502.
Carl Bean. "I Was Born This Way," 1977, Motown TMG1108.
Earlene Bentley. "The Boys Come to Town," 1983, Record Shack SOHO08.
———. "I'm Living My Own Life," 1984, Record Shack SOHO14.
Boys Town Gang. "Cruisin' the Streets," 1981, Moby Dick BTG231.
Miquel Brown. "So Many Men, So Little Time," 1983, Record Shack SOHO06.
———. "Close to Perfection," 1985, Record Shack SOHO48.
Cerrone. "Call Me Tonight" from *Angelina*, 1979, Atlantic SD9917.
Charlie & Ray. "I Love You Madly," 1954, Herald 438.
Chocolat's. "The Kings of Clubs" from *Kings of Clubs*, 1977, Tom n' Jerry TJS4500.
Patrick Cowley. "Menergy," 1981, Fusion FPSF003.
———. *Megatron Man*, 1981, Megatone M1002.
———. *Mind Warp*, 1982, Megatone M1004.
Betty Davis. "Game Is My Middle Name," and "If I'm in Luck, I Might Just Get Picked Up" from *Betty Davis*, 1973, Just Sunshine Records JSS5.
Hazell Dean. "Searchin'," 1983, Proto 13542.
Dynamic Superiors. *Pure Pleasure*, 1975, Motown STML12007.
Eastbound Expressway. "Primitive Desire," 1983, Record Shack SOHO09.
Marvin Gaye. *What's Going On*, 1971, Tamla Motown TS310.
Yvonne Gidden. "In Orbit," 1984, Electricity ELECT02.
Frankie "Half-Pint" Jaxon. *Frankie "Half-Pint" Jaxon Volume 1, 1926–1929*, 1994, Document DOC5258.
———. *Frankie "Half-Pint" Jaxon Volume 2, 1929–1937*, 1994, Document DOC5259.
———. *Frankie "Half-Pint" Jaxon Volume 3, 1937–1940*, 1994, Document DOC5260.
Le Pamplemousse. "Le Spank," 1977, AVI 153.
Linda Lewis. "You Turned My Bitter Into Sweet," 1984, Electricity ELECT05.
Love Unlimited Orchestra. "Love's Theme," 1973, 20th Century 2069.
Bill Motley & Trip Ringwald. "Bitchin' 50s Medley," 1979, Disconet Volume 3, Program 6 MWDN306.
Laura Pallas. "Emergency," 1984, Record Shack SOHO16.
Paul Parker. "Right on Target," 1983, Megatone MT101.
Billy Sha-Rae. "Do It," 1970, Laurie 117.
Marlena Shaw. "Touch Me in the Morning," 1979, Columbia AS678.
Stainless Steal. *Can-Can*, 1978, Warner Bros. 3274.
Candi Staton. "Young Hearts Run Free," 1976, Warner Bros. 8181.
Donna Summer. "I Feel Love"/"I Feel Mega Love (The Patrick Cowley MegaMix)," 1979, Disconet Volume 3, Program 7 MWDN307.
Supremes, The. "Love Is Like an Itching in My Heart," 1966, Motown 1094.
Sylvester. *Sylvester & the Hot Band*, 1973, Blue Thumb BTS6018.

———. *Bazaar*, 1973, Blue Thumb BTS6059.
———. *Sylvester*, 1977, Fantasy F9531.
———. *Step II*, 1978, Fantasy F9556.
———. *Stars*, 1979, Fantasy F9579.
———. "Do Ya Wanna Funk," 1982, Megatone MT102.
———. *Rock the Box*, 1984, Megatone M1015.
———."Take Me to Heaven," 1985, Megatone MT133.
Tavares. "Heaven Must Be Missing an Angel," 1976, Capitol 4270.
Evelyn Thomas. "High Energy," 1984, Record Shack SOHO18.
Tasha Thomas. "Shoot Me (With Your Love)," 1978, Atlantic 3542
Valentino. "I Was Born This Way," 1975, Gaiee 90001.
Velvette. "Nothing Worse Than Being Alone," 1984, Electricity ELECT04.
Bill Withers. "Harlem," 1971, Sussex SUX219.

3. "LIKE CLONES AND ROBOTS THAT WE ARE": Automating the Beat
Amon Düül II. *Viva La Trance*, 1973, United Artists A198.
Arpeggio. "Love and Desire," 1978, Polydor POSPX40.
Claudja Barry. "Boogie Woogie Dancin' Shoes," 1979, Chrysalis 2313.
Dave Bartholomew. "Messy Bessy" from *In the Alley*, 1991, Charly 273.
Beautiful Bend. "Boogie Motion," 1979, Marlin 3327.
Bee Gees. *Main Course*, 1975, RSO 4807.
———. "You Should Be Dancing," 1976, RSO 853.
Hamilton Bohannon. "South African Man," 1974, Dakar 4539.
———. "Foot Stompin Music," 1975, Dakar 4544.
———. "Disco Stomp," 1975, Dakar 4549.
Boney M. *Take the Heat Off Me*, 1976, Atco 36143.
———. *Love for Sale*, 1977, Atlantic 19145.
———. *Nightflight to Venus*, 1978, Sire 6062.
———. *Oceans of Fantasy*, 1979, Hansa 50610.
Pattie Brooks. "Don't Make Me Wait"/"Pop Collage Medley," 1977, Casablanca 904.
James Brown. "I've Got Money," 1962, King 5701.
———. *Live at the Apollo*, 1963, King 826.
———. "Papa's Got a Brand New Bag," 1965, King 5999.
James Brown and His Orchestra. "Out of Sight," 1964, Smash 1919.
Cerrone. "Love in 'C' Minor," 1977, Cotillion 44215.
———. *Cerrone's Paradise*, 1977, Cotillion SD 9917.
———. *Cerrone 3 (Supernature)*, 1977, Cotillion SD 5202.
———. "Rocket in the Pocket," 1978, Atlantic 4802.
Chakachas, The. *Jungle Fever*, 1972, Polydor 2480084.
Chicory. "Son of My Father," 1972, Epic 10837.
Chocolat's. *King of Clubs*, 1977, Tom 'n' Jerry TJS4500.
Eddie Cochran. "Somethin Else," 1959, Liberty 55203.
Alec R. Costandinos and the Syncophonic Orchestra. *Romeo & Juliet*, 1978, Casablanca 7086.
Darby & Tarlton. "Freight Train Ramble" from *Complete Recordings*, 1995, Bear Family BCD15764.
Bo Diddley. "Bo Diddley," 1955, Chess 814.
———. "Who Do You Love?," 1956, Checker 842.

———. "Hey Bo Diddley," 1957, Checker 860.
Einzelgänger. *Einzelgänger*, 1975, Oasis 5001.
El Coco. "Cocomotion," 1977, AVI 147.
Equals, The. "Viva Bobby Joe," 1969, President PT260.
Fantastic Johnny C, The. "Waitin' for the Rain," 1973, Phil-LA of Soul 361.
Festival. *Evita*, 1979, RSO 3061.
Ace Frehley. "New York Groove," 1978, Casablanca 941.
French Kiss. "Panic," 1979, Polydor PRO094.
Funkadelic. *Uncle Jam Wants You*, 1979, Warner Bros. WB3371.
Gloria Gaynor. "Never Can Say Goodbye," 1974, MGM 14748.
Gaz. "Sing Sing," 1978, Salsoul SG206.
Giorgio & Chris. *Love's in You, Love's in Me*, 1978, Casablanca 7104.
Nico Gomez. "Baila Chibiquiban" from *Ritual*, 1970, Carina.
Heart and Soul Orchestra, The. "Love in 'C' Minor," 1977, Casablanca 876.
Willie Henderson. "Dance Master," 1974, Now Sound 101/Playboy 50057.
Hot Butter. "Popcorn," 1972, Musicor 1458.
Hot Chocolate. "Mindless Boogie," 1979, Infinity 50048.
Thelma Houston. "Don't Leave Me This Way," 1976, Tamla 54278.
Dee D Jackson. *Cosmic Curves*, 1978, Epic 90523.
Jackson 5. "Forever Came Today," 1975, Motown 1356.
Jacno. "Rectangle," 1980, Dorian CEL6201.
Jesse James. "Red Hot Rockin' Blues," 1958, Kent 314.
Jean-Michel Jarre. *Oxygène*, 1976, Polydor 6112.
Joneses, The. "Sugar Pie Guy," 1974, Mercury 73614.
Patrick Juvet. *Still Alive*, 1980, Barclay 96112.
Madleen Kane. "Forbidden Love," 1979, Warner Bros. 8772.
Roberta Kelly. "Kung Fu's Back Again," 1974, Contempo 2044.
———. *Trouble Maker*, 1976, Oasis 5005.
———. *Zodiac Lady*, 1977, Casablanca 7069.
Kongas. "Jungle," 1972, Barclay 61719.
———. "Anikana-O," 1974, Barclay 61802.
———. *Africanism*, 1977, Polydor 6138.
———. *Anikana-O*, 1978, Salsoul 8512.
Kraftwerk. *Autobahn*, 1975, Vertigo VEL2003.
———. *Trans-Europe Express*, 1977, Capitol ST11603.
LaBelle. *Nightbirds*, 1974, Epic KE33075.
Suzi Lane. *Ooh La La*, 1979, Elektra 6E207.
Eddy Lang. "I'm Beggin' With Tears," 1956, RPM 476.
Lead Belly. "Rock Island Line" and "The Midnight Special" from *Take This Hammer Down*, 2003, Blue Bird 82876509572.
Le Pamplemousse. "Le Spank," 1977, AVI 153.
Love and Kisses. *How Much, How Much I Love You*, 1978, Casablanca 7091.
———. *You Must Be Love*, 1979, Casablanca 7157.
Masquerade. *Pinocchio*, 1979, Prelude 12169.
George McCrae. "Rock Your Baby," 1974, T.K. 1004.
Harold Melvin and the Blue Notes. "The Love I Lost," 1973, Philadelphia International 3533.
Memphis Jug Band. "KC Moan," 1929, Victor V38558.
Meters, The. "Cissy Strut," 1969, Josie 1005.

———. "Look-Ka Py Py," 1969, Josie 1015.

Midnight Express, 1978, Casablanca 7114.

Munich Machine. *Munich Machine*, 1977, Casablanca 7058.

———. *A Whiter Shade of Pale*, 1978, Casablanca 7090.

Giorgio Moroder. "Mendocino" from *That's Bubblegum, That's Giorgio*, 1970, Hansa 80052.

———. "Son of My Father," 1972, Dunhill/ABC 4304.

———. *Knights in White Satin*, 1976, Oasis 5006.

———. *From Here to Eternity*, 1977, Casablanca 7065.

———. *E=MC²*, 1979, Casablanca 7169.

Shuggie Otis. "Island Letter" from *Inspiration Information*, 1974, Epic 33059.

Parliament. *Funkentelechy vs. the Placebo Syndrome*, 1977, Casablanca 7084.

Patti Jo. "Make Me Believe in You," 1973, Wand 11255.

Peppers, The. "Pepper Box," 1974, Event 213.

Rhythm Makers. "Zone," 1976, Vigor 1726.

Rinder & Lewis. *Seven Deadly Sins*, 1977, AVI 6035.

Diana Ross. "Love Hangover," 1976, Motown 1392.

Shalamar. "Uptown Festival," 1977, Soul Train 10885.

Shirley and Company. "Shame, Shame, Shame," 1975, Vibration 532.

Silver Convention. "Save Me" from *Save Me*, 1975, Midland International BKL11129.

———. "Fly, Robin, Fly," 1975, Midland International 10339.

———. "Get Up and Boogie (That's Right)," 1976, Midland International 10571.

Sly & the Family Stone. "Everyday People," 1968, Epic 10407.

———. *There's a Riot Goin' On*, 1971, Epic KE30986.

Huey "Piano" Smith and the Clowns. "Rocking Pneumonia and the Boogie Woogie Flu," "High Blood Pressure," "Little Liza Jane," and "Everybody's Whalin'" from *Havin' a Good Time*, 1959, Ace 1004.

Space. "Magic Fly," 1977, United Artists 1076.

Sparks. *Nº 1 in Heaven*, 1979, Virgin V2115.

Donna Summer. "The Hostage," 1974, Delta 811011.

———. "Love to Love You Baby" from *Love to Love You Baby*, 1975, Oasis 5003.

———. *A Love Trilogy*, 1976, Oasis 5004.

———. "Could It Be Magic," 1976, Oasis 405.

———. "Try Me, I Know We Can Make It," 1976, Oasis 406.

———. *Four Seasons of Love*, 1976, Casablanca 7038.

———. "I Feel Love," 1977, Casablanca 2884.

———. *Once Upon a Time . . .* , 1977, Casablanca 7078.

———. *Live and More*, 1978, Casablanca 7119.

———. *Bad Girls*, 1979, Casablanca 7150.

———. "State of Independence," 1982, Geffen 29895.

———. "She Works Hard for the Money," 1983, Mercury 812370.

Sylvia & the Moments. "Sho Nuff Boogie," 1974, All Platinum 2350.

T-Connection. "Do What You Wanna Do," 1977, Dash 5032.

Temptations, The. "Law of the Land" and "Masterpiece" from *Masterpiece*, 1973, Gordy 965.

Thank God It's Friday, 1978, Casablanca, 7099.

Timmy Thomas. "Why Can't We Live Together," 1972, Glades 1703.

Trax. *Watch Out!*, 1977, Polydor 2393162.

Tribe. "Koke" from *Ethnic Stew*, 1974, ABC ABCX807.

Tuxedo Junction. *Tuxedo Junction*, 1977, Butterfly 007.

Two Man Sound. "Qué Tal America," 1979, JDC 1204.
Village People. "San Francisco (You've Got Me)," 1977, Casablanca 7064.
Wing and a Prayer Fife and Drum Corps, The. "Baby Face," 1975, Wing & a Prayer 103.

4. "ZIPPIN' UP MY BOOTS, GOING BACK TO MY ROOTS": Disco and the Soul
  Continuum
Aural Exciters. *Spooks in Space*, 1979, Ze 3303.
Joe Bataan. *Mericana*, 1973, Salsoul XMS124.
———. *Afrofilipino*, 1975, Salsoul 4101.
———. "The Bottle (La Botella)," 1975, Salsoul 8701.
Carl Bean. "I Was Born This Way," 1977, Motown TMG1108.
Black Ivory. "Mainline," 1979, Buddah 132.
Blue-Belles, The. "I Sold My Heart to the Junkman," 1962, Newtown 5000 (actually
  sung by the Starlets although credited to the Blue-Belles).
———. "Down the Aisle (Wedding Song)," 1963, Newtown 5777.
———. "Danny Boy," 1964, Parkway 935.
Dee Dee Bridgewater. "Bad for Me," 1979, Elektra 46031.
Jerry Butler. "Only the Strong Survive," 1969, Mercury 72898.
Charlie Calello. "Dance, Dance, Dance," 1976, Ariola 7614.
———. "Sing, Sing, Sing," 1982, Profile 7005.
Cab Calloway. "There's a Cabin in the Cotton" from *The Chronological Classics 1931–32*,
  1966, Melodie Jazz Classic 532.
Judy Cheeks. "Mellow Lovin'," 1978, Salsoul SG2063.
Chic. "Dance, Dance, Dance (Yowsah, Yowsah, Yowsah)," 1977, Buddah 583.
———. *Chic*, 1977, Atlantic 19153.
———. *C'Est Chic*, 1978, Atlantic 19209.
———. *Risqué*, 1979, Atlantic 16003.
———. *Real People*, 1980, Atlantic 16016.
———. *Take It Off*, 1981, Atlantic 19323.
———. *Tongue in Chic*, 1982, Atlantic 80031.
———. *Believer*, 1983, Atlantic 80107.
———. *Chic-Ism*, 1992, Warner Bros. 26394.
———. *Live at the Budōkan*, 1999, Sumthing Else Music Works 1003.
The Chi-Lites, "(For God's Sake) Give More Power to the People," 1971, Brunswick
  55450.
Creative Source. "Who Is He and What Is He to You," 1974, Sussex 509.
Gary Criss. "Rio De Janeiro," 1977, Salsoul SG2059.
Cristina. "La Poupée Qui Fait Non," 1980, Ze 600235.
Delfonics, The. "La-La Means I Love You," 1968, Philly Groove 150.
Dr. Buzzard's Original Savannah Band. *Dr. Buzzard's Original Savannah Band*, 1976,
  RCA 11504.
———. *Meets King Pennett*, 1978, RCA 12402.
———. *Dr. Buzzard's Original Savannah Band Goes to Washington*, 1979, Elektra 218.
Don Armando's Second Avenue Rhumba Band. "Deputy of Love," 1979, Ze 6557.
Double Exposure. "Ten Percent," 1976, Salsoul 12D2008.
Lamont Dozier. "Fish Ain't Bitin'"/"Breaking Out All Over," 1974, ABC 11438.
———. "Going Back to My Roots" from *Peddlin' Music on the Side*, 1977, Warner Bros.
  3039.

Bob Dylan. "Gotta Serve Somebody," 1979, Columbia 11072.

Ebonys, The. "You're the Reason Why"/"Sexy Ways," 1971, Philadelphia International 3503.

———. "It's Forever," 1973, Philadelphia International 3529.

Electric Indian. "Keem-O-Sabe" and "Land of 1000 Dances" from *Keem-O-Sabe*, 1969, United Artists 6728.

Ethics, The. "Think About Tomorrow," 1968, Vent 1001.

First Choice. "Doctor Love," 1977, Gold Mind 12G4004.

———. "Let No Man Put Asunder" from *Delusions*, 1977, Gold Mind GZS7501.

Four Tops. "Reach Out I'll Be There," 1966, Motown 1098.

———. "Standing in the Shadows of Love," 1966, Motown 1102.

———. "Bernadette," 1967, Motown 1104.

———. "Are You Man Enough," 1973, Dunhill/ABC 4354.

Marvin Gaye. *In the Groove*, 1968, Motown 11091.

———. "I Heard it Through the Grapevine," 1968, Tamla 54176.

———. *What's Going On*, 1971, Motown 11190.

Gichy Dan's Beachwood #9. *Gichy Dan's Beachwood #9*, 1979, RCA 2938.

Edwin Hawkins Singers. "Oh Happy Day," 1969, Pavilion 20001.

Isaac Hayes. *Hot Buttered Soul*, 1969, Enterprise 1001.

Eddie Holman. "This Can't Be True," 1966, Parkway 960.

Honeydrippers, The. "Impeach the President," 1973, Alaga 1017.

Hues Corporation, The. *Freedom for the Stallion*, 1973, RCA 0323.

Willie Hutch. "Theme of Foxy Brown," 1974, Motown 1292.

Inner Life. "I'm Caught Up (In a One Night Love Affair)," 1979, Prelude 8004.

Intruders, The. "(We'll Be) United," 1966, Gamble 201.

———. "Cowboys to Girls," 1968, Gamble 214.

———. "(Love Is Like a) Baseball Game," 1968, Gamble 217.

Weldon Irvine. "Watergate" from *Time Capsule*, 1973, Nodlew 1002.

Isley Brothers, The. "Fight the Power," 1975, T-Neck 2256.

Tamiko Jones. "Can't Live Without Your Love," 1979, Polydor 14580.

Kain. *Blue Guerrilla*, 1971, Juggernaut 8805.

Paul Kelly. "Stealing in the Name of the Lord," 1970, Happy Tiger 541.

Kid Creole & the Coconuts. *Off the Coast of Me*, 1980, Antilles 7078.

——— *Fresh Fruit in Foreign Places*, 1981, Ze 3534.

———. *Tropical Gangsters*, 1982, Island 7016.

———. *Doppelganger*, 1983, Ze 9743.

Gladys Knight & the Pips. "I Heard It Through the Grapevine," 1967, Soul 35039.

LaBelle. *LaBelle*, 1971, Warner Bros. 1943.

———. *Moonshadow*, 1972, Warner Bros. 2618.

———. *Nightbirds*, 1974, Epic KE33075.

Loose Joints. "Is It All Over My Face," 1980, West End WES22129.

Machine. "There but for the Grace of God Go I," 1979, RCA 11456.

Barbara Mason. "Yes, I'm Ready," 1965, Arctic 105.

Van McCoy. "The Hustle," 1975, Avco 4653.

McFadden & Whitehead. "Ain't No Stoppin' Us Now," 1979, Philadelphia International 3681.

Harold Melvin and the Blue Notes. "If You Don't Know Me By Now," 1972, Philadelphia International 3520.

———. "The Love I Lost," 1973, Philadelphia International 3533.

————. "Bad Luck," 1975, Philadelphia International 3562.

————. "Wake Up Everybody," 1975, Philadelphia International 3579.

Ethel Merman. *The Ethel Merman Disco Album*, 1979, A&M 4775.

MFSB. "TSOP," 1974, Philadelphia International 3540.

Garnet Mimms & the Enchanters. "Cry Baby," 1963, United Artists 629.

Mutant Disco, 1981, Ze/Island 4001.

New York Citi Peech Boys. "Don't Make Me Wait," 1982, West End WES22140.

New York City. "I'm Doin' Fine Now," 1973, Chelsea 0113.

New York Rubber Rock Band. "Disco Lucy," 1976, Henry Street 10001.

Norma Jean. *Norma Jean*, 1978, Bearsville 6983.

Odyssey. "Going Back to My Roots," 1981, RCA 12240.

O'Jays, The. *Back Stabbers*, 1972, Philadelphia International 31712.

————. "Don't Call Me Brother" from *Ship Ahoy*, 1973, Philadelphia International 32408.

————. "For the Love of Money," 1974, Philadelphia International 3544.

————. "I Love Music," 1975, Philadelphia International 3577.

————. "Use Ta Be My Girl," 1978, Philadelphia International 3642.

Gene Page. *Blacula*, 1972, RCA LSP4806.

Billy Paul. "Me and Mrs. Jones," 1972, Philadelphia International 3521.

Teddy Pendergrass. "You Can't Hide from Yourself," 1977, Philadelphia International 34390.

Pentagons, The. "Until Then," 1961, Jamie 1210.

The Persuaders. "Thin Line Between Love & Hate," Atco 6822, 1971.

Wilson Pickett. "Don't Let the Green Grass Fool You," Atlantic 2781, 1971.

Lou Rawls. "You'll Never Find Another Love Like Mine," Philadelphia International 3592, 1976.

Ripple. "The Beat Goes On and On," Salsoul SG2057, 1977.

Salsoul Orchestra. "Salsoul Hustle," Salsoul 2002, 1975.

————. "Tangerine," Salsoul 2004, 1976.

————. "You're Just the Right Size," Salsoul 2007, 1976.

————. "Nice 'N' Naasty," Salsoul 12D2011, 1976.

————. "Magic Bird of Fire," Salsoul 12D2028, 1977.

Silvetti. "Spring Rain," Salsoul 2014, 1977.

Joe Simon. "Drowning in the Sea of Love," Spring 120, 1971.

Sister Sledge. "Love Don't You Go Through No Changes on Me," Atco 7008, 1975.

————. *We Are Family*, Cotillion 5209, 1979.

Sly & the Family Stone. "Thank You (Falettinme Be Mice Elf Agin)," Epic 10555, 1970.

————. *There's a Riot Goin' On*, Epic KE30986, 1971.

Smoggs, "Gotta Have a Little Talk With the Peanut Man," Event 254, 1977.

Staple Singers, The. "I'll Take You There," Stax 0125, 1972.

Edwin Starr. "War," Gordy 7101, 1970.

Taco. "Puttin' on the Ritz," RCA 13574, 1983.

The Temptations, "Cloud Nine," Gordy 7081, 1968.

Temptations, The. "Runaway Child, Running Wild," Gordy 7084, 1969.

————. "Don't Let the Joneses Get You Down," Gordy 7086, 1969.

————. "I Can't Get Next to You," Gordy 7093, 1969.

————. "Message From a Black Man" from *Puzzle People*, 1969, Gordy 949.

————. "Ball of Confusion," 1970, Gordy 7099.

————. "Smiling Faces Sometimes" from *Sky's the Limit*, 1971, Gordy 957.

————. "Papa Was a Rollin' Stone" from *All Directions*, 1972, Gordy 962.

Three Degrees, The. "When Will I See You Again," 1974, Philadelphia International 3550.

Trammps, The. *Trammps*, 1975, Golden Fleece KZ 33163.

Tuxedo Junction. "Chattanooga Choo Choo," 1978, Butterfly 1205.

Undisputed Truth, The. "Smiling Faces Sometimes," 1971, Gordy 7108.

————. "Papa Was a Rollin' Stone," 1972, Gordy 7117.

Volcanoes, The. "Storm Warning," 1965, Arctic 106.

————. "Help Wanted!," 1965, Arctic 111.

War. "Get Down" from *All Day Music*, 1971, United Artists 5546.

Fred Wesley & the JB's. "You Can Have Watergate Just Gimme Some Bucks and I'll Be Straight," 1973, People 627.

Anthony White. "I Can't Turn You Loose/Block Party," 1977, Salsoul 12D2030.

James White & the Blacks. *Off White*, 1979, Ze 3303.

Bill Withers. "Who Is He and What Is He to You?" from *Still Bill*, 1972, Sussex 7014.

Stevie Wonder. "Superstition," 1972, Tamla 54226.

5. PRISONERS OF THE NIGHT: The Disco Craze

Ace Spectrum. "Don't Send Nobody Else," 1974, Atlantic 3012.

Ahzz. "New York Movin'," 1981, Land of Hits 903.

Clyde Alexander. "Got to Get Your Love," Heavenly Star 612.

Phylicia Allen. *Josephine Superstar*, 1978, Casablanca NBLP 7108.

Herb Alpert. "Rise," 1979, A&M 2151.

Arpeggio. "Love and Desire," 1979, Polydor 14535.

Jorge Ben. "Taj Mahal" from *África Brasil*, 1976, Philips PH 4235.

Blackbyrds, The. "Party Land" from *Unfinished Business*, 1976, Fantasy 9518.

Black Ivory. *Don't Turn Around*, 1972, Today TLP 1005.

————. *Baby Won't You Change Your Mind*, 1972, Today TLP 1008.

Bloodstone. "Just Like in the Movies," 1976, London 1067.

Brainstorm. "Lovin' Is Really My Game," 1977, Tabu 10961.

Brass Construction. "Movin'," 1976, United Artists 775.

James Brown. "Give It Up or Turnit a Loose," 1969, King 6213.

Peter Brown. "Do Ya Wanna Get Funky With Me"/"Burning Love Breakdown," 1977, Drive 6258.

————. "Dance With Me"/"For Your Love," 1978, Drive 6269.

Bumble Bee Unlimited. "Love Bug," 1976, Mercury 73864.

Jimmy Castor Bunch, The. "It's Just Begun" from *It's Just Begun*, 1972, RCA 4640.

Chapter Three. "I'll Never Be the Same," 1975, New Moon NM 8500.

Cher. "Hell on Wheels," 1979, Casablanca NB 2208.

Citi. *Roller Disco*, 1979, De-Lite DSR 9515.

Cloud One. "Disco Juice," 1977, P&P 777.

————. "Spaced Out," 1977, P&P 1818.

————. *Funky Disco Tracks of Cloud One*, 1978, Queen Constance 4040.

Norman Connors. "This Is Your Life"/"Captain Connors," 1978, Arista 0343.

Johnny Copeland (Cloud One) Orchestra. "Atmosphere Strutt," 1976, P&P P111.

Alec R. Costandinos. *The Hunchback of Notre Dame*, 1978, Casablanca NB 7124.

————. *Romeo & Juliet*, 1978, Casablanca NB 7086.

Cymande. "Bra," 1973, Janus 215.

Steve Dahl and Teenage Radiation. "Do You Think I'm Disco?" 1979, Ovation 1132.

Charlie Daniels Band. "The South's Gonna Do It," 1975, Kama Sutra 598.

———. "The Devil Went Down to Georgia," 1979, Epic 50700.

Rick Dees and His Cast of Idiots. "Disco Duck," 1976, RSO 857.

John Denver. "Thank God I'm a Country Boy," 1975, RCA 10239.

Disco Tex & His Sex-O-Lettes. "Get Dancin'," 1974, Chelsea 3004.

Carl Douglas, "Kung Fu Fighting," 1974, 20th Century 2140.

Carol Douglas. "Doctor's Orders," 1974, Midland International 10113.

Don Downing. "Lonely Days, Lonely Nights," 1973, Roadshow 7004.

Eli's Second Coming. "Love Chant," 1976, Silver Blue 7302.

Fajardo '76. "C'mon Baby Do the Latin Hustle" from *La Raiz de la Charanga*, 1976, Coco Records.

Flakes. "Sugar Frosted Lover," 1980, Magic Disc MD 1980.

Flame and the Sons of Darkness. "Solid Funk"/"Something," P&P PP222.

Four Below Zero. "My Baby's Got E.S.P.," 1976, Roulette R7186.

Foxy. "Get Off," 1978, Dash 5046.

Gloria Gaynor. "Honeybee," 1973, Columbia 45909.

———. "Honey Bee," 1974, MGM 14706.

———. "I Will Survive," 1978, Polydor 14508.

———. "I Am What I Am," 1983, Silver Blue 720.

Merle Haggard. "Okie From Muskogee" from *Okie From Muskogee*, 1969, Capitol ST 384.

———. "Are the Good Times Really Over? (I Wish a Buck Was Still Silver)" from *Big City*, 1981, Epic 37593.

Heatwave. "The Groove Line," 1978, Epic 50524.

Thelma Houston. "Don't Leave Me This Way," 1976, Tamla 54278.

Incredible Bongo Band, The. "Apache" from *Bongo Rock*, 1973, MGM 2315 255.

Indeep. "Last Night a D.J. Saved My Life," 1982, Sound of New York SNY 5102.

———. "When Boys Talk," 1983, Sound of New York SNY 5104.

———. "The Record Keeps Spinning," 1983, Sound of New York SNY 5109.

Inner Life. "I'm Caught Up (In a One Night Love Affair)," 1979, Prelude 8004.

———. "Ain't No Mountain High Enough," 1981, Salsoul SG 350.

Isley Brothers. "Get Into Something," 1970, T-Neck 924.

Debbie Jacobs. "Hot Hot (Give It All You Got)," 1979, MCA 1857.

Bob James. *Three*, 1976, CTI 6063.

Rick James. "Be My Lady" from *Come Get It!*, 1978, Motown 5263.

Patrick Juvet. "I Love America," 1978, Casablanca NBD 20134.

———. "Lady Night"/"Swiss Kiss," 1979, Casablanca NBD 20160.

KC and the Sunshine Band. "Sound Your Funky Horn," 1974, T.K. 1003.

———. "Queen of Clubs," 1974, T.K. 1005.

———. "Get Down Tonight," 1975, T.K. 1009.

———. "That's the Way (I Like It)," 1975, T.K. 1015.

———. "(Shake, Shake, Shake) Shake Your Booty," 1976, T.K. 1019.

———. "I'm Your Boogie Man," 1977, T.K. 1022.

KC and the Sunshine Junkanoo Band. "Blow Your Whistle," 1973, T.K. 1001.

Herman Kelly & Life. "Dance to the Drummer's Beat," 1978, Alston 3742.

Evelyn "Champagne" King. "Shame," 1978, RCA 11122.

Kinky Foxx. "So Different," 1983, Sound of New York SNY 5107.

Kiss. "I Was Made for Lovin' You," 1979, Casablanca 983.

Eartha Kitt. "Where Is My Man," 1983, Record Shack SOHOT 11.
Kleeer. "Keep Your Body Workin'," 1979, Atlantic 3559.
Kool & the Gang. "Hollywood Swinging," 1974, De-Lite 561.
D. C. LaRue. "Indiscreet," 1977, Pyramid P 8011.
Licky. "African Rock," 1979, Queen Constance 9292.
Love Deluxe With Hawkshaw's Discophonia. "Here Comes That Sound Again" from *Here Comes That Sound Again*, 1979, Warner Bros. BSK 3342.
Love Unlimited Orchestra. "Love's Theme," 1973, 20th Century 2069.
Cheryl Lynn. "Got to Be Real," 1978, Columbia 10808.
Loretta Lynn. "Coal Miner's Daughter" from *Coal Miner's Daughter*, 1971, MCA 936.
Lynyrd Skynyrd. "Sweet Home Alabama," 1974, MCA 40258.
Herbie Mann. "Superman," 1979, Atlantic 3547.
Kelly Marie. "Feels Like I'm in Love," 1981, Coast to Coast 02023.
Vaughan Mason and Crew. "Bounce, Rock, Skate, Roll," 1980, Brunswick 211.
Mass Production. "Welcome to Our World (of Merry Music)," 1977, Cotillion 44213.
Mastermind. "Hustle Bus Stop," 1977, Prelude 71090.
Van McCoy & the Soul City Symphony. *Disco Baby*, 1975, Avco AV-69006-698.
Bob McGilpin. "54" from *Get Up*, 1979, Butterfly FLY 3104.
Mercury Disco Sampler, 1976, Mercury MK 20 (features Tony Silvester and the New Ingredient's "Pazuzu" and "Cosmic Lady").
Miracles, The. "Love Machine," 1975, Tamla 54262.
Walter Murphy & the Big Apple Band. "A Fifth of Beethoven," 1976, Private Stock 45,073.
Musique. "In the Bush," 1978, Prelude 71110.
———. "Keep on Jumpin'," 1978, Prelude 71114.
Originals, The. "Down to Love Town," 1976, Soul 35119.
Gene Page. *Hot City*, 1975, Atlantic 18111.
Dennis Parker. "Fly Like an Eagle"/"New York By Night," 1979, Casablanca NBD 20153.
Teddy Pendergrass. "Get Up, Get Down, Get Funky, Get Loose" from *Life Is a Song Worth Singing*, 1978, Philadelphia International JZ 30595.
Phreek. "Weekend," 1978, Atlantic DSKO 123.
Ritchie Family, The. *Brazil*, 1975, 20th Century T498.
———. "The Best Disco in Town," 1976, Marlin 3306.
———. *Arabian Nights*, 1976, Marlin 2201.
———. "Quiet Village," 1977, Marlin 3316.
———. *African Queens*, 1977, Polydor 454.
Vicki Sue Robinson. "Turn the Beat Around," 1976, RCA Victor PB 10562.
Rolling Stones, The. "Miss You," 1978, Rolling Stones 19307.
Rose Royce. "Pop Your Fingers," 1980, Whitfield 49274.
Diana Ross. "Love Hangover," 1976, Motown 1392.
———. "Upside Down," 1980, Motown 1494.
Saturday Night Fever, 1977, RSO 4001.
Side Effect. "Always There," 1976, Fantasy 769.
Sine. "Just Let Me Do My Thing," 1978, CBS 6351.
Skipworth & Turner. "Thinking About Your Love," 1985, 4th & B'way 7414.
Slave. "Slide," 1977, Cotillion 44218.
Sons of Darkness. "What It Look Like?"/"Black Ice," P&P PP444.
Sphinx. *Judas Iscariot Simon Peter*, 1977, Casablanca NB 7077.
Rod Stewart. "Do Ya Think I'm Sexy?," 1978, Warner Bros. 8724.

Stone. "Crazy," 1983, Sound of New York SNY 5106.

Barbra Streisand/Donna Summer. "No More Tears (Enough Is Enough)," 1979, Columbia 11125.

Sugarhill Gang. "Rapper's Delight," 1979, Sugar Hill 542.

Sun. "Sun Is Here," 1978, Capitol 4587.

Johnnie Taylor. "Disco Lady," 1976, Columbia 10281.

Titanic. "Sultana," 1971, CBS 5365.

Tribe. "Koke" from *Ethnic Stew*, 1974, ABC/Dunhill ABC 807.

Andrea True Connection. "More, More, More," 1976, Buddah 515.

Tanya Tucker. "I Believe the South Is Gonna Rise Again" from *Would You Lay With Me (In a Field of Stone)*, 1974, CBS 32744.

Universal Robot Band. "Dance and Shake Your Tambourine," 1977, Red Greg 207.

Village People. *Village People*, 1977, Casablanca NBLP 7064.

———. *Macho Man*, 1978, Casablanca NBLP 7096.

———. *Cruisin'*, 1978, Casablanca NBLP 7118.

———. *Go West*, 1979, Casablanca NBLP 7144.

———. *Can't Stop the Music*, 1980, Casablanca NBLP 7220.

Voyage. "Souvenirs," 1979, Marlin 3330.

Narada Michael Walden. "I Don't Want Nobody Else (To Dance With You)," 1979, Atlantic 3541.

Anita Ward. "Ring My Bell," 1979, Juana 3422.

Wild Honey. "At the Top of the Stairs," 1976, T.K. TKD 1.

Hank Williams Jr. "The South's Gonna Rattle Again" from *High Notes*, 1982, Elektra 60100.

Wish featuring Fonda Rae. "Touch Me (All Night Long)," 1984, KN1001.

Wood, Brass & Steel. *Wood, Brass & Steel*, 1976, Turbo TURB 7016.

Michael Zager Band. "Let's All Chant," 1978, Private Stock 45, 184.

6. "SO WHY SHOULD I BE ASHAMED?": Disco Goes Underground

Black Uhuru. *Black Uhuru in Dub*, 1977, Jammy's 227A.

Cabaret Voltaire. "Nag Nag Nag," 1979, Rough Trade RT018.

C-Bank. "One More Shot," 1983, Next Plateau NP50011.

Certain Ratio, A. *The Graveyard and the Ballroom*, 1980, Factory FACT16C.

———. "Shack Up" from *The Double 12″*, 1981, Factory FACT42.

Clash, The. "Magnificent Dance," 1981, Epic 4802036.

Jimmy Cliff. "Treat the Youths Right," 1982, Columbia 03507.

Dinosaur. "Kiss Me Again," 1978, Sire 0785.

Dinosaur L. "Go Bang #5," 1982, Sleeping Bag SLX000.

Divine. "Love Reaction," 1983, Bobcat 813 821.

Dominatrix. "The Dominatrix Sleeps Tonight," 1984, Streetwise SWRL2220.

"D" Train. "You're the One for Me," 1981, Prelude PRL539.

———. "Keep On," 1982, Prelude PRL547.

Brian Eno & David Byrne. *My Life in the Bush of Ghosts*, 1981, Sire SRK6093.

ESG. *ESG*, 1981, 99 Records 9904.

Marianne Faithfull. "Why d'Ya Do It?" from *Broken English*, 1979, Island 201018.

Freez. "I.O.U.," 1983, Streetwise SWRL2210.

Glaxo Babies. *Limited Entertainment*, 1980, Y Y6.

Manuel Göttsching. *E2-E4*, 1984, Racket Records 15037.

Indian Ocean. "School Bell"/"Tree House," 1986, Sleeping Bag SLX23.
Jah Wobble/the Edge/Holger Czukay. *Snake Charmer*, 1983, Island IMA1.
Kano. "I'm Ready"/"Holly Dolly," 1980, Emergency EMDS6504.
Kinky Foxx. "So Different," 1983, Sound of New York SNY 5107.
Liquid Liquid. *Optimo*, 1983, 99 Records 9911.
Lisa Lisa and Cult Jam, with Full Force. "I Wonder If I Take You Home," 1984, Columbia 05203.
Lola. "Wax the Van," 1985, Jump Street JS1007.
Loose Joints. "Is It All Over My Face?"/"Pop Your Funk," 1980, West End WES22128.
———. "Is It All Over My Face? (Male/Female)," 1980, West End WES22129.
———. "Tell You Today," 1983, 4th & B'way BWAY401.
Maximum Joy. "Stretch"/"Silent Street"/"Silent Dub," 1981, 99 Records/Y 9908/Y11.
J Walter Negro & the Loose Jointz. "Shoot the Pump," 1981, Zoo York/Island 12WIP6765.
New Order. "Blue Monday," 1983, Factory FACT73.
Normal, The. "Warm Leatherette," 1978, Mute 001.
Number of Names, A. "Sharevari," 1982, Quality QRFC027.
Peppers, The. "Pepper Box," 1973, Spark Records SRL100.
Pigbag. "Papa's Got a Brand New Pigbag," 1981, Y Y10.
PiL. "Death Disco," 1979, Virgin VS274.
Pulsallama. "Ungawa Part II," 1982, Y Y25.
Arthur Russell. *World of Echo*, 1986, Rough Trade 114.
———. "Let's Go Swimming," 1986, Rough Trade RTT184.
Section 25. "Looking From a Hilltop," 1984, Factory FAC108.
Shriekback. "My Spine Is the Bassline," 1982, Y Y27.
———. "Lined Up," 1983, Y Y(T)102.
TW Funkmasters. "Love Money" from Various Artists, *Re-Mixture*, 1981, Champagne CHAMP1.
Was (Not Was). "Wheel Me Out," 1980, Ze/Antilles AN805.
———. "Tell Me That I'm Dreaming," 1981, Ze/Island 50011.

7. "STAYIN' ALIVE": Disco Today
Alcazar. "Cryin' at the Discoteque," 2000, BMG 18934.
All Saints. "Lady Marmalade," 1998, London 408.
DJ Harvey. "Cosmic," 1997, Black Cock 068.
Faze Action. *Full Motion*, 1995, EP Nuphonic 102.
Idjut Boys & Laj. *Beard Law*, 1995, EP U Star 007.
Barry Manilow. "Could It Be Magic," 1975, Arista 0126.
Metro Area. *Metro Area*, 1999, EP Environ 008.
———. *Metro Area*, 2002, Environ ENVCD002.
Pet Shop Boys. "Go West," 1993, Parlophone 6356.
Take That. "It Only Takes a Minute" and "Could It Be Magic" from *Take That and Party*, 1993, RCA 66221.
Take That featuring Lulu. "Relight My Fire," 1993, RCA 67722.
Tavares. "It Only Takes a Minute," 1975, Capitol 4111.
Daniel Wang. *Look Ma No Drum Machine*, 1993, Balihu BAL001.
———. *Aphroasiatechnubian*, 1995, Balihu BAL003.
———. *The Probe, the Strobe*, 1996, Balihu BAL006.
———. *Silver Trophies*, 1999, Environ ENV009.

NOTES

Chapter 1. THE ROTTEN APPLE

1. Vincent Canby, "New York's Woes Are Good Box Office," *New York Times*, November 10, 1974, Section 2, p. 1.
2. David Caute, *The Year of the Barricades: A Journey Through 1968* (New York: Harper, 1968).
3. Mark Rudd, leader of the Columbia University chapter of Students for a Democratic Society (SDS), quoted in Terry Anderson, *The Movement and the Sixties* (New York: Oxford University Press, 1995), p. 195.
4. Six and a half million African Americans migrated northward between 1910 and 1970. Mary Pattillo-McCoy, *Black Picket Fences: Privilege and Peril Among the Black Middle Class* (Chicago: University of Chicago Press, 1999), p. 16.
5. Bruce J. Schulman, *The Seventies* (Cambridge, MA: Da Capo, 2002), p. 68.
6. Vincent J. Cannato, *The Ungovernable City: John Lindsay and His Struggle to Save New York* (New York: Basic Books, 2001), p. 549. Between 1969 and 1977, New York lost 16 percent of its jobs, and in just one year, from 1970 to 1971, the city's unemployment rate jumped from 4.8 percent to 6.7 percent.
7. The white population of New York City declined by 617,127 during the 1960s; at the same time, the minority population increased by 702,903. See ibid., p. 447.
8. Kenneth T. Jackson, ed., *Encyclopedia of New York City* (New Haven: Yale University Press, 1995), pp. 165–67. Beginning in 1965, New York City was required to pay 25 percent of welfare and Medicaid costs of all New Yorkers receiving these benefits. Especially when coupled with the demographic changes in the city, this not only drove up municipal spending but also forced the city to greatly expand its bureaucracy in order to meet the new federal and state regulations. Furthermore, higher interest rates on both the city's debt and the bonds it issued to cover its costs increased the city's budget by another $1.5 billion.
9. Sam Roberts, "1977; Summer of Paranoia," *The New York Times*, July 1, 1999, p. E1.
10. Cannato, *Ungovernable City*, p. 526.
11. Jim Fricke and Charlie Ahearn, *Yes Yes Y'All: The Experience Music Project Oral History of Hip-Hop's First Decade* (Cambridge, MA: Da Capo, 2002), p. viii.

12. Cannato, *Ungovernable City*, p. 533.
13. Ibid., p. 533.
14. Jackson, *Encyclopedia of New York City*, pp. 345–46.
15. David Burnham, "The Changing City: Crime Reports Rise Despite More and Modernized Police," *The New York Times*, June 3, 1969, p. 1.
16. See Christopher Mele, *Selling the Lower East Side: Culture, Real Estate and Resistance in New York City* (Minneapolis: University of Minnesota Press, 2000), and Joshua B. Freeman, *Working-Class New York: Life and Labor Since World War II* (New York: New Press, 2000).
17. Cannato, *Ungovernable City*, p. 528.
18. See www.derechos.net/paulwolf/cointelpro/churchfinalreportIIIc.htm for the Senate's Church Commitee report on the COINTELPRO programs targeting black nationalist groups.
19. Street gangs in New York peaked in 1973, when there were 315 gangs and more than 19,000 members. See Nelson George, *Buppies, B-Boys, Baps and Bohos: Notes on Post-Soul Black Culture* (New York: Harper, 1992).
20. Ibid., p. 11.
21. Nelson George, *The Death of Rhythm & Blues* (New York: Omnibus, 1988), p. 98.
22. *Time*, January 5, 1970.
23. Cannato, *Ungovernable City*, p. 389.
24. Quoted in Peter Carroll, *It Seemed Like Nothing Happened: The Tragedy and Promise of America in the 1970s* (New Brunswick, NJ: Rutgers University Press, 1990), p. 61.
25. Ibid., p. 58. From 1960 to 1970, nationwide welfare lists ballooned by 225 percent, most of which occurred after 1968 when Nixon's anti-inflation strategy produced higher unemployment.
26. Ibid.
27. Pete Hamill, "The Revolt of the White Lower Middle Class," *New York*, April 14, 1969, pp. 29, 24.
28. Francis X. Clines, "For the Flag and for Country, They March," *The New York Times*, May 21, 1970, p. 1. Homer Bigart, "War Foes Here Attacked by Construction Workers," *The New York Times*, May 9, 1970, p. 1; "After 'Bloody Friday,' New York Wonders If Wall Street Is Becoming a Battleground," *The Wall Street Journal*, May 11, 1970, p. 1; Pete Hamill, "Hard Hats and Cops," *New York Post*, May 12, 1970, p. 47.
29. Carroll, *Nothing Happened*, p. 59.
30. Ibid., p. 58.
31. Jackson, *Encyclopedia of New York City*, pp. 165–67.
32. See Homer Bigart, "Negro School Panel Ousts 19, Defies City," *The New York Times*, May 10, 1968, p. 1; Leonard Buder, "Parents Occupy Brooklyn School As Dispute Grows," *The New York Times*, May 15, 1968, p. 1; Fred M. Hechinger, "Racism and Anti-Semitism in the School Crisis," *The New York Times*, September 16, 1968, p. 46; Martin Mayer, "Frustration Is the Word For Ocean Hill," *The New York Times Magazine*, May 19, 1968, p. 28; Irving Spiegel, "Jews Troubled Over Negro Ties," *New York Times*, July 8, 1968, p. 1.
33. Roberts, "1977."
34. Studio We (193 Eldridge Street) was the first of the lofts and was owned by James DuBois and Juma Sultan; Studio Rivbea (24 Bond Street) and Ali's Alley (77 Greene Street) were probably the two most important lofts and were owned,

respectively, by Sam Rivers and his wife Bea and Rashied Ali. Other important loft spaces included Environ at 476 Broadway, Axis at 463 West Broadway, Ladies Fort/Cafe NoHo at 2 Bond Street, Brook on West Seventeenth Street, and Jazzmania at 14 East 23rd Street. For more on the jazz loft scene, see Stanley Crouch, "Jazz Lofts: A Walk Through the Wild Sounds," *The New York Times Magazine*, April 17, 1977, pp. 40–42, and Tom Roe, "Generation Ecstasy: New York's Free Jazz Continuum," in Rob Young, ed., *Undercurrents: The Hidden Wiring of Modern Music*, Continuum, 2002, pp. 241–62. The best available audio document of the loft jazz scene is the *Wildflower* series released on Douglas/Casablanca in 1978.

35. The "prehistory" of disco that follows is only a sketch. A decent history of the context of music consumption, particularly discotheques, house parties, record hops, and sound systems, has yet to be written. The journalistic accounting of nightlife has largely been left to the society and gossip columnists, skewing the focus toward the jet set and Eurotrash. As Sarah Thornton has suggested, the culture of the discotheque has been largely ignored by music writers because the discotheque is often seen as part of the leisure and service industries rather than part of the music industry and it is a site of music consumption rather than production. See Sarah Thornton, "Strategies for Reconstructing the Popular Past," *Popular Music*, Vol. 9, No. 1, 1990, pp. 87–97.

36. The association of desperation and the discotheque can also be seen in the *salsotecas* of Cali, Colombia, during the '70s and '80s. Here, at clubs called Congo Bongo and Impacto Afro-Latino, men who couldn't afford to take dates to the dance halls where live bands played would gather to listen to records both old and new and drown their sorrows in the local firewater. In the mid- to late '80s, when the Cali drug cartel overtook the notorious Medellín cartel as Colombia's top supplier of cocaine, the town's sudden wealth, and the cartel's sponsorship of many local groups, meant that the *salsotecas* were no longer needed. For more, see Lise A. Waxer, *The City of Musical Memory: Salsa, Record Grooves and Popular Culture in Cali, Colombia* (Middletown, CT: Wesleyan University Press, 2002).

37. Report by the Reich Youth Leadership, September 1942, quoted in Uta G. Poiger, *Jazz, Rock, and Rebels: Cold War Politics and American Culture in a Divided Germany* (Berkeley: University of California Press, 2000). See also Mike Zwerin, *La Tristesse de Saint Louis: Swing Under the Nazis* (New York: Morrow, 1987), the excellent Swing Kids Web site at www.return2style.de/amiswhei.htm, and Arvo Vercamer and Marcus Wendel's history of the Hitlerjugend at www.skalman.nu/third-reich/youth-historyof-1939.htm.

38. Quoted in Zwerin, p. 150.

39. The African-American rent parties, "buffet flats," and after-hours joints of the 1920s and 1930s also often featured recorded music, but the music that was played was what was popular and not necessarily targeted at a very specific audience with specific tastes.

40. Zwerin, *Tristesse*, p. 147.

41. W. D. Halls, *The Youth of Vichy France* (Oxford: Clarendon Press, 1981), p. 178.

42. Ludovic Tournès, *New Orleans Sur Seine: Histoire du Jazz en France* (Paris: Librairie Arthème Fayard, 1999).

43. Albert Goldman, *Disco* (New York: Hawthorn Books, 1978). While his book was undoubtedly learned and was certainly written with some pizzazz, Goldman is a problematic figure. Most irritatingly for the writer and historian, he doesn't list any of his sources in his book. This might not be such a problem if it wasn't for

his reputation. His tabloid character assassinations of Elvis Presley and John Lennon have an infamy in the rock community comparable only to Southern preachers warning of the dangers of "jungle music." But more crucial for disco scholars are his comments made during a 1967 debate with Gore Vidal that featured in a documentary on homosexuality made by the American CBS television network. "We're in the course of gradually rolling back from our former cultural values or cultural identifications to a more narcissistic, more self-indulgent, more self-centered, essentially adolescent lifestyle," he said, predating the neoconservative attack on popular culture by some fifteen years. "The homosexual thing cannot really be separated from a lot of other parallel phenomena in our society today . . . We have all sorts of fun-and-game approaches to sex. We have rampant exhibitionism today in every conceivable form. We have a sort of masochistic, sadistic vogue. We have a smut industry that grinds out millions of dollars of pornography a year. We have a sort of masturbatory dance style that's embraced as if it were something profoundly sexual, whereas actually, all those dances do is just grind away without any consciousness of other people or their partners. And homosexuality is just one of a number of such things all tending toward the subversion, toward the final erosion, of our traditional cultural values. After all, when you're culturally bankrupt, why you fall into the hands of receivers."

By the time he wrote *Disco*, Goldman seemed to have made peace with narcissism—he even downright praises this aspect of disco culture. However, thorny sentiments still abound throughout the book, with barely disguised racism and misogyny giving an added piquancy to his homophobia. "To the ghetto-inspired pleasure grabbing, multiple drug abuse, and off-the-wall fucking of the '60s have been added all those refinements that come with money and maturity"; "The moment you hit the room, your nostrils were distended by the stench of black sweat"; and "demonstrating unwittingly how totally unfulfilling it is to dance by yourself as opposed to how frustrating and infuriating it is to have to work out something as intimate as the way you dance with some cranky bitch" are but three examples.

Despite poring over countless accounts of Paris during the occupation, numerous histories of jazz in France and queries to the Académie Française, and numerous scholars specializing in the history of jazz in France, I have been unable to uncover any other source that confirms the existence of La Discothèque. The record lending arm of La Bibliothèque Française, which started in the 1930s, however, was called La Phonothèque. In *The Last Party: Studio 54, Disco, and the Culture of the Night* (New York: Morrow, 1997) Anthony Haden-Guest writes that "credit for coining the word 'discothèque'—a play on cinémathèque—has been claimed by Brigitte Bardot's director-husband Roger Vadim."

44. Halls, *Youth of Vichy France*.
45. Regine Zylberberg, *Call Me By My First Name* (London: Andre Deutsch, 1988).
46. Ibid., p. 130.
47. Donald Goddard, "It's Only 640 Miles From Paris to Vienna, But They Are Atmospheres Apart," *The New York Times*, June 25, 1972, Section 10, p. 1.
48. Vanessa Grigoriadis, "Regine's Last Stand," *New York*, April 19, 1999.
49. Goldman, *Disco*, p. 30.
50. Record hops were popular during the early years of the rock-and-roll era. Local radio DJs would play the latest releases at a town's dance hall with the occasional appearance of a performer who usually lip-synched along with his or her latest hit.

51. Louis Calta, "Party to Mark Closing of Arthur Discotheque," *The New York Times*, June 21, 1969, p. 16; Angela Taylor, "Arthur, Once a Hairdo, Is Now a Discotheque," *The New York Times*, May 7, 1965, p. 44.
52. Author's interview with Cherry Vanilla, August 22, 2003.
53. Jackson, *Encyclopedia of New York City*, pp. 315–16.
54. John Gruen, "Cerebrum, 'Designed to Soothe the Spirit,'" *Vogue*, January 1969.
55. Goldman, *Disco*, p. 112.
56. Author's interview with Barry Lederer, October 22, 2003.
57. For more on Stonewall and the gay rights movement, see Chapter 2.
58. Goldman, *Disco*, p. 118.
59. "State Asking for Shutdown of 43d Street Discotheque," *The New York Times*, March 25, 1972, p. 34; "Discotheque Ordered Closed," *The New York Times*, April 5, 1972, p. 49.
60. Gamelan is a heavily percussive Indonesian music featuring hammered metallophones that sound like an orchestra of xylophones but considerably less twee and tinkly.
61. Radio DJs had used slip-cueing for some time prior to Grasso's bringing it to the club environment. Grasso himself was taught the technique by an engineer for WCBS, DJ Bob Lewis. See the Francis Grasso interview at www.djhistory.com.
62. Whether Grasso was the first DJ to use two copies of the same record is in dispute. Pete DJ Jones, who was Grandmaster Flash's biggest influence, claims to have started using two copies of the same record in 1969. Other uptown DJs who were formative influences on the hip-hop DJs, like Maboya and Grand Master Flowers, claimed to have originated the technique as well.
63. Bill Brewster and Frank Broughton, *Last Night a DJ Saved My Life*, Grove Press, 2000, p. 130.
64. Peter Braunstein, "Disco," *American Heritage*, November 1999, p. 53.
65. Carroll, *Nothing Happened*, p. 3.
66. "The Story of the Loft," XFM London, aired October 2000.
67. Vince Aletti, "SoHo Vs. Disco," *The Village Voice*, June 16, 1975, p. 124.
68. "The Story of the Loft."
69. Robert McG. Thomas Jr., "Weekly Parties for 500 Chill Tenants," *The New York Times*, May 21, 1974, p. 45.
70. Aletti, "Sotto Vs. Disco," p. 1.
71. Author's interview with Danny Krivit, March 11, 2003.
72. Aletti, "Sotto Vs. Disco."
73. Ibid.
74. Author's interview with Danny Krivit.
75. Aletti, "Sotto Vs. Disco."
76. Author's interview with Danny Krivit.
77. Steven Harvey, "Behind the Groove: New York City's Disco Underground," *Collusion 5*, September 1983, p. 30.
78. Another popular Loft record with similar vibes was Ozo's *Listen to the Buddha* album, particularly "Anambra River." Ozo was a multiracial band tending toward the fourth-world fusions conjured up by Brian Eno and Jon Hassell and featuring expressly Buddhist lyrics.
79. There are also those who say that "Soul Makossa" was discovered by DJ Alfie of the Glitter Palace (see Mark Jacobson, "Hollyw-o-o-o-d! The Return of the New York Disco," *New York*, July 1, 1974), but given Mancuso's well-documented championing of Caribbean and African music, it seems likely that he found it. Another

discovery from his trawls through Nostrand Avenue's record shops was Jamaican Boris Gardiner's version of Booker T. & the MG's' "Melting Pot," whose break featured more percussion than the original. Mancuso's love affair with Jamaican music would continue well into the '80s as he played records like Joe Gibbs's dub classic "Chapter Three," and Nicodemus' version of the "Mad Mad" riddim, "Boneman Connection."

80. While this was the first record pool, it wasn't the first attempt to organize DJs as a unified workforce. See "Disco DJs Form Union in Poland," *Billboard*, January 11, 1975, p. 4.

81. For more on "Love Is the Message," see Chapter 4.

82. Sheila Weller, "New Wave of Discotheques," *New York Sunday News*, August 31, 1975, pp. 20–26.

83. Author's interview with Tom Moulton, March 12, 2003.

84. Ibid.

85. Ibid.

86. Author's interview with Barry Lederer.

87. Author's interview with Tom Moulton.

88. See I. S. Horowitz, "'Illegit' Disco Tapes Peddled by Jockeys," *Billboard*, October 12, 1974, p. 1.

89. Linda M. George, liner notes to *Disco Par-r-r-ty*, Spring Records SPR 6705, 1974.

90. Ibid.

91. Author's interview with Tom Moulton.

92. Quoted in Tony Cummings, Robert Gallagher, Denise Hall, and Davitt Sigerson, "Dance and Discomania," *Black Music*, January 1976, p. 12.

93. Many DJs made their own edits of songs (usually boosting the breaks with additional percussion) and pressed them up on acetates so that they could play them at clubs and often distributed copies of their new mixes to other DJs. The most famous of these early remix "labels" was Sunshine Sound, which was the studio where most acetates were cut in New York at the time. DJs like François Kevorkian (a mind-boggling tribal remix of Donna Summer's "I Feel Love"), Keith Dumpson, and John Morales contributed edits to Sunshine Sound, which also released the legendary "Hollywood" mix. DJ Rick Gianatos released his edits on his own Disco Queen label, which featured his mixes of records like Juggy Jones's "Inside America" and MFSB's "Love Is the Message."

94. Author's interview with Danny Krivit.

95. Haden-Guest, *The Last Party*, pp. xvii–xviii.

96. George Melly, *Revolt into Style* (New York: Oxford University Press, 1989), pp. 106–07.

97. Author's interview with Ian Levine, November 2, 2003.

98. Ibid.

99. Ibid.

100. Tony Cummings, "Blue-Eyed Soul," *Black Music*, September 1975, p. 17.

101. Ibid.

Chapter 2. "I'M JUST AN OUTLAW, MY NAME IS DESIRE": Disco and Sexuality

1. The Mattachine Society pressured the New York City Police Department to stop using undercover cops to entrap homosexuals (not that this seemed to affect the

Continental Baths, which was raided in February and December 1969 by cops who wore handcuffs underneath their towels) and forced a change in the New York Liquor Authority law that stated that if a group of three or more homosexual men met in a bar, the bar could lose its license.

2. In the late '60s/early '70s, rampant homophobia was hardly the exclusive preserve of religious zealots and bigots. It was enshrined in the dictates of "science." The American Psychiatric Association wouldn't strike homosexuality from its list of mental disorders until 1973.

3. Charles Kaiser, *Gay Metropolis, 1940–1996* (San Diego: Harcourt, 1999), pp. 148–49.

4. Ibid., p. 149.

5. Quoted in Mark Jacobson, "Live From New York," *New York*, October 22, 2001, p. 42.

6. The fame of the Continental Baths was largely thanks to Bette Midler, who sang the club's praises on her three appearances on the *Tonight Show* in 1970 and 1971.

7. Robert Amsel, "A Walk on the Wild Side of Stonewall," *The Advocate*, September 15, 1987.

8. Martin Duberman, *Stonewall* (New York: Dutton, 1993), p. 185.

9. Lucian K. Truscott IV, "Gay Power Comes to Sheridan Square," *The Village Voice*, July 3, 1969, p. 1.

10. Ibid., p. 18.

11. Jerry Lisker, "Homo Nest Raided, Queen Bees Are Stinging Mad," *Daily News*, July 6, 1969.

12. Author's interview with Barry Lederer.

13. Ibid.

14. See Felix Guattari, *Molecular Revolution: Psychology and Politics* (New York: Penguin, 1984).

15. John Whyte, the owner of the Botel in the Pines, disputes this account and says it was the other way around: The first DJ setup in Fire Island was at his establishment. See Esther Newton, *Cherry Grove, Fire Island: 60 Years in America's First Gay and Lesbian Town* (Boston: Beacon Press, 1993), p. 244.

16. Author's interview with Barry Lederer.

17. Cherry Grove and the Pines are linked by a path that cuts across the sand dunes' shrubbery, which acquired the nickname of the Meat Rack because of the startling amount of anonymous sex that went on in those bushes.

18. Author's interview with Barry Lederer.

19. Andrew Holleran, *Dancer from the Dance* (New York: Penguin, 1978), p. 114.

20. Quoted in Mel Cheren, *Keep on Dancin': My Life and the Paradise Garage* (New York: 24 Hours for Life, 2000), p. 108.

21. Author's interview with Barry Lederer.

22. See Cheren, *Keep on Dancin'*, p. 162.

23. Andrew Kopkind, "The Dialectic of Disco: Gay Music Goes Straight," *The Village Voice*, February 12, 1979, p. 13.

24. Edmund White, *States of Desire: Travels in Gay America* (New York: Penguin, 1991), pp. 269–70.

25. Author's interview with Ian Levine.

26. Ibid.

27. Ibid.

28. Chris Kirk, "What a Difference a Gay Makes," *Collusion*, No. 4, February–April 1983, p. 18.
29. See Danny Wang, "Tee Scott," *Underground News*, No. 20, p. 15.
30. David Diebold, *Tribal Rites: San Francisco's Dance Music Phenomenon 1978–1988* (Northridge, CA: Time Warp Publishing, 1988), p. 5.
31. Diebold, p. 125.
32. Fittingly, Pete Bellotte and most of the Munich Machine covered "Can Can" under the guise of Stainless Steal in 1978.
33. Author's interview with Ian Levine.
34. Ibid.
35. Ibid.
36. Ibid.
37. Ibid.
38. Ibid.
39. Author's interview with Ian Levine.
40. See Kimberley Leston, "The Story of O," *The Face*, May 1987, p. 32–35.
41. Ibid.
42. Ibid.
43. Kaiser, *Gay Metropolis*, p. 283.
44. Rodger McFarlane quoted in David W. Dunlap, "As Disco Faces Razing, Gay Alumni Share Memories," *The New York Times*, August 21, 1995, p. B3.

Chapter 3. "LIKE CLONES AND ROBOTS THAT WE ARE": Automating the Beat
1. David Toop, "Throbbery With Intent," *The Wire*, April 1992, p. 21.
2. Quoted in Simon Reynolds, *Energy Flash* (London: Picador, 1998), p. 3.
3. David Toop, *Ocean of Sound: Aether Talk, Ambient Sound and Imaginary Worlds* (London: Serpent's Tail, 1995), p. 204.
4. Ibid., p. 205.
5. George, *Death of Rhythm & Blues*, p. 154.
6. Rickey Vincent, *Funk: The Music, the People, and the Rhythm of the One* (New York: St. Martin's Press, 1996), p. 209.
7. Toop, "Throbbery," p. 21.
8. Walter Hughes, "In the Empire of the Beat: Discipline and Disco," in *Microphone Fiends: Youth Music & Youth Culture*, ed. Andrew Ross and Tricia Rose (New York: Routledge, 1994), p. 151.
9. Toop, "Throbbery," p. 22.
10. Adam White and Fred Bronson, *The Billboard Book of Number One Rhythm & Blues Hits* (New York: Billboard Books), 1993, pp. 183–85.
11. Abe Peck, *Dancing Madness* (New York: Anchor Books, 1976), p. 6.
12. Interview with Laurin Rinder at www.discomusic.com/people-more/41_0_11_0_M/.
13. Davitt Sigerson, "A Splice of History," *Black Music*, September 1977, p. 40.
14. Haden-Guest, *The Last Party*, p. xxii.
15. Vince Aletti, "Electric Dreams," *Numéro 39*, December 2002. Reprinted at www.discostepbystep.com/giorgio_moroder.htm.
16. Angus MacKinnon, "The Importance of Not Being Earnest," *New Musical Express*, December 9, 1978, p. 30.

Chapter 4. "ZIPPIN' UP MY BOOTS, GOING BACK TO MY ROOTS": Disco and the Soul Continuum

1. Kaiser, *Gay Metropolis*, p. 136.
2. In 1968, gay activist Frank Kameny coined the slogan "Gay is good" after witnessing Stokely Carmichael and fellow protesters chanting, "Black is beautiful." At the "Gay-In" in Central Park celebrating the first anniversary of Stonewall, marchers chanted, "Say it loud, gay is proud." See ibid., pp. 147, 216.
3. Author's interview with Vicki Wickham, November 2003.
4. Ibid.
5. Ibid.
6. Much of this account comes from Cecil Adams's "Straight Dope" column, April 23, 1993, reprinted at www.straightdope.com/classics/a4_031.html.
7. See Ben Edmonds, *What's Going On?: Marvin Gaye and the Last Days of the Motown Sound* (Edinburgh: Mojo Books, 2001).
8. The report is printed at www.dol.gov/asp/programs/history/webid-meynihan.htm.
9. Peter Kihss, "'Benign Neglect' on Race Is Proposed by Moynihan," *The New York Times*, March 1, 1970, p. 1.
10. Carroll, *Nothing Happened*, p. 41.
11. Ibid.
12. For a discussion of the Philadelphia Plan, see ibid., pp. 45–46.
13. Ibid., p. 49.
14. Frank Robertson, "Disco Tech: An All-American DJ Fights the Power," in Peck, *Dancing Madness*, p. 27.
15. Holleran, *Dancer from the Dance*, pp. 38–39.
16. This account is based on White and Bronson, *Number One Rhythm & Blues Hits*, pp. 58–59.
17. Ibid., p. 85.
18. Tony Cummings, *The Sound of Philadelphia* (London: Methuen, 1975), p. 89.
19. Davitt Sigerson, "Philly '76," *Black Music*, July 1976, p. 37.
20. Interview with Joe Tarsia at geosound.org/joetarsiainterview.htm.
21. Harvard Business School, "A Study of the Soul Music Environment Prepared for Columbia Records Group," quoted in George, *Death of Rhythm and Blues*, pp. 136, 137.
22. David Sanjek, "Tell Me Something I Don't Already Know: The Harvard Report on Soul Music Revisited," in Norman Kelley, ed., *Rhythm and Business: The Political Economy of Black Music* (New York: Akashic Books, 2002), p. 66.
23. Harvard Business School, quoted ibid., p. 63.
24. Ibid., p. 66.
25. Sigerson, "Philly '76," p. 37.
26. Ibid.
27. For more on Young and the ur-disco beat, see Chapter 3.
28. Salsoul advertisement, *Billboard*, January 22, 1977, p. 82.
29. Sigerson, "Philly '76," p. 37.
30. For more on this record, see Chapter 1.
31. George, *Death of Rhythm & Blues*, pp. 154–55.
32. Sigerson, "Philly '76," p. 37.
33. Ibid.
34. Jacobson, "Hollyw-o-o-o-d!," p. 48.
35. Author's interview with Danny Krivit.

36. Jacobson, "Hollyw-o-o-o-d!," p. 51.
37. Racliffe A. Joe, *The Business of Disco* (New York: Billboard Books, 1980), p. 40.
38. Peck, *Dancing Madness*, p. 6.
39. William Julius Wilson, *The Declining Significance of Race* (Chicago: University of Chicago Press, 1978), p. 130.
40. George, *Death of Rhythm & Blues*, p. 121.
41. Ibid.
42. Ellis Cose, *The Rage of a Privileged Class* (New York: Harper, 1993), p. 79.
43. Bart Landry, *The New Black Middle Class* (Berkeley: University of California Press), 1987, pp. 75, 195.
44. Wilson, *Declining Significance*, p. 139.
45. Joe, *Business of Disco*, p. 34.
46. Ibid., p. 36.
47. Haden-Guest, *The Last Party*, p. 81.
48. Ibid.
49. Ibid., p. 82.
50. Ibid., pp. 82–83.
51. Ibid., p. 83.
52. Author's interview with Nile Rodgers, June 18, 2003.
53. Ibid.
54. Ibid.
55. Ibid.
56. Marc Taylor, A *Touch of Classic Soul 2* (Jamaica, NY: Aloiv Publishing, 2001), pp. 51–52.
57. Author's interview with Nile Rodgers.
58. Ibid.
59. Quoted in David Nathan, "The Art of Being Chic," *Blues & Soul*, October 9–22, 1979, p. 7.
60. Author's interview with Nile Rodgers.
61. Ibid.
62. Ibid.
63. Geoff Brown, "Qui Sont Ces Gens? C'est Chic," *Black Music*, March 1979, p. 27.
64. Author's interview with Nile Rodgers.
65. Quoted in Davitt Sigerson, "Dr. Buzzard's Original Savannah Band," *Black Music*, January 1977, p. 25.
66. For a measure of how original the brothers Browder were, check out Charlie Calello's own disco revival pap "Dance, Dance, Dance" (essentially a disco "Havah Nagilah") (Ariola, 1976) and a cover of Louis Prima's "Sing, Sing, Sing" (Profile, 1982).
67. Sigerson, "Dr. Buzzard," p. 24.
68. Quoted in Robert Palmer, "Kid Creole: He Mixes a Heady Brew of Styles," *The New York Times*, June 10, 1981, p. C23.

Chapter 5. PRISONERS OF THE NIGHT: The Disco Craze
1. Vince Aletti, "Discotheque Rock '72: Paaaaarty!," *Rolling Stone*, September 13, 1973, pp. 60–61; "Discotheques Break Singles," *Billboard*, October 6, p. 3.
2. Jacobson, "Hollyw-o-o-o-d!," p. 50.

3. Although the ribbon was cut in 1973, the building's first tenants moved in on December 16, 1970.

4. In 1962, a report titled "The Wastelands of New York City" called lower Manhattan a vast commercial slum, and it was earmarked for wholesale demolition by Robert Moses to make way for his Lower Manhattan Expressway project. But in the face of a campaign waged by urbanist Jane Jacobs, the expressway project was turned down and the cast iron buildings of SoHo and TriBeCa were granted a reprieve.

5. Roger Cohen, "Casting Giant Shadows: The Politics of Building the World Trade Center," *Portfolio: A Quarterly Review of Trade and Transportation*, Winter 1990/1991, reprinted at www.greatbuildings.com/buildings/World_Trade_Center_History. html.

6. Quoted in Fred Bronson, *The Billboard Book of Number One Hits* (New York: Billboard Books, 1988), p. 410.

7. This account is a composite of several conflicting stories that have appeared in ibid.; Bronson and White, *Number One Rhythm & Blues Hits*; Brian Chin, "In the Beat of the Night," liner notes to *The Disco Box*, Rhino 75595, 1999; Wayne Jancik, *The Billboard Book of One-Hit Wonders* (New York: Billboard Books, 1998).

8. One measure of how important the hustle and "The Hustle" were to disco's mainstream success is the number of hustle records that appeared in its wake: Salsoul Orchestra's "Salsoul Hustle," the Kay-Gee's' "Hustle Wit Every Muscle" and "Tango Hustle," Eddie Drennon's "Let's Do the Latin Hustle," Joe Cuba's "Latin Hustle," James Brown's "Hustle!!! (Dead on It)," Fajardo '76's "C'mon Baby Do the Latin Hustle," the Fatback Band's "Spanish Hustle," Alcatraz Black Band's "The Dynamic Hustle Samba," Sweet Charles's "Hang Out and Hustle," Tommy Stewart's "Bump and Hustle," Rice & Beans Orchestra's "Blue Danube Hustle," Hidden Strength's "Hustle on Up (Do the Bump)," Mastermind's "Hustle Bus Stop," and Hi-Tension's "British Hustle" to name but a few.

9. William Safire, "On the Hustle," *The New York Times*, August 4, 1975, p. 19.

10. Dena Kleiman, "The Hustle Restores Old Touch to Dancing," *The New York Times*, July 12, 1975, p. 27.

11. Safire, "On the Hustle."

12. Ibid.

13. Kopkind, "The Dialectic of Disco," p. 25.

14. Goldman, *Disco*, p. 11.

15. Maureen Orth, with Betsy Carter and Lisa Whitman, "Get Up and Boogie," *Newsweek*, November 8, 1976, p. 98.

16. For a poetic explanation of the fascination that pigeon flying has on New York street culture, see Jim Jarmusch's film *Ghost Dog: The Way of the Samurai*.

17. Author's interview with Michael Corral, February 3, 2004.

18. Lasch quoted in J. David Hoeveler Jr., *The Postmodernist Turn: American Thought and Culture in the 1970s* (New York: Twayne, 1996), p. 12.

19. Author's interview with Michael Corral, February 3, 2004.

20. Ibid.

21. Ibid.

22. Ibid.

23. Ibid.: "The only hip-hop parties I would go to was the Kool Herc parties . . . When I went to Herc parties, they was cool, but I wasn't wanted there because

I was a light-skinned child and everybody was black in there. It was like a racial thing going on, so I felt intimidated in a way, and I couldn't wear colors in there because I would get my ass kicked. So when I went there I wasn't feeling that vibe, I was feeling uncomfortable."

24. Mikal Gilmore, "Disco!," *Rolling Stone*, April 19, 1979, p. 54.
25. Jan Hoddenfield, "Cruising the Scene in the Discotheques," *New York Post*, August 9, 1975, p. 39.
26. Author's interview with Nile Rodgers.
27. *The Tonight Show*, June 5, 1974.
28. Le Jardin flyer from 1974.
29. Ed McCormack, "No Sober Person Dances, in Which a Suburban Prole Decadent Visits a Hot Manhattan Disco and Learns That Cicero Was Right," in Peck, *Dancing Madness*, p. 11.
30. Richard Szathmary and Lucian K. Truscott IV, "Inside the Disco Boom," *The Village Voice*, July 21, 1975, p. 6.
31. McCormack, "No Sober Person Dances," p. 11.
32. Robert Roth, "N.Y. Club Scrutiny Again Draws Liquor Board Fire," *Billboard*, December 17, 1977, p. 68.
33. Sally Helgesen, "Disco: Phosphorescent Shapes Pass Through the Night, Leaving Nothing Behind," *Harper's*, October 1977, p. 20.
34. Ibid., p. 21.
35. Ibid.
36. Author's interview with Ian Levine.
37. While this figure is pretty staggering, it is also worth noting that in 1925 there were 786 licensed dance halls in New York City, 238 of them in Manhattan, and that 14 percent of men and 10 percent of women aged seventeen to forty visited one at least once a week. See Jackson, *Encyclopedia of New York City*, pp. 315–16.
38. "Discomania," *Forbes*, June 1, 1976, p. 47.
39. Szathmary and Truscott, "Inside The Disco Boom," p. 7.
40. Orth, "Get Up and Boogie," *Newsweek*, p. 95.
41. For a discussion of inflation and how it presaged the '80s credit and speculation boom, see Schulman, *The Seventies*, pp. 131–43.
42. Quoted in Hoeveler, *The Postmodernist Turn*, p. 11.
43. John Sippel, "Ramada Tests Disco Appeal in North Dakota," *Billboard*, December 14, 1974, p. 63.
44. Quoted in Cummings, Gallagher, Hall, and Sigerson, "Dance and Discomania," p. 12.
45. See Tom Moulton, "Disco Action," *Billboard*, November 23, 1974, and Radcliffe Joe, "The L.A. Scene: Growing, But Second to N.Y.," *Billboard*, December 16, 1978, p. 53. With disco proliferating out of control and the inevitable thinning of the DJ talent pool, New York's Sugarscoop Records came to the rescue of dancers in provincial outposts everywhere forced to listen to lousy transitions and clunky mixing. In October 1977 they started a DJ subscription remix service called Disconet that offered premixed medleys and special remixes of individual tracks by New York's most talented DJs. The first Disconet record featured a mix by 12 West DJ Tom Savarese that included Chic's "Dance, Dance, Dance (Yowsah, Yowsah, Yowsah)," Sheila & B. Devotion's "Love Me Baby," and the Hues Corporation's "Telegram of Love."
46. See Moulton, "Disco Action."

47. Brian Chin, "The Disco Beatmasters: From the Studio to the Dance Floor," liner notes to *The Disco Box*, Rhino 75595, 1999.
48. Quoted in Denise Hall, "Lookin' White/Bein' Black/Soundin' Brown," *Black Music*, September 1976, p. 43.
49. Davitt Sigerson, "The Great Disco Debate," *Black Music*, September 1978, p. 23.
50. Quoted in Chin, "The Disco Beatmasters."
51. Nik Cohn, "Another Saturday Night," in Hanif Kureishi and Jon Savage, eds., *The Faber Book of Pop* (London: Faber & Faber, 1995), pp. 425, 431.
52. Nik Cohn, "Fever Pitch," *The Guardian*, September 17, 1994, Weekend Section, p. 12.
53. Jon Savage, *England's Dreaming: Anarchy, Sex Pistols, Punk Rock, and Beyond* (New York: St. Martin's Press, 2002), pp. 433–34.
54. Carroll, *Nothing Happened*, p. 266.
55. Author's interview with Nile Rodgers.
56. McCormack, p. 13.
57. Aletti, "SoHo Vs. Disco," p. 124.
58. Anna Quindlen, "What's New in Discotheques," *The New York Times*, November 11, 1977, p. C18.
59. Ibid.
60. Al Corley, a sometime doorman: "You know Steve's basic line? 'Just make sure you don't let in anyone like me!' Basically what he was saying was, I would not let myself in. It was a joke, but there was some truth to that. Or Ian. I mean, you would never let Ian in. If Ian wasn't in, he would never get in. And he knows that." Quoted in Haden-Guest, *The Last Party*, pp. 52–53.
61. Orth, "Get Up and Boogie," p. 94.
62. William H. Chafe, *The Unfinished Journey: America Since World War II* (New York: Oxford University Press, 1999), p. 449.
63. Quindlen, "What's New in Discotheques."
64. Haden-Guest, *The Last Party*, p. 50.
65. Helgesen, "Disco," p. 23.
66. Kaiser, *Gay Metropolis*, p. 258.
67. Gloria Gaynor, *Soul Survivor* (London: Fount Paperbacks, 1995), p. 94.
68. Arnold H. Lubasch, "Two Studio 54 Owners Are Given 3½ Years for Evading U.S. Taxes," *The New York Times*, January 19, 1980, p. 1.
69. "Talk of the Town," *The New Yorker*, October 3, 1977, p. 33.
70. Vita Miezitis, *Night Dancin'* (New York: Ballantine Books, 1980), p. 118.
71. Quindlen, "What's New in Discotheques."
72. Ibid.
73. Miezitis, *Night Dancin'*, p. 25.
74. Joe, "The L.A. Scene," p. 53.
75. Andy Blackford, *Disco Dancing Tonight* (London: Octopus, 1979), p. 24.
76. Author's interview with Ian Levine.
77. Jamake Hightower, "Dancing in the Seventies," *Horizon*, May 1977, p. 31.
78. Holleran, *Dancer from the Dance*, p. 12.
79. "With Jamaica," *The New Yorker*, February 25, 1974.
80. The record was originally released promotionally on Brown's P&P label.
81. Brown started the P&P label in the early '70s with a record of driving, primal funk by Flame & Sons of Darkness called "Solid Funk." Flame was longtime underground soul presence Oscar Richardson of the group Flame 'N' King, while Sons

of Darkness was a teenaged group that Brown had discovered playing in the base-ment of his apartment building. The group featured Emmanuel Rahiem LeBlanc and Keith "Sabu" Crier, who would later become part of the Rhythm Makers (see Chapter 3) and GQ, who had a huge disco hit with "Disco Nights (Rock-Freak)" in 1979.

82. Adams's more commercial side was evidenced by his work with Main Ingredient's Tony Sylvester and producer Bert DeCoteaux on soft soul records by Bloodstone ("Just Like in the Movies") and Ace Spectrum ("Don't Send Nobody Else"); as the house arranger at Greg Carmichael's Red Greg Records, where he worked on records as diverse as Universal Robot Band's "Dance and Shake Your Tambourine," Bumble Bee Unlimited's "Love Bug," and Tony Sylvester and the New Ingredient's "Pazuzu"; and his work on more than one hundred commercial jingles—most important for disco devotees was the one of Windsong Perfume: "I can't seem to forget her, her Windsong stays on my mind."

83. Abe Peck, "The Cartoon That Conquered the World," *Rolling Stone*, April 19, 1979, p. 12.

84. Jacques Attali, *Noise: The Political Economy of Music* (Minneapolis: University of Minnesota Press, 1985).

85. David Toop, "Throbbery," p. 21.

86. Frederic Dannen, *Hit Men: Power Brokers and Fast Money Inside the Music Business* (New York: Times Books, 1990), pp. 162–63.

87. Jesse Kornbluth, "Merchandizing Disco for the Masses," *New York Times Magazine*, February 18, 1979, p. 8.

88. I. S. Horowitz, "Symphony and Disco Join in Rochester," *Billboard*, December 16, 1978, p. 47.

89. Gilmore, "Disco!," p. 9.

90. Kopkind, "The Dialectic of Disco," p. 12.

91. Author's interview with Danny Krivit.

92. Tara Rogers, "Take Me 'Out' to the Ballgame," www.pinknoises.com/ymca.shtml.

93. Bill Straub, "With a Nail-Biting Playoff Season, Baseball Bounces Back," *The Washington Post*, October 16, 1997.

94. Insane Coho Lips membership card reprinted at www.outernetweb.com/focal/disco/coholips/jpgs/vicoho.jpg.

95. Abe Peck, "Hangover at Dahl House," *Chicago Sun-Times*, July 14, 1979, p. 6; Bill Gleason, "The Horror at Comiskey," *Chicago Sun-Times*, July 14, 1979, p. 85; "Disco Demolition," whitesoxinteractive.com/History&Glory/DiscoDemolition.htm.

96. DREAD was started by DJs Jim Johnson and George Baier, who originally called their antidisco army the Disco Ducks Klan and were going to wear white sheets at a rally at a disco that had decided to turn back into a rock club.

97. Frank Rose, "Discophobia: Rock & Roll Fights Back," *The Village Voice*, November 12, 1979, p. 36.

98. Joe Nick Patoski, "Disco Showdown in Oklahoma," *Rolling Stone*, November 2, 1978, p. 33.

99. Quoted at www.jahsonic.com/DiscoSucks.html.

100. Bill Brewster and Frank Broughton, *Last Night a DJ Saved My Life* (New York: Headline, 1999), p. 249.

101. Billy Sunday, "Dancing, Drinking, Card Playing," reprinted at www.bibleteacher.org/bs_6.htm.

102. Much of this account is from Rose, "Discophobia," pp. 36–37.
103. Ibid.
104. Steve Hogan and Lee Hudson, *Completely Queer: The Gay and Lesbian Encyclopedia* (New York: Henry Holt, 1998), p. 291.
105. Schulman, *The Seventies*, p. 121.
106. Robert Worth, "Guess Who Saved the South Bronx?," *Washington Monthly*, Vol. 31, No. 4, April 1999, pp. 26–32; Robert Caro, *The Power Broker: Robert Moses and the Fall of New York* (New York: Random House, 1975); Joshua B. Freeman, *Working-Class New York: Life and Labor Since World War II* (New York: New Press, 2000); "City on a Hill: The South Bronx: From Urban Planning Victim to Victor" at www.demographia.com/db-sbrx-txt.htm.
107. Fricke and Ahearn, *Yes Yes Y'All*, p. viii.
108. Worth, "Guess Who," p. 27.
109. Joseph P. Fried, "City's Housing Administrator Proposes 'Planned Shrinkage' of Some Slums," *The New York Times*, February 3, 1976, p. 35.
110. Worth, "Guess Who," p. 28.
111. Fricke and Ahearn, *Yes Yes Y'All*, p. viii.
112. See Freeman, *Working-Class New York*, p. 276, and Jonathan Mahler, "Summer of '77," *The New York Times*, June 30, 2002, Section 14, p. 1.
113. Quoted in Freeman, *Working-Class New York*, p. 281.
114. Herbert C. Gutman, "As for the '02 Kosher-Food Rioters . . . ," *The New York Times*, July 21, 1977, p. 23.
115. Freeman, *Working-Class New York*, p. 281.
116. Fricke and Ahearn, *Yes Yes Y'All*, pp. 131–33.
117. Vince Aletti, "The Dancing Machine," in Shelton Waldrep, ed., *The Seventies: The Age of Glitter in Popular Culture* (New York: Routledge, 2000).
118. Author's interview with Danny Krivit.
119. Fricke and Ahearn, *Yes Yes Y'All*, p. 28.
120. For more on the rise of the South, see Kirkpatrick Sale, *Power Shift* (New York: Vintage, 1975) and Bruce J. Schulman, *From Cotton Belt to Sunbelt* (New York: Oxford University Press, 1991).
121. Quoted in Schulman, *The Seventies*, p. 107.
122. Ibid.
123. Ibid., p. 121.
124. Ibid., pp. 102–17.

Chapter 6. "SO WHY SHOULD I BE ASHAMED?": Disco Goes Underground
1. Haden-Guest, *The Last Party*, p. 226.
2. Michael Gross, "The Latest Calvin: From the Bronx to Eternity," *New York Magazine*, August 8, 1988, pp. 20–29.
3. Frank Rich, "The Gay Decades," *Esquire*, November 1987, p. 98.
4. Ibid.
5. Vince Aletti, "I Won't Dance, Don't Ask Me," *The Village Voice*, April 29, 1976, p. 158.
6. Liner notes to *Streets*, Beggars Banquet BEGA1, 1977.
7. Author's interview with Bob Blank, January 7, 2003.
8. Savage, *England's Dreaming*, pp. 433–34.

9. British label Stiff was associated with the punk movement and had plenty of records that alluded to the dance floor and predated "Contort Yourself"—Nick Lowe's "I Love the Sound of Breaking Glass" and Roogalator's "Cincinnati Fatback"—but they were more punk by association than by sound. The same was true for the label's early Ian Dury & the Blockheads records like "Sex and Drugs and Rock 'n' Roll" and "Wake Up and Make Love With Me," where the only punk element was Dury's Cockney accent.

10. Quoted in Glenn O'Brien, liner notes to *Irresistible Impulse*, Tiger Style Records TIG60037, 2003.

11. For more on Max's Kansas City, see Yvonne Sewall-Ruskin, *High on Rebellion* (New York: Thunder's Mouth Press, 1998).

12. Steven Harvey, "ESG: The Family Jewels," *Collusion*, No. 4, February 1983, p. 15.

13. "Why Are Lines Shorter For Gas Than the Mudd Club in New York? Because Every Night Is Odd There," *People*, July 16, 1979, p. 33.

14. Ibid.

15. John Rockwell, "Rock Comes to the Aid of Art," *The New York Times*, June 13, 1982, Section 2, p. 31.

16. Author's interview with Bob Blank.

17. Robert Palmer, "Concert: Russell and Marti," *The New York Times*, April 26, 1987, Section 1, p. 67.

18. Jonathan Fleming, *What Kind of House Party Is This?* (Slough, UK: MIY Publishing, 1995), p. 191.

19. Author's interview with Bob Blank.

20. Ibid.

21. See Steven Harvey, "Behind the Grove: New York City's Disco Underground," *Collusion*, No. 5, September 1983, p. 29.

22. Haden-Guest, *The Last Party*, p. 211.

23. Cheren, *Keep on Dancin'*, p. 198.

24. Harvey, "Behind the Grove," pp. 29–30.

25. Ibid., p. 30.

26. Author's interview with Danny Krivit.

27. Ibid.

28. Ibid.

29. Chin, "The Disco Beatmasters."

30. Ibid.

31. Paul Hofmann, "Inquiry in Drug Case a Worry to the Dolce Vita Set in Rome," *The New York Times*, February 20, 1972, p. 16.

32. It is important to note that "Italo-disco," a term coined in 1984 by Bernhard Mikulski of the record label ZYX, refers to a specific type of disco rather than disco of Italian origin. It's just that the overwhelming majority of these records came from Italy. Nor does the term cover all Italian disco—disco records by Italians like La Bionda, Raffaella Carra, Adriano Celentano, and Umberto Tozzi, or most of those made by Italian production duo of Jacques Fred Petrus and Mauro Malavasi.

33. Another important French influence on the Italo sound was an obscurity called *Black Devil Disco Club*, an EP made in Paris by Bernard Fevre and Jackie Giordiano. Originally released in 1978, the record sounded like the house band from the Terre Haute Holiday Inn playing the *Doctor Who* theme with conguero Coke Escovedo sitting in for the session—oh, so Italo.

34. Author's interview with Daniele Baldelli, courtesy of Daniel Wang, March 2003.
35. Ibid.
36. Another important, although slightly later, club in the same region was Gatto Giallo, where the DJ played a lot of Italo records. Since the Lake Garda area was popular with German and Dutch holiday makers, the music played at these clubs spread up to Northern Europe and were particularly influential on DJs/mixers like Dutch mastermixer Ben Liebrand.
37. Author's interview with Daniele Baldelli.
38. Ibid.
39. Ibid.
40. See Sheryl Garratt, "Sample and Hold: The House Sound of Chicago," *The Face*, September 1986, pp. 18–23.

Chapter 7. "STAYIN' ALIVE": Disco Today
1. Author's interview with Daniel Wang, March 11, 2003.
2. Ibid.
3. Ibid.
4. None of this criticism is meant to single out Wang—he is far from the worst offender—or to suggest that his music, which is often wonderful, is tainted with moldy fig-ism. His comments are merely illustrative (not to mention well articulated) of a mind-set that is pervasive among a stratum of musicians, writers, and fans.
5. Author's interview with Daniel Wang.
6. Kaiser, *Gay Metropolis*, pp. 243, 283.
7. Andrew Holleran, *Ground Zero* (New York: Morrow, 1988), pp. 21–22.
8. Simon Napier-Bell, *Black Vinyl, White Powder* (London: Ebury Press, 2001), p. 344.

BIBLIOGRAPHY

Abbott, Kinglsey, ed. *Calling Out Around the World: A Motown Reader.* London: Helter Skelter, 2001.

Abraham, John Kirby. "Manu's Afrodisiac." *Black Music,* June 1977.

Aletti, Vince. "The Dancing Machine." In Waldrep, *The Seventies.*

———. "Discotheque Rock '72: Paaaaarty!" *Rolling Stone,* September 13, 1973.

———. "Electric Dreams." *Numéro 39,* December 2002.

———. "I Won't Dance, Don't Ask Me." *The Village Voice,* April 29, 1976.

———. "SoHo Vs. Disco." *The Village Voice,* June 16, 1975.

Amsel, Robert. "A Walk on the Wild Side of Stonewall." *The Advocate,* September 15, 1987.

Anderson, Terry. *The Movement and the Sixties.* New York: Oxford University Press, 1995.

Attali, Jacques. *Noise: The Political Economy of Music.* Minneapolis: University of Minnesota Press, 1985.

Bell, Michael J. *The World From Brown's Lounge: An Ethnography of Black Middle-Class Play.* Champaign: University of Illinois Press, 1983.

Benson, Richard, ed. *NightFever: Club Writing in* The Face: *1980–1996.* London: Macmillan, 1997.

Berman, Marshall. "Ruins and Reforms: New York Yesterday and Today." *Dissent,* Fall 1987.

Bigart, Homer. "Negro School Panel Ousts 19, Defies City." *The New York Times,* May 10, 1968.

———. "War Foes Here Attacked by Construction Workers." *The New York Times,* May 9, 1970.

Blackford, Andy. *Disco Dancing Tonight.* London: Octopus, 1979.

Bourget, Pierre. *Paris 1940–44.* Paris: Plon, 1979.

Brassaï. *The Secret Paris of the 30's.* Trans. Richard Miller. New York: Pantheon, 1976.

Braunstein, Peter. "Disco." *American Heritage,* November 1999.

Brewster, Bill, and Frank Broughton. *Last Night a DJ Saved My Life.* New York: Grove Press, 2000.

Bronson, Fred. *The Billboard Book of Number One Hits.* New York: Billboard Books, 1988.

Brown, Geoff. "It's the (Mighty) Real Thing." *Black Music*, November 1978.
———. "Qui Sont Ces Gens? C'est Chic." *Black Music*, March 1979.
Browne, Zambaga. "New Disco Stirs Muslim Protest." *Amsterdam News*, July 29, 1978.
Buder, Leonard. "Parents Occupy Brooklyn School As Dispute Grows." *The New York Times*, May 15, 1968.
Burnham, David. "The Changing City: Crime Reports Rise Despite More and Modernized Police." *The New York Times*, June 3, 1969.
Burrin, Philippe. *France Under the Germans: Collaboration and Compromise*. Trans. Janet Lloyd. New York: New Press, 1996.
Butler, Albert and Josephine. *Encyclopedia of Social Dance*. New York: Albert Butler Ballroom Dance Service, 1980.
Calta, Louis. "Party to Mark Closing of Arthur Discotheque." *The New York Times*, June 21, 1969.
Canby, Vincent. "New York's Woes Are Good Box Office." *The New York Times*, November 10, 1974.
Cannato, Vincent J. *The Ungovernable City: John Lindsay and His Struggle to Save New York*. New York: Basic Books, 2001.
Caro, Robert A. *The Power Broker: Robert Moses and the Fall of New York*. New York: Random House, 1975.
Carroll, Peter. *It Seemed Like Nothing Happened: The Tragedy and Promise of America in the 1970s*. New Brunswick, NJ: Rutgers University Press, 1990.
Caute, David. *The Year of the Barricades: A Journey Through 1968*. Harper, 1988.
Chafe, William H. *The Unfinished Journey: America Since World War II*. New York: Oxford University Press, 1999.
Cheren, Mel. *Keep on Dancin': My Life and the Paradise Garage*. New York: 24 Hours for Life Inc., 2000.
Chin, Brian. Liner notes to *The Disco Box*. Rhino 75595. 1999.
Clines, Francis X. "For the Flag and for Country, They March." *The New York Times*, May 21, 1970.
Coffey, Dennis. *Guitars, Bars & Motown Superstars*. Ann Arbor: University of Michigan Press, 2004.
Cohen, Roger. "Casting Giant Shadows: The Politics of Building the World Trade Center." *Portfolio: A Quarterly Review of Trade and Transportation*, Winter 1990/1991.
Cohn, Nik. "Another Saturday Night." In Hanif Kureishi and Jon Savage, eds., *The Faber Book of Pop*. Boston: Faber & Faber, 1995.
———. "Fever Pitch." *The Guardian*, September 17, 1994.
———. "Tu Sweet, No Sweat." In Nik Cohn, *Ball the Wall: Nik Cohn in the Age of Rock*. New York: Picador, 1989.
Cose, Ellis. *The Rage of a Privileged Class*. New York: Harper, 1993.
Crichton, Kyle. "Peel That Apple!" *Collier's*, December 4, 1937.
Crouch, Stanley. "Jazz Lofts: A Walk Through the Wild Sounds." *The New York Times Magazine*, April 17, 1977.
Cummings, Tony. "Blue-Eyed Soul." *Black Music*, September 1975.
———. "Gay Soul." *Black Music*, August 1975.
———. "Gloria Gaynor and the Disco Boom." *Black Music*, June 1975.
———. *The Sound of Philadelphia*. London: Methuen, 1975.
———. "The Thom Bell Story." *Black Music*, January 1974.
Cummings, Tony, Robert Gallagher, Denise Hall, and Davitt Sigerson. "Dance and Discomania." *Black Music*, January 1976.

Cummings, Tony, and Denise Hall. "Home Grown Soul." *Black Music*, April 1975.

Dannen, Frederic. *Hit Men: Power Brokers and Fast Money Inside the Music Business*. New York: Times Books, 1990.

De Dubovay, Diane. "New York After Hours: Infinity's the Limit." *Los Angeles Times*, March 7, 1976.

DeSouza, Cheryl. "Complaint From a Disco Buff." *Amsterdam News*, June 23, 1979.

Diebold, David. *Tribal Rites: San Francisco's Dance Music Phenomenon 1978–1988*. Northridge, CA: Time Warp Publishing, 1988.

Dougherty, Philip H. "Now the Latest Craze Is 1-2-3, All Fall Down." *The New York Times*, February 11, 1965.

Duberman, Martin. *Stonewall*. New York: Dutton, 1993.

Dunlap, David W. "As Disco Faces Razing, Gay Alumni Share Memories." *The New York Times*, August 21, 1995.

Dyer, Richard. "In Defence of Disco." In Richard Dyer, *Only Entertainment*. New York: Routledge, 2002.

Edmonds, Ben. *What's Going On?: Marvin Gaye and the Last Days of the Motown Sound*. Edinburgh: Mojo Books, 2001.

Edwards, Henry. "Disco Dancers Are Back, and the Kung Fu Has Got Them." *The New York Times*, December 29, 1974.

Emery, Lynne Fauley. *Black Dance From 1619 to Today*. London: Dance Book Publishers, 1988.

Farber, Jim. "The Mudd Club: Disco for Punks." *Rolling Stone*, July 12, 1979.

Feron, Jean Clare. "Roller Skating + Disco Dancing = Two Hot Rinks." *The New York Times*, December 24, 1978.

Fikentscher, Kai. *You Better Work! Underground Dance Music in New York City*. Middletown, CT: Wesleyan University Press, 2000.

Fleming, Jonathan. *What Kind of House Party Is This?* Slough: MIY Publishing, 1995.

Freeman, Joshua B. *Working-Class New York: Life and Labor Since World War II*. New York: New Press, 2000.

Fricke, Jim, and Charlie Ahearn. *Yes Yes Y'All: The Experience Music Project Oral History of Hip-Hop's First Decade*. Cambridge, MA: Da Capo Press, 2002.

Fried, Joseph P. "City's Housing Administrator Proposes 'Planned Shrinkage' of Some Slums." *The New York Times*, February 3, 1976.

Frum, David. *How We Got Here: The 70's—The Decade That Brought You Modern Life, For Better or Worse*. New York: Basic Books, 2000.

Gallagher, Bob. "Adams' Family." *Black Music*, January 1979.

Gallagher, Robert. "Miami's Foundation Stone." *Black Music*, August 1977.

Garratt, Sheryl. "Sample and Hold: The House Sound of Chicago." *The Face*, September 1986.

Gaynor, Gloria. *Soul Survivor*. London: Fount Paperbacks, 1995.

Gendron, Bernard. *Between Montmartre and the Mudd Club*. Chicago: University of Chicago Press, 2002.

George, Nelson. *Buppies, B-Boys, Baps and Bohos: Notes on Post-Soul Black Culture*. New York: Harper, 1992.

———. *The Death of Rhythm & Blues*. New York: Omnibus, 1988.

Gilmore, Mikal. "Disco!" *Rolling Stone*, April 19, 1979.

Gleason, Bill. "The Horror at Comiskey." *Chicago Sun-Times*, July 14, 1979.

Goddard, Donald. "It's Only 640 Miles From Paris to Vienna, But They Are Atmospheres Apart." *The New York Times*, June 25, 1972.

Goldman, Albert. *Disco.* New York: Hawthorn Books, 1978.

Grigoriadis, Vanessa. "Regine's Last Stand." *New York*, April 19, 1999.

Gross, Michael. "The Latest Calvin: From the Bronx to Eternity." *New York*, August 8, 1988.

Gruen, John. "Cerebrum, 'Designed to Soothe the Spirit.'" *Vogue*, January 1969.

Guattari, Félix. *Molecular Revolution: Psychology and Politics.* New York: Penguin, 1984.

Gutman, Herbert C. "As for the '02 Kosher-Food Rioters . . ." *The New York Times*, July 21, 1977.

Haden-Guest, Anthony. "Isn't This Where We Came In?" *New York*, June 13, 1978.

———. *The Last Party: Studio 54, Disco, and the Culture of the Night.* New York: William Morrow, 1997.

Hager, Steven. "Beatin' It With the Juice Crew (Saturday Night at the Funhouse)." *The Village Voice*, May 17, 1983.

Hall, Denise. "Lookin' White/Bein' Black/Soundin' Brown." *Black Music*, September 1976.

Halls, W. D. *The Youth of Vichy France.* Oxford: Clarendon Press, 1981.

Hamill, Pete. "Hard Hats and Cops." *New York Post*, May 12, 1970.

———. "The Revolt of the White Lower Middle Class." *New York*, April 14, 1969.

Haraway, Donna J. *Simians, Cyborgs, and Women: The Reinvention of Nature.* New York: Routledge, 1991.

Harvey, Steven. "Behind the Groove: New York City's Disco Underground." *Collusion*, no. 5, September 1983.

———. "ESG: The Family Jewels." *Collusion*, no. 4, February 1983.

Hazzard-Gordon, Katrina. *Jookin': The Rise of Social Dance Formations in African-American Culture.* Philadelphia: Temple University Press, 1990.

Hechinger, Fred M. "Racism and Anti-Semitism in the School Crisis." *The New York Times*, September 16, 1968.

Helgesen, Sally. "Disco: Phosphorescent Shapes Pass Through the Night, Leaving Nothing Behind." *Harper's*, October 1977.

Hent, Dennis. "Ban Sex-Rock, Minister Asks." *Los Angeles Times*, December 28, 1976.

Hightower, Jamake. "Dancing in the Seventies." *Horizon*, May 1977.

Hill, Dave. "Boystown Nights." In Benson, *NightFever*.

Hoddenfield, Jan. "Cruising the Scene in the Discotheques." *New York Post*, August 9, 1975.

Hoeveler, J. David., Jr. *The Postmodernist Turn: American Thought and Culture in the 1970s.* New York: Twayne, 1996.

Hofmann, Paul. "Inquiry in Drug Case a Worry to the Dolce Vita Set in Rome." *The New York Times*, February 20, 1972.

Hogan, Steve, and Lee Hudson. *Completely Queer: The Gay and Lesbian Encyclopedia.* New York: Henry Holt, 1998.

Holden, Stephen. "The Evolution of a Dance Craze." *Rolling Stone*, April 19, 1979.

Holleran, Andrew. *Dancer from the Dance.* New York: Penguin, 1978.

———. *Ground Zero.* New York: William Morrow, 1988.

Horowitz, I. S. "'Illegit' Disco Tapes Peddled by Jockeys." *Billboard*, October 12, 1974.

———. "Symphony and Disco Join in Rochester." *Billboard*, December 16, 1978.

Howell, Chauncey. "Salvation!" *Holiday*, August 1968.

Hughes, Walter. "In the Empire of the Beat: Discpline and Disco." In Ross and Rose, *Microphone Fiends*.

International Gay Information Center Archives. New York Public Library, Manuscripts and Archives Division.

Jackson, Kenneth T., ed. *Encyclopedia of New York City*. New Haven: Yale University Press, 1995.

Jacobson, Mark. "Hollyw-o-o-o-d! The Return of the New York Disco." *New York*, July 1, 1974.

———. "Live From New York." *New York*, October 22, 2001.

Jancik, Wayne. *The Billboard Book of One-Hit Wonders*. New York: Billboard Books, 1998.

Joe, Radcliffe. "The L.A. Scene: Growing, But Second to N.Y." *Billboard*, December 16, 1978.

Joe, Racliffe A. *The Business of Disco*. New York: Billboard Books, 1980.

Johnson, Herschel. "Discotheque Scene." *Ebony*, February 1977.

Johnston, Laurie. "Christopher Street: From Farm to Gay Center." *The New York Times*, July 26, 1971.

Kaiser, Charles. *The Gay Metropolis: 1940–1996*. San Diego: Harcourt, 1999.

Kelley, Norman, ed. *Rhythm and Business: The Political Economy of Black Music*. New York: Akashic Books, 2002.

Kempster, Chris, ed. *History of House*. London: Sanctuary, 1996.

Kihss, Peter. "'Benign Neglect' on Race Is Proposed by Moynihan." *The New York Times*, March 1, 1970.

Kirk, Chris. "What a Difference a Gay Makes." *Collusion*, no. 4, February 1983.

Kleiman, Dena. "The Hustle Restores Old Touch to Dancing." *The New York Times*, July 12, 1975.

Klemesrud, Judy. "Discotheque Fanatics Mob Latest Addition to Scene." *The New York Times*, June 9, 1978.

———. "Queen of French Nightclubs Hopes to Reign Here." *The New York Times*, November 16, 1975.

Knight, Frida. *The French Resistance 1940 to 1944*. London: Lawrence & Wishart, 1975.

Kopkind, Andrew. "The Dialectic of Disco: Gay Music Goes Straight." *The Village Voice*, February 12, 1979.

Kornbluth, Jesse. "Merchandizing Disco for the Masses." *The New York Times Magazine*, February 18, 1979.

Landry, Bart. *The New Black Middle Class*. Berkeley: University of California Press, 1987.

Le Boterf, Hervé. *La Vie Parisienne Sous L'Occupation, 1940–1944*. Paris: Éditions France-Empire, 1974.

Leston, Kimberley. "The Story of O." *The Face*, May 1987.

Lichtenstein, Grace. "Steve Ostrow's Satyricon." *Saturday Review of the Arts*, April 1973.

Lisker, Jerry. "Homo Nest Raided, Queen Bees Are Stinging Mad." *Daily News*, July 6, 1969.

Lubasch, Arnold H. "Two Studio 54 Owners Are Given 3½ Years for Evading U.S. Taxes." *The New York Times*, January 19, 1980.

MacKinnon, Angus. "The Importance of Not Being Earnest." *New Musical Express*, December 9, 1978.

Mahler, Jonathan. "Summer of '77." *The New York Times*, June 30, 2002.

Marzano, Dale A. *Roller Disco*. Chicago: Domus Books, 1979.

Mayer, Martin. "Frustration Is the Word For Ocean Hill." *The New York Times Magazine*, May 19, 1968.

McCormack, Ed. "No Sober Person Dances, in Which a Suburban Prole Decadent Visits a Hot Manhattan Disco and Learns That Cicero Was Right." In Peck, *Dancing Madness*.

McDonough, Jack. "Unprecedented Boom Enlivens the Bay Area." *Billboard*, July 15, 1978.

Melanson, Jim. "Discos Demand Five-Minute Singles." *Billboard*, December 14, 1974.

Mele, Christopher. *Selling the Lower East Side: Culture, Real Estate and Resistance in New York City*. Minneapolis: University of Minnesota Press, 2000.

Melly, George. *Revolt Into Style*. Oxford: Oxford University Press, 1989.

Miezitis, Vita. *Night Dancin'*. New York: Ballantine Books, 1980.

Miller, Jim, ed. *The Rolling Stone Illustrated History of Rock & Roll*. New York: Picador, 1981.

Moore, Marie. "Dynamic Superiors Lead Gay Music Crusade." *Amsterdam News*, August 13, 1977.

Moulton, Tom. "Disco Action." *Billboard*, November 2, 1974.

Napier-Bell, Simon. *Black Vinyl, White Powder*. London: Ebury Press, 2001.

Newton, Esther. *Cherry Grove, Fire Island: 60 Years in America's First Gay and Lesbian Town*. Boston: Beacon Press, 1993.

Nowell, David. *Too Darn Soulful: The Story of Northern Soul*. London: Robson Books, 2001.

O'Brien, Glenn. Liner notes to *Irresistible Impulse*. Tiger Style Records TIG60037. 2003.

Orth, Maureen, with Betsy Carter and Lisa Whitman. "Get Up and Boogie." *Newsweek*, November 8, 1976.

Palmer, Robert. "Concert: Russell and Marti." *The New York Times*, April 26, 1987.

———. "Kid Creole: He Mixes a Heady Brew of Styles." *The New York Times*, June 10, 1981.

Patoski, Joe Nick. "Disco Showdown in Oklahoma." *Rolling Stone*, November 2, 1978.

Pattillo-McCoy, Mary. *Black Picket Fences: Privilege and Peril Among the Black Middle Class*. Chicago: University of Chicago Press, 1999.

Peck, Abe. "The Cartoon That Conquered the World." *Rolling Stone*, April 19, 1979.

———. *Dancing Madness*. New York: Anchor Books, 1976.

———. "Hangover at Dahl House." *Chicago Sun-Times*, July 14, 1979.

Penrose, Roland. *In the Service of the People*. London: William Heinemann, 1945.

Phillips, Paul. "UK Union Denies Purge Against 'Non-Live' Niteries." *Billboard*, December 3, 1977.

Poiger, Uta G. *Jazz Rock, and Rebels: Cold War Politics and American Culture in a Divided Germany*. Berkeley: University of California Press, 2000.

Poschardt, Ulf. *DJ Culture*. Trans. Shaun Whiteside. London: Quartet, 1998.

Post, Henry. "Sour Notes at the Hottest Disco." *Esquire*, June 20, 1978.

Quindlen, Anna. "What's New in Discotheques." *The New York Times*, November 11, 1977.

Reynolds, Simon. *Energy Flash*. New York: Picador, 1998.

Rich, Frank. "The Gay Decades." *Esquire*, November 1987.

Rimmer, Dave. *The Rare Soul Bible: A Northern Soul A–Z*. London: Bee Cool, 2002.

Roberts, Sam. "1977: Summer of Paranoia." *The New York Times*, July 1, 1999.

Robertson, Frank. "Disco Tech: An All-American DJ Fights the Power." In Peck, *Dancing Madness.*

Rockwell, John. "Rock Comes to the Aid of Art." *The New York Times*, June 13, 1982.

Roe, Tom. "Generation Ecstasy: New York's Free Jazz Continuum." In Young, *Undercurrents.*

Rose, Frank. "Discophobia: Rock & Roll Fights Back." *The Village Voice*, November 12, 1979.

Ross, Andrew, and Tricia Rose, eds. *Microphone Fiends: Youth Music & Youth Culture.* New York: Routledge, 1994.

Ross, Tim. "Something Like a Phenomenon: The 99 Records Story." *Tuba Frenzy*, no. 4, Spring 1998.

Roth, Robert. "N.Y. Club Scrutiny Again Draws Liquor Board Fire." *Billboard*, December 17, 1977.

Safire, William. "On the Hustle." *The New York Times*, August 4, 1975.

Sale, Kirkpatrick. *Power Shift.* New York: Vintage, 1975.

Sanjek, David. "Tell Me Something I Don't Already Know: The Harvard Report on Soul Music Revisited." In Kelley, *Rhythm and Business.*

Savage, Jon. *England's Dreaming: Anarchy, Sex Pistols, Punk Rock, and Beyond.* New York: St. Martin's Press, 2002.

Schulman, Bruce J. *From Cotton Belt to Sunbelt.* New York: Oxford University Press, 1991.

———. *The Seventies.* Cambridge, MA: Da Capo, 2002.

Sewall-Ruskin, Yvonne. *High on Rebellion.* New York: Thunder's Mouth Press, 1998.

Shapiro, Peter. "'All He Left Us Was Alone': Disco Music and Masculinity." Master's thesis, Sussex University, 1993.

———. "Primer: P-Funk." *The Wire*, no. 172, June 1998.

———. *The Rough Guide: Soul 100 Essential CDs.* New York: Rough Guides, 2000.

———. "Smiling Faces Sometimes." *The Wire*, no. 203, January 2001.

———. "The Tyranny of the Beat." *The Wire*, no. 187, September 1999.

Shapiro, Peter, ed. *Modulations: A History of Electronic Music.* New York: DAP, 2000.

Sigerson, Davitt. "Bitches and Bummers." *Black Music*, February 1977.

———. "The De-Lite Records Saga." *Black Music*, September 1976.

———. "Dr. Buzzard's Original Savannah Band." *Black Music*, January 1977.

———. "The Great Disco Debate." *Black Music*, September 1978.

———. "Philly '76." *Black Music*, July 1976.

———. "A Splice of History." *Black Music*, September 1977.

Sippel, John. "Ramada Tests Disco Appeal in North Dakota." *Billboard*, December 14, 1974.

Slesin, Suzanne. "Designed for Dancing." *New York*, June 13, 1978.

———. "Making the Scene at the Mudd Club." *The New York Times*, April 21, 1979.

Smith, Howard. "Full Moon Over the Stonewall." *The Village Voice*, July 3, 1969.

Spiegel, Irving. "Jews Troubled Over Negro Ties." *The New York Times*, July 8, 1968.

Storm Roberts, John. "The Latin Soul of Joe Bataan." *Black Music*, August 1976.

———. *The Latin Tinge: The Impact of Latin American Music on the United States.* New York: Oxford University Press, 1999.

Straub, Bill. "With a Nail-Biting Playoff Season, Baseball Bounces Back." *The Washington Post*, October 16, 1997.

Szathmary, Richard, and Lucian K. Truscott IV. "Inside the Disco Boom." *The Village Voice*, July 21, 1975.

Taki. "Studio 54 Is Over." *Esquire,* April 24, 1979.

Tantner, Anton. "Jazz Youth Subcultures in Nazi Europe." *ISHA Journal,* February 1994.

Taylor, Angela. "Arthur, Once a Hairdo, Is Now a Discotheque." *The New York Times,* May 7, 1965.

Taylor, Marc. *A Touch of Classic Soul 2.* Jamaica, NY: Aloiv Publishing, 2001.

Taylor, Steve. "Inside August Darnell's Wardrobe." *The Face,* February 1982.

Terry, Clifford. "What Is This Thing Called Disco?" *Stereo Review,* September 1976.

Thomas, Robert McG., Jr. "Weekly Parties for 500 Chill Tenants." *The New York Times,* May 21, 1974.

Thornton, Sarah. "Strategies for Reconstructing the Popular Past." *Popular Music,* Vol. 9, no. 1, 1990.

Toop, David. "Disco." *The Face,* September 1992.

———. *Ocean of Sound: Aether Talk, Ambient Sound and Imaginary Worlds.* New York: Serpent's Tail, 1995.

———. "Throbbery With Intent." *The Wire,* April 1992.

Tournès, Ludovic. *New Orleans Sur Seine: Histoire du Jazz en France.* Paris: Librairie Arthème Fayard, 1999.

Truscott, Lucian K., IV. "Gay Power Comes to Sheridan Square." *The Village Voice,* July 3, 1969.

Vincent, Rickey. *Funk: The Music, the People, and the Rhythm of the One.* New York: St. Martin's Press, 1996.

Wagenheim, Karl. *A Survey of Puerto Ricans on the U.S. Mainland in the 1970s.* Westport, CT: Praeger, 1975.

Waldrep, Shelton, ed. *The Seventies: The Age of Glitter in Popular Culture.* New York: Routledge, 2000.

Wang, Danny. "Tee Scott." *Underground News,* no. 20, 1994.

Waxer, Lise A. *The City of Musical Memory: Salsa, Record Grooves and Popular Culture in Cali, Colombia.* Middletown, CT: Wesleyan University Press, 2002.

Weller, Sheila. "New Wave of Discotheques." *New York Sunday News,* March 1975.

Werner, Craig. *A Change Is Gonna Come: Music, Race and the Soul of America.* New York: Plume, 1998.

White, Adam, and Fred Bronson. *The Billboard Book of Number One Rhythm & Blues Hits.* New York: Billboard Books, 1993.

White, Edmund. *States of Desire: Travels in Gay America.* New York: Penguin, 1991.

Wilson, William Julius. *The Declining Significance of Race.* Chicago: University of Chicago Press, 1978.

Worth, Robert. "Guess Who Saved the South Bronx?" *Washington Monthly,* Vol. 31, no. 4, April 1999.

Young, Rob, ed. *Undercurrents: The Hidden Wiring of Modern Music.* New York: Continuum, 2002.

Ziegler, Mel. "They're Behind the Disco Beat." *San Francisco Chronicle,* July 10, 1978.

Zwerin, Mike. *La Tristesse de Saint Louis: Swing Under the Nazis.* New York: William Morrow, 1987.

Zylberberg, Regine. *Call Me By My First Name.* London: Andre Deutsch, 1988.

INDEX

Arpeggio, 106, 201
Arthur (New York City), 21–22, 23
Ash, Bill, 69–70
Ashford, Jack, 81, 82
Ashford, Nickolas, 77
Atkins, Juan, 280
Attali, Jacques, 227
Auger, Brian, 27, 272
Aural Exciters, 177
Aux Puce (New York City), 22–23, 255
Avalon, Frankie, 139, 206
Ayers, Roy, 72

B-52, 257
B. T. Express, 44
Babe Ruth, 273
Backstreet Boys, 289
Badham, John, 202
Bahlman, Bill, 260
Baia Degli Angeli (Italy), 276–77
Bailey, David, 50
Baker, Arthur, 259–60, 272, 273
Baker, Ronnie, 46, 96–97, 139, 141,
    148, 149
Baldelli, Daniele, 276–78
Ball, Harvey, 120, 132
Ballard, Hank, 19, 40, 159
Bambaataa, Afrika, 241, 243, 259, 274
Banbarra, 259
Bangs, Lester, 227
Banks, Darrell, 50
Banks, Kenny, 96
Barnes, J. J., 51
Barrabas, 35, 36, 45, 54, 99, 103
Barry, Claudja, 85, 102
Barry, Len, 148
Barthes, Roland, 268
Bartholomew, Dave, 90
Bascomb, Wilbur, 262
baseball, 231–34, 235, 236, 237–39,
    281
Basie, Count, 17, 154, 165, 175
Basquiat, Jean-Michel, 257
Bataan, Joe, 146–47
bathhouses, 57–65, 73, 87, 88. *See also*
    Continental Baths
Batiste, Rose, 51
Baxter, Les, 34
"be-ins," 24–25, 59

Bean, Carl, 75, 137
Beasley, David, 142
Beastie Boys, 200
Beatles, 106, 171, 205, 235, 248, 251
Beautiful Bend, 105
Bee Gees, 106, 107, 171, 172, 202, 203,
    235, 237, 244, 285
Bell, Al, 129
Bell, Arthur, 63
Bell, Madeline, 104
Bell, Thom, 130, 141, 143, 148, 149
Bellotte, Pete, 109, 110–11
Belolo, Henri, 223–26
Beltram, Joey, 206
Ben, Jorge, 229, 278
Benatar, Ralph, 103
Benecke, Marc, 158, 211, 228
Benitez, John "Jellybean," 263, 271–72,
    273–74
Benjamin, Benny, 82
Bennett, J. B., 235
Benson, Carla, 148
Bentley, Earlene, 84
Benton, Evette, 148
Berger, Miles, 270
Berry, Chuck, 19, 37
Better Days (New York City), 70, 74–75
Biddu, 55, 56
Big Apple Band, 160, 230
Birkin, Jane, 113
Bishop, Jimmy, 139
Black Blood, 35, 103
Black Ivory, 136, 220, 221
Black Panthers, 7, 160, 161, 173
Black Parties, 71–72
Blackpool Mecca (England), 51, 52, 217
Black Power movement, 117, 126–27,
    129, 133, 134, 161–62
black pride, 150–57
black radio, 150–52
Black Sabbath, 38
Black Uhuru, 263
Blackbyrds, 200
Blackford, Andy, 216–17
blacks. *See* African Americans
Blank, Bob, 252, 261–62, 263, 264
Blecman, Marty, 80
Blondie, 254
Blow, Kurtis, 243
Blue-Belles, 118–19

Blue Notes. *See* Harold Melvin & the Blue Notes
Bogart, Neil, 100–101, 228
Bogosian, Eric, 260
Bohan, Marc, 19
Bohannon, Hamilton, 95–96, 261
Boncaldo, Mario, 278
Bones, Frankie, 206
Boney M., 102, 105
Bonfiglio, Joey, 61
Bongiovi, Tony, 199
Bongo Band, 244
Bonham, John, 169
"Boo!" (disco hallmark), 201
Booker T. & the MG's, 27
Botel in the Pines (Fire Island, New York), 40–41, 67, 68, 70
Bowie, David, 22, 191, 255, 257
boy bands, 288–89. *See also specific band*
Brahms, Maurice, 193, 214–15
Brainstorm, 86, 202
Branco, Glenn, 260
Brandt, Jerry, 228
Brass Construction, 202, 274
Braunstein, Peter, 29
Breakout, 241
Bridgewater, Dee Dee, 136
Briley, Alex, 224
Bristol, Johnny, 86
Brody, Michael, 267, 269
Bronson, Fred, 101
Bronx (New York City), 219, 238–39, 241, 242
Brooks, Pattie, 105–106
Browder, Stony Jr., 174–75, 176
Browder, Tommy. *See* Darnell, August
Brown, Genie, 39
Brown, Geoff, 171
Brown, James, 50, 199; and automating the beat, 90, 94–95, 98, 110, 111; and disco-soul, 131, 135, 138, 165, 167; and disco underground, 263, 265; and Edwards and Rodgers' music, 165, 167; and Loft sound, 33, 34, 35; and mixing, 40, 43; and prehistory of disco, 27, 28, 29
Brown, Jocelyn, 220, 221, 222
Brown, Julie, 258
Brown, Miquel, 83, 86
Brown, Peter, 199, 220–21

Brown, Peter (DJ), 220–21
Brown, Polly, 55
Brown, Sam "Little Sonny," 140, 142
Bruce, Lenny, 265
Bruie, David, 69
Buari, 35
Buchanan, Shaun, 86–87
Buggles, 56
Bumble Bee Unlimited, 220, 221
Bump (dance), 26–27, 216
Burgess, Jim, 86, 193, 194, 271
Burgess, LeRoy, 275
Burke, Clem, 281
Burnham, David, 7
Burton, Jenny, 272, 273
Butler, Bill, 219
Butler, Jerry "The Iceman," 110, 124–25, 138, 142
Buzzard, Carrash, 174
Byrne, David, 261, 265
Byron, Dennis, 106–107

Cabaret Voltaire, 256
Cage, John, 38, 111
Calello, Charlie, 106, 175
Calloway, Cab, 15, 133, 165, 174
Calvin, Billy Rae, 125, 128, 129
Camison, Mat, 276
Can, 257, 264
Canby, Vincent, 4
Cannato, Vincent J., 8–9
Capote, Truman, 190, 191, 206, 211
Cappello, Michael, 37, 205
Capricorn, 279
Carleo, Vincent, 72
Carlos, Walter/Wendy, 111
Carpenter, John, 104
Carroll, Peter, 9, 10–11, 29–30, 127, 129, 204
Carstairs, 52
Carter, Jimmy, 181, 237
Carter, Ralph, 45
Casablanca Records, 100–101, 104, 227–28, 229
Casanova Fly, 241
Casella, Paul, 36, 37, 207, 209
Casey, Bob, 193, 199
Casey, Harry Wayne, 99, 197–98
Castor, Jimmy, 244, 272

Copeland, Johnny, 220
Coquelin, Olivier, 20, 22
Corley, Al, 211
Cornelius, Don, 44
Corr, Frank, 73
Corral, Michael "Lucky Strike," 186–87, 188–89
Cortez, Dave "Baby," 117, 219
Cose, Ellis, 154
Cosmic (Italy), 277–78
Cosmic music, 277–78
Costa, Jenny, 253
Costandinos, Alec R., 102, 103, 104–105, 230
Costello, Elvis, 54
country music, 245–46
County, Wayne/Jayne, 255
Cowley, Patrick, 78–80, 83, 84, 111, 260, 273
Craig, Carl, 93, 280
Creative Source, 125
Creatore, Luigi, 184
Creole, Kid, 177, 178–80
Crisco Disco (New York City), 73–74, 188, 189
Criss, Gary, 148
Cristina, 177
Crocker, Frankie, 35, 146–47, 151, 153, 156
Crosby, Stills & Nash, 168
Cross, Christopher "Criss," 255, 256
crossover, 146, 149, 150–57, 271
Crusaders, 155
Cult Jam, 274
Cummings, Tony, 140
Curry, Tim, 266
Curtis, Clem, 53
Curtis, Ian, 259
Curtis, King, 152
Curtis, Tiger, 65
Cut Glass, 87
Cymande, 220, 254
Czukay, Holger, 264

da Costa, Paulinho, 155
Dahan, Pierre Alain, 276
Dahl, Steve, 232–34, 235, 236, 237, 244, 249
D'Alessio, Carmen, 208, 209, 210

Dalida, 103
Dami, Maurizio, 280
dance: crazes, 165, 181–248; and prehistory of disco, 19–20, 30; see also type of dance
Danceteria (New York City), 260–61
Daniels, Charlie, 245–46
D'Aquisto, Steve, 36, 190, 205, 262
Darby & Tarlton, 92
Darnell, August, 173–80
Dash, Sarah, 86, 118
Davis, Betty, 77
Davis, Clifton, 44
Davis, Clive, 143–44
Davis, Miles, 77, 110, 160, 167
Day, Bob, 276–77
Daye, Cory, 135–36, 174, 175–76
DC LaRue, 241, 243, 262
Dean, Hazell, 85, 284
Deans, Mickey, 21
Dee, Joey, 19
Dees, Rick, 203
Deleuze, Gilles, 65, 69
Delfonics, 130, 141
Denny, Martin, 34
Denver, John, 246
DePaul, Nilo, 22
Depeche Mode, 277
Descloux, Lizzy Mercier, 177
Detroit Emeralds, 41
Detroit, Michigan, 27, 234, 236–37, 279–80, 286
Devizia, Tony, 86
Dibango, Manu, 35
Diddley, Bo, 91, 92, 96, 99
Diebold, David, 79–80
Diga Rhythm Band, 34
Dimanda Galás, 258
Dinger, Klaus, 92
Dinosaur, 261, 262
disco: abandonment of original constituency and values by, 227; anonymity of, 229–30; and antidisco campaign, 53, 232–41, 244; and automating the beat, 89–115; birth of, 30, 58, 65; canon of, 285; characteristics of, 3, 30, 74, 100, 251, 289; commercialization of, 218–20, 227–31; as dance craze, 181–227; dark side of, 254; and decadence, 3, 286;

disco (*cont.*)
decline of, 85, 172, 227–48, 249–50, 251–58, 260–71; democratic nature of, 21–22, 30, 74, 100, 189–90, 191–93, 207, 251, 282–83, 289; and disco as craze, 181–248; and disco-soul, 116–80; and discontent, 13; in early twenty-first century, 281–89; as emblematic of America's dwindling power, 237; as emblematic of new kind of political resistance, 65; emergence of, 13; feminizing influence of, 234; first disco record as #1 hit, 67; first records of, 95; foundation of sound of, 34; height of, 146–50; as liberalism's last hurrah, 247–48; mundanity of, 227; as musical genre, 28, 145; and New York City in 1960s and early 1970s, 3–13; nostalgia about, 282, 285, 286–87; as part of establishment, 282; as people's entire social lives, 195; pleasure principle of, 253; prehistory of, 13–30; profitability of, 230–31; as "quality music," 285; as representing ideal of integration, 153; as retreat back into body, 29–30; sanitization of, 237; and sexuality, 57–88, 244; spread of, 205; subgenres of, 202; superstar billing in, 229–30; as theater, 208–209, 215–16; ultimate aim of, 93; as underground, 249–80; and visions of the world, 244, 289
Disco Demolition Derby (Comiskey Park), 232–34
Disco Sally, 211, 216
"disco sucks" movement, 53, 232–41, 244
Disco Tex & His Sex-O-Lettes, 36, 97, 191
Disco Wiz, 241
discotheques: admission to, 21, 22–23, 192–93; and business networking, 195; characteristics of typical New York DJ in, 205–206; and disco craze, 194–95, 206–17; and disco-soul, 153; egalitarianism in, 207; exclusivity and inclusivity at, 192; expansion in number of, 194, 216; images of, 3; as means for selling records, 36; mix at, 21–22, 24; in 1970s, 13; popularity

of, 196; in postwar Europe, 17; profitability of, 194; rise of, 194–96; social mix at, 192–93; as success, 182; *see also* clubs; *specific club, city, or nation*
Distel, Sacha, 18
Divine, 85, 260
DJ Harvey, 285
DJ Thomas (aka the Mammal), 285
DJs: in Britain, 217; characteristics of typical New York, 205–206; club, 36–37; combination of live performance and, 256; and disco in early twenty-first century, 285; and hip-hop, 241, 242, 243–44; Mancuso organizes New York, 36–37; in Miami, 197; and mixing, 39–48; new breed of, 241; punk, 253; and race, 70; radio, 36; and reel-to-reel tapes, 42–43; and Swing Kids, 15; women as, 253; *see also* mix; *specific person*
DNA, 261
Dodd, Alan, 73, 86
Doggett, Bill, 138, 139
Dominatrix (aka Stuart Argabright), 257–58
Don Armando's 2nd Ave. Rumba Band, 177
Donghia, Angelo, 214
Donovan, Terry, 50
doo-wop, 271
Doobie Brothers, 37, 230–31
Doors, 23, 27, 161
Dorritie, Kathy, 22–23, 253, 255
Dorsey, Lee, 23
Dorsey, Thomas, 75
Double Exposure, 46, 148
Douglas, Carl, 36, 55, 191
Douglas, Carol, 153, 200
Downes, Geoff, 56
Downing, Al, 45
Downing, Don, 43, 45, 199, 200
Dozier, Lamont, 154–56
Dr. Buzzard's Original Savannah Band, 82, 106, 135–36, 174, 175–77
Drach, Ted, 65
Drifters, 53
drugs, 3, 13, 24, 29, 79, 115, 158, 286; and decline of disco, 251, 266; and

81–88; *see also* bathhouses; gay clubs; *specific person or club*

Gaytones, 35

Gaz, 102

Gazebo, 278

Gedda, Laurence J., 192

Gefter, Philip, 285

Geist, Morgan, 285

Geno Washington & the Ram Jam Band, 53

George, Nelson, 8, 97, 149, 153–54, 157

Germany, Swing Kids in, 13–15

Gibb, Barry, 106–107

Gibb, Maurice, 106–107

Gibb, Robin, 106–107

Gibbons, Walter, 46–48, 262–63, 264

Gibson Brothers, 103

Gibson, Walter, 284

Gichy Dan's Beachwood #9, 177

Gidden, Yvonne, 85

Gilmore, Mikal, 230

Ginsberg, Allen, 261

Gladys Knight & the Pips, 122

Glass, Philip, 260

Glaxo Babies, 258

Glover, Sue, 104

Go-Go's, 54

Goblin, 278

Godin, David, 51

Goldman, Albert, 16, 19, 26–27, 186

Gomez, Nico, 103

Gonella, Nat, 14

Gonzalez, Jerry, 147

Gooding, Cuba, 272

Gordon, Peter, 261, 262

Gordy, Berry, 123, 139, 154

Gorney, Karen Lynn, 282

gospel, 76–77, 94, 212–13, 243; and automating the beat, 109, 110; and disco-soul, 116, 118, 125, 145–46, 154, 169, 180

Göttsching, Manuel, 268

Graham, Larry, 107

Grand Wizard Theodore, 241

Grandmaster Caz, 241

Grandmaster Flash, 167, 241, 243, 244, 257

Grandmaster Flash & Melle Mel's, 257

Grant, Eddy, 54, 284

Grasso, Francis, 27–29, 32, 33, 37, 38, 39, 68, 205, 230

Grateful Dead, 29, 34

Gray, 257

Green, Al, 109

Green, Jerome, 92

Greenberg, Jerry, 168, 169

Griffey, Dick, 105

Griffith, Roni, 84, 85

Gross, Michael, 250

Gruen, John, 25

Guattari, Felix, 65, 69

Gucci. *See* Halston, Gucci, Fiorucci

Guthrie, Woodie, 201

Gutman, Herbert, 240

Guttadaro, Bobby "Bobby DJ," 36, 60–61, 67, 68, 72, 191, 193, 205, 271

Guttenberg, Steve, 223

Gypsy Lane, 225

Haazen, Guido, 34

Haden-Guest, Anthony, 49, 113, 158, 211, 265

Haggard, Merle, 8, 245, 248

Haircut 100, 258

Halen, Van, 234

Hall, Daryl, 148

Hall, Denise, 201

Hallyday, Johnny, 224

Halston, 70, 210, 211, 212, 250

Halston, Gucci, Fiorucci, 3, 166, 287

Hamill, Pete, 9

Hamlyn, Chris, 258

Hancock, Herbie, 262

Hannett, Martin, 259

"happenings," 24–25

Haraway, Donna, 111–12

"Hard Hat Riots" (1970), 10, 205

Hardy, Françoise, 23

Hardy, Ron, 279

Harlem Hamfats, 75

Harlow, Jean, 18

Harold Melvin & the Blue Notes, 96–97, 142, 144–45, 157

Harpo, Slim, 91

Harris, Alan, 72

Harris, Charles "Valentino," 75

Harris, Dennis, 140, 141, 148

Harris, Ennis. *See* Trammps

Indeep, 221, 275
Indian Ocean, 262
Infinity (New York City), 193–94, 208, 209
Ingram, Barbara, 148
Ingram, Jimmy, 262
Ingram, John, 262
Inner Life, 136, 180, 222
Instant Funk, 270
Intruders, 140, 141, 142, 145
Iron Butterfly, 23
Irvine, Weldon, 155
Isherwood, Christopher, 65
Isley Brothers, 38, 122, 135, 138, 177
Italian Americans, role in dance music culture of, 205–206
Italo-disco, 272, 275–80
Italy, clubs in, 276–78

Jack, Wolfman, 60
Jacks, Cheryl, 223
Jackson 5, 107
Jackson, "Big Bank Hank," 244–45
Jackson, Dee D, 102
Jackson, Jermaine, 47
Jackson, Michael, 134, 202
Jackson, Tony, 55
Jacno, 104
Jacobs, Debbie, 201
Jacobson, Mark, 151, 152
Jacobson, Sam, 213–14
Jagger, Bianca, 3, 209, 210, 211, 234
Jagger, Mick, 209–10, 229, 234
Jam & Lewis, 275
Jamerson, James, 142
James, Bob, 217
James Chance & the Contortions, 177
James, Rick, 201, 256
James, Sylvester. See Sylvester
James, Tommy, 199
James White & the Blacks, 253, 254
Jarre, Jean-Michel, 104, 225, 278
Jarrett, Keith, 155
Jaxon, Frankie "Half Pint," 75
Jaymes, Jesse, 91
jazz, 12, 15, 16, 17, 30, 31, 90; and disco craze, 188, 217; and disco-soul, 117, 138–39, 160, 164, 174
JB's, 155

Jeremy, Ron, 61, 67
Jesrani, Darshan, 285
Jessup, Jim, 69
Jesters, 55
jet set, 18, 21, 32, 103, 276
J. Geils Band, 37
Jiani, Carol, 86
Jimmy James & the Vagabonds, 53
Joey Dee & the Starliters, 20
John, Elton, 288–89
Johnny Johnson & the Bandwagon, 54
Johnson, Donald, 259
Johnson, L. J., 52
Johnson, Lyndon B., 20–21, 123–24
Johnson, Syl, 41
Johnstone, James, 258
Jonas, Joan, 12
Jones, Aled, 109
Jones, Bob, 217
Jones, Casey, 79
Jones, E. Rodney, 123
Jones Girls, 150
Jones, Grace, 113, 158, 169
Jones, LeRoi, 49
Jones, Philly Joe, 138, 139
Jones, Quincy, 112
Jones, Randy, 224
Jones, Raymond, 169
Jones, Tamiko, 136
Jones, Tom, 53
Jones, Uriel, 82
Joneses, The, 97, 153
jook, 24, 32
Joplin, Janis, 23
Joshua, 106
Joy Division, 259
Juvet, Patrick, 102, 223, 225–26, 283

Kaczor, Richie, 37, 45, 209, 212
Kaiser, Charles, 59, 60, 116–17, 213, 285
Kamins, Mark, 260
Kane, Madleen, 102
Kane, Terry, 197
Kano, 280
Kaprow, Allan, 24
Kasenetz, Jerry, 99
Katz, Jeff, 99
KC and the Sunshine Band, 99, 198–99, 202, 226

Levene, Keith, 254
Levenson, Larry, 61
Levert, Eddie, 130, 142
Levine, Ian, 51–53, 73–74, 82–84, 85, 86–87, 194, 217, 288, 289
Levy, Morris, 220
Lewis, Linda, 85
Lewis, Michael, 106
Lewis, Pat, 51
Lewis, Terry, 265
Libran, Tito, 256
Licky, 221
Lilo, 104
Lindsay, Arto, 261
Lindsay, John, 8–9, 63, 64
Lipps, Inc., 257
Liquid Idiot, 257
Liquid Liquid, 256–57
Lisa Lisa, 274
Little All-Stars, 262
Little Richard, 40, 75, 91, 98
Little Sister, 28, 33
Lloyd Webber, Andrew, 105, 201
Lockett, Bert, 74, 253
Loft, The (New York City), 40, 181, 262, 267; admission to, 31, 32; aesthetic of, 193–94; background about, 30–31; gays at, 32; "Love Saves the Day" party at, 31–32; music/sound systems at, 33–36, 70, 72, 77, 96, 254; and race, 32; Record Pool DJs at, 36–38, 243; see also Mancuso, David
Logg, 275
Lola, 263
Lollipops, 55
London, England. See United Kingdom
Long, Richard, 209, 267, 269, 270
Loose Joints, 74, 136, 262
Lopez, Bernard, 106
Lord, Arnie, 25–26
Los Angeles, California, 83, 197, 216
Los Bravos, 105
Love Deluxe, 201
Love and Kisses, 104
Love of Life Orchestra, 262
Love Saves the Day party (1970), 31–32
Love Unlimited, 202
Love Unlimited Orchestra, 36, 67, 102, 191, 198
LSD, 29, 31, 160, 161, 189

Lunch, Lydia, 57, 177, 252
Luongo, John, 197
Lydon, John, 254, 256
Lynn, Cheryl, 229
Lynn, Loretta, 245
Lynyrd Skynyrd, 246

Maas, Steve, 257
MacDonald, Jeanette, 79, 112
Machine, 177
machinic rhythms, 89–115
MacKinnon, Angus, 115
Madame, 60
Madara, Jon, 148
Madonna, 221, 260, 273–74, 284
Mahavishnu Orchestra, 263
Mailman, Bruce, 85, 86, 87
Main Ingredients, 272
Makeba, Miriam, 278
Malcolm, Ron, 42, 66
Malle, Louis, 18
Mamas and the Papas, 22
Mammal (aka DJ Thomas), 285
Man Parrish, 272
Mancuso, David, 30–39, 40, 48, 68, 69, 191, 205, 242, 267, 285
Mandre, 33
Mangual, Bacho, 61
Manilow, Barry, 57, 60, 112, 256, 289
Manley, Cynthia, 81, 83
Mann, Herbie, 222, 227
marching band sound, 90, 91–92, 95
Mardin, Arif, 106, 202, 203
Marie, Kelly, 86, 201
Marketts, 27
Marks, Johnny, 159
Marotta, Rick, 184
Mars, 177
Marsh, Dave, 100
Martha & the Vandellas, 50, 81
Martin, Carlos, 201
Martin, Jay, 23
Martin, Luci, 165, 166, 167, 168, 169, 172
masculinity, 225, 231, 232–34, 236–37, 247
Mason, Barbara, 139
Mason, Vaughan, 222, 275
Mass Production, 202

Mastermind, 200
Masters At Work, 274
Matmos, 111
Matta-Clark, Gordon, 12
Mattachine Society, 58
Matthews, Eric, 47
Maximum Joy, 258–59
May, Derrick, 280
MC5, 265
McCormack, Ed, 191–92, 205
McCoy, Van, 134, 145, 153, 183–84, 187, 188, 202, 232
McCrae, George, 99, 153, 198
McCrae, Gwen, 198
McCullers, Carson, 65
McDonald, Ralph, 199
McDougal, Weldon III, 139, 140
McFadden, Gene, 131, 150
McFarlane, Rodger, 88
McGilpin, Bob, 206
McGriff, Jimmy, 138
McGuire, Richard, 256–57
McLean, Penny, 102
McPhatter, Clyde, 53
"Me Decade," 186–87, 252
mechanical rhythms: and black music, 89–90, 93, 96, 97, 98, 109, 110; and Eurodisco, 97–108; and marching band sound, 90, 91–92, 95; and Moroder, 100–101, 102, 108, 109, 110–11, 113–15
Mekas, Jonas, 24
Melly, George, 50
Melton, Elva, 28
Melvin, Harold, 96–97, 142, 144–45, 157
Memphis Jug Band, 92
Merman, Ethel, 112, 174, 229
Merritt, Howard, 72, 80, 86
Merry, Jimmy, 65, 66
Meters, 90, 95
Metro Area, 285
MFSB Orchestra: beginnings of, 143; and Belolo, 223; as house band of Philadelphia International Records, 46, 117; members of, shift to Salsoul label, 146, 147, 148; records of, 38, 46, 55, 98, 116, 145, 149; and T.K. label, 199
Miami, Florida, 51, 52, 98, 197
Miami sound, 202

Michael, George, 117, 259
Michael Zager Band, 201
Micioni, Paolo, 278
Midler, Bette, 57, 60, 119
Midney, Boris, 105
Miezitis, Vita, 215
Mighty Tomcats, 35
Mimms, Garnet, 138
Minelli, Liza, 210, 211, 212, 215
Minneapolis funk, 275
Minnelli, Liza, 21
Miracles, 202
Miranda, Carmen, 76, 177
mix, 22, 24, 28–29, 37, 39–48, 116, 217. *See also specific DJ or song*
Mizell brothers, 274
Modeliste, Joseph "Zigaboo," 95
Mods, 50–51, 56, 203–204
Moment of Truth, 45
Monardo, Meco, 199, 200
Monroe, Bill, 92
Montana, Vince, 139, 141, 142, 145, 147–48, 149, 283
Montclairs, 52
Monteagudo, Frank, 72
Montgomery, Wes, 138
Moods, 140
Moonglows, 77
Moore, Bobby, 45
Moore, Rudy Ray, 81
Morali, Jacques, 223–26
Morgan, Glen, 234–35
Morgan, Julia, 76
Moribito, Susan, 253
Moroder, Giorgio: and automating the beat, 100–101, 102, 108, 109, 110–11, 113–15; and disco in early twenty-first century, 284; and Eurodisco, 100–101, 102; and Hi-NRG, 82, 85; and Italo-disco, 276, 278, 279; and punk disco, 259, 260
Morricone, Ennio, 273, 278
Morse, Tiger, 255
Motley's Boys, 81
Motown: and automating the beat, 95–96, 99, 101, 106, 114; and disco-soul, 122, 123, 124, 139, 140, 142, 143, 154, 167; and Eurodisco, 106; and Hi-NRG, 82; and prehistory of disco, 23, 27; and San Francisco

sound, 81; and soul in United Kingdom, 50, 51, 53, 54, 56; and twelve-inch singles, 47, 48
Moulton, Tom, 40–45, 46, 52, 67, 68, 196–97, 202
Mountain, 29
MTV, 36
Mudd Club (New York City), 257–58
Munich Machine, 102, 114–15
Munich Philharmonic, 101
Munich sound, 102, 114–15
Musique, 221–22, 252, 264
Musto, Tommy, 206

Nairobi Afro Band, 35
Nam June Paik, 12
Nance, Kevin, 177
Napier-Bell, Simon, 288
Nayobe, 273
Neptunes, 287
Neu!, 92
Nevada, Gaz, 279
New Jack Swing, 275
New Jersey, clubs in, 195, 222, 270–71
New Kids on the Block, 288
New Order, 259–60, 272, 279
New Orleans, Louisiana, 90–92, 93–94, 95, 197
New Wave, 86, 260, 272, 278, 279
New York Citi Peech Boys, 78, 136, 180, 270
New York City: as center of disco, 196–97, 237; clubs in, 12, 17, 20–29, 32, 36, 37, 46, 60–63, 69–76, 80, 85–88, 119, 151, 175, 181, 184, 188, 189, 191, 193–96, 199, 205–16, 222, 224, 229, 243, 250, 253–58, 260–61, 263, 264, 266–75, 279, 282; Cohn's views about discotheque culture in, 203–204; and decline of disco, 237; demographic changes in, 5–6; and disco craze, 182–83, 196–97; economy of, 11–12, 160; overview about, 4–13, 160, 182–83, 238–41; power failures in, 240–42; problems facing, 4–13; terrorism in, 239–40; see also specific club or bathhouse
New York City (vocal group), 141, 160

New York Dolls, 84, 191, 255
New York Rubber Rock Band, 174
Newman, Colin, 281
Niblock, Phill, 261
Nichols, Wade, 226
Nixon (Richard M.) era, 8, 121, 124, 127, 129, 131, 132, 133, 154–55, 184, 236, 248, 251
No Wave, 261
Noel, Terry, 21–22, 23, 28, 255
Nordine, Ken, 23
Normal, 256
Norman, Jeremy, 216
Northern Soul, 48–53, 55, 56, 82, 84, 85, 105, 139, 203
nostalgia, 173–74, 187, 248, 282, 285, 286–87
'N Sync, 289
Numan, Gary, 104, 273
Number of Names, A, 280

Oak Ridge Boys, 245
O'Brien, Glenn, 257
O'Dell, Dick, 258
Odyssey, 72, 155
Oh Romeo, 85
O'Harro, Mike, 194
O'Jays, 130, 131, 132, 142, 143, 144, 146, 150, 220, 224, 268
Olatunji, Babatunde, 27, 35
Oliver, Gwendolyn, 223
O'Neil, Sue, 234–35
Oquendo, Manny, 147
Originals, 153, 202
Orlando, Bobby, 84–85, 111, 260
Orloff, Gene, 169, 184
Osibisa, 27, 35
Ostrow, Steve, 58, 60, 61
Otis, Shuggie, 99
Ottawan, 103
Owles, Jim, 63

Pacine, Paul, 17
Pagano, Tony, 205
Page, Gene, 202
Page, Jimmy, 28
Pallas, Laura, 84
Palmer, Earl, 90–91, 93

Palmer, Robert, 263
Palmieri, Eddie, 273
Pampianelli, Richard, 205
Panda, Andy, 273
Paradise Garage (New York City), 70,
72, 151, 222, 243, 254, 266–68,
269–70, 271, 275, 279
Parikhal, John, 235
Paris, France. *See* France
Parker, Alan, 69, 115
Parker, Dennis, 206, 226
Parker, Melvin, 94
Parker, Paul, 79, 83
Parker, Walter, 17
Parliament, 109–10, 225, 259, 280
Parsons, Alan, 278
Parsons, Chuck, 86
Parsons, Gram, 77
Parton, Dolly, 245
Passenger, 86
Passion & Pain, 39
Pat the Cat, 219
Pate, Johnny, 132
Patti Jo, 52
Paul, Billy, 145
Paycheck, Johnny, 245
Pearls, 55
Peck, Abe, 102, 153
Peebles, Ann, 41
Pendergrass, Teddy, 137, 142, 145, 150,
201
Penguins, 40
Pennington, Barbara, 52
Pentagons, 138
Pepitone, Joe, 60
Peppermint Lounge (New York City),
20, 21, 37, 196
Peppers, 43, 104, 276
Peretti, Hugo, 184
Perren, Freddie, 47
Perrey, Jean-Jacques, 104, 108
Perry, Fred, 50
Perry, Lee "Scratch," 47
Persuaders, 134
Pervis, Claude, 255
Pet Shop Boys, 85, 287
Pettibone, Shep, 283–84
Philadelphia International Records, 34,
46, 55, 101, 223, 279; and automating
the beat, 96, 101, 105–106; and CBS,

144–45; decline of, 150; and disco-
soul, 117, 126, 143–45, 146, 150–51,
168; early years of, 143; *see also*
Gamble, Kenny; Huff, Leon; MFSB
Orchestra
Philadelphia Philharmonic Orchestra,
138
Philly soul, 96, 106, 113, 137–46, 147,
199. *See also* Philadelphia
International Records
Philly sound: and disco craze, 200, 223;
and disco-soul, 137–46, 150–57; and
Italo-disco, 277; and Salsoul Records,
146–50; and subgenres of disco, 202
Phreek, 220, 221, 268
pickanninny caricature, 132–33
Pickett, Wilson, 142
Picking, Johnny C., 97
Pieper, Rudolf, 260
Pierce, Bradley, 20
Pigbag, 258
PiL, 256, 258, 264, 265
Pine, Seymour, 62
Pink Floyd, 205, 258, 278
Planet Patrol, 272
Plant, Robert, 28
Pointer Sisters, 37, 76–77
politics, 65, 135, 150–57, 161, 200–201,
227, 237. *See also* civil rights
movement; Nixon (Richard M.) era;
race; Reagan (Ronald) era; Vietnam
War
Pop Group, 258
postpunk, 256, 260, 265
President Eisenhower, 265
Presley, Elvis, 19, 248
Preston, Peter, 218
Principato, Salvatore, 256–57
prog rock, 276, 278, 279
psychedelic era, 22, 24, 27, 29, 31
Public Enemy, 135
Public Image Limited, 254
Puente, Tito, 260, 273
Pulsallama, 258–60
Punches Delegates of Pleasure, 75
punk, 251–60, 278, 286, 287

Quant, Mary, 50
Quashie, Mike, 23

Timebox, 27
Típica, 260
Titanic, 35–36, 37, 54, 99, 103,
243–44
T.K. Records, 197, 198, 199, 220
Todd, David, 184
Tokens, 179
Tonto's Expanding Head Band, 108
Toop, David, 92, 93, 100, 101, 227–28
Torales, Hippie, 270
Traitors, 265
Trammps, 13, 140–41, 244, 257
Travolta, John, 202, 203, 204, 227,
282
Trax, 102
Trench, Fiachra, 83
Tribe, 243–44
Tripoli, Andy "Panda," 273
Trovajoli, Armando, 35
True, Andrea, 228
Trumbull, Douglas, 215
Truscott, Lucian IV, 63
Tucker, Tanya, 246
Turner, Mel, 53
Tuxedo Junction, 174
TW Funkmasters, 264
twelve-inch records, 45–48
12 West (New York City), 72–73, 86,
250, 267
twist, 19–20
Two Man Sound, 103
Two Tons o' Fun, 77
Tyler, Bonnie, 86, 114
Tyrone & Carr, 55
Tyson, Mike, 220

Underwood, Simon, 258–60
Undisputed Truth, 125, 128, 129
United Kingdom: antidisco sentiment
in, 235; clubs in, 48–53, 81–88, 189,
216–17, 256, 258; disco craze in,
216–17; disco in early twenty-first
century in, 288–89; DJs in, 217; gays
in, 81–88; and Hi-NRG, 81–88; pop
music in early twenty-first century in,
288–89; punk-disco merger in,
258–60; radio in, 31, 256; roller disco
in, 218; soul in, 48–56; see also
Northern Soul

Universal Robot Band, 220, 221
USA-European Connection, 199

Van Der Graf Generator, 256
Van Dyke, Earl, 51, 123
Van Tiegham, David, 261
Vandross, Luther, 160
Vaness, Theo, 87
Vangelis, 278
Vanini, Peppo, 215
Vartan, Sylvie, 23
Vee, Vivien, 278
Vega, Eddie, 188, 189
Vega, Lil' Louie, 274
Velez, Lisa, 274
Velours, 55
Velvet Underground, 24, 255
Velvette, 85
Ventures, 35
Vesaas, Tarjei, 65
Vietnam War, 5, 10–11, 29–30, 31,
121, 123, 161, 231, 248
Village People, The, 84, 107, 223,
224–25, 226, 232, 281, 282,
287–88
Vincent, Rickey, 97
Vincent, Robbie, 217
Viteritti, Bobby, 80, 86
Volcanoes, 139–40
Voyage, 86, 87, 199
Vreeland, Diana, 21

Wade, Stanley, 140. See also
Trammps
Wakeman, Rick, 229
Walden, Narada Michael, 222
Walker, Jr., 152
Waness, Theo, 87
Wang, Daniel, 283–85, 289
War, 33, 129
Ward, Anita, 199, 201
Warhol, Andy, 3, 22, 24, 191,
211, 212, 255, 257
Warhol Superstars, 255
Warner, Allan, 53
Warwick, Dionne, 112
Was (Not Was), 265–66,
287

INDEX OF SONGS

"Treat the Youths Right," 264
"Try Me, I Know We Can Make It," 107
"TSOP," 145
"Turn the Beat Around," 201
"Tuxedo Junction," 106
"Twist, The," 19, 159
"Two Pigs and a Hog," 47

"UFO," 256
"Underwater," 272
"Until Then," 138
"Up in a Puff of Smoke," 55
"Upside Down," 231
"Uptown Festival," 105
"Uranium," 260
"Use Ta Be My Girl," 144
"Utopia—Me Giorgio," 115

"Valentino," 75
"Viva Bobby Joe," 99

"Waitin' for the Rain," 97
"Wake Up Everybody," 145
"Walking Into Sunshine," 275
"Warm Leatherette," 256
"Warm Summer Night," 168
"War," 124
"Watergate," 155
"Wax the Van," 263
We Are Family (album), 169–71
"We Are Family," 150, 169, 171, 237–38
"We Shall Overcome," 131, 155
"Weekend," 221–22, 268
"Wela Wela," 103
"(We'll Be) United," 140
"West End Girls," 85
"Westchester Lady," 217
"Wham! Rap," 259
"What Can I Do For You?," 95, 116, 118, 120
"What a Fool Believes," 231
"What's Going On," 67
"Wheel Me Out," 265
"When Will I See You Again," 145
"When the World's at Peace," 131
"When You're Young and in Love," 45

"Where Is My Man," 226
"White Lines (Don't Do It)," 257
"Who Do You Love?," 92
"Who Is He (And What Is He to You?)," 125
"Whole Lotta Love," 28
"Why Can't We Live Together?," 98, 99, 198
"Why d'Ya Do It?," 268
"Wild Horses," 119
"Wild Safari," 35
"Without Your Love," 87
"Woman," 35
"Won't Get Fooled Again," 119
"Working with Fire and Steel," 86

"Yes, I'm Ready," 139
"Yes We Can Can," 37
"Yesterday," 248
"Y.M.C.A.," 225, 227, 281
"You Better Keep Her," 52
"You Can Have Watergate Just Gimme Some Bucks and I'll Be Straight," 155
"You Can't Hide From Yourself," 137
"(You Caught Me) Smilin'," 134
"You Don't Bring Me Flowers," 230
"You Make Me Feel (Mighty Real)," 77–78
"You Should Be Dancing," 106–107, 205
"You Turned My Bitter Into Sweet," 85
"You'll Never Find Another Love Like Mine," 145
"Young Hearts Run Free," 73
"You're a Friend to Me," 171
"You're Gonna Make Me Love You," 84
"You're Just the Right Size," 148
"You're No Good," 256
"You're the One," 28, 33
"You're the Reason Why," 142, 143

"Zing Went the Strings of My Heart," 141
"Zone," 96

PERMISSIONS ACKNOWLEDGMENTS

Grateful acknowledgment is made to the following companies and individuals who have granted permission to reprint excerpts from articles, books, periodicals, and compositions. Every effort has been made to contact copyright holders of both text and images reproduced in this book. If any have been inadvertently overlooked, the publishers will be pleased to make restitution at the earliest opportunity.

Lyrics from "Get Down" by Sylvester Allen, Harold Ray I. Brown, Morris D. Dickerson, Leroy L. Jordan, Charles W. Miller, Lee Oskar, Howard Scott, Jerry Goldstein © 1971, renewed 1999 by Universal—PolyGram Int. Publ., Inc./ASCAP used by permission. International copyright secured. All rights reserved; "Fish Ain't Bitin'" by McKinley Terrell Jackson, James Reddick © 1974, renewed 2002 by Songs of Universal, Inc., on behalf of Bullet Proof Music/BMI used by permission. International copyright secured. All rights reserved; "Are You Man Enough" by Dennis Lambert, Brian Potter © 1973, renewed 2001 by Universal—Duchess Music Corporation/BMI used by permission. International copyright secured. All rights reserved; "I'll Take You There" by Alvertis Isbell © 1972, renewed 2000 by Irving Music, Inc./BMI used by permission. International copyright secured. All rights reserved.

Lyrics from "Freak of the Week" by George Clinton, Jr., Peter Bishop, DeWayne S. McNight © 1979 by Bridgeport Music Inc. (BMI) used by permission. All rights reserved.

Lyrics from "Hard Times," "Cherchez La Femme," "I'll Play the Fool" by August Darnell and Stony Browder, Jr. © 1976, renewed 1995 Raineyville Music (BMI) / Administered by BUG used by permission. All rights reserved; "Animal Crackers" by August Darnell and Giampietro Favero © 1981 Raineyville Music (BMI) / Administered by BUG used by permission. All rights reserved; "Going Places," "In the Jungle," "Latin Music" by August Darnell © 1981 Raineyville Music (BMI) / Administered by BUG used by permission. All rights reserved; "No Fish Today," "Annie, I'm Not Your Daddy," "Stool Pigeon" by August Darnell © 1982 Raineyville Music (BMI) / Administered by BUG used by permission. All rights reserved.

Lyrics from "Back Stabbers" by Leon Huff, Gene McFadden, and John Whitehead © 1972, renewed, Warner-Tamerlane Publishing Corp. and Mijac Music. All rights administered by Warner-Tamerlane Publishing Corp. used by permission. All rights reserved; "Don't Call Me Brother" by Kenneth Gamble and Bunny Sigler © 1974, renewed, Warner-Tamerlane Publishing Corp. used by permission. All rights reserved; "When the World's at Peace" by Kenneth Gamble, Bunny Sigler, and Phil Hurtt © 1972, renewed, Warner-Tamerlane Publishing Corp. used by permission. All rights reserved; "Cruisin' the Streets" by Bill Motley © WB Music Corp. used by permission. All rights reserved; "Thin Line Between Love & Hate" by Richard Poindexter, Robert Poindexter, and Jackie Poindexter © 1971, renewed, Cotillion Music, Inc., and Win or Lose music. All rights administered by Cotillion Music Inc. used by permission. All rights reserved; "You Can't Hide From Yourself" by Kenneth Gamble and Leon Huff © 1977 Warner-Tamerlane Publishing Corp. used by permission. All rights reserved; "Ain't No Stoppin' Us Now" by Gene McFadden, John Whitehead, and Jerry Cohen © Warner-Tamerlane Publishing Corp. used by permission. All rights reserved; "Hell on Wheels" by Bob Esty and Michelle Aller © Rightsong Music Inc. used by permission.